Peter and Mary Ha...

SUPERNAT...
THE CHILDREN
& OTHER STRANGE TRUE STORIES

COMPENDIUM

Sinclair Publishing Ltd

A Sinclair Compendium

© Peter and Mary Harrison 1990

SUPERNATURAL:
THE CHILDREN THAT TIME FORGOT
& OTHER STRANGE TRUE STORIES

THE CHILDREN THAT TIME FORGOT
First published in 1983 (entitled 'Life Before Birth') by
Futura
Published by Sinclair Publishing Ltd 1989
ISBN 1-872149-01-4

MYSTIC FORCES
First published by Sinclair Publishing Ltd 1989
ISBN 1-872149-00-6

SPINECHILLER
First published by Sinclair Publishing Ltd 1990
Reprinted 1990
ISBN 1-872149-03-0

To our late parents
Esme, Wilfred, Margaret and James

Sinclair Publishing Ltd
123 Midland Road, Wellingborough NN8 1LU

British Library Cataloguing in Publication data
Harrison, Peter
    Supernatural: The Children That Time Forgot
    & Other Strange True Stories
    1. Supernatural
    I. Title II. Harrison, Mary
    133

    ISBN 1-872149-08-1

Printed and bound in Great Britain by
Cox & Wyman Ltd, Reading

Peter and Mary Harrison

THE CHILDREN THAT TIME FORGOT

Sinclair Publishing Ltd

Acknowledgements

The authors appreciate all the help received from people in the media who willingly gave of their time and energy to assist with the research of this book including newspaper reporters, radio and television producers, magazine editors and secretaries of various organisations, also the Southend Police, the Bradford Archives and countless members of the public.

A special mention must be given to the many people in the medical profession for their patience and advice, in particular Dr Peter Fenwick, Neurophsychiatrist, Inst. of Psychiatry, London, Dr Paul Pandarakalam of the Kottayam Medical College, South India and Dr David Stevenson, Senior Lecturer in International Community Health at the Liverpool School of Tropical Medicine.

The religious chapter could not have been written without the co-operation of the various priests, vicars and spokesmen from all denominations, especially Rabbi Louis Jacobs of St. Johns Wood, London.

A very special thanks must go to Miss Lorna Hinwood for her ingenious contribution.

Most of all we owe a tremendous vote of thanks to all the children and their relatives who were the essence of kindness and co-operation in the researching of the case histories.

Contents

Introduction 7

PART 1: CASE HISTORIES
  LIFE BEFORE BIRTH 9
Small girl remembers being killed by a train 11
Girl remembers her own funeral 19
Boy remembers assassination of Thomas Becket 28
Girl remembers being a nineteenth-century nurse 32
Young boy remembers being a German bomber
  pilot 41
Girl remembers being her own
  great-grandmother 47
Girl remembers previous life in South Africa 53
Boy remembers being a garage mechanic 58
Two-year-old girl remembers being a mother 63
Boy remembers being in his aunt's womb 70
Girl remembers being lady of the manor 77
Girl remembers being a witch 81
Girl remembers being in Tay Bridge disaster 84
Boy remembers being drowned off sailing ship 90
Girl remembers being a boy 95
Boy remembers being a commando 102
Girl remembers Jesus 108
Girl remembers being a musician 115
Boy remembers being his own grandfather 118
Boy remembers being a ghost 123
Girl remembers watching silversmith at work 129
Girl remembers being a nun 133
Girl remembers pet horse from previous life 137
Boy remembers waiting to be reborn 140
Girl remembers being hit by previous mother 143
Two-year-old girl remembers being born 146

LIFE AFTER DEATH   151
Mother sees daughter six weeks after child's death 151
Mother sees dead baby slowly progressing   154
Woman sees dead grandchild   158

PART 2: HYPNOPTIC REGRESSION   161

PART 3: MEDICAL AND RELIGIOUS VIEWS   173
Medical Views   175
Religious Views   185

Introduction

Many people are so terrified at the prospect of death that they become introverted, despondent and victims of nervous tension, becoming totally incapable of relaxing and enjoying this life to the full.

The following case histories reveal a clue to the true nature of human consciousness, an indication that the personality exists not only on the earth plane during our present lives, but also on a pre-birth dimension of time and space. Many children remember the days and months spent in their mother's womb before being born, and more amazingly, some remember further back than that to an existence before physical conception in a realm which, although similar to earth in as much as this region contained houses, schools, rivers, trees, etc., differed in material density, i.e. life operated according to a different set of laws and principles to those vibrations by which life is lived on earth.

The great majority of case histories deal with children's memories of former lives on earth brought to the notice of their parents by spontaneous flashes, usually triggered off by some ordinary every-day activity or experience. In no case was hypnosis or any other form of age regression used, and in every case the parents were hesitant to jump to conclusions about their children's statements. Only after repeated spontaneous recollections of places, people and objects which were outside the knowledge of the children, did these parents concede that there might be an element of truth in their children's remarks.

It could be significant that in every case history, the child was pre-school age, almost all being two to three years of age when their memories were first voiced. By the time they reached six the memories seemed to vanish

Possibly by the time a child has learnt to speak coherently, these memories have already started to diminish, and by the time they reach school age their brains are so occupied with the increased amount of data to be absorbed that the pre-birth memories are pushed to the back of the brain into the subconsciousness.

According to the case histories there seems little doubt that in some instances life does indeed exist before earthly birth, either in a non-physical realm, or on the physical material earth plane. If this is so, then the idea of life after death seems like a natural following on and continuation of the personality.

If we have managed to spread the joyous message that physical death is not the end, then we have succeeded in our objective.

PART ONE
CASE HISTORIES

LIFE BEFORE BIRTH
AND
LIFE AFTER DEATH

Small girl remembers being killed by a train
Nicola Wheater, Keighley

Kathleen, mother of five-year-old Nicola, is convinced her child has lived before. From the age of two the child has been describing her previous life near the West Yorkshire village of Haworth, famous as the birth-place of the Bronte sisters, Charlotte, Emily and Anne, and where Emily's book Wuthering Heights is set.

The strange story began when Nicola was given a pullalong toy dog on her second birthday. The child got very excited as she told her mother, 'I'll call it Muff, the same as the other dog I had before.' Kathleen laughed at what she thought was the over-active imagination of her little girl. They had once owned a dog before, but never one called Muff. She played along with the child's game of make-believe, and agreed that Muff would make a lovely name for her little toy dog.

As the days went on, Kathleen noticed that Nicola became more and more engrossed with Muff and continually asked her toy dog if he could remember various incidents and experiences that they were supposed to have shared in the past. Assuming that it was all just a childish fantasy, Kathleen attached no importance to her daughter's so-called reminiscences, until suddenly Nicola asked her mother a strange question which made Kathleen stop and think. Being unusually articulate for her age, Nicola asked her mother, 'Why am I a little girl this time, Mummy? Why am I not a boy like I was before?'

When Kathleen asked Nicola what she meant, she answered, 'When Mrs Benson was my mummy I was a little boy and I played with Muff.' This remark left Kathleen puzzled, especially the reference to a Mrs Benson. Nicola did not know anyone called Mrs Benson, and in fact the name was not that of anyone known to the family.

As the references to what Nicola had done 'before'

became more and more frequent, Kathleen was forced to take note of what her daughter was saying, as the child never varied her story, even slightly. Nicola insisted that she used to be a boy, and although she could not remember her Christian name, she knew that her second name had been Benson and that her mother had been known as Mrs Benson and her mother's first name had been something like Elspeth or Elsie. She was certain that she had lived near Haworth and that she had had two sisters and of course her pet dog Muff. She remembers that her father, Mr Benson, worked on the railway and that they lived in a little house near the railway lines.

She described the house in detail to her mother. 'It was grey stone in the middle of four houses joined together in a row. There were lots of fields at the back where I used to play with Muff.' Nicola was able to relate in the most amazing detail how her mother wore a long skirt: 'It was like a kind of pinny, just like the one that my doll wears.' She recalls how her mother wore her hair, and describes it as 'All tied up funny'. Her father wore big heavy boots and for some reason which Nicola has refused to talk about, she did not like her father much. 'He always had a dirty black face,' she tells, but when asked any other questions about Mr Benson she clams up.

She remembers sitting on the floor eating butties which her mother used to make for her and her friend who, along with Muff, was her constant companion. She knows her friend was another boy, but she cannot remember his name. 'He was smaller than me,' recalls Nicola, 'about one or two years smaller. Not one year and not two years,' she explains in an effort to describe her friend, 'and we always went to the railway together and we played in the fields behind my house.'

The little girl has vivid recollections of how as a boy she used to wander along the lanes and pathways surrounding her home with her beloved Muff. 'We played funny games all the time. I would throw my ball in the air and Muff would run and catch it and bring it back to me.'

Apparently her two sisters were much younger than Nicola, and she didn't have over-much to do with them, as would be the case with any other normal healthy little boy. 'They were too little for me,' she says, then adds 'One was just a baby and was too small to come out and play with me.'

Nicola told Kathleen of how her other Mummy always told her that she mustn't play on the railway; then she said, 'But I didn't listen to her and I used to go down to the railway with Muff and my friend.'

The child has clear memories of the day she was knocked down by a train. 'I was playing on the railway lines with Muff and my friend and I saw a man walking along swinging a lamp. After that a train came up fast and knocked me over.' When Kathleen asked her daughter what happened after that, Nicola replied, 'I got taken to hospital. Everyone kept asking me if I was all right but I couldn't walk or talk so I couldn't answer them.'

'What happened after that?' asked Kathleen.

'I went to sleep and died and I saw God in Heaven before I was born.' Then Nicola added, 'But I didn't really die. I came to you instead and you got to be my other Mummy.' When asked what God was like Nicola replied, 'I don't know how to say it to you. He was really beautiful but I don't remember what clothes he had on.' Then in an enthusiastic tone she assured her mother, 'He's much nicer than in his pictures.'

Because Nicola's story was so consistent, her mother decided to take her daughter to Haworth where they had never been before, in an attempt either to verify the little girl's words, or to put an end to the incredible story once and for all.

They travelled along desolate country lanes, through the bleak windswept moorland and Kathleen, who was unfamiliar with that part of the country, took a wrong turning and got hopelessly lost. Nicola, who like her mother had

13

never been to the area before, came to the rescue, and directed Kathleen down some lonely unmarked roads straight into Haworth village. Nicola explained to her mother, 'I know the way because Muff and I used to walk all around here.'

After following Nicola's instructions, Kathleen was guided towards the outskirts of the village and was flabbergasted to find herself looking at what Nicola said was her other home: one of four old grey-stone terraced houses, exactly as Nicola had previously described and in the precise spot where the child said it would be. The physical details of the surrounding countryside matched Nicola's description perfectly, with the back of the house looking out over open fields. Kathleen noted that the address was 12 Chapel Lane, Oakworth.

Kathleen then went to the Haworth Parish Church to see if she could find any trace of a Benson family in the church records. The rector told her that she would be unlikely to find any Bensons in the parish registers as it was a very unusual name for those parts. However, he gave Kathleen permission to look through the birth and marriage registers, although he expressed his personal opinion that he thought the exercise would be a waste of time.

Kathleen's heart skipped a beat when she turned over the aging yellowed pages of an old birth register. Her eye caught the name Benson. The entry recorded the birth of a baby boy, John Henry Benson, on the 20th June, 1875. His father's name was given as Thomas Benson, whose occupation was a railway plate-layer. The boy's mother's name was given as Lucey Benson.

Kathleen looked down at little Nicola's face, then at the register of births, wondering if her daughter and the baby John Henry could really be one and the same person. The mother's name, Lucey, caused Kathleen to wonder even more. Nicola was of the opinion that her previous mother had been called Elspeth or Elsie. Could there be some mistake due to the similarity of the words Elsie and Lucey? The

14

father's occupation as a railway plate-layer tied in with Nicola's story, a plate-layer being someone who lays the tracks down on the railway.

A further line of research provided even more startling results. In the Archives Department at the City of Bradford Metropolitan Council offices, the reference librarian, Mr Ian Dewhirst, has in his charge the census for the Haworth district. By law, the census, which is taken only once in every ten years, must remain confidential for a hundred years, so the latest details which could be consulted were the results of the 1881 census. The following information came to light:

12 Chapel Lane, Oakworth

		Age		*Born*
Thomas Benson	Head	29 yrs	Railway Plate-layer	Kildwick (Yorks)
Susy(?) Benson	Wife	30 yrs		Bradford (Yorks)
Hephyibah(?) Benson	Daughter	3 yrs	Scholar	Keighley (Yorks)
Sellis Benson	Daughter	6 mths		Keighley (Yorks)

The most significant point about the above entry is that although it represents the same Benson family of 12 Chapel Lane, Oakworth, as mentioned in the Haworth church birth register, there is no mention of the son John Henry. As it was required by law that each and every member of the family must be included in the census, this means that the boy John Henry must have died before the census was taken in 1881.

Taking into account the fact that Nicola remembers having had two sisters when she lived before as a boy and that the second benson daughter Sellis was only six months old when the 1881 family details were recorded, this points to John

15

Henry's death being between 1880 and 1881, when the child would have been between five and six years of age.

Unfortunately the hospital for the Haworth/Oakworth area in 1880-81 has long been closed down and so it is impossible to check to see if there had ever been any record of a child having been admitted after being knocked down by a train.

Again there is some discrepancy regarding the name of the mother. The census seems to show Thomas Benson's wife as Susy, but according to Ian Dewhirst, there is some doubt attached to this. The entries are in handwriting which is very difficult to decipher. He thinks the handwriting gives the name of Susy, but he does admit that it could just as easily be Lusy with a flourishing capital L. He goes on to remark that the Bensons seemed to go in for unusual names for their children, i.e. Hephyibah and Sellis, and he adds that he's not entirely sure that he read the name Hephyibah correctly. This highlights the problem of having to depend upon roughly written documents in order to establish the facts.

Let us for a moment suppose that the census entry for Thomas Benson's wife is Lucy. This would fit in with the entry in the Haworth birth register of Lucey: the same name with a different spelling. However, this still doesn't resolve the matter of Nicola thinking that her previous mother's name was Elsie. Perhaps buried in the store of information in young Nicola's unconsciousness is the name Lucy, but her conscious mind has interpreted the name as Elsie.

One thing which is very much to the fore of Nicola's consciousness is the terrifying experience of being knocked down by a train. Kathleen explains how one night the family were sitting together watching a film on television called The October Man, starring John Mills. There was a sequence in the film where a man was standing on top of an old railway bridge ready to throw himself down on to the railway lines. There was a shot of a train thundering down the railway track, and instantly Nicola started to scream hysterically. She threw herself down on to the carpet gasping for breath and throwing her arms in the air wildly. Her mother thought that the child was having a fit or a heart attack and rushed to help her. Little Nicola could not be consoled, and cried out, 'The train, the train', repeatedly. It was only when her mother switched the television off that the child calmed down.

'She seemed to be re-living the time when the train knocked her down,' explains Kathleen. 'I had no idea that the film would have affected her like that.'

One possible explanation for Nicola's story, unless, of course, it is truly a straightforward example of reincarnation, is that it could be a case of temporary spirit overshadowing, which is not to be confused with spirit possession, whereby the spirit of a member of the 19th century Benson family has latched on to young Nicola. But Nicola's strange behaviour when she watched the train on television thunder down the track would seem to point to a more personal involvement, and would suggest that she was re-living a terrible past experience, so overwhelming that it caused her to go into a convulsion-like frenzy.

Nicola's mother is in no doubt whatsoever that her daughter's story points to reincarnation. Kathleen did not know of the research being carried out at the Archives Department in Bradford, and when she was told that Nicola's story did in fact check out and that the boy John Henry who had lived in the old grey-stone house had been killed before the 1881 census had been taken, and that his father had worked on the railway she became absolutely convinced that Nicola had been re-born. 'I always thought that she was telling the truth. I realized that if she was making it up, the story would probably alter, but it never did. Now I know the results of the census I know she has been telling the truth. There is no explanation of how she could have had so many details in her head of a place she had never ever seen in her life. '

As far as Nicola herself, now a bubbly cuddly five year-old with chubby rosy cheeks and a head of tousled golden

17

curls, is concerned, the nicest thing she remembers about her previous life is all the fun she had with Muff.

Girl remembers her own funeral
Mandy Seabrook, Hitchin

Gillian had just finished her usual afternoon cup of coffee when she felt the stab of her first contraction. A gush of excitement rushed through her as she realized that at last the long months of waiting were over. Already her mind was buzzing with visions of how she would enjoy the late summer with her new baby. Like any happy mother-to-be she carefully checked over the little pastel-coloured baby clothes she had so lovingly set aside in preparation for the great day.

A short time later, after a perfectly normal labour, a beautiful baby girl was born in the modern delivery room of the Women and Children's Hospital in Leeds. The baby's parents were overjoyed as they welcomed the child into the world, and her four-year-old sister Carol was bubbling with excitement at the prospect of having a real live baby to play with. During that first euphoric day there was a stream of friends and relatives armed with flowers and baby cards, all showering their congratulations on the proud family.

Unfortunately the celebrations were short lived. When the baby was given the routine medical inspection by the hospital paediatric doctor, Gillian's smiles dissolved into tears as she was told that little baby Mandy had been born with a double hernia behind the heart. The infant was moved to the intensive care unit where she was given constant attention by the nursing staff. The following few days were like a nightmare for the parents, who hovered between hope and despair as they listened to the doctors whose responsibility it was to prepare such parents for any frightening developments which might occur. The distraught mother and father were forced to face the fact that they might lose their precious new-born baby.

However, the crisis eventually passed and much to the relief of her parents, little Mandy's condition became stable and she started to gain weight, the first sure sign of improvement. She was discharged from hospital and the family settled down to a normal existence.

Five months later the baby caught a common cold, and although her mother was somewhat alarmed by this, her fears soon subsided as she watched her tiny daughter bounce back to relative good health again, after only two days. Mandy appeared to be particularly exuberant during this period, so much so that the child's grandmother who was a nurse, made the prophetic remark 'I've seen babies like that before. They get energetic before they die.' The chilling words pierced Gillian's heart.

Later that afternoon, the child's mother thought that she had heard a choking sound. She rushed to the cot and was horrified to find that her baby's face had turned purple and she was gasping for breath. An alarm call went out for the family doctor who came immediately. He examined little Mandy and informed Gillian that her child had just suffered a severe heart attack. Even as he spoke, the life was ebbing from the tiny body.

Suddenly the heartbeat and pulse stopped completely. The doctor's grim expression told Gillian that the end had come. As she stared at her baby in stunned silence, Gillian saw the doctor bend over the child, force her tiny lips apart, and breathe deeply into her mouth. Tears of joy streamed down Gillian's face as she saw her infant's chest start to rise and fall in response to the doctor's kiss of life. She took the daughter who had come back from the dead into her arms and held the fragile frame close to her heart in an attempt to regulate the baby's heartbeat by using her own heart as a pacemaker. Mandy's face had become relaxed and her eyes were open, staring up at her mother.

Sadly, the reprieve lasted for only a few short minutes. 'I kissed her, but when I looked down at her eyes I realized that they had gone dry. I knew she had slipped away.' A second heart attack had taken the baby's life. The doctor tried mouth-

20

to-mouth resuscitation again, but without success. The baby lay dead in her mother's arms and it seemed like the end of the world to Gillian.

Mandy's death had a chaotic effect on her family. The months of worry and anxiety had taken their toll on her parents' relationship which had been slowly deteriorating. While the baby's life had tottered precariously in the balance, the couple had managed to put their differences to one side, but when the slender bonding thread was severed, their relationship suffered irredeemable damage and they decided to go their separate ways.

Gillian, her heart heavy with bereavement and the breakup of her home, tried desperately to pick up the pieces of her shattered life. She became acquainted with a kindly sympathetic man called George Seabrook on whom she started to rely more and more. Eventual;y she married George and once again her existence took on a semblance of harmony and normality. Like Gillian, George had also been through a traumatic time and had recently become divorced. Determined to put their troubles behind them, they made a pact that no mention would be made of the past. They agreed to make a fresh start.

The couple had four children: Wendy, Sean, John, and the fourth, another girl, born in May, 1972, they decided to call Mandy, after the baby who had died, because the new baby looked remarkably like the first Mandy, with bright blue eyes and jet-black pupils. They were adamant, however, that they should adhere to their agreement not to tell their children about the first Mandy.

One day, two years later, the Seabrooks were travelling from Leeds down the M1 motorway on a family outing. It was a sunny spring afternoon. Little Mandy was sitting on her mother's knee in the front passenger seat of the car and the other children were singing songs in the back seat. They passed the cemetery where the first Mandy had been buried, at Hunslet on the outskirts of the city, an area totally unknown to the children who had never been taken to that part of the city before.

Mandy suddenly jumped up from her mother's lap. 'Look, Mummy,' she cried excitedly, pointing through the car window. 'That's the place you put me in the ground that time, and you nearly fell on top of me, remember?' Her parents looked at each other in absolute horror, neither of them able to utter a word. 'Mandy sent shivers up my spine,' recalls Gillian, who had been so upset over the loss of the first Mandy that she had always found it impossible to talk about her. George who was at the driving wheel remembers that he got such a shock that the hairs at the back of his neck stood up on end. 'I felt as if I'd been struck by an electric current,' he recollects. 'There was just no way that my little girl could have known anything about the cemetery, its location, or any of the other details.'

Mandy then went on to describe a tiny silver bracelet engraved with crosses, roses and words which she remembered wearing in her coffin. This bracelet had been fastened round Mandy Number One's tiny wrist when she was buried. It was indeed silver, engraved with roses and crosses. It had been given to the first Mandy as a present from the brother of the first baby's father, a man called Patrick whom the second Mandy never knew. Mandy remembered that the bracelet had words on it. The inscription read: 'To darling Mandy from Uncle Patrick.'

At the time of the first Mandy's death, Gillian had been treated for shock by her doctor and had been given some tablets to help calm her down. She remembers being in a state near to collapse while standing at her baby's grave and with the combination of the tablets and grief, she lost her balance, slipped on the wet soil and in fact almost fell into the grave on top of the miniature white coffin.

Before the lid of the coffin was closed on the baby, it was noticed that a tiny half tooth had cut through the gum on the bottom left hand side. Another thing noticed was a solitary curl on the crown of the baby's head, but no sign of any other hair. When Mandy Number Two was born, the same half tooth was visible on the bottom left hand side of her gum and the same solitary curl crowned her head, although there was no sign of any other hair at birth.

In spite of Mandy Number Two's striking resemblance to the first Mandy, and the fact that the tooth and curl were present at birth, the family didn't think that there was anything strange about it at the time. As Gillian says, 'We weren't looking for a connection between the two Mandys. None of us believed in reincarnation and it wasn't until much later that we began to see that there might be a connection between the two girls.'

The second Mandy has since grown into a bright energetic girl with a happy-go-lucky disposition. She sports long shining brown hair, straight as a poker, but for the one solitary curl which can still be seen on the crown of her head.

When Mandy Number Two was three years old, she was walking with her father across the forecourt of Leeds railway station. They were making their way to the coffee bar when Mandy caught sight of a boy in a wheelchair being pushed through the bustling crowds. She suddenly turned to her father and said, 'Stevie's OK and he can walk now.'

George Seabrook was astounded at these words because unknown to Mandy he had had a spastic son by his previous marriage called Stephen who had died when Mandy was just a few months old. He had never even mentioned Stephen's name to his daughter or to any of the other children because of the agreement which he and Gillian had come to when they married, whereby they had decided to put their past lives behind them. The spastic child had never lived with him but had been cared for by his former wife's parents. The name of Stephen was more or less taboo.

When Mandy mentioned Stevie, George Seabrook was so incredulous that he got Mandy to explain her remark, asking her, 'What do you mean, love? What Stevie?'

She answered, 'You know, your own Stevie. Stephen. He can walk now.'

Bearing in mind that Mandy had never been told about Stephen's existence, Mr Seabrook was thunderstruck, most of all by the words 'He can walk now'. The child was too young to understand what spastic meant. He also' wondered at Mandy referring to the boy as Stevie, the name by which George had always called his son.

Just before Mandy's fifth birthday, Gillian was preparing lunch in the kitchen when her small daughter ran in and tugged at her skirt.

'Mummy, why did you cry when I died?' she asked.

Gillian replied, 'But you're not dead, darling.'

Mandy persisted. 'Oh, you remember, Mummy, when I was very little. I couldn't live long because I was poorly. Now I've come back. I'm Mandy Number Two.'

There is a twist to this story. The first Mandy's sister Carol had only just reached her fifth birthday when the baby had died. Carol had not long started school, and on the day of the funeral it was thought best that the child should be sent to school as usual.

When Gillian later married George Seabrook, Carol was naturally included as part of the family. The crucial question arises: could Carol have related the story to Mandy about having had a baby sister called Mandy who died? That two half sisters, one a two-year-old toddler, and the other an eleven-year-old girl, could have had such conversations is physically possible, but is it logically probable?

In the first place, Carol was not at the funeral and was never told the location of the cemetery, so there is no explanation for Mandy's first statement about being put in the ground. Bear in mind that the child was in a fast car on a motorway, and they passed the cemetery in a flash, yet it was in that same lightning flash that the two-year old pointed towards the graveyard and announced, 'That's the place you put me in the ground that time.'

Secondly the child Carol was not at the funeral service, so she did not witness her mother almost falling into the grave. It is hardly feasible that this kind of information would be passed on to a five-year-old child. There still remains the possibility that Carol had overheard a conversation regarding the grave-side mishap, lodged this information in her brain, then fed it into the second Mandy's. brain to be used at the appropriate time, either wittingly or unwittingly.

The main obstacle to this line of reasoning is the time factor involved. When Mandy Number One was buried, Carol had just reached her fifth birthday. When Mandy Number Two made her first statement in the car as they passed the graveyard, Carol was eleven and Mandy was two. Even if the toddler had been carefully tutored by her half-sister, would a child of this age act perfectly on cue and make her statement at precisely the moment when the car flashed passed the cemetery? Remember, Mandy was in the front of the car on her mother's lap, and the other children were in the back of the car taking part in a sing-song at the time. Would the child then follow up her first remark with the accurate statement about how her mother almost fell into the grave? This seems unlikely, and considering that Carol did not attend the funeral and did not know where the cemetery was, impossible.

Thirdly, there is the matter of the eyes, tooth, and the curl. There is no possible way that Carol could have had any influence whatsoever over Mandy Number Two's physical traits.

Again, how can this explanation be applied to the remarks about George Seabrook's son Stephen? Stephen was the child of Mr Seabrook and his first wife. Mandy was the child of Mr Seabrook and his second wife. Mandy had never met, or known about, Stephen, who died when she was only four months old. In addition, there are the words 'He can walk now'. How can these be explained?

And now to the tail piece. George Seabrook had been collecting cardboard milk bottle tops, and one day he gave them to the children to play with. Gillian, who was busy with the household chores at the time, remarked casually to the children that the cardboard milk bottle tops could be used to make pom-poms or fluffy wool balls. Immediately Mandy asked her mother why she had buried her other fluffy wool ball. At first Gillian did not know what Mandy was talking about, and being engrossed in her washing up, she vaguely replied, 'It must be in the garden, love,' thinking to herself that if some toy or another had been buried, then the garden would seem the obvious place to look.

Mandy would not be fobbed off and insisted that her mother had buried her fluffy ball.

'What fluffy ball are you talking about, Mandy?' asked her mother.

'You know, the yellow one. The one that you put in the ground with me,' came Mandy's reply.

Gillian's mind raced back to the time of the first Mandy's funeral. Little Carol had just started school and had been taught how to make fluffy wool balls. She brought the little ball home from school as a present for her baby sister. The baby died, and Carol had asked her mother if she could still give the present to Mandy. She wanted to put the fluffy wool ball into the coffin but Gillian had decided against the idea and said 'No'. As far as everyone knew, that was the end of it.

When Mandy Number Two mentioned the fluffy ball being put in the ground with her, Gillian had only one course of action. She asked Mandy to go and find Carol who was not in the room at the time and had had no part in the foregoing conversation.

Carol was duly brought before her mother and was asked to try to remember when the first Mandy had died. She was then asked to describe what really happened to the fluffy wool ball. Carol admitted that although she had been told that the ball should not go into the coffin with the baby, she managed to hide the ball underneath the dead baby when no one was looking. The coffin lid had been left open for a whole day and night, so there would have been ample opportunity for the girl to accomplish this without being noticed by anyone, especially when the household was in such disarray. Her mother was in a state of shock at the time, and would not have been watching Carol's every move. The yellow fluffy wool ball was in fact buried with baby Mandy, against Gillian's wishes.

Gillian says that Mandy has an unnerving habit of dropping reminders of the past, completely out of the blue. When she was six, she said to her mother, 'Do you remember the night I died? There was a bright star shining in the sky.' Her mother turned her mind back to the time she had tried so hard to forget. 'Suddenly it came back to me,' says Gillian. 'I had gone to close the curtains when I saw an unusually bright star hovering over the garden. I commented on it at the time because it was so bright and so low. But after that I never gave it another thought. Then Mandy said, "That was my star. It was my way of telling you that I would be back".'

Mandy is quite matter-of-fact about her previous life. She says, 'I remember very well when I was Mandy One, but I didn't like it when everyone cried when I died. It was nice to come back.'

Mandy's father, George Seabrook, a sensible, levelheaded man, used to be extremely sceptical about such matters. 'I used to think when you're dead you're dead and that's the end of it, but I don't think that now. I know in my heart that my little girl has lived before.'

Says Gillian, 'We really are convinced that Mandy has been reborn. They say that after you've lost a child, having another baby fills the gap, but it doesn't. Admittedly it takes your mind off it a lot, but it never makes up for the loss. I withdrew into myself and would not talk to anyone for days on end. If I had known then that Mandy would come back, I might have been much more philosophical about her death, though if someone had told me that all this would happen, I wouldn't have believed it possible. I certainly believe it now.'

27

Boy remembers assassination of Thomas Becket
Philip Harding, Milton Keynes

As a special treat, two-and-a-half-year-old Philip was taken on a day outing to Oxford by his Aunt Rosemary. The child had never been to Oxford in his life, and Rosemary had only been there once before when she passed through the town on a coach trip.

They set off on a bright sunny morning and no sooner had they arrived in Oxford when little Philip asked his aunt, 'Can we go and see the clock, Aunty Rosie?'

Thinking it was just idle chatter Rosemary humoured the child by saying that they would probably pass a clock on the way. Philip answered, 'But I mean the funny clock.' His aunt asked him, 'What funny clock?' Philip then gave a full description to his aunt of a large clock on the side of an old church which had strange markings on the face.

'I always went to see the funny clock,' said Philip. Rosemary explained to him that he couldn't have seen any clock in Oxford because he had never been there before. The child told her, 'I saw it when I lived here when I was Andrew.'

'Of course I thought he was just talking a lot of rubbish, ' said Rosemary, 'especially as the so-called clock he described to me was so off-beat. By what he said it sounded to me more like a sun dial.'

Rosemary then suggested that they should go shopping, but Philip became very upset and started to cry, saying that he really wanted to see his clock again. Rosemary remembers, 'He looked so dejected that I started to wonder what was going on. There was definitely something niggling him.'

In spite of Rosemary's promises of ice-cream and sweets when they went shopping, Philip would not be moved. He only wanted to see his clock, which he said was on the old church. 'I felt helpless as I didn't know what to do or where to turn to,' she says. Then Rosemary told Philip, 'I don't know where your clock is, love.'

Philip sparked up and replied, 'I know where it is. I'll show you.'

Philip took his aunt's hand and led her all round the side alleys and back streets of Oxford. 'He seemed so intent on finding his clock and he was so definite in leading me round the streets that I just resigned myself to go along with it. All of a sudden there it was. The old church and the most peculiar looking clock I've ever seen in my life. I couldn't believe my eyes.'

Philip had taken his Aunt Rosemary to the old clock, which was exactly as he had described it to her. Rosemary explains, 'It was the strangest thing in the world, because I thought that Philip's description was bound to be completely out as I thought that he'd got it all mixed up, but he was absolutely correct. The clock had a large sundial incorporated onto the face, as well as the regular hands and numbers. That was why Philip's description sounded confused!'

When Rosemary asked Philip how he knew about the clock he assured her that he remembered it from when he lived before as a little boy called Andrew.

Rosemary never told anyone at all about what Philip had told her — not even his parents. 'I knew that it would sound so far-fetched that they would probably think I was going crazy.'

About a year later when Rosemary was looking after Philip for his parents he suddenly said, 'When I was Andrew I saw Thomas Becket being assassinated.'

Rosemary was astounded because although the Andrew part was not a surprise to her, she just couldn't believe that she had heard the words 'Thomas Becket' — and 'assassinated'. These words were totally outside the range of the three-year-old's vocabulary and the historical event was beyond the horizon of his knowledge. 'I could hardly speak I got such a shock,' says Rosemary. Philip told his aunt that when he was

29

Andrew he was bigger than he is now because he was six years old and he could write.

Philip says, 'I wrote down everything I saw. I had lots of notebooks then but I think they got lost.' The child remembers that he had been taken to Canterbury for some reason from his home in Oxford, and it was during this visit to the city that the archbishop was murdered. He remembers seeing lots of people rushing about and he especially remembers that there were lots of soldiers in the city. He says, 'The soldiers had giant swords and big long shields with drawings on them and they wore funny masks on their faces. Some of them were on fancy horses and some were just standing about. They were very noisy and shouted a lot.'

Philip says that at the time of the murder he was actually in Canterbury Cathedral. 'Lots and lots of people were there,' he says. He remembers the clothes that the people wore: he describes them as 'long dresses'. He told his aunt, 'The men wore short dresses and the ladies wore long ones.'

It seems that although he had only been six years old at the time, the little boy was acutely aware that something terrible was taking place. He says, 'I knew it was a very bad thing and that's why I wrote it in my notebook. There was lots of noise and screams in church. It was very dark and I couldn't see very well. I was squashed with all the people. I couldn't see Thomas Becket because the big people were in front of me but I know that he was there and the soldiers murdered him then they ran out.' After that, Philip says, 'Everybody was pushing and screaming and frightened.'

When Philip described the scene to his Aunt Rosemary there was no doubt in her mind that her nephew's memories were real, and that he had lived before in the 12th century. 'No child of his age could have such knowledge of events which took place so long ago. We never discuss history or anything like that — we're just not that kind of family — and in any case we would never talk about a murder in front of a three-year-old child. As for Thomas Becket, I don't think any of us know anything about him. I just know that he existed once and that he was murdered but I've got no idea of how or why. In fact I know nothing at all about the man.'

Rosemary says, 'I think the whole thing is a bit creepy. The thing that puzzles me most is that when Philip first mentioned Becket he used the word assassination, not murder, which would be more like the thing a kid would say, and what's more, he seemed to know exactly what assassination meant.'

There is one link with Oxford in the story of Thomas Becket. Robert of Cricklade, prior of St Frideswide's in Oxford from 1140 to 1180, wrote the life of Thomas Becket but since the prior would not have been married it is unlikely that he would have been in the company of a six-year-old boy at the time of the murder. It is more probable that Andrew was one of the congregation gathered for the service on that fateful winter evening in 1170. The events of that night made such an impression on the young mind that they are still vivid more than 800 years later.

Girl remembers being
a nineteenth-century nurse
Angela Mahony, Poole

Angela Mahony was born in Cork in the South of Ireland and when she was twenty-two months old her parents moved to Poole in Dorset, England. This was the first time Angela or her parents had been outside Ireland. In fact baby Angela had never even been outside her native city of Cork. It took a few days for the family to settle in to their new home, but on the third day Angela's mother Kathleen thought she would take her little girl on a walk round Poole to look at the shops.

On that very first visit they passed Barclay House, the huge bank building. The child became very excited and started to shout out wildly, 'Look, Mummy, that's my hospital. That's where I was a nurse.'

Her mother explained to the child that the big building was not a hospital but the office of a large bank. She told Angela that the people in the bank look after other people's money. Then she said to her daughter, 'So you see, Angie, they don't have any nurses in there.'

Angela would not accept her mother's explanation but got more and more excited and repeated her first statement, saying, 'It is a hospital.' Then pointing towards the building she added, 'I was a nurse in there when I was here before.'

Her mother asked her what she meant, reminding Angela that they had only been in the country three days and that this was the first time that either of them had ever walked down that particular road. Angela then said, 'When I was a nurse I always came down this road with my long dress on and my nurse's hat.' She described her uniform as being long, with a long white apron and a funny-shaped hat.

Kathleen took the child home and thought no more about what the child had said, but a few days later when they passed Barclay House for the second time, Angie again became highly excitable and repeated her story about having lived before as a nurse.

This time Angela's father Desmond was with them. When he heard his little girl's remarks he turned to his wife and asked, 'What's she on about?' Kathleen told him what had happened on their previous walk past the bank building.

'But that's ridiculous,' said Desmond. 'Where did she pick up stuff like that?'

Kathleen told her husband that she was just as puzzled as he was and that since they had no friends or relatives who were nurses Angela couldn't have been told anything about them. 'Besides,' said Kathleen, 'she seems to recognize this area and she insists that there should be a hospital here.'

Desmond is a man who likes to get to the bottom of things, so he asked Angela, 'What's all this silly stuff you've been telling Mammy, Angie? You know you've never been a nurse, darling. Have you been playing at nurses with your dollies?'

Angela was quite definite in her reply to her father. She told him, 'Not with my dollies, Daddy, with big people.' Then again she pointed towards the bank building and said, 'It was in there when I was here the last time. That's where I was a nurse.'

From that day on every single time the child passed the bank building she said the same thing. As the months went on and little Angela's speech became more coherent she was able to communicate more and more details of her past life to her bewildered parents. She said that she had a lot of sick people to look after and she had to work very long hours. Angela remembers that she did her share of night duty and she told her mother, 'Sometimes I had to sit up all night to look after the sick people. It was very dark and I didn't like it much '

Because Angela never changed her story her mother wonders if there might be something in her little girl's memories. Kathleen says, 'It makes me wonder because Angie has never said anything else remotely like her story about having been a nurse. If she was always making up yarns about herself then of course I would just put it all down to fantasy. But she has always given the exact same account of her days as a nurse and has never come out with any similar stories about other lives. So I'm inclined to believe that she really does remember something from her past.'

Kathleen says that all mothers are well aware of how their children can lapse into little day-dreams and at times they can come out with the most far-fetched stories. 'The thing about this,' says Kathleen, referring to Angela's story, 'is that they always forget things and when they repeat the story they either leave some of their previous details out or else they get completely muddled up and invariably you end up with about four or five versions of the same story. That's always the give-away. But whenever Angie talks about being a nurse the story never alters. That's why I feel that her memories are real and she is not just making it up.'

On researching Angela's story, it was found that totally unknown to the child's parents, next to the site presently occupied by Barclay House there used to be an old workhouse. It was known as the Union Workhouse and it was built in 1838, and of course, as in all workhouses, nurses were employed in the building to take care of the sick. It was then discovered that in 1900 the workhouse was converted into an infirmary. The guardians of the infirmary are on record as having stated that they were 'very particular about the calibre of nurses they employed'.

The infirmary eventually became part of the old Poole hospital, which in those days was known as 'The Cornelia Hospital' after Lady Cornelia Wimborne who financed it.

So Angela could well have worked as a nurse in any one of the three establishments - the workhouse, the infirmary or the Cornelia hospital. There was a large turnover of nurses through the Poor Law system which governed the workhouse and the infirmary. The minimum age for a nurse employed in the workhouse was set at twenty-five in 1873. In 1900 when the workhouse was converted to an infirmary the age restriction for nurses was lowered to twenty-one, and nurses were not allowed to continue their employment when they married.

Although general conditions in Poor Law workhouses were very rough up and down the country, on the inmates and on the nursing staff alike, the Poole workhouse had a better reputation than most. The children were treated slightly better than in many workhouses and they received more individual attention. They were taught net-making and were kept occupied at producing nets for Poole's considerable fishing trade with Newfoundland and Labrador.

A young girl wishing to enter the nursing profession in those days could do so either by being accepted as a trainee in a teaching hospital, where she would take a three year course, or she could go directly to the workhouse as an untrained assistant.

Normally the workhouses would be run by a master and matron, usually a husband-and-wife team who took care of the all-over day-to-day running of the building, the master being responsible for the incoming stores and goods and the matron - who was really more of a housekeeper- supervising the laundry, food, hygiene, etc. However the nursing division was run on an independent system within the workhouse. A superintendent nurse was in charge of all the nursing administration and activities and she took the role of the present-day matron. She was usually a fully-trained nurse of good education and social standing in the true tradition of Florence Nightingale.

The superintendent nurse took charge of all the trainee and assistant, or half-trained nurses, and she generally was able to command respect from nursing staff, doctors and patients alike.

In the early days of the workhouse the nurses were more often than not the inmates themselves. Many kindly souls, known as pauper nurses, who were half dying themselves of a multitude of diseases, were left to care for their companions in conditions of squalour. These untrained, diseased women had to cope with every type of illness and they also acted as midwives. It was only when many new-born babies were discovered to be suffering from high temperatures and diseased eyes that measures were taken to improve the system.

It was difficult to effect any improvements within the Poor Law system to the workhouses, not least because these establishments were houses of deterrent for people convicted of various crimes. L many cases it was argued by the workhouse guardians that the conditions in the workhouses, however shabby and unhygienic, were far superior to the homes that some of the inmates had come from. The guardians were afraid that if the workhouses were improved to the degree whereby the inmates were more comfortably cared for and better fed than in their own homes, then the buildings would cease to be effective in as much as they would no longer deter would-be offenders. For this reason, life in the workhouse was kept to such a standard as to bring the inmates to task and to have a punishing effect on them.

The few trained nurses had been paid such low wages that they usually left the workhouse system to go on to the better conditions offered by the infirmaries and voluntary hospitals. Such nurses looked upon their stint in the workhouse just as a stepping stone towards a more lucrative career in private nursing. The standard wage for a union workhouse nurse and trainee at a teaching hospital in 1849 was an incredible five shillings per week (equivalent to 25 pence). Because the nurses were supplied with food and accommodation of sorts, the five shillings was not looked upon as a wage, but as mere pin money.

The idea was to attract young women of stable financial backgrounds to the nursing profession, and to discourage girls from becoming nurses for the wrong reasons. Although fine enough in theory, this did not quite work out as expected

36

in practice because many young girls of sub-standard education looked upon the nursing profession as nothing more than a way of filling in their time before marriage. Because of the shortage of nurses the standards in the workhouses were so low that at one time the only requirement for a nurse was that the girl be educated enough to read the doctor's prescription.

Such women were a thorn in the flesh of the newly thriving nursing profession in England. They often treated their patients with downright cruelty and were inclined to look upon the inmates as prisoners who did not deserve any decent treatment. This attitude became so widespread amongst untrained nurses that a rule was passed to demand that workhouse patients should be treated in accordance with their disease, and not in accordance with their morals. After this the cruelty to patients by the untrained nurses was replaced by what was described as passive cruelty whereby certain patients were more or less ignored and left to suffer unattended.

There was a stigma attached to unmarried mothers and they would be given a particularly rough time in the workhouse. Their hair would be cut in. a short cropped style and they were invariably made to wear a straight yellow sackcloth which was the sign of a fallen woman. Even amid the unsavoury community of thieves, thugs and villains of all descriptions, the unmarried mother ranked as the lowest form of life. Such was the moral code of Victorian workhouse society.

There were stringent rules laid down by the workhouse guardians regarding the personal behaviour of the nursing staff. They were not allowed to talk to male staff unless under extremely urgent circumstances. Their living accommodation was nothing more than a tiny room with only the minimum essentials and was often referred to as the nurse's hutch: a small cupboard-like compartment with a bed and a small locker. They were forbidden to decorate their hutches or put up any pictures or ornaments. The reason given for this was that it inflicted extra cleaning duties on the already over-burdened cleaning staff. The nurses were forbidden to smoke, talk loudly or take part in improper conversation, and they had to be in bed asleep by 11 pm every night.

They had to work from 7.30 am to 8 pm six days a week with one half day off from 2 pm to 11 pm. Even on their nights off they were still ordered to be in bed at 11 pm. The night duty was on a strict rota from 8 pm to 7. 30 am and often one nurse had to manage up to thirty beds on her own, with many patients suffering from highly contagious diseases. In the poorer or smaller workhouses, the nurse did not even have her own separate accommodation but just bedded down in the ward along with her patients, and often the one nurse would be on duty day and night.

In the infirmaries conditions were slightly better, but there was still a desperate shortage of trained nurses. The First World War drained the country of nursing staff and was responsible for a complete upheaval of the system. The best of the infirmaries were taken over by the government to care for the war casualties. All of the patients from these institutions were transferred to neighbouring infirmaries which had at the same time to cope with the ever-increasing demand for beds and they had to take the overspill of civilian patients who would normally have been scheduled for admission to the war-casualty infirmaries. This put a tremendous pressure on the nurses who were already stretched to breaking point. Unlike the better organized and prestigious voluntary hospitals, the infirmaries could not refuse admittance to any patient needing hospital treatment. The voluntary hospitals could pick and choose their patients, but the over-worked infirmaries were left to cope with all the terminally ill, geriatric and imbecile patients, those cases being generally considered uninteresting by the voluntary hospital staff.

Also because the rates of pay and the general conditions of

the voluntary hospitals were so much better than the infirmaries they attracted more highly trained nurses. These nurses would receive good food, properly cooked, and lived in comfortable staffquarters. This again reflected on the poorer standard of nursing staff in the infirmaries compared to the voluntary hospitals.

By 1913 nursing staff from the training hospitals could expect a wage of fourteen to nineteen shillings per week (equivalent to 70 pence to 95 pence per week), while the semi-trained nurses in the small country areas were only paid in the region of ten shillings per week (equivalent: 50 pence).

As time went on and the Welfare State system took over, the old workhouses gradually faded out of existence, and even the antiquated infirmaries were replaced by modern efficient hospitals as we know them. The life of a nurse became easier, though it has to be said that nurses' wages did not keep up with the ever-increasing national average.

It will be interesting to see if little Angela Mahony goes into the nursing profession when she grows up. At the moment she is too young to even think about what her future job might be, being only four years old. If she does become a nurse she will find herself living a very different lifestyle to that experienced by the nurses in the nineteenth-century workhouses.

Angela is a very intelligent child and is very well behaved and seems to possess her own self-discipline, not usual in a child so young. She has been able to read and write from the age of three and has an awareness which surprises most adults.

Kathleen says, 'More than once, when I have been out shopping with Angie, people have stopped me in the street to remark on how old-fashioned Angie is. They always seem to wind up saying the same thing: "Oh, she's been here before".'

Angie's mother smiles to herself when she hears these remarks. She wonders what these strangers would think if they heard Angie's story about being a nurse in her previous life.

Young boy remembers being a German bomber pilot

Carl Edon, Middlesbrough

When young Carl Edon plays with his toy planes, his parents believe that it is not purely childish behaviour but is an action replay of the time when Carl remembers he was a pilot in the German Air Force.

'As soon as he could talk he used to tell us that he once crashed his plane into the windows of a building,' says his mother Valerie. 'We gather that he eventually died from multiple injuries sustained in the crash. We thought it strange that he should say such a thing, for as a tiny toddler he never showed any real interest in adventure stories and he had no time for looking at war films or such things.'

Valerie Edon went on to explain that as he grew older and started to gain more command over his speech the story became more detailed and he told it in such a matter-of-fact sort of way that she and her husband felt that they could no longer dismiss it out of hand as a little toddler's day-dream.

The incident which really persuaded the Edons that Carl's story had a ring of truth to it occurred when Carl first learnt to draw and to colour. Like most small children he went through the stage of experimenting with his coloured pencils and crayons and he had the usual colouring-in books and children's puzzle books in which he used to join up the dots to make a picture. One day he sat with his crayons and colouring-in book, but instead of colouring in the drawings, his mother noticed that he had drawn peculiar-looking badges and motifs all over the page.

The neatness of the drawing was the thing that most caught Valerie's attention. Unlike the normal scribbles of a three-year-old, Carl's little drawings were definite precise examples of various badges and insignia which Valerie confesses were completely foreign to her, except for one little

drawing. Thereon the top corner of his colouring book Carl
had drawn a perfect German swastika inside a circle, thus
making it look like a badge. There were other small badges
drawn with the expertise of a professional artist.

When Valerie questioned her son about the badges he
replied, 'That's the kind of badges I wore on my uniform
when I used to drive my plane.'

More surprises were in store when shortly after Carl's
fifth birthday he drew the cockpit of his plane. He remembered the exact positions of all the various controls and he
explained to his bewildered parents the function of each
lever, dial and gauge. He even knew the location of the but-
ton which he remembers having to press in order to release
the bombs.

Carl's father was intrigued with the amount of minute
detail in his small son's drawings, particularly as he knew
that Carl had never ever been in a plane of any description,
and had certainly never been in a cockpit. 'I don't see how he
could have got the information,' said his father. 'He certainly
couldn't have got it from a picture book because he would
have had to study the subject so thoroughly that we would
have noticed, and in any case he did not possess any picture
books containing German planes or cockpits.'

The little boy can remember how he enlisted in the
Luftwaffe, the German Air Force, when he was nineteen
years of age and he was stationed on a large air-force camp
with a lot of huts in rows. Carl explains, 'The huts had sinks
in them but no taps for the water. The water came out of a
pump.' The boy recalls that he and his comrades were all
trained in first aid and anyone who was injured was treated
by the men themselves. All of them were called upon to perform this duty.

Valerie and her husband were taken aback when their
young son suddenly told them that he had been made to
salute a framed picture of Hitler. 'I couldn't believe my ears,'
said Valerie. 'I had no idea that he ever knew, or had even

heard of, the name Hitler. It certainly was never a topic of conversation at home.'

According to Carl, the troops were ordered to gather in a large assembly hall. He says, 'There was a picture of Hitler on the wall and we all had to stamp our feet and salute to this picture.' He can demonstrate the stamp and the salute, which he executes as if they were second nature to him.

In reply to his mother's question about what he wore when he was in the hall, he says, 'Grey trousers tucked into knee-high leather boots and a black jacket.' His parents did not really believe that what their son described was a proper German uniform, so without telling their child they went along to their local library and looked up some books, only to find that Carl had given a perfectly correct description of his uniform, badges, and the cockpit of his plane.

His parents were able to check even the smallest details of Carl's drawings against photographs which they found in an old book on German planes of the last war.

Carl can reconstruct in chilling detail his crash into the windows of the building. He was flying low over some buildings and he must have lost consciousness for a few moments: as he described things, 'It went all black for a moment.' When he came round in the cockpit of his plane he was aware of a building rushing towards him at great speed. He desperately wrenched at the controls in a gigantic effort to avert the collision, but he was too late. The plane bulldozed its way right through the large glass windows of the building.

Carl remembers the horrendous sensation which swept over him as he realized that he had lost his right leg. The shock of the crash, and the loss of his limb, combined with his other injuries, affected him so severely that he died very shortly after the crash.

Sadly the fatal blow affected not only Carl, but a pretty young fraulein from Carl's village back in Germany, to whom he was engaged to be married. They had been childhood sweethearts and had grown up together, although she was several years younger than he. He remembered his thoughts just before he died and how he felt great compassion for his young fiancee, knowing that she would ultimately be given the shattering news of his death. In Carl's typical understatement, 'I felt so sorry for her.'

Although Carl cannot recall much of what happened after he died, he is acutely aware of having had a younger brother who was also a pilot, and the strange thing is that he is convinced that this younger brother died shortly after he himself bled to death amongst the twisted debris of his wrecked plane.

He has clear memories of his father in his previous life, whose name was Fritz. Carl seems to have been very fond of the man, who appears to have been a jovial character. Carl says of him, 'He was so funny and always made me laugh, and he took me for nice walks in the woods.' He told Carl all about the trees and the flowers and plants that they would see on their rambles in the woods near their home in Germany. The village they lived in was picturesque, and nestled among hills and lush woodlands. 'It was not a very big place,' says Carl, 'but I liked it.'

His mother was the disciplinarian of the family and Carl remembers her as being small and plump with dark curly hair and smallish glasses which she used to wear on the end of her nose. 'She was a bit bossy,' says the boy, 'and I always had to do what I was told.'

He was made to do his share of the household tasks and he remembers that his regular chore was to gather the wood for the large open fires in their home. He has distinct memories of chopping up long tree trunks into small logs, then carting them home in his barrow to be stored as fuel. The smell of the newly-chopped logs made a vivid impression on the young boy. He describes it as 'a nice fresh smell which always reminds me of the woods.'

Other smells which linger in Carl's consciousness are those of cooking. He remembers how he used to be served a type of

44

soup. 'It wasn't like the soup I get now,' he says. 'It was a dark red colour and was quite thick. My mother made it nearly every day.' Then Carl added with a laugh, 'I used to get other things to eat as well, only I can't remember what the other things were like. But I know I got them as well as the soup.'

Valerie Edon wonders if there could be any connection between Carl's memories of his past life, and other members of her family. She says, 'My sister-in-law is German by birth and her father was a German pilot during the last war.' She wonders if it is only coincidence that this man was also killed in action, being brought down by the British while he was at the controls of his plane.

While this sister-in-law was still a baby, her mother remarried an Englishman in Germany and then moved to England where the family have since settled. The baby was adopted by the English step-father. Valerie muses over the possibility that by some strange twist of fate, she has given birth to the child who was really meant for her sister-in-law to bear.

Valerie's other two children, Darren and Angela, are completely different from their brother Carl. Both are well built with dark hair and tan complexions, whereas Carl is of a slight build with pale blond hair and white eyelashes.

The Edons are still wondering why they felt compelled to call their little boy by the name of Carl. 'It is a most incredible thing,' says Valerie, 'because we decided to call him Carl not knowing that he would have any connections with Germany.'

At a visit to Carl's school on a parents' evening recently, Valerie spoke to Carl's teacher who said, 'He has strange eyes, and when I am talking to him about anything his eyes pierce straight through me.' The teacher went on to tell Valerie that if she gives Carl a sum to do, he gives her the correct answer in a flash. 'When I ask him how he worked it out, he just doesn't answer me. He seems to think that there is no need to bother working things out when he knows the answer already.'

Carl, now an extremely bright nine-year-old, has a perfectionist streak in him which belies his years. He is ultra precise in his manner, and is more than particular about his appearance and clothes. His mother takes great pains to have everything just so for him: the collars of his shirts must be beautifully ironed, and everything has to be scrupulously clean at all times. Could this possibly be a hangover from his strict military days?

'We had a visitor in for tea recently,' laughed Valerie, 'and Carl almost frightened the life out of her by solemnly describing in amazing detail all about Adolf Hitler, accompanied by goose-steps and salutes.

'As he gets older, though,' says Valerie, 'Carl doesn't say too much about his mysterious past life. It's as though he only remembers the odd flash every now and then.' His mother has noticed that he is not particularly interested in watching war films on television but when he does he sometimes points out a mistake in the German uniform. Once he pointed to an actor playing a German NCO and said, 'He is just like my sergeant.'

Perhaps the reason for Carl's lack of enthusiasm for war films could be that they remind him too much of the real thing. Who could blame him for not wanting to bring back to his conscious mind those horrific days of violence and death?

Girl remembers being her own great-grandmother
Kelly Williams, Defen

When Mrs Diane Williams was expecting her third child, the only cloud which overshadowed the happy coming event was the fact that the baby's great-grandmother, a gentle old lady called Nanny Wyatt, had just died, and sadly she would not see her new great-grandchild. She had passed away on 4 October, 1974, at the ripe old age of 89.

When baby Kelly was born on 4 May, 1975, Diane was acutely aware of a great sense of contentment and from that moment she ceased to mourn for her much loved lost grandmother. Since then, after countless inexplicable incidents, Diane feels that her nan has returned to her in the form of her daughter Kelly.

It all started when Kelly was only two. One day she was sitting on her aunt Pam's lap when she turned to Pam and asked, 'Do you remember when you used to sit on my lap like this?' Both Diane and her sister Pam just laughed, thinking that the child was talking gibberish, but they were soon silenced when Kelly went on to describe how Pam used to wear her hair in a Cleopatra style, and added, 'And I used to comb it for you.'

Pam had indeed worn her hair in a straight sleek Cleopatra style, but that was twenty years earlier, when she was only four or five years old, and the person who used to comb it for her was Nanny Wyatt.

Kelly went on to tell the dumbfounded Pam that she remembered her freckled face, and then she asked Pam if she could please have the lovely red-and-white spotted dress because that was her favourite. Pam and Diane exchanged incredulous looks, as they realized that the dress to which Kelly was referring was one which Nanny Wyatt had bought for Pam many years before. It was a fresh white cotton frock with red polka-dots on it and frills round the sleeves and neck.

How could Kelly possibly now anything about clothes long since discarded by her aunt? Her mother Diane admits that she was something of a non-believer before Kelly was born, but since the birth of her daughter she has completely reversed her opinions. 'I never believed in life after death or reincarnation,' says Diane, 'but since I have had Kelly I do believe. My husband Clive and I have become convinced that somehow Nanny Wyatt lives on - in our daughter. I know it sounds completely ridiculous, but Kelly actually speaks as if she really is Nanny Wyatt - as if she is one and the same person with the same store of memories.'

Clive has no explanation for Kelly's behaviour. 'It's just uncanny,' he says. 'Sometimes she leaves me feeling a bit creepy after listening to the things she comes out with.' Clive went on, 'I'm no expert on this kind of thing, but there's definitely something more to it than meets the eye.'

Pam in particular is awed by Kelly's remarks about things, places and events which took place years and years before the child was born. 'It was weird the way she described my dress and hairstyle, especially when she couldn't have seen a picture of me when I was young, because we just don't have one.' Another thing that puzzles Pam is the fact that the two-year-old referred to Pam's hairstyle as a 'Cleopatra' style. 'How did she know the style was called Cleopatra?' she asks. 'After all, that fashion is years out of date and the word Cleopatra has never been uttered by any of us in front of Kelly - there was just no reason to mention it.'

Diane noticed that even Kelly's speech and mannerisms were those of Nanny Wyatt. She says, 'Strangely, Kelly seems to know all about her great-grandmother, even though she has never asked me anything about the old lady. When she sits down in an armchair, she always fetches her toy handbag, and places it on the floor, tucked between one leg and the side of the chair, just like Nanny Wyatt used to. Most people would just plonk their handbags on the floor any old way, but not Nanny, or Kelly.'

Most of the people who knew the old lady, remark on the close similarity between Mrs Wyatt and Kelly. Diane says, 'Kelly is a neat and fussy little girl, exactly like my nan was. Like most little girls she loves to play with her dolls and handbags, but unlike most, the contents of her bag are always so neatly organized, with everything in the right compartment. Nanny Wyatt was constantly cleaning out and rearranging her handbag, so much so that it became almost an obsession with her. She could not bear a crumpled tissue or an odd sweet paper to clutter up her bag, and she would get really upset if she could not find a waste-paper bin instantly.'

'It is mystifying sometimes when Kelly talks about my grandmother,' says Diane, 'as she will refer to the old woman in the first person as if she was talking about herself. Then she will go on to relate things which happened before she was born and about which she could have no knowledge whatsoever.' Diane has noticed that her little girl has developed a fascination for fashions of the Victorian times, the clothes Nanny Wyatt would have worn when she was a young girl. 'Kelly can describe them all in great detail, talking about the clothes as "the clothes we wore then".' She seems to have definite objects in her mind which she will talk about every so often. Says Diane, 'There is a particular black dress which she has described so many times that I could almost run it up on my sewing machine.'

'My dress went right down to the ground,' insists Kelly, 'and it was black and the neck came right up to my chin. It had a white collar and long sleeves and the skirt could whirl out wide when I turned around quickly.'

Her parents just cannot understand where Kelly gets her information from. 'We have no books or pictures at home which could have told her so much,' says Clive. Then he added, 'Even if I came across any odd old papers or magazines containing photographs of Victorian times, I think I would be inclined to get rid of them straightaway, so that Kelly would not be influenced by them.' Diane says, 'Whenever I ask her where she gets so much information, she says that she used to watch the ladies in the ballroom and that she was peeping through the window and nobody saw her!' Diane is completely baffled by this and has not got the faintest idea of what her daughter means. 'The funny thing is,' laughed Diane, 'she never changes her story. No matter how I frame the question, she always comes out with the exact same answer: she was peeping through the ballroom window. As far as we are concerned ballrooms really are a thing of the past. In fact I don't think I've ever been in one in my life, so heaven knows where she gets it from.'

Some of Kelly's memories are-connected with events which even her own mother had forgotten. Diane explains, 'One day Kelly told me that she enjoyed living in her little bungalow that time.' Diane is used to Kelly referring to herself as though she was Nanny Wyatt, so naturally she cast her mind back to see if she could remember her grandmother ever having lived in a bungalow. 'I was sure my grandmother had never lived in such a place, but Kelly kept on and on about it, even describing the curtains as being blue with little flowers. Then it suddenly came to me: Nanny had lived in a bungalow, but only for a few weeks and that was many years ago when I was just young myself. I had even visited her there.'

Diane's mother passed away suddenly on 13 March this year and left the whole family heartbroken. It was little Kelly who proved to be the strong one, and astounded the family by announcing, 'Nanny's at rest now with all the people she loved as much as us. She is with grandad Wyatt.' This summing up of the situation seemed to be coming from the lips of a much more mature person than a seven-year-old girl.

'She had a very special attachment to my mother, who 50 was Nanny Wyatt's daughter, of course,' says Diane. 'Mum had five grandchildren, including Kelly's brother and sister,

Spencer, aged ten, and twelve-year-old Tracey, and they all used to play happily around her - except for Kelly. She used to mother my mum.'

On 12 June, Diane's sister got married and it was a very emotional occasion for the entire family, who were still grieving over the death of Kelly's grandmother. 'We are an extremely close family,' explains Diane, 'and at the wedding service, mum was sorely missed. We were all deeply upset because we knew how much she had been looking forward to the wedding.' Diane continued, 'There were a lot of tears in church. Kelly and my elder daughter were bridesmaids. She kept a firm eye on me and had such a courageous expression on her little face that I knew she was working overtime, willing me to smile and to keep up a brave front. I'll never forget the uncanny feeling I got when her eyes looked directly into mine. I got the distinct impression that if I broke down, I would be letting her down in some odd way. If it hadn't been for Kelly, I don't think I would have got through the service.'

Recently Diane was chatting to a friend about their teenage days. The two girls had been close companions at that time, but had somehow lost touch when Diane had become engaged to Clive. They became so engrossed in their reminiscences that they forgot for a moment that Kelly was sitting in the comer playing with her toys. Diane started to talk about a particularly enjoyable holiday she had had somewhere back in 1958 or 1959. Out of the blue, Kelly called out, 'Oh I remember it. That was the year we had the plague of ladybirds.'

Diane, who by this time had become quite used to Kelly's unexpected revelations just took the remark in her stride and acknowledged her small daughter's contribution to the discussion as being correct, but Diane's friend who was unaware of the child's extraordinary gift for accurately recalling past events, looked quite stunned as she asked Diane, 'Did you hear what she said?'

Diane laughed. 'Yes, she comes out with things like that from time to time.'

The friend was even more surprised at Diane's attitude of mild acceptance. She asked Diane, 'But how does she know about the ladybirds?'

Kelly's answer left her mother's friend totally perplexed. The little girl explained, 'I know it was the year of the ladybirds because when you went on that holiday to the seaside you wore that big funny hoop thing under your dress to make it stand out more, and your mother and I kept teasing you about it. Remember we called you a walking bell tent?'

Now it was Diane's turn to be left open-mouthed and speechless. She thought that by this time she had become shock-proof with Kelly, but this really took her unawares. Everything Kelly had said was true. It had been the late fifties when wide flouncy hula-hoop skirts with lots of frilly petticoats underneath were all the rage. Diane's mother did tease her, and the other person present at the time had been Nanny Wyatt.

Another insight into Kelly's peculiar sense of the past came to light when some members of the family were sitting in the lounge discussing the troubles in the Falklands. Someone expressed a fear that there might be some bombings on the British mainland, and immediately Kelly said, 'It was just the same during the last war, when they dropped the bombs. It was awful, and everyone knows Birmingham was badly hit during the war.'

'Nanny Wyatt's death was a great personal loss,' says Diane, 'but since Kelly began to demonstrate this inexplicable supernatural link with her, I have had a deep conviction that the old lady is still here.'

Kelly, now a chirpy seven-year-old, is a very self-confident child, perceptive and thoughtful, and she can hold a proper conversation with an adult as if she is on equal terms.

Girl remembers previous life in South Africa
Justine Shillito, Reading

One sunny summer afternoon when Justine was playing happily in the garden of her home in Reading, Berks, she turned to her mother and said, 'When I lived in Africa we had sunshine like this every day.'

As Justine was only three years old at the time and had never been out of England, her mother Beverly got quite a shock. Says Beverly, 'I went cold when she said this because I'd never read her any stories mentioning Africa and she never bothered to watch television apart from the odd children's programme.'

Beverly asked her daughter what her name had been when she lived in Africa and she was told Mary. As a test question, Beverly then asked Justine, 'Were the people black or white?' The child's answer confirmed her mother's suspicions that Justine's remarks were not just childish fantasy. Justine replied, 'Black poor ones and white ordinary ones.'

Over the course of the next few weeks Justine told her parents that when she lived in Africa she had two brothers and her mother had been called Ann. Her father had been a farmer of some type. They lived on a farm or a small holding and they had lots of chickens and dogs.

Justine said that when she was Mary she did not go to school but just played around her house with a pet brown and white dog called Bimbo, which she fondly remembers. She is vividly aware of the climate being always dry and hot.

The family must have been reasonably well off because Justine says, 'We had our own pool in the garden and I went in it when I got very hot.' She remembers that her mother had domestic assistance and she described a Negro woman called Daisy who was 'very fat and black with lots and lots of little woolly curls in her hair.' Justine says

'Daisy helped my mummy and did the housework for her.'

Daisy lived with the family, but according to Justine the woman did not sleep in the main house but had her own quarters in a small hut at the end of the garden. There was also a black house-boy called Tom-Tom.

Daisy and Tom-Tom were most probably related in some way, possibly as husband and wife, or maybe as mother and son, because Daisy seemed to be very much in authority over Tom-Tom. According to Justine's memory, Daisy's word was law in the servants' quarters. Also Justine recalls just one wooden hut at the bottom of the garden, another factor which would indicate that the two servants were probably related.

Justine was very fond of Daisy but she had reservations about Tom-Tom. 'He stole my mummy's ring once,' said Justine. 'He pretended he didn't but Daisy found it in the hut.' Tom-Tom used to do the gardening, and help generally around the house. 'He liked to eat mealie,' says Justine. 'But I didn't like that, so Mummy never gave it to me.' Mealie is a slang term used to describe a meal of maize mixed with potatoes which is eaten by the natives of South Africa. This food was always eaten by Daisy and Tom-Tom in the wooden hut and never in the house.

Justine told her mother, 'The black people were over the other side.' This comment, together with the reference to the mealie suggests that Justine's former life may have been in South Africa.

Another point which bears this out is that Justine is absolutely petrified of what she calls 'baubies' . Her mother Beverly had no idea what a bauby was but she was alarmed at her little girl's fear which expressed itself each time the child raised the subject.

Beverly tried time and time to comfort her daughter but the fear of the terrible baubies caused the child to go into near hysterics. Beverly says, 'Each time I asked her what she meant by baubies she would just burst into tears with a look of absolute terror in her eyes.'

Unknown to Beverly or Justine, some research was carried

out with the co-operation of South Africa House. At first there was no success whatsoever, and no one had even heard of anything called a bauby. It looked as if every avenue of investigation had been exhausted, and the terror that had menaced Justine's former life was destined to remain a mystery. As a final attempt to find an explanation, the question was put to a Negro employee at South Africa House who had spent many years living in the South African bush. She was asked, 'Have you ever heard of a bauby?' Immediately she replied, 'You mean boerbee? Of course. It's another name for Afrikaaner cattle.'

Boerbees are a particularly tough brand of cattle with extra-long, ferocious-looking horns, specially bred to survive in drought conditions. They are not like the normal docile cattle which we in the UK are accustomed to seeing grazing peacefully in our fields, but are left to roam wild, and appear to be extremely menacing. There would be every reason for a small girl to react with terror if she happened to find herself confronted with or attacked by a boerbee.

The words bauby and boerbee sound so alike, it is clearly possible that the child was referring to the latter word. This again would support the South Africa theory.

Another remark made by Justine which her mother did not understand was, 'I didn't get to go beside the kafas.' Beverly thought that Justine was talking about calves, because she had previously mentioned the fact that the family lived on a sort of farm, but the little girl said, 'No, not calves, Mummy. Kafas.' When Beverly asked her daughter what she meant by kafas Justine replied, 'You know, the black kafas.' Beverly didn't know that a kaffir is another word for a member of the South African Bantu and is also used in a wider context by white South Africans as a derogatory reference to any member of the Negro community. Perhaps what Justine meant to say was the word kaffir, which sounds so much like the little girl's word: kafa.

Beverly cannot understand how little Justine has such

knowledge of a country and way of life which could not be more different from her lifestyle in Berks. The girl describes her garden in Africa with big fruit trees, the big swimming pool, and the large elegant white house with the flight of steps leading down to the pool, all in great detail.

'There were snakes in the garden sometimes,' recalls Justine, as she tells her mother how one day she was sitting with her mother when a snake appeared just inside the door which led directly out on to the back garden. She remembers that her mother was afraid and screamed to her father who was outside in the garden. The father rushed into the house carrying a huge boulder or heavy stone. 'He came in and saved us,' says Justine. She explains, 'Daddy hit the snake on the head with the big stone. Then he killed it.'

'Justine does not appear to be particularly frightened of snakes, at least no more so than anyone else,' says her mother, 'because although she said that her mother Ann had been afraid when the snake entered the kitchen, Justine made no mention of being afraid herself.' Beverly says, 'I'm sure that if she had experienced fear, it's the first thing she would have told me, especially since she mentioned the fact that her mother had been afraid. Perhaps she saw snakes quite regularly, or she may have been too small at the time to realize the danger, considering that she said that she did not go to school when she lived in Africa.'

The servants' hut at the bottom of the garden seemed to be out of bounds for Justine - or Mary as she was then called. 'Mummy told me I mustn't go down there,' the child remembers.

When Beverly was making an apple pie one day and Justine was watching her, supposed to be helping as all little girls like to do from time to time, the child said, 'That's not how Daisy made our pies.' When Beverly asked what was different about Daisy's pies, Justine replied, 'Daisy didn't cover them over on top like that. She just put lines over the apples.' 'She was obviously trying to describe an open tart,' said Beverly.

Justine told her mother that they had lots of apple trees in their garden and there was a big ladder which TomTom used to climb up to collect the apples. It was also his job to spray the lawn and flowers with water using a long rubber hose-pipe. 'It was like a long snake,' says Justine.

Justine is sure that she had two brothers in her previous life in Africa but she does not recall their names or whether they were younger or older than herself. She remembers playing in the swimming pool with them and having fun being sprayed with the hose-pipe. Justine and her brothers used to gather the eggs from the chickens every morning and bring them to Daisy.

Justine's mother says, 'I often wonder what would happen if we ever took our little girl to South Africa. I wonder if she would be specially drawn to any particular part of the country. But I don't think we will manage such a trip in the fore-seeable future.'

Maybe that's just as well for Justine's sake, when we remember her reaction to the Afrikaaner cattle. She is now a bubbling exuberant six-year-old who enjoys nothing more than tucking into her mother's English apple pie and fresh Devon cream.

Boy remembers being a garage mechanic
Jonathan Pike, Leigh-on-Sea

When Jonathan was three-and-a-half years old his parents moved from Hulbridge in Essex to the Priory Park area of Prittlewell on the outskirts of Southend-on-Sea. The first time his mother Anne took him out walking through the park little Jonathan had fun running through the thick carpet of red and rust-coloured leaves which had fallen from the trees. It was a glorious afternoon and the sun was streaming through the trees, highlighting the natural beauty of the autumn colours. There was a pleasant hint of burning wood in the air, and Anne noticed some men busy gathering up leaves and twigs into heaps to throw into a crackling brazier.

Jonathan turned to Anne and with a broad reminiscent smile on his face told her, 'When I was ten we used to come over here, and we set a bonfire alight and a policeman came and chased us away.'

Anne thought that the sight of the burning leaves had just set her little boy's imagination on a make-believe trip, making him think that he had been in the park before. She thought no more about the remark and didn't even tell her husband.

Some time later Anne was busy with her ironing. It was early evening and little Jonathan who was all ready for bed was watching her. He had been allowed to stay up just a little later than usual that evening, but as it was now well past his usual bedtime his father Tom decided that it was time to take his son upstairs and tuck him in for the night. After kissing his mother goodnight, Jonathan jumped up on his father's back piggy-back style and was taken upstairs. On the way up, the child said to his father, 'When I was a little boy the last time, my other mummy did ironing.' Tom was mildly surprised to hear this, but he didn't over-react. He remembers, 'At first I thought that I must have heard the wrong thing, or that he had got a bit jumbled up in what he was trying to say.'

Tom asked Jonathan, 'You mean you've been watching mummy do the ironing.' The child replied, 'Not this mummy, my other mummy.' His father asked him, 'What other mummy?' Jonathan replied, 'The one that I had when I was here before.' Tom says, 'He seemed so definite that it made me wonder, so I asked him what he meant when he had said that he'd been here before.' Jonathan told his father, 'I used to live near here before when I was a little boy the last time with my other mummy and daddy.'

Because Tom had never heard Jonathan say anything vaguely like that before, he really began to feel uneasy. He says, 'I put him into his bed, and I remember feeling very odd. I looked at him lying there relaxed and smiling away as if he'd said something quite ordinary and normal. I could see that he wasn't in the least bothered by having been here before.' Tom then tucked his little boy in and kissed him goodnight. Just as he got to the bedroom door, Jonathan called to his father, 'Daddy, when my other mummy did her ironing she showed me how to put creases in my trousers.'

A bewildered Tom made his way back downstairs to join his wife. He told Anne all about what Jonathan had been saying and then she told him about the child's remarks in the park about having been there before when he was ten.

Jonathan's parents could well imagine how a little boy might make a remark about a bonfire, and that he had been watching ironing, but the one thing they couldn't fathom was how Jonathan could know anything about putting creases in trousers. Tom usually wears jeans around the house and any time his trousers need to be pressed they are sent to the dry cleaners. Anne says, 'I wouldn't even attempt to press his good trousers in case I made a mess of them.' She has never ever pressed creases in trousers and Jonathan, being only three years old, had always worn children's permanently pressed trousers. Anne says, 'All the kids' trousers nowadays come either permanently creased, or else like his little shorts with no creases in them at all.' They were surprised that Jonathan even knew what the word crease meant.

Shortly after that Anne took Jonathan out on a bus past some very large white houses in Chalkwell. Suddenly Jonathan pointed over to the houses and said, 'That's where Angela lived.' Anne asked him who Angela was and he replied, 'She was my wife.' Anne couldn't believe her ears. She said to Jonathan, 'How could you have a wife? You're only three.' Jonathan answered, 'Yes, but when I was here the last time I grew up into a big man and Angela was my wife.'

The child then went on to say that when he had been living before, he had had a son and daughter and the little girl was also called Angela after her mother. Jonathan remembered that his little girl had lots of long curls in her hair and she used to have them tied at each side with ribbons. This seemed to stick in his mind. He told Anne that before little Angela would be put to bed his wife used to brush the child's hair and put what he described as long cloth bandages in her hair. He went on to explain that in the morning when the bandages would be taken off, Angela's hair would be all covered in long curls.

Later that same day when Anne was returning on the bus by the same route, they travelled down Chalkwell Avenue and when they came to the crossroads where Crosby Road crosses the Ridgeway, Jonathan became very agitated and he looked very upset. Anne was watching him but she didn't say anything. He suddenly turned to her and said, 'That's where my little girl got killed.' Anne says, 'He looked really sad and I thought he was going to cry. I asked him if he was all right and he nodded and then said, "My little girl Angela got killed by a car there." '

After that first bus journey Jonathan always said the same thing about his little girl being killed and each time they would go down that road on the bus he always pointed to the same spot by the crossroads. He never once changed his mind or got confused about this. He remembered that little Angela had run out on to the road and a car had run over her, killing her outright.

On another occasion, again when they were on a bus travelling between the Bell Public House and Cuckoo Corner, Jonathan pointed to a big garage called Earl's Hall Motors and said, 'That's where I used to work as a mechanic.' He told his mother that he had to fix all the cars and that he knew how to fit engines.

Jonathan has two smaller sisters, Elizabeth and Louise, and one day when Anne was bathing the girls, Jonathan said to her, 'I used to bath Angela like that.' His little sisters were one and two at the time, and Elizabeth, the two-year-old, asked Jonathan who Angela was. Then she giggled. 'Is she your dollie?' she asked. Jonathan became quite indignant at this question and in a superior manly voice he informed his little sister, 'I didn't have dollies. Angela was my daughter.' Of course Elizabeth didn't know what her brother was talking about and just splashed about merrily in her bath, but Anne understood what he meant. She said to Jonathan, 'Did you really have a little girl called Angela?' He replied firmly, 'Yes, and she got killed.' Anne then asked him, 'What about your little boy?' Jonathan said, 'I can't remember what his name was. I only remember Angela's name because it was the same as my wife's.'

Jonathan told his mother that when he was married to Angela he went to live in the Chalkwell area in one of the big white houses. He said that he had a nice big garden and he used to grow lots of flowers and vegetables. He couldn't remember the actual address or number of the house but he was certain that it was somewhere in Chalkwell.

Because the family had only just moved to the area, Anne cannot understand how Jonathan knew the name Chalkwell, where it was, or that such a place even existed. They were totally new to the entire district and Jonathan had never been taken to Chalkwell apart from the times when he was on the bus with his mother.

Although there are four garages in the area, three are simply filling stations. Earl's Hall Motors, the oldest garage in the area, is the only one where mechanics were employed. Because Jonathan cannot remember his previous name it is difficult to check back to see if there ever was a mechanic employed there who would fit the description of the man Jonathan thinks he used to be.

The main lead was the fact that his little girl had been killed in a road accident at the crossroads on Chalkwell Avenue. There is no one living in the area at present who can recall an accident at that spot involving a small girl called Angela, but again because there is no surname people find it difficult to think back. Very often when a small child is knocked down and killed on the road, the people will remember the incident according to the family name, as it were, the Jones girl, or Billy Smith's daughter. They would not necessarily remember the child's Christian name.

Prior to 1960 the Southend police were an independent force but then they merged with the county police and all the old records from the Southend station have been stored away in vaults. Again, in the absence of a date or surname, it would be an almost impossible task to try to dig up details of such a fatal accident. However, a long serving police officer, Sergeant Ernie Dark of Southend Traffic Police, does remember a fatal accident involving a child at that very spot some thirty years ago, and he recollects that the child who was killed was a little girl.

Two-year-old girl remembers being a mother
Gaynor Marsh, Isle of Man

When Mrs Margery Marsh, a busy mother with two children, ran out of the family's favourite breakfast cereal, she decided to give the children porridge, hoping that they would find it a pleasant change from their usual morning fare.

Seven-year-old Laurie who was rushing to get ready for school made little comment on the change of menu but his two-year-old sister Gaynor was quite nonplussed about having to eat porridge.

'I don't like porridge,' she told her mother.

'How do you know you don't like it?' asked her mother. 'You've never had it before.'

'Oh yes I have,' insisted Gaynor. 'When I was a little girl before I had it and I didn't like it then either.'

The harassed mother sighed, although she couldn't help smiling to herself as she heard Gaynor's remarks about when she was a little girl before. Margery assumed that this was just a trumped-up argument against having to eat porridge, and she marvelled at the ingenuity of it. 'I certainly hadn't heard that one before,' says Margery, 'but I just thought it was Gaynor's imagination providing her with an excuse not to eat breakfast, so I didn't pay too much attention to it, and in fact I didn't even comment on her words.'

Gaynor's mother tried to convince her that she could not possibly know whether or not she liked the porridge until she had tasted it. Margery suggested that perhaps if she added some raspberry jam it would brighten up the meal, which she admitted didn't look all that enticing. In spite of her mother's efforts, Gaynor was adamant. She didn't like porridge and that was that. She then turned tearfully to her mother and remarked, 'When I was a mummy I didn't make my little girls eat things they didn't like.'

'What little girls?' snapped Margery impatiently as she

reluctantly threw Gaynor's porridge in the bin. Her daughter answered, 'My two little girls, when I was a mummy.' She added, 'And I didn't shout at them. When I was a mummy I was nice to my little girls.'

Margery did not know what to think of her child's remarks, but over the following weeks and months the story of Gaynor's two little girls did not alter. Gaynor remembered how she used to play with the little girls and how she used to teach them to sew and how to make things. She said that she only gave them the things to eat which they liked and that the one special treat that the girls loved was when she took them out to pick blackberries and they got to eat some on the way home. She used to let the girls watch her make jam with the berries but she wouldn't let them stir the jam when it was hot in case they got their fingers burnt, although she did allow them to help her prepare the fruit.

Gaynor used to make unprompted comments about what her girls used to do and how they all got on together and what they looked like. Gaynor remembers them as having 'nice long frocks right down to the ground'.

'It's funny,' says Gaynor's mother. 'Every time I used to ask her any questions about her little girls she would never answer me. I didn't press the questioning. I realized that if I asked her any specific question it might put the idea into her head and give her some material upon which to build, so I purposely kept off the subject.'

Gaynor's mother feels that the memories were sparked off by various happenings in everyday life. For example, when the child was offered porridge for breakfast it reminded her of how she had disliked porridge in her previous life. She says, 'She seems to have been very close to her daughters.'

Before all this developed, something very odd happened. For the first time Gaynor managed to say a complete sentence. It was shortly after her second birthday. Her mother recalls, 'We were out for a walk one afternoon, and I decided to take Gaynor along a narrow country road where she had never been before, just for a change of scenery.' As they ambled down the road, they came to an old cemetery. 'Immediately Gaynor set eyes on the graveyard she got very excited,' says Margery. 'At first I thought it was something to do with the flowers which had been left at the various tombstones, but I soon realized that the flowers had nothing to do with Gaynor's reaction. She kept jumping up and down and pointing towards the cemetery. Then to my amazement she yelled out her first complete sentence: "That is where I was born."

'The words hit me in an odd way,' says Margery. 'There was something in her tone - a sort of conviction, which left me stunned. She had never ever said a complete sentence like that before, just the usual baby talk, and it struck me as very strange that she should choose such unusual words with which to make her break-through. I got such a shock that I couldn't get away from the cemetery quick enough.

When Gaynor was only a few months old, Margery had had an unforgettable experience which left her convinced that she had been given a glimpse of the past. In view of Gaynor's remarks about a previous life, Margery feels that what she saw could be linked up with her daughter's past.

'We had gone to bed, and baby Gaynor was fast asleep in her crib in the corner of our bedroom,' says Margery. She goes on to explain that she suddenly found herself in the doorway of a room totally unknown to her. She could see into the room which was illuminated by a pinkish orange light, and there inside was a family she had never seen before in her life - a father, mother, and two or three young children.

'The first thing that impressed me,' says Margery, 'was the fact that they were all wearing very old-fashioned clothes. They were simple and looked as though they had been hand-made.' Margery remembers that the woman's ankle-length dress was of a coarse type of deep brown linen or cotton and was perfectly plain. It was gathered at the neckline and waist by some type of cord or rope, and there was a long white apron over the dress, like an old-fashioned pinafore.

The father sat by a great blazing fire and the children were playing on the floor. Margery was aware of the children laughing and talking but she could not make out what was being said; in fact she is not sure whether she actually heard any sounds or not, and she feels that she received more of an impression of laughter and sound rather than actually hearing it.

The room was sparsely furnished, giving the impression that the family must have been rather poor. The bits and pieces of furniture were very crude, and like the clothes, they too seemed to have been home-made. There was a large wooden table, a couple of rough looking wooden benches. The father sat on one of the benches smoking a peculiar looking pipe with an extra long stem. Margery recalls that she was puzzled about the pipe because it was not a type usually seen in England. She says, 'It was more of a Continental pipe, like the ones you see in Holland. '

The man wore a lightish coloured shirt and a dark brown jacket. Margery could not see his face because he had his hand up to it as he held the pipe.

'I got the feeling of the 17th century, for some reason,' says Margery, 'and although the family seemed to be poor, it was not abject poverty, and I think they probably managed to get by O.K.' As Margery stood in the doorway watching the family, she expected them to notice her and ask her what she wanted. She says, 'The strange thing was they didn't pay the slightest bit of attention to me. They just acted as if I wasn't there.'

Margery felt herself strongly drawn towards the mother. 'I just couldn't take my eyes off the woman,' she explains. 'The mother was setting a meal out on the big table, using wooden plates and bowls and very large coarse-looking wooden platters. She was standing with her back to the fire, facing the table and I could distinctly see that she must have been in her twenties. Her hair was tied back from her face and she wore a little scarf or kerchief on her head, tied back behind her neck and underneath her hair. I was looking at a side view of the woman,' says Margery, 'and I could see that her apron hung loosely from her shoulders, and she had her sleeves rolled up as she worked with the food.'

Suddenly Margery felt herself being pulled backwards, but she was still unable to take her eyes off the woman. The doorway became smaller and smaller until it looked like a black tunnel, then it seemed like a small black hole and she realized that she was looking into the pupil of an eye. She then became aware of the fact that the eye was that of her baby daughter Gaynor, who was quietly lying in her cot.

For a moment Margery stood looking at the baby, then she turned away from the cot to go back to bed. She became petrified with fear when she saw herself lying in the bed fast asleep beside her husband. 'I'll never forget how afraid I felt at that moment,' says Margery. 'The next thing I knew, I was awake, sitting up in bed looking around me. I think the shock woke me up.'

Margery had had what is known as an out-of-the-body experience, known as O.O.B.E. for short, in which her etheric or astral body separated from her physical body during sleep. Her entire consciousness and personality were present with her ego in the etheric body, leaving the physical shell housing only the material components - flesh, bones, blood, etc. The physical body still continues to function normally during an O.O.B.E. but at a very subdued level, i.e. the heart still beats, the blood continues to circulate, but these things happen automatically, rather like when an aeroplane is flying on automatic pilot.

Margery believes that the scene she witnessed actually took place in her daughter Gaynor's previous life. She feels that Gaynor was the mother of the family - the woman to whom Margery felt inexplicably drawn, and she feels that the children playing on the floor were in fact the little girls that Gaynor constantly referred to. She is almost certain that there were three of them ranging in age from two to five. Although she could not see them clearly she has the strong impression that they were Gaynor's daughters.

The interesting point about this is that Margery's out-of-the-body experience happened when Gaynor was only four months old, long before the child started to relate her memories of her previous life. So the scene which margery witnessed could not possibly have been implanted in her mind by any of Gaynor's comments. She sums up the experience as, 'almost as if I had been inside my daughter and was able to tune into her past'.

For a long time Gaynor used to talk to two invisible friends. Her mother often heard the child engrossed in conversation in her bed at night. 'I could only, of course, hear a one-way conversation,' says Margery, 'but it always seemed to follow a logical format. It wasn't just a string of random ideas or words. The things she said seemed to tie up with inaudible questions and answers. It appeared as if she really was talking to people in the room unseen by me but apparently quite visible to her. I would watch her expressions and her eye movements and it seemed as if she was focusing on someone while she directed her speech to that particular area'.

Whenever Margery asked Gaynor who she was speaking to she would only reply, 'Just my lady and gentleman.' The child would never volunteer any further information, and Margery thought it wise not to question her on the matter.

One of Gaynor's oddest remarks came when she was sitting on her brother Laurie's knee. She said, 'I'm sitting on my daughter's friend's knee.' Margery thinks that this remark indicates that the family were all known to each other, or even related, in some previous life.

Margery had suffered a miscarriage before Gaynor was born but when she was carrying her daughter, she had a strange dream in which she clearly saw the baby that was in her womb. She remembers the little face and how the child seemed to speed forward in time. One moment she was holding a tiny new-born baby with not a hair on her head and the next moment the child leapt down from Margery's arms and started to run about. The face of the child in the dream was identical to the face of Gaynor when she was born, and again when she developed into a toddler. Margery was so impressed by the dream that she told her husband that she was sure that this time she would not have a miscarriage and that the baby would be born. She described the baby in her dream to her husband, telling him that she was convinced that she had been shown the baby waiting to be born. In the dream Margery thought that Gaynor was one of twins. She did not have twins when her daughter was born, but some time later she was diagnosed as expecting twins, though sadly she suffered a miscarriage and lost them. She is certain that Gaynor was meant to be born to her in response to some long-forgotten link between them in the past.

Boy remembers being in his aunt's womb
Desmond Sanderson, Coventry

Three-and-a-half-year-old Desmond was playing on the floor with his toy cars one day when completely out of the blue he looked up at his mother Dorothy and said, 'You know, Mummy, I went to Aunty Ruth before I came to you, but I didn't stay there very long.'

The words made Dorothy stop in her tracks because her sister-in-law Ruth, the Aunty referred to by Desmond, had given birth to a still-born son almost ten years previously.

Dorothy says that her sister-in-law suffered a double tragedy because shortly after she lost her baby, her husband was killed in an accident. Dorothy says, 'It was all too much for poor Ruth and she almost had a nervous breakdown. It took her a long time to recover, but she has never been able to talk about her baby or her husband. As a mark of respect, the rest of the family took their cue from Ruth and to this day no one has ever mentioned either the baby or the husband.

'That is why I am absolutely certain that my small son could never have heard about the dead baby, let alone interpret it in the way he did,' explains Dorothy.

As his mother listened quietly, little Desmond told her that he remembered everything quite clearly, and that he was very warm when he was with Aunty Ruth. 'It was quite bouncy,' he said, 'and I used to turn round and round all the time.'

He remembered feeling very happy and comfortable and very wet. It was always dark but it didn't frighten Desmond. It all seemed perfectly natural. He used to get sleepy sometimes, and said, 'One time I just went to sleep but when I woke up again I wasn't with Aunty Ruth any more.

His mother asked him where he was then. His reply surprised her: 'I went back home, of course.' Dorothy laughed. 'He said it in such a tone of voice that it made me feel quite foolish, as if I should have known that he went home - wherever that was!'

When his mother asked him where his home was, Desmond said, 'The place that I lived in before I went to Aunty Ruth, where all the nice fields are, and all the other little boys and girls. I went back to Robert and Samantha.'

Over the following weeks Dorothy heard more of her son's story of how he had special friends at home before he went to his Aunt Ruth called Robert and Samantha, and that there were also bigger people who looked after the children. He described how all the children were together and that they played lots of games.

The games were sometimes organized as in the case of the boat races which the child described, but mostly the children just played at what they liked. The boat races were evidently part of some type of gala or celebration, because Desmond was aware of dressing in a special robe for the occasion. 'He described taking part in a regatta with Samantha and Robert. He was in the same boat as Robert, but Samantha was with some of her other friends in another boat. There were lots of decorations on the boats - mostly flowers. He said that it was easy to make the boats go, but they didn't have any sails because there was no wind.

'On holidays we all had to sing,' said Desmond. He told how sometimes they got important visitors who came to play music for them. Desmond said that he never got any sweets in his other home but he remembered eating fruit. 'It was juicy and nice,' he said, and went on to describe what his mother thought must have been some kind of plum but bigger, and with no stone in the centre. He made an odd remark about the fruit when he told his mother, 'Some of the sick people got fruit to make them better after they died.'

There were pets in Desmond's home, and many of the children played with rabbits and dogs. He was friends with a tiny green and yellow bird which used to accompany him everywhere. The bird always stayed with him.

It is interesting to note that there was some continuity in Desmond's story regarding the period which was spent waiting to be born in his aunt's womb. 'I didn't like to question him too closely,' says Dorothy, 'but it seems that somehow he remembers some of the incidents as having happened before he went to his Aunty Ruth, and some afterwards. I mean after he left Ruth and before he came to me, although there does seem to be some mix-up regarding time. I get the feeling that the time element in Desmond's previous life is not based on the same principles as our earthly time. He seems to have some difficulty sorting out exactly when the various incidents occurred, but he is in no doubt as to the reality of his experiences.'

The fact which suggests that there is some continuity in the chain of events remembered by Desmond is that he vividly remembers saying goodbye to his pet bird before he left his home to go to his Aunt Ruth. He then had an awareness of being in the womb and he seemed to know the identity of his mother at that time. Then after falling into a sleep he remembers going home again, and then he remembers meeting his little green and yellow bird - the same bird to which he had said goodbye before.

This also seems to suggest that the conception of Desmond in Ruth's womb was a carefully planned affair. He was well advised of what was about to happen to him and he prepared for a parting from his friends and his pet bird. Desmond also seemed to be aware of being called away from his permanent home when it was time for him to go to his present mother. He said, 'I knew I was coming to you and Daddy, because they told me.' This would strongly suggest that nothing happens by chance.

According to Desmond, there was something very special about the water at his other home. Says Dorothy, 'He told me about how the children used to play in pools of water, but when I asked him if he went swimming he said no. Then I asked him if he meant that he had gone paddling in the water the way he does now. Again he said no. I thought at that point that he was just playing me up, but when I heard his next remark I realized that there must be something more to it.'

Desmond's explanation of the water was, 'We didn't have to swim because we didn't sink and we never got wet.' He went on to tell his mother that when he went into the water with his friends they used to float on top of the water which seemed to support them and the drops of water just fell off them when they got out of the pool. 'Sometimes we went underneath the water,' said Desmond, 'but it didn't go in my mouth or in my eyes.'

'The most incredible thing of all,' says Dorothy, 'is that Desmond told me that the water made some sort of sound - like music.' Her son had said, 'The water played songs for us, Mummy, but not with words in them. When we picked up some water it went tinkle tinkle.' Desmond said that as well as sounds, the water had colours in it 'like little rainbows, but sometimes just one colour at a time.' The water was described as being soft to the touch and did not penetrate clothes or objects. It just seemed to bounce off in drops and made its own way back to the pool. 'When we got out of the water we were all dry straightaway without towels,' said Desmond, as if it was the most natural thing in the world.

Another time Desmond suddenly said, 'I've been to school, Mummy.' At that time the child had just started to attend play-school so of course Dorothy thought that Desmond was referring to that. She made some casual answer about hoping that he liked his play-school, but then he said, 'No, I mean the big children's school when I was at home with all my friends.'

Desmond related his story about how the children attended school and were taught lots of things. The teachers also looked after the children as guardians and all of them lived at the school. 'It seems that it was like a kind of school village,' says Dorothy. 'Not exactly a boarding school and certainly not as strict. The way Desmond describes it it appears almost like a holiday-camp with lessons thrown in.'

'He cannot remember the things he was taught,' says Desmond's mother, 'but he seems to know that there were lots of books. It's funny, but although Desmond is something of a tear-away little fellow he does have a great respect for books. I belong to a book club myself and I treasure my books very much, yet I feel quite confident when Desmond looks at them. I know that he wouldn't dream of tearing them or scribbling on them. He can't read, of course, but he enjoys looking through the books. Sometimes I have to laugh at his serious expression as he looks up and down the printed pages. I often wonder what is going on in his mind.'

Dorothy has never told Ruth about Desmond's remarks because more and more she is becoming convinced that her little boy must have been the child Ruth was expecting.

'She has no children of her own at all,' explains Dorothy, 'so I am afraid to tell her about Desmond in case she feels that he really belongs to her. In any case, I couldn't bear to start digging up the past again. Ruth has come to terms with her circumstances and it would be unfair and cruel of me to remind her of what she obviously would prefer to forget.'

As Desmond gets older the stories of his other home become fewer and fewer. 'Now that he's six he seems to have forgotten most of it,' says his mother, 'but every now and then he comes out with some odd remark which leaves me puzzled.'

Apart from these remote flashes, the last complete incident to be related by Desmond was when he was almost five. 'We were in the garden at the time,' says Dorothy, 'and I was showing Desmond how to plant some flower seeds. He took my breath away when he told me he used to make his own singing flowers when he lived with his friends.'

When his mother asked him what he meant by singing flowers he replied, 'You know, the flowers with the music coming out of them.' It seems that Desmond and one of his friends had been taught how to make flowers by some man

74

who knew all about them. He was taught that all he had to do was to think of the flower, stage by stage, and the flower would appear. Apparently the stem would materialize, followed by the leaves and petals, etc., and the colour of the flower would correspond to the colour willed by Desmond. If he wanted a pink flower it would become pink. 'The shapes of the flowers were different to the ones in our garden,' said the child.

'Like the water, these flowers had some kind of sound attributed to them,' says Dorothy. Seemingly, after the flowers were completed, some kind of force instilled itself into them and came from the petals in the form of sound or music. 'I may have some of it wrong,' says Dorothy, 'but that's the way I can describe it from what Desmond has told me. I know the whole thing sounds too ridiculous for words, but for that very reason, I am certain Desmond must have had some strange experiences.' Then Dorothy added with a laugh, 'He's certainly never seen musical flowers in our garden. We're lucky if we manage a few dandelions.'

Desmond's father John is taking his son's remarks seriously. He says, 'We don't really discuss it much, especially since he's started school, because the kid seems to have forgotten most of it now - at least he never mentions much about his other life. But at the time I remember thinking that there was no way that a youngster of his age could possibly have such things in his head unless he had lived through it all. It's not just the stuff about the water and the flowers,' says Desmond's father, 'but how he could tell us that he went to his Aunt Ruth before he came to us is unbelievable. If she had never lost a baby, then it would be different, but that one fact casts a whole new light on the matter. There's no doubt in my mind that the kid must have experienced life beforehand and those memories stayed with him during his first three or four years on the earth.'

Going to school was the turning point for Desmond, as that was the period when the memories seemed to fade into the background and the stories all but ceased, apart from occasional isolated remarks. Possibly the reason for this could be that when he went to school, the child had to absorb an increased amount of knowledge, facts and figures at a comparatively accelerated pace, and his brain was too busy dealing with this new information to allow the older memories to manifest themselves.

Girl remembers being lady of the manor
Gayle Woodward, Liverpool

Since Gayle Woodward was only two she has had a very advanced vocabulary for her age. Her mother Edna describes Gayle as petite and fairy-like, and a little old-fashioned in her ways.

The family always ate lunch in the kitchen and one day when they had just finished eating, Gayle said, 'I will have my coffee in the lounge, please, Mummy.' Gayle's father was tickled at this remark from his two-year-old, and jokingly asked her, 'What were you before, Gayle, a lady?' To the surprise of her parents, the child replied, 'Yes of course, why?'

Edna then asked Gayle what made her think that she had been a lady. Gayle replied, 'When I lived at the big house with all the rooms I was a lady.' When her mother asked her what house she meant, Gayle said, 'The big house with lots of steps going down from the door. The one with the big rooms and tall roofs, remember?' Gayle's mother told her that she didn't know any big house like that, but the child insisted that she used to live in the house, saying, 'It was when I was a big lady and I used to wear my pretty long dresses.'

Edna knew that Gayle had never visited or known about such a house, but she and her husband listened while Gayle described her memories of her former life. She said that there were lots of people at the big house who did all the work, and there was a man whose job it was to carry the bags. There were several horses, some of which were used to pull a coach which belonged to her family.

Gayle remembers how the coach was always kept in shining condition. She says, 'One of the helpers used to keep polishing it to keep the lanterns shiny.' She describes the coach as being black with lanterns on each side. There was one seat inside the coach and there was a high seat up on the top at the front where the man used to sit 'to drive the horses'. Gayle distinctly remembers lots of brasswork on the coach, which was always gleaming. 'The inside seat was red,' she says, 'and there was red on the inside of the doors at the bottom, but at the top of the doors it was glass, just like the windows.'

She remembers that sometimes one horse was used to pull the coach and sometimes two. She says, 'But Gypsy never went in front of the coach, only some of the other horses. Gypsy was my special horse and he was lovely.'

The coach was used by the family all the time, and Gayle says, 'Sometimes it would be sent to collect people who wanted to come to visit us at our house, especially when we used to have the big parties.' Gayle remembers that her family did a lot of entertaining, but she does not remember specific members of her family. She seems only to be aware of the fact that she lived in the big house as part of the family, and that there were lots of people around. 'It's more the lifestyle that she remembers,' says her mother, 'rather than individual relatives.'

'I liked it when we had the big parties because I got to wear my best dresses,' recalls Gayle. She described her dresses as being long with lots and lots of frills on them and little ribbons and bows on the sleeves. 'I had lots of pretty dresses in different colours and they all had big fat bits at the back,' says the little girl.

It would seem that Gayle was describing a bustle which was very much in fashion in the eighteenth century. She describes how they had a very large room where all the guests would gather. She explains, 'We always had dancing and there were men who played music.' Gayle says that the dancing took place after all the food and tables were cleared away so that there was plenty of space. 'There were lots of men with funny jackets on with big long bits down the back, and they had sticking up collars and fancy ties like butterflies.'

There was one particular horse, Gypsy, which Gayle was

very attached to. One day she asked her mother if she could have another horse just like Gypsy. Her mother thought at first that she was talking about her rocking horse and she asked the child why she needed another one. Gayle replied, 'Not Rocky. I mean my other horse that I had at the big house.' Rocky is the name Gayle gives to her rocking horse. She described Gypsy as being 'very big and black and I used to go on his back'.

Edna says, 'At first we thought that she had a lively imagination, but she described everything so fully that her father and I began to wonder. She was so emphatic about the big house and the horse that we felt sure that she must have had some kind of experience to match her story. She only watches children's programmes on television and we are sure that she could not have picked up so much detail from the television. We now believe that she has lived on this earth before. Each time she mentions anything to do with the big house she always ends up with the same thing: "And I always used to have my coffee in the lounge." '

Gayle has shown a great fascination for old-fashioned jewellery and she loves the ballet. She has started to hoard things, especially old brooches, and she has quite a collection now, built up mainly through going to jumble sales.

Once Edna thought she would give Gayle a new hairstyle, but as soon as she produced the scissors to start clipping, the little girl adamantly refused to have her hair cut. She told Edna, 'I like it long the way I always used to have it when I was a big lady.' Gayle told her mother that when she was a lady her hair was very long and she never had to brush it herself. She had a special maid - or helper, as she put it - who used to look after her and take care of her clothes. The maid always brushed her hair for her and put it in curls with 'a funny hot stick thing' - Gayle's words for curling tongs. She wore a variety of hats and these were kept in pretty boxes, which her maid looked after. She remembers a little black hat which she only wore when she went riding on Gypsy.

'Sometimes my helper put other hair on top of my head,' remarks Gayle. 'It was white, not like my own hair.' This other hair which Gayle refers to would seem to be a powdered wig such as was worn by eighteenth century ladies of high rank.

Gayle is very demure and ladylike and has a sense of dignity which is highly unusual for such a small child. She accepts her previous life as part of her background which to her appears perfectly natural, as if everyone has lived before.

Says Edna, 'She takes the whole thing so for granted, she seems to know that there is nothing extraordinary in remembering her past life. I think she assumes that we have all been here before.'

Perhaps Gayle is right and we do have memories of our previous lives buried deep down in our subconscious minds, just waiting to be sparked off by some key word or experience which acts as a trigger to release the flood of memories.

Girl remembers being a witch
Julie Tomlinson, Dagenham

Long before little Julie reached her second birthday she was able to produce very distinctive drawings, not of flowers or houses or any of the usual efforts of a tiny child, but very elaborate detailed sketches, always on the same subject: witches!

Julie's grandmother was so intrigued by watching the child feverishly drawing what looked suspiciously like a witch one day, that she asked, 'What is that you're drawing, Julie?' The answer was more than Granny had bargained for, 'It's me of course, when I used to be a witch.'

Mrs Tomlinson just stared at the child in disbelief, wondering where on earth she had got the word witch from. It was certainly not the kind of thing anyone in the family ever discussed, and since Julie was not even two years old she couldn't have read about witches anywhere. Julie could never have heard the word at home because her parents don't like that sort of thing. In fact Julie's mother is a bit wary of anything she doesn't understand, and witches definitely come into that category.

One of the strangest things about Julies's drawings is the speed at which she can complete them. Her grandmother says, 'Ever since she has been able to hold a pen in her hand she has been drawing the witches. She completes a picture so fast it's almost as if she doesn't have to think about what she is doing. It all comes out sort of automatically, but despite the speed, she still manages to put in a wealth of detail. It's really uncanny for someone so young.'

Julie's drawings follow a distinctive style - full of individuality and not like the rough scribbles of other children of her age. She has a peculiar way of drawing the people in the background of her pictures. They seem to be done more in some type of symbol language than as straightforward sketching. Also the trees and flowers are done in the same manner. Mrs Tomlinson explains, 'They are always queer shapes, more as if they are meant to represent the trees and flowers rather than actually picture them as they look.'

Although the background material to Julie's pictures is in symbol form, there is no mistaking the main subject of the drawings. The witches are drawn fully and in perfect detail. No symbolism is shown here and it is almost as though the background is done in such a way as purposely to subdue the minor details in order that the main focal point of the work will be enhanced.

'When I lived before I used to drink blackbirds' blood,' Julie informed her granny, much to the woman's horror. She then went on to say that it tasted sweet.

In some of the drawings there are tiny blackbirds, sometimes seen in flight and sometimes on the ground. The blackbirds are not just standing on the ground as one would expect in a child's drawing, but they are lying down on their backs, or on their sides, as if to indicate that these birds are dead. This probably has some connection with Julie's remarks about drinking blackbirds' blood. The whole idea repels Mrs Tomlinson who says, 'I just can't bear to think about the business of drinking such a thing. Who could imagine anything more ghastly?'

Julie's family never ask her any questions. Says her grandmother, 'It has become a family policy. I think we're all a little bit afraid of what we might hear. There are some things you're better off not knowing.'

Julie was born in Wellingborough, a small town in Northamptonshire, and it is known that many centuries ago there was a strong witch cult in that part of the country. There are records of several witches having been burnt at the stake, but by all accounts this was not the normal method of dealing with them, as they were accepted as a part of life by the community and were more or less allowed to get on with it, unless, as must have been the case in the stake burnings, there had been proven malice to a member of the public. The witches of Wellingborough were allowed to gather in the area which lies behind what is now known as Sheep Street, to the rear of the old Hind Hotel (which is rumoured to be haunted by Oliver Cromwell who once lived there).

One of the most telling of little Julie's drawings shows an odd-looking tree in a field and a witch standing beside a large blazing fire. In the centre of the flames there is a small naked baby. Julie's grandmother just can't understand this at all because normally the little girl loves babies, and like most children of her age she mothers her baby dolls and makes a great fuss of them. 'It doesn't make sense,' says Mrs Tomlinson.

Julie has described how she used to go into the woods at night and light big fires. 'We used to kill sheep,' she says. From what Mrs Tomlinson gathers, the sheep were involved in some kind of sacrifice. 'Julie is absolutely certain that she has lived before as a witch,' says her grandmother, 'and when I hear some of the things she comes out with I'm beginning to think she must indeed have been here before because she certainly never got it from us.'

Girl remembers being in Tay Bridge disaster
Diane Brownlea, Darlington

On the evening of 28 December, 1879, as a howling gale ravished the east coast of Scotland, steam engine number 24 pulled out of Bumtisland station after picking up the Edinburgh passengers from the ferryboat William Muir which had crossed the River Forth to connect with the Dundee train.

Six months earlier the journey from Edinburgh to Dundee would have necessitated two river ferryboat crossings, firstly over the Firth of Forth and then across the River Tay. However, since 1 June the impressive new Tay rail bridge had been open for passenger trains.

The bridge was a stupendous work of engineering, a distance of two miles long and eighty feet above the high water mark of the turbulent Tay. The return fare from Edinburgh to Dundee was seven shillings - equivalent to thirty-five pence.

In one of the carriages on that nightmare journey over a century ago sat a man with four small children - one was a baby boy on his knee, the three other toddlers being two girls and another boy - all huddled round their father on their way to see their grandmother in Dundee.

Inside the compartment the children became restless when the carriage was blasted by the wind and sleet, making it sway heavily from side to side. The roar of the storm frightened the children who one by one started to cry.

In the next compartment a Mr Linton was travelling alone from Edinburgh to St Andrews. Because it was a Sunday the normal rail connection from Leuchars Junction was not scheduled to run, so Mr Linton had arranged for his coach to pick him up at Leuchars to take him on to St Andrews.

When Mr Linton heard the screams of the children in the next compartment, he was moved to go and offer his assistance to the distraught father, whose wife had stayed behind

84

in Edinburgh with relatives because she was expecting her fifth child.

The young father was trying hopelessly to calm his children who were all four crying pitifully. Mr Linton took one of the little girls on his knee and tried to convince her that everything would be all right but the child could not be comforted.

At Leuchars Junction, the train rattled to a halt and Mr Linton jumped off to check with the station master, Thomas Robertson, that the coach had arrived to take him to St Andrews. 'No, sir,' boomed the station master's voice above the roar of the storm. 'There's no sign of any coach. It's more than likely been held up with the weather. '

Linton then got back on board the train resigning himself to the fact that his coach was not going to arrive. He decided that instead of waiting at the desolate station in such dreadful conditions he would go on to Dundee and take a room at a hotel for the night, then make his way back to St Andrews the following morning by which time he hoped the storm would have subsided.

During this time the stationmaster ordered a check on all the carriage wheels to make sure that everything was in order for the arduous journey over the bridge. It was duly reported to Robertson that the wheel check had been completed, and that he could give the go-ahead for the train to set off on the next lap of the journey which would take them to one more station, St Fort, then on across the bridge and into Dundee.

Before he authorized the departure, Robertson, being a thoughtful conscientious man, braved the elements to take one last look down the winding country road to see if there was any sign of Linton's coach. There, sure enough, in the distance the stationmaster could see the faint glimmer of lights and he recognized that the overdue coach was at last rumbling along towards the station.

He immediately ran to the train to inform Mr Linton that his coach was about to arrive. Then he helped the man off the train with his baggage and gave the signal for the engine driver to set off towards St Fort and then on to the southern approach to the bridge.

The train slowed down as it passed the signal box on the south bank of the river and signalman Thomas Barclay held out the bridge baton to the fireman on board, a man called John Marshall, who leaned out of his open cab and exchanged a quick greeting with the signalman as he took the baton. Marshall then called over to the engine driver, David Mitchell, to let him know that he had picked up the baton, giving the driver his cue to increase the speed of the engine to the stipulated twenty-five miles an hour which was the maximum speed allowed for passenger trains crossing the bridge.

At precisely 7. 14 p.m. Thomas Barclay put through his signal to the box on the northern end of the bridge confirming that the train had safely entered the bridge section. The signalman on duty in the north box was expecting the train to clear his box at 7.19 p.m. The train with seventy-five people on board set out over the Tay Bridge that dark night, never to reach the other side.

The engine driver clung on to his controls in the open cab as he and his fireman tried to shield themselves from the wind and sleet. They braced themselves as the train shuddered on to the most precarious part of the bridge - the part everyone referred to as the 'high girders', so called because at this point the bridge took on the form of a tunnel of iron lattice-work girders over the centre of the River Tay.

As the old engine struggled on, a sudden deafening roar was heard all along the creaking, swaying bridge. Then with one furious blast the supporting columns split apart under the tremendous pressure of the pounding waters. The girders were wrenched loose and the train with all its crew and passengers plunged deep down into the murky waters of the Tay far below.

On the road to St Andrews, as Mr Linton's coach struggled against the howling storm, he could see the curve of the mighty bridge in the distance and he watched the train, nothing more than a moving line of lights, slowly progress across the bridge.

He was watching the line of lights enter the high girders when suddenly from his coach he saw the horrendous sight of the engine with all five carriages and guard's van plough downwards with the heavy girders into the foaming river. He instantly thought of the family of small children as they fell to certain death.

He later described the scene as follows: 'The great gale seemed to gather itself together for one mighty effort and tore down on the bridge with one tremendous thunderous roar and crash.'

Linton stopped his coach and stood horrified as he traced the black line of the bridge to a point where it became nothingness, just a giant space above the waters of the Tay.

A sailor from the training ship Mars had been on deck watch on the River Tay fairly near to the bridge at the time and saw the entire incident. He had an excellent view of the train as it moved across the bridge, but as soon as the line of moving lights entered the central girders, the lights suddenly disappeared and there was a long break in the outline of the bridge structure. The sailor heard nothing above the deafening howl of the wind.

Of the seventy-five people who lost their lives in one of the most tragic rail disasters in history, only forty-six bodies were recovered from the river.

More than a hundred years later, a small three-and-a-half-year-old girl from Darlington has strange recurring memories of that winter night so long ago.

Diane Brownlea was playing with a toy case that her grandmother had bought her in Woolworth's. The toddler dressed up two of her dolls and carefully packed her toy case with odds and ends, then announced to her grandmother, 'I'm going to visit my granny in Dundee now.'

Diane's grandmother, Mrs Pemberton, said to her grandchild, 'But I don't live in Dundee, love, I live here in Darlington.' Then thinking for a moment that Diane was referring to her paternal grandmother whom she called Nanny

Brownlea, she said, 'You don't mean Nanny Brownlea, do you? She doesn't live anywhere near Dundee. Aren't you thinking of Newcastle?'

Diane then said, 'No, I mean my other granny that I used to go to see in Dundee when I was a little girl before, when I went on the train over the big bridge.'

Mrs Pemberton tried gently to explain to her grandchild that she had never been to Dundee before. She told Diane, 'Dundee isn't even in this country, it's in Scotland. You know you've never been to Scotland, love.'

Diane answered, 'I lived in Scotland when I was here before and my granny lived in Dundee.' Again she insisted that she used to go to visit her granny on the train.

Her grandmother says that she was surprised that Diane could know anything about a bridge and she swears that Dundee had never been mentioned to the child. She explains, 'We have absolutely no connection with Dundee - no relations, no friends, absolutely no one - so no one in the family ever had cause to mention the place. And as far as the granny part goes - well, I'm one of her grannies and Mrs Brownlea, her father's mother, is the other one. She's a Geordie like the rest of her family, with no ties in Scotland at all, and I'm a Darlington woman, born and bred. I've never even been out of England in all my years .'

Then one day about a month later Diane told her, 'I fell into the water when I went to see granny in Dundee.' When her grandmother asked Diane what she meant, she said, 'I was with my other daddy and we all fell into the water when we were on the train.'

From then on Diane constantly repeated that she fell into the water when she was in the train going to see her granny in Dundee. The child of course is too young to know anything about the 1879 disaster. She cannot read and the subject has not been covered on television. In any case Diane is only interested in the children's programmes and that is all she watches.

The child has not mentioned anything about having had brothers or sisters but she does refer to her previous family as 'we all fell into the water'. This would indicate that there were more people involved than just herself and her father who is vivid in her memory. She makes no mention of her mother, only her father.

Apart from Mr Linton who travelled on the doomed train, other people witnessed the family of father and four children on the train on the night of the disaster. At St Fort station, the final stop before the bridge, all the tickets had to be collected from the passengers who were alighting at Dundee, and other travellers going further north through Arbroath, Stonehaven, Aberdeen and even further up the Scottish east coast had their tickets checked.

William Friend, the ticket collector, remarked to the stationmaster after the train pulled out of St Fort station that he had seen a man with three or four small children with him huddled together in one of the compartments. He remembered thinking at the time that the man had a lot on his hands with so many young children on such a foul night. He had collected the man's ticket and noticed that the family were bound for Dundee. He also remarked that there was no sign of the mother in the compartment and it was this fact that had drawn the collector's attention to the plight of the father.

From this it would seem that there was only the one family of small children on the train that night. The family on the train consisted of a father, two boys (including the baby) and two girls. Could it be that little Diane Brownlea was one of those girls?

Although it is heart-breaking to think of those children going to their watery graves it surely must bring comfort to know that little Diane is a happy, contented, well adjusted, normal little girl who plays with her dolls and toy case like all little girls love to. If she was one of the girls on that nineteenth-century train then she certainly has come through with flying colours.

Boy remembers being drowned off sailing ship
Simon Brown, Chelmsford

Shortly after two-year old Simon had learnt to hold a conversation, he turned to his mother Susan and surprised her by saying, 'Mummy, I've been here before. I was on a big boat with sails and ropes on it and I fell into the water. I went under the water and died.'

His mother thought that Simon might have been day-dreaming, but six months later he repeated the same story, and added that he remembers being in the water, which was very dirty, with his dog who always went everywhere with him.

Simon described the boat as having lots of sails and three masts and hundreds of ropes. He remembers that there had been a fierce storm and he fell overboard. He told his mother that the boat had a giant wheel with spokes all round it and he said that some of the other men used to steer the ship using the wheel. From his reference to other men it would seem that Simon was a grown man in his other life.

Susan says that every now and then Simon comes out with words which she has never heard before, like the time he accidentally knocked over a pot of Susan's freshly-made blackcurrant jam, sending it crashing to the kitchen floor.

When he saw how harassed his mother was at having to clean up the sticky mess of jam and broken glass, he looked up at her apprehensively and said, 'I hope I don't have to do haze now, Mummy.' Susan was in no humour for wisecracks and thinking that the child had picked up some slang word she started to tell him off, saying that he must speak properly. Then she asked him what he meant.

Simon answered, 'When I was a sailor I hated doing haze but sometimes I had to.' 'What's haze?' demanded Susan. Her son answered, 'It was what happened when we were naughty. We had to scrub all the decks and do all the work.'

Susan mentioned the incident to Simon's father Greg, after which it was more or less forgotten till one evening an old friend of Simon's father paid a visit to the Brown household. The man, Peter Eawlings, had emigrated to Australia several years previously, and had never seen little Simon as the child had been born since his departure. Peter was an ex-merchant seaman.

After Simon was put to bed the adults settled down to talk about old times. Naturally the conversation got round to ships and the sea. Greg asked Peter if he had ever heard the word haze. Peter replied, 'Of course. Every sailor knows what haze is. It's extra work given on board as punishment. '

Peter explained that in the old days sailors used to dread haze, as it usually meant that they would not only be subjected to incessant hard work, but more often than not they would be refused their quota of rum and often would have to go without regular meals for the period of probation - or haze. As conditions on board were far from ideal even at the best of times, this extra penalty inflicted extreme hardship on a man.

When Simon's parents heard Peter's explanation, they bean to take their son's remarks more seriously. They realized that the little boy must have got the unusual word from somewhere, yet they had never heard of the expression before and they were certain that Simon had never been told about haze by anyone. Susan says, 'He knows absolutely no one who could have told him. His father and I can only assume that he really has remembered it from a previous life as a sailor.' Greg is impressed with the way young Simon can describe the ship that he sailed in and some of the places he visited. He says, 'He knows more about a sailing ship than I do. He can tell you all about the different sails and rigging and all that. He's mentioned some things I've never even heard of, like a spanker. He says his boat had a spanker on it - whatever that is.'

Simon must hive been a regular crew member although he

cannot remember any name or special rank. From the fact that he had been given haze it would appear that he was not an officer.

Susan says, 'He can be playing away as usual and he might look at something, or pick up some object which sets things off in his head and he starts remembering things. The other day he was playing around with an old toy clock. He was staring at it intently and turning it round and round in his hands. He looked up at me and told me that the clock reminded him of the wheel of his ship. He seemed to be in a kind of daze as if he was away in another world.'

Simon remembers being on board the ship for long periods at a time. He must have been on long voyages because he told his mother that when they had been away on the ship, sometimes the men got fed up and would start fighting with each other. He remembers that they were given horrible jobs to do to keep them busy.

Although Simon does not remember any names of places he visited in his sea-faring days, he has vivid pictures in his mind of landing on some kind of island. He says there was lovely sand all round the land and lots of trees, flowers and fruit. They made fires on the shore and they spent some time walking around looking for food, but they slept in their cabins on board.

'The ship was kept near the edge of the water and we had to go back to it every night to sleep,' he says. He remembers eating bananas and other fruits which he could not describe. He told his mother that he has never seen them in the fruit shop.

'It was always hot on the land but we needed to light fires because another sailor told us to.' Simon had no idea why the fires were lit. Perhaps it was to cook their food, or possibly to ward off any wild animals.

When Susan asked her son if he met any people on the land, he replied, 'Lots and lots. They didn't have any clothes on, but they had lots of colours on them and beads.' His mother then asked him if he spoke to the people. He replied, 'They tried to talk to us but we didn't know what they were saying. They talked funny words. They gave us the bananas and other fruit and things.'

Susan asked him if these people looked like him. He told her yes, but they were very sunburnt. From this, Susan is not sure if her little boy meant that the people were coloured, but she gets the impression that they were not. She thinks this, because Simon has a little West Indian friend called Wesley and when she asked Simon if the people looked like Wesley, he said no. She feels that if the natives had been West Indian or Negro then Simon would have said straight away that they were like his little coloured friend,

'I've got a feeling that he may have gone to some of the Polynesian islands,' says Susan. 'Of course that's a long shot as it could be anywhere really. ' She comes to the Polynesian conclusion because Simon describes the land as being lush in vegetation, with flowers and fruit in abundance and he says it was very very hot.

Simon told his mother that they played drums and sang funny songs, which according to the boy's description were more of a slow chant. 'The people danced for us and gave us nice things to eat,' he recalls. Susan says, 'This sounds as if they were invited to some kind of feast or celebration. The natives seemed to be very friendly as Simon has no memories of any hostility on the part of the islanders.'

Simon seems to have come to terms with his drowning. Greg explains, 'I would have thought that something as traumatic as being drowned would cause all kinds of havoc in a person's mind - that's assuming that they remember it all as Simon seems to. The peculiar thing is that it doesn't seem to bother him in the slightest. He remembers that his dog was with him throughout the whole ordeal but he doesn't seem to be too put out by the fact that he died. If anything, he makes more fuss about the fact that the water was dirty - as if that makes any difference.'

Greg is somewhat puzzled by Simon's comment about the dirty water. He feels that if the storm had taken place while the ship was out on the open sea then the water would hardly be described as dirty. He wonders if the ship was docked in some big port at the time, because that might explain the dirty water. The argument against that is the obvious one that if the ship was in port during the storm, then there would be no need for the crew to stay aboard. They could easily have gone ashore to safety.

Of course there is always the possibility of Simon having some kind of mishap in these very conditions, i.e. the ship was docked in a big port during a violent storm and while trying to get ashore with his dog, he could have fallen overboard.

Regarding the actual drowning, Simon calmly says, 'It went all black when I went underneath the water. It was very quiet. After a long time I woke up and my dog was with me. We were in a bright place but I was very tired. I went to sleep again.'

He does not remember much about what happened in the interim period but he does remember that he was then reborn and Susan and Greg were his parents. He said to his mother, 'After a long time I came back here and you were my new mummy.'

Susan asked Simon if he was English when he was a sailor. The boy replied, 'I think so. I talked the same as I do now.'

Greg was interested to hear that the odd words used by his young son in connection with his ship are not really so odd to anyone familiar with sailing ships. A spanker, for instance, is a term used to describe the fore-and-aft sail of a ship.

Young Simon is unperturbed about his previous life, and although he knows all about ships he is no more or less enthusiastic about them than anyone else. He takes a very philosophical view and regards his past life as over and done with. He doesn't have any special hankerings for a life at sea. Perhaps he feels that once is enough for anyone.

Small girl remembers being a boy
Sharon Prescott, Lanark

Three-and-a-half-year-old Sharon was out shopping with her mother in the small Scottish market town where they live when she said to her mother, 'When I was a boy I lived up round the back of the old church.'

The child's mother Judy looked slightly surprised but just dismissed it as the ramblings of a child with a vivid imagination. A few weeks later Judy was in the same market place and once more little Sharon pointed towards the old church and repeated that when she was a little boy she used to live up the road behind it.

Out of curiosity, Judy said, 'OK. Come on, then. Show me.' With that Sharon took her mother's hand and led her up behind the church, past a children's play park and over a couple of roads. Then Sharon stopped but she seemed to be bewildered, Is she stood looking around her.

Judy remembers her reaction at that moment. 'Come on, Sharon,' she said to the child. 'Let's not waste any more time with all this nonsense.'

Although Sharon was looking puzzled she wouldn't move away from the spot. She told her mother, 'But it's all different now, Mummy.' Her mother was quickly losing patience and took hold of her little girl to take her back to the shopping area of town.

Sharon pulled back and said to her mother, 'But I did live here when I was a little boy. I remember it, Mummy, but the houses are all different now.'

That evening Judy told her husband Glen all about the episode with Sharon earlier that day. As the couple talked it over, and Judy described the route that Sharon had led her, it became apparent that they had gone to the area of town where Glen had lived for a short time when he was a small baby.

Judy says, 'I knew that my husband's family had come

from that area, but at the time I didn't think anything of it. It was only when Glen and I started to talk things over that we realized that Sharon had stopped at the exact same road where the old family cottage used to stand. You see, I had never known the family when they lived there so I didn't know the district where they used to live.'

Glen and his family had long since lost touch with that area of town and in fact in his early childhood everyone had to be moved out when the entire district came under new development. The old houses were pulled down and all the residents were scattered to various districts of the town and surrounding area.

The whole place was completely gutted and brand new modern homes were built on the site of the old tumbledown cottages. Judy now wonders if this is why Sharon looked so lost when she stood and looked around her at the new different houses. 'She seemed to be completely bewildered because the houses were different,' says Judy. 'But she was adamant that she was in the correct road. She seemed to recognize the route from the main shopping centre of town to where her father used to live without any difficulty whatever. It was just the new buildings that threw her.'

The re-development of the area could well explain why little Sharon was mixed up. Before the new houses the old cottages were home to her great-grandparents for many years. When Glen's father left the family home to get married, he lived for a few years in a neighbouring village with his new wife. He then moved back to the family cottage when Glen was a small baby while they waited for a few months until they got another house of their own. It was only during this short few months that Glen had lived in his grandparent's cottage, but the old couple had lived there for more than thirty years.

Glen wonders if there could be any connection between Sharon and his grandparents, whom the child never met. One day Glen asked Sharon, 'Can you remember what your name was when you were a little girl before?' Sharon answered instantly, 'Oh I wasn't a little girl, Daddy, I was a little boy.' This answer was more than her father had bargained for because he was sure that she had just got mixed up somehow when she had talked before of being a boy, but here again she was quite definite and stated clearly that she was a boy in her previous life. Her father then asked her, 'What are you talking about, Sharon? How could you be a little boy?' His daughter assured him that she had been a boy. Then she added, 'And when I grew up I was a man, and I worked at a big place down the road past Forbes Farm.'

Glen says, 'The Forbes Farm bit shook me because that did exist at one time but it disappeared off the face of the earth years and years ago. It was taken over by the redevelopers when all the old cottages were knocked down. It all happened so long ago that nearly everyone's forgotten all about it. Nobody even mentions Forbes Farm any more. I remember hearing my father talking about it.'

He wonders how Sharon would know that there had once been a place called Forbes Farm which was situated in the vicinity of the old cottages. He honestly doesn't feel that anyone could have told the little girl about such a place because she only mixes with the small children of a few of their immediate neighbours - all young couples who came to the district long after Forbes Farm was knocked down.

Glen explains, 'It's not as if the people still call that part by its old name or anything as often happens. When the developers took over they made a clean sweep and renamed all the roads. Forbes Farm was never used as a reference term for any part of the area.'

As for Sharon saying that she worked in a big place down the road past Forbes Farm, Glen can think of two or three possibilities. 'There are a couple of big factories down that way,' he said. 'But the thing that sticks in my mind most is that my old grandfather used to work in a big bakery for a while and that was down past where the old farm road used to be.'

Another link between Sharon and her great-grandfather? Perhaps. The old man used to leave his cottage very early in the mornings to walk down the quiet country road, past the part where the Forbes Farm lane met the road, and down another few hundred yards to the old bakery which also has been long since demolished.

Sharon told Judy that she remembers being a little boy very well. She says, 'I had a lovely cat called Nutty.' She remembers how Nutty used to scamper around the cottage looking for mice. She used to run after Nutty and help him find the mice for her mother.

Sharon says, 'My other mummy cried when I was a little boy.' When Judy asked her what had happened to make her mother cry, Sharon answered, 'It was a bad woman that made her cry.' The child would not say anything further at that point. judy could see that her little daughter was becoming quite upset. She says, 'Sharon went very quiet and her face became deadly serious. She had tears in her eyes as if she was remembering something which had upset her deeply at some time.'

Several weeks after, while Glen was pushing Sharon on her garden swing, she suddenly shouted to her father, 'Stop. Stop, Daddy, I want to get off' Glen says, 'She sounded so frightened I stopped the swing instantly. I couldn't understand it because she always loves to be pushed on her swing, and usually I'm the one that gets fed up with it before she does.'

From Sharon's swing, she could see out beyond the back garden of their home on to the roadway. She had spotted something which seemed to terrify her. As soon as she got off her swing she grabbed her father's hand and pulled at him to go into the house.

She kept crying, 'Bad woman's coming- bad woman's coming.' Glen looked out towards the roadway but could see no one. Because Sharon was getting herself worked up into such a state he took the child into the house and tried to calm her down. He assured the little girl that there was no bad woman anywhere. Sharon shouted in a frightened tone, 'I saw her, Daddy. She's coming to get us. She's the bad woman.'

The next moment someone knocked on the side door of the house. At this, little Sharon started screaming uncontrollably as she ran to Judy. She kept repeating to her parents, 'Don't answer. Don't go to the door.'

Glen answered the door to find a middle-aged gypsy woman standing there trying to sell him some trinkets out of a small case and offering to read his fortune. Glen looked at the woman suspiciously. He had never seen her in the area before but he felt compelled to ask her if she had been down their road before. The woman told him that she had not and that it was all new territory to her.

She was an Irish gypsy, well graced with the gift of the gab, and promised Glen every good fortune under the sun, providing he would cross her palm with silver, just, as she put it, 'to help keep an oul' woman's body and soul together'.

Glen told the woman that he wanted no fortune read and he warned her not to come back near the house ever again, and he told her to tell her friends to stay away as well.

When he went back inside he found his little daughter crying her eyes out. He told her that everything was fine and that she had nothing to worry about. Sharon sobbed, 'That's the bad woman that made my other mummy cry.' The story came out that when Sharon was a little boy, a gypsy woman had knocked at the door of their cottage and when her mother answered it the woman said that she was a fortune teller. Sharon remembers the woman asking for her hand to be crossed with silver, but as soon as the gypsy saw that there was no sale for her fortune-telling she screamed abuse and said that she was going to cast an evil spell on the family.

This had upset and frightened Sharon's other mother so much that the woman had burst into tears. The memory of that event was so strongly stamped on the child's mind that as soon as she saw the gypsy walking up the road towards their house something sparked in the little girl's head and rekindled the memory of what had happened with the gypsy and her mother in her previous life.

Glen explains, 'We hardly ever get peddlars or gypsy fortune-tellers around here, but seemingly years ago they were quite common. There was a camp of Irish gypsies on some waste ground not far from the old cottages. They were harmless enough but they became a nuisance, always trying to flog things. The fortune-telling was quite a novelty at first, but the people soon got tired of it. There were too many gypsies and they were constantly knocking on doors begging for money. The people in the cottages hardly had any money themselves. These gypsy women had fierce tempers and they had a nasty habit of casting what they reckoned were evil spells if they didn't get what they wanted.'

Glen continues, 'Of course it was all a lot of old bunk, but the old biddies could be so convincing with their threats that it would have been very unpleasant to be on the receiving end of their wrath.'

There is no question that Sharon recognized the same woman, but there must have been something familiar about the gypsy who walked up their back garden path and knocked on the side door of their house that day.

Judy says, 'Most of those women look the same anyway. They all have red cheeks and high cheekbones and they usually wear their hair tied back behind their ears, and they nearly all wear scarves over their heads. Because they spend so much time out of doors their complexions are ruddy and rather coarse-looking. They are usually on the hefty side.'

It is not so surprising, then, that as Sharon spied the gypsy woman from her swing her memory immediately raced back to the time that she had seen a woman who looked very similar say upsetting things to her previous mother.

Little Sharon's parents have since explained to her that although the woman who frightened her other mummy was not a very nice sort of person that doesn't mean that all gypsy women are the same. They told her gypsies are just like everyone else: some of them are nice and some are a bit silly.

'I think she understands,' says Judy. 'She's fine now, but she still talks about how that bad woman made her other mummy cry. I don't think she'll ever forget that.'

Glen has a feeling that there is some kind of bond between his grandfather and his daughter. 'I can't say definitely what it is,' he says, 'but so many things seem to click together.'

There is always the possibility, of course, that the link could be with some other member of the family who lived in the little cottage at some period in their lives. The mystery remains unsolved, but it doesn't seem to bother little Sharon, whose fondest memories seem to centre round Nutty her cat.

Boy remembers being a commando
Stephen Ramsay, Blackpool

From the time that Stephen was only twelve months old he has had a terrible fear of planes. Any time a plane would pass over his home he would become hysterical. At first, his mother Tessa thought that it was just the noise that was upsetting her baby and that he would eventually grow out of it.

Very early one morning, before the alarm clock went off, Stephen, who was then two years old, scrambled out of his little bed and ran into his parents' room, climbed into the bed beside his mother and shook her to wake her up, calling out, 'There's a plane coming, Mummy. There's a plane coming.' His mother could hear nothing and she told the child that he must have been dreaming. Stephen then said, 'I don't like planes because a plane hurt my tummy once.'

Stephen's mother listened carefully, and again she could hear nothing, so she said, 'No, love, there's no plane and anyway you are safe with me.' Within one minute a jet screamed overhead. Tessa hugged Stephen tightly as she wondered how on earth he could have known that a plane was coming. She says, 'He seemed to be able to sense that the plane was on its way. I can't believe that he could have heard anything because it was so early in the morning and there wasn't a sound. I'm sure I would have heard it if he heard it.'

Tessa remembers feeling very odd one sunny afternoon when they had just finished lunch. Her husband Bill, Stephen and herself were just about to get up from the table when a jet screamed over the house. Stephen instantly dropped onto his stomach and crawled commando-style under the table. Tessa remembers, 'He did it with such speed and in such a professional way that it really made my hair bristle, although I know that sounds silly.' After the noise of the jet died away Stephen, still lying flat out under the table, called out, 'OK. It's all clear now.' Then the little boy crawled out from under the table.

About a year after that incident, when Stephen was three, Bill was playing around the house with him when the child started to rub his stomach and said to his father, 'I got my tummy hurt with a plane once, Daddy.' Bill just laughed and picked his little boy up, thinking that this was just another example of the child showing his fear of planes. 'Oh, you don't want to worry about planes,' said his father. 'You'll see when you get older; they just look big and they sound very loud but they won't come near you or hurt you.'

'A plane hurt me in my tummy,' repeated Stephen. Bill tried to talk things through with his little son to explain to him that he was only imagining that he had hurt his tummy because he was afraid of planes. Bill said, 'So you see a plane didn't really hurt your tummy, you just think it did.' Stephen started to nod his little head frantically saying, 'It did, Daddy, it did. The plane did hurt my tummy.' Bill looked at his child seriously and was just about to make another attempt to reason with Stephen, when the little boy said, 'It was when I lived the last time, before I died.'

Bill was taken aback at Stephen's words and repeated aghast, 'Before you died?' Stephen went on to say, 'I died when that plane hurt my tummy.' By now Bill was beginning to think that there might be something in what Stephen was saying. He recalls, 'It was the way that he came right out with it without any hesitation that made me think twice. When he said that he had died I got a bit of a shock because that's not the kind of thing he would be likely to say. In fact he had never said anything like that before - about having died - although he had always been absolutely terrified of planes.'

Stephen then told his father, 'I was a big man then and we had to hide from the planes.' Bill remembered how Stephen had crawled under the table the time that he heard the jet and he wondered if there could be a connection. The two incidents seemed to match up.

'Why did you hide from the planes?' asked his father. The

child answered, 'Because the planes were trying to hurt us.' His father asked Stephen, 'But why should they want to hurt you?' Stephen explained, 'Because we were all fighting in the trees.' Bill asked him, 'Where were these trees?' Stephen told him, 'I don't know, but there were lots of trees and it was hot all the time.'

With a question here and there, Bill learnt from Stephen that he had been fighting in a very hot place which sounded as if it could be a jungle and that Stephen was with a crowd of other men. They were being attacked from the air by low-flying planes, but there was also some fighting on the ground. The planes would sweep down towards Stephen and his men and drop bombs.

The little boy remembers, 'The planes made loud bangs and they tried to kill us.' He told his father, 'We tried to hide in the trees when we heard the planes coming but one time a plane came down and hurt my tummy.' 'What happened then?' asked Bill. Stephen replied, 'That was when I died. My tummy got hurt and it was bleeding.' Bill asked Stephen if he knew what happened then and the little boy replied, 'I just went to sleep in the trees. ' Bill asked him, 'Do you remember what happened then?' Stephen replied, 'After I was sleeping I woke up and my tummy was all better.' Bill asked him where he was then and his son said, 'I was still in the trees.' When asked what happened after that Stephen told his father, 'A lady came to see me.'

'What lady?' asked Bill. The child replied, 'She was a nice lady and she told me to follow her. She took my hand and took me with her.' Bill asked what happened next and Stephen replied, 'She took me to a nice place and told me to go back to sleep again.' When asked where the place was, Stephen replied, 'It was where lots of beds and seats were.'

Bill thought for a moment that his child was trying to describe some kind of hospital. He said, 'Was it a hospital with sick people in it, Stephen?' His son replied, 'No. The people weren't sick, they were just tired.' Bill asked his son if he remembered anything about after that and Stephen said, 'I wakened up sometimes and went back to sleep again.'

'Did you see anyone in this place?' asked Bill. Stephen said, 'Oh yes, the nice lady was with me all the time.' When Bill asked if he knew the lady's name or anything about her, Stephen said thoughtfully, 'I don't know her name, but she told me that I had to sleep because I had died.' Then he added, 'She said I had to get strong again.'

When asked what the lady looked like, Stephen said, 'She had a blue dress on.' 'Was it an ordinary dress?' asked Bill, 'or was it long?' After a few moments of thinking, Stephen said, 'It wasn't too long and it wasn't too short.' Bill asked Stephen if the lady's dress was like his mummy's dresses and the boy replied, 'Kind of like them. '

'Do you remember what happened after that?' asked Bill, and Stephen told him, 'I had to wait around for a long time.' His father asked him, 'Well, what were you waiting for?' and the little boy replied, 'Till it was time for me to come to you and Mummy.'

'Really?' exclaimed Bill, not knowing quite what to think. Then he asked Stephen, 'Well, how did you know when it was time for you to be born again?' Stephen said, 'Oh, they always come and tell you when you're going to be born.' 'Who's they?' asked Bill. His son told him, 'They're the men who looked after all the people.' Bill said, 'So there were lots of other people in this place?' and Stephen replied, 'Oh yes, Daddy. I had lots and lots of friends there.' 'Well, what did you and your friends do?' asked Bill. 'Did you work or play or what?' 'Oh we had work to do if we wanted to do it,' said Stephen. Then he added, 'But we didn't have to do it.' His father asked him, 'Well, what work did you do then?' Stephen's answer left Bill really puzzled. The child told his father, 'I worked in the library.'

Bill didn't think that Stephen really knew what a library was, but he thought perhaps the child had heard his mother talk about their local library because both he and his wife were members. Bill said, 'Are you thinking about Mummy's and Daddy's library, Stephen?' The child replied, 'No, my library was much bigger than yours. It was a giant library.'

Still wary, Bill said, 'Well what did you do in the library, Stephen?' Again the child's answer left his father very bewildered. Stephen said, 'I had to put all the new bits into the books.' Bill asked, 'What do you mean by the new bits?' The child answered, 'Sometimes the books were wrong and I had to make them right for people.'

'For what people?' asked Bill. Stephen answered, 'For the people who wrote the books, of course.' Bill asked Stephen if he knew the names of these people and the child hesitantly replied, 'I can't remember. I don't know. I didn't talk to them much.' Bill asked him how he knew what to change in the books and the child replied, 'I got to know.' Bill asked him if the people who wrote the books told him what new bits he had to put into them and Stephen answered, 'Not them, the other people told me. The ones who looked after us all.'

Stephen went on to explain to his father that there were lots of people living together but over these people there resided a few other men in charge of them. When Bill asked him if he meant that the people in charge were like kings, Stephen said that they didn't call the men kings. He told his father that the men who instructed him on what he had to add into the library books were the same men that informed him about when he was to be born again. He said that he thinks he called the men by their names but he couldn't remember what the names were.

When the child started play-school at the age of four, most of his memories were pushed to the back of his mind, although it took him quite a while to get over his fear of planes.

Tessa says, 'It's funny because although Stephen was terrified of planes right up until recently when he started school, he seemed just to have the feeling of fear without knowing why. Yet when he was much younger he would say that he was afraid because a plane hurt his tummy. He never seemed to associate the planes he heard later on with the business about being killed by a plane in his previous life.' Then Tessa adds, 'I suppose now that he's coming to terms with the fear of planes, I wouldn't be surprised if eventually he forgets that he was ever even afraid at all. He seems to be so taken up with school and all the new things that he's learning that he doesn't have much room for anything else in his head.'

Girl remember Jesus
Lorna Taylor, Plymoth

From the time she was an eighteen-month-old baby, little Lorna has been able to hear and see people outside the range of normal perception. She used to laugh and giggle in her cot, and wave her arms in the air as if she was reaching for some toy which was being dangled in front of her then taken away suddenly, making the child miss catching the invisible object each time. This game would never fail to send the baby into hoots of happy laughter, but the strange thing was that Lorna's mother Margaret could never see anyone else in the baby's room.

Margaret says, 'It was just as if someone was waving a toy in front of her then pulling it back suddenly just before she could grab it. She would throw out her arms quickly and stretch out her little fingers just as if she was trying to catch something.' Margaret says that she could see by studying her baby's face that the child was definitely focusing on someone. 'Her gaze was fixed on an area just above her cot as if someone was standing there playing with her. Sometimes her eyes would move slightly but she seemed to be holding someone in focus all the time. It was as if the person would move slightly and Lorna's eyes would follow. I often wondered who my baby's mystery playmate was. I imagine whoever it was must have been an adult because of the way Lorna would look upwards above the top rail of her cot at much the same angle as she would look up at me. One thing's for sure, she was very much at home with her playmate, as she had such a happy contented expression on her face every time I would find her playing her little game.'

Margaret says that she can't remember a time when Lorna didn't understand what was being said to her. 'She has always been completely aware of what was going on around her, and whatever I said to her I got the impression that she under-

108

stood my message. Something in her eyes and her knowing expression would tell me that she was following my words and that she knew what they meant.'

When Lorna was two years old Margaret's father died. Even at that young age, Lorna seemed to have an inner knowledge of death and birth and she seemed to accept these things as being perfectly natural and nothing to get alarmed about. Margaret said that Lorna came up to her, put her arms around her mother's neck and said, 'I know you're sad, Mummy, but Grandad's with Jesus and his mummy and daddy now and all his pain has gone.'

A few days after, Lorna said to her mother, 'I expect when I'm old I'll be quite glad to die, because everybody I love will be with Jesus and I'll want to be there too.' Margaret asked Lorna what made her think that, and the child replied, 'Because I used to be with Jesus before I was born.' Margaret asked Lorna how she knew that it was Jesus and the child replied, 'Everybody knew it was Jesus when He came to see us. Everybody talked about Him coming.' Margaret then asked Lorna where she was when she saw Jesus and Lorna answered, 'It was when I was at my other home before I was born.'

Margaret persevered, asking her daughter, 'But where was this other home?' Lorna replied, 'It's where everyone lives before they're born.' 'I don't remember being there,' said Margaret. Her daughter told her, 'Of course you were there and so was Daddy but you're too old to remember.' In spite of herself Margaret had to laugh. She then went on to tell Lorna that she has never remembered being in a place with Jesus, even when she was a little girl. Lorna's answer staggered Margaret. The child told her mother, 'Of course you remembered when you were a baby, but you've forgotten it all now you're old.'

Lorna's father David was bemused when Margaret told him what their little girl had been saying. He thought that he would try to find out what was putting those thoughts into the child's mind. She had been taken to Sunday school a couple of times and he thought that perhaps something had been said which Lorna had possibly misinterpreted.

David asked Lorna, 'Remember that time when you went to Sunday school, love? Was that when you heard all this about Jesus?' Lorna replied instantly, 'No. I didn't see Jesus at Sunday school, only Mr Edwards.' (Mr Edwards is the local vicar.) Lorna's father was quite glad that his small daughter recognized the difference.

David then asked Lorna, 'But did you see any pictures of Jesus, and did that make you think you'd seen him?' Lorna answered, 'Oh I did see pictures of Him in my book, but I liked Him better when I saw Him really.' Again David pressed on to try to get to the bottom of the question. He said, 'But didn't you just imagine you saw Him? Like when you have a dream?' Lorna was emphatic in her reply. 'No, Daddy, I didn't dream about Jesus. He came to see us when I lived at my other home.'

'What other home?' asked her father. She replied sharply, 'The home I lived in before I was born.' Lorna was getting slightly peeved at having to repeat herself so many times, so her father thought that he would let things rest for a while.

When the child started play-school her teacher told Margaret that she was very much ahead of the other children and that she didn't really act like a child at all. She never had to be disciplined and she seemed to know instantly what to do with everything. Her teacher particularly noticed that Lorna was very considerate of the other children's feelings, and says, 'She is acutely aware of when anyone is upset. Sometimes when I get a bit harassed if the children get boisterous or have tiffs with one another, I notice that Lorna looks at me in such an understanding way as if she really appreciates how I must be feeling. She has such a lovely comforting face that I always feel better. I feel as if she is more of a little friend than a child.'

Margaret says that since Lorna started play-school it is almost as if she is slowly learning to become a child.

However she constantly says things that reveal a mind which is far from child-like.

Once Margaret and Lorna were in the centre of Town waiting in the parked car for David to join them. Margaret recalls how they were just sitting quietly, looking out of the windows when all at once Lorna turned to her mother and said, 'I know where all these people came from.' Then she went on to say, 'There was a time once when there were no people, no cars or houses, just trees and grass and sky. I wonder where the first lady and man came from to make all these people?' Lorna had just turned three when she said this.

Lorna seems to have a deep understanding about personal relationships and she can analyse these. When she started play-school she met lots of other children for the first time. She told her mother, 'As soon as I saw Georgina I knew I liked her, and although I was shy at first, the more I knew her the more I liked her. That's what being friends is, isn't it?' Margaret told Lorna that she was glad that she had a nice new friend at play-school. Then Lorna said, 'I thought Noreen was a friend but she just stands in the doorway, and the first person who comes up, she says hello to, and that's her friend for the playtime.' Then Lorna added, 'That's not a real friend, is it, Mummy?'

When Lorna was three-and-a-half she was sitting with her father, and she suddenly said, 'Jesus wasn't with us all the time, you know, Daddy.' 'Oh really?' answered her father. She went on, 'No. He only came to see us on special days and we all went out to see Him.'

Again David thought that he would try to find out just what was making her say such things. Now she had started play-school he realized that there were more people influencing her life, and her levels of knowledge were rising all the time. He wondered if someone had said anything to start her talking about Jesus again.

He asked her, 'Have you been getting stories about Jesus at play-school, love?' She answered, 'We were practising for

111

our Christmas play about Jesus, and Mrs Dodds (her play-school teacher) said that when we die and go to Heaven, Jesus is with us all the time.' Then she added in a confident tone, 'He's not, you know - not all the time. We can't see Him all the time but I think He can see us.'

'How do you know He's not?' asked her mother. 'Because I remember. He only used to come to see us sometimes,' came the reply. David argued, 'But you haven't died yet, Lorna, so how could you know?' She replied, 'I died the last time, but when I went to my other home I didn't see Jesus all the time.' Then she added most adamantly, 'Not all the time.'

'What do you mean by when you died the last time?' David asked her. She replied, 'The last time I died when I was here before.' He argued, 'But you've never been here before, love.' She looked him straight in the eye and said slowly, 'Oh yes I have, but you weren't my daddy then.'

David just looked at his little daughter, not quite knowing what to say next. He remembers feeling a funny sensation flow over him as she said the words. He recalls, 'There was just something in the slow deliberate way she said it that made my blood creep. It was as if she was letting me in on some deep mysterious secret. I wasn't sure that I wanted to hear any more right at that moment.'

After he pulled himself together, Lorna's father said to her, 'Oh really? Well, who was your daddy?' She looked very thoughtful and then she said, 'I don't know, but I know I had another mummy as well.' David asked her, 'How do you know that, then?' She replied, 'I know I had because I had a daddy and a mummy.' David continued, 'O.K., who was your mummy then?' Again the child hesitated, then said, 'I don't know who she was but I know I had one.' Her father asked her, 'What happened to them?' She answered, 'I don't know. When I was little I got sick and then that was when I died and went back to Jesus.' Then as an afterthought she added quite categorically, 'But He wasn't with us all the time, Daddy.'

By that time David had got the message. In the afterlife

which Lorna had often talked about, Jesus only came to visit her and her friends sometimes, not all of the time.

He said, 'O.K., O.K. So He only came to see you sometimes. What was He like when He did visit you?' Lorna replied, 'He didn't visit me to come to my house like Aunty Jane visits me. He just came to see us.'

'O.K.,' said David, smiling at this. 'When He came to see you, what was He like?' Little Lorna's face lit up into a delightful smile. She told her father, 'He was laughy.'

David roared with laughter when he heard this. He explains, 'The last thing I expected her to say was that.' He put the question to his small daughter another way and asked her, 'What else was He like?' She replied, 'He was pretty and had shiny eyes and He made us all glad, and He had some other people with Him.' When David asked Lorna who the other people were, she told her father that she didn't know their names but that they were Jesus's friends.

David asked Lorna if Jesus said anything. She replied, 'He doesn't talk the same way as we do here. He did talk in a different way but not with saying words.' David asked her what Jesus had said and she hesitated, then replied, 'He came to bring us some light, I think.' Then she repeated slowly, 'He came with bright light to help us.'

David got a feeling that his little daughter was remembering something of profound supernatural value. He remembers, 'She seemed to be awestruck and her face had the most unusual expression on it. She had been smiling a moment earlier when she mentioned about Jesus being laughy but now she had a strange mystified look on her face.'

As Lorna grew older, the memories of Jesus and her life in her other home seemed gradually to vanish, although she is still very much aware of everything around her.

She is now a lively five-year-old and has just started infants' school which she loves. She has two smaller brothers who, as Margaret puts it, are 'much loved and very normal little boys who came into the world with puckered faces, and although very special to my husband and me they are in no way extraordinary.' Recently, Lorna's two-year-old brother Duncan was quite naughty. Margaret told him off and the little boy began to cry, saying that his mummy didn't love him any more. Lorna took her brother's hand in a comforting way and in a worldly voice told him, 'Yes she does love you. She always loves you, she just doesn't like you very much at the moment.' Despite Margaret feeling cross, she was forced to laugh at the way her five-year-old had summed things up absolutely correctly. She says, 'Lorna just seems to know the score. It makes me wonder where she got all this inner knowledge from, as she couldn't have learnt everything since she came to us.'

Girl remembers being a musician
Charlotte Middleton-Million, Leeds

Ever since tiny Charlotte could stand up she has had a most amazing sense of rhythm, and when looking through her mother's mail order catalogues she always used to go straight to the guitar sections and sit and stare at them and try to finger the instruments.

Although Charlotte still hasn't reached her second birthday, so many unaccountable incidents have taken place that her mother Alyson is certain that her baby must have been here before.

'I feel that in Charlotte's past life she must have been involved with music, ' says Alyson, 'because apart from her fascination with guitars, a strange thing happened which made me feel more sure than ever that this must be so. '

Alyson says, 'When Charlotte was eighteen months old, I was doing the housework one day and she was playing about with her dolls. The radio was on and a particular record was being played, which featured a prominent piano. Charlotte immediately threw her dolls down and sat upright, her arms out in the air, and started to mime to the music. She moved her fingers separately as if she actually was playing the piano. I was tickled at this, and also surprised because she has never even seen a piano let alone played one - not even a toy one.'

Jokingly, Charlotte's mother asker her, 'Who do you think you are - Chopin?' 'She became very excited, her face became flushed and she started nodding her head furiously as if she was trying to tell me that I was nearly correct. Then she blurted out in her baby voice, "Me playing, me playing." And then she went on miming to the piano music.'

Alyson says that her baby was trying so hard to tell her something, but the child did not know the correct words to use to express herself. 'It was as if she was in agony trying so desperately to communicate with me,' says her mother.

When the child heard the name Chopin she seemed to recognize it even though the name had never been mentioned in her presence before.

'Her reaction really was incredible,' says Alyson. 'I feel deeply that I was on the right track when I said the word Chopin to her, because I saw her eyes instantly light up and her expression was strange as if she was trying to encourage me to keep guessing so I would have eventually hit upon the right name.'

Charlotte's mother feels that it would be all too easy to say that Charlotte had been Chopin in a previous life. She does not believe this, as she explains. 'I'm certain that the name Chopin is only a clue, not the answer. There was something in the way that Charlotte was trying to guide my thoughts, as if her eyes were willing me to keep talking just a little longer and I would have discovered her former identity.' Alyson wonders what would have happened if she had tried another few names.

Other incidents also make Alyson think that her baby has lived before, like the many times the child picks up a baby vest, but instead of putting it on herself or on her dolls as one might expect a child of her age to do, she bundles the vest up and very efficiently goes round all the furniture dusting it. Most people would say that Charlotte must have seen her mother dust the furniture but Alyson thinks that there is more to it than that. 'If the dusting was just an isolated incident then it would not mean much, but when this is seen in an all-over context and all the other things are taken into consideration, it takes on a certain significance,' says Alyson.

Another time they went visiting to Alyson's parents' home, which has a large fireplace in the lounge. Although the chimney has been boarded up for several years, the mantelpiece, grate and hearth are still the main centre feature in the room. Charlotte picked up a small ornamental brass shovel and began to push this back and forward under the grate as one would do when trying to clean out the ashes of a coal fire. Alyson says that Charlotte could not possibly have copied those actions from anyone because they know absolutely nobody with a coal fire.

Although the child is still very young in earthly terms, Charlotte's mother gets the impression that her little girl is really a very mature person in a baby shell. She says, 'A few days after Charlotte was born I was being visited by my parents who were seated one at each side of the bed. Charlotte was facing my mother when my father made a comment about Charlotte, and the baby turned her head and looked him directly in the eyes. Charlotte has always supported her own head and she has been able to focus properly from day one.'

When her mother first let Charlotte see money, the child seemed to know instinctively what it was for, and when she is given a pen and paper she doesn't scribble as most tiny children of her age would do. She makes a lot of carefully written marks that look like shorthand, all set out in neat rows.

Charlotte is meticulously tidy and clean and has a fantastic sense of humour. Since the age of three months she has had an infectious cheeky laugh, and when she wakes up in the mornings she has a look in her eyes that tells her mother that she is truly glad to be alive. One evening her mother heard giggles coming from her cot and when she went to find out what was so funny Charlotte said, 'Pretty lady makes Charlotte laugh.' Alyson could see no lady.

Her mother says, 'Each day she seems so eager to show me how much she already knows.' The little girl's latest achievement is to stand on a table with her hands on her hips doing a clog dance.

'There are so many things that she does,' says Alyson, 'that I can't believe she has just picked them up in the short time she has been with us. Some of her actions are so automatic that it makes me feel that she has an inbuilt knowledge of what things are all about.'

Boy remembers being his own grandfather
Richard Williamson, Wootton Bassett

Richard's parents were discussing an event which had taken place several years before he was born. The two-and-a-half-year-old boy was tinkering away on the floor with his toy cars and seemed to be fully absorbed in what he was doing, so much so that his parents almost forgot that he was in the room.

They had been talking about Richard's grandfather who had died nine months before Richard was born, and they were recalling the time when the old man had suffered a minor accident and had cut his hand when a chisel he had been working with had slipped under the weight of a hammer. Richard's grandfather had to go to the local hospital casualty department where he had four stitches put in his hand.

The boy looked up from his toy cars and said, 'My hand was sore that time.' His mother Frances corrected him and said, 'You mean your grandad's hand was sore.' Richard replied, 'No, my hand, Mummy.' Then he stretched out his left hand and pointed to a spot between his thumb and forefinger and said, 'It was just there, and it was sore, but it's all better now.'

There was no mark or scar of any description on the child's hand but he had pointed to the exact spot which corresponded with the injury received by his grandfather.

Frances had never discussed her father's accident before and she couldn't understand how Richard could have known the location of the injury. She says, 'It wasn't as if my dad's accident had been a major catastrophe or anything like that, so there was never any real reason to mention it. It was just something that had happened to him during his lifetime. The only reason I had been talking about it was that a friend of my husband had hurt his hand the day before and had to have it stitched and that reminded me about my father's similar experience.'

When Richard's father Len asked him how he knew which hand his grandfather had to have the stitches in, the little boy replied, 'I know because it was my hand. I remember.' 'How could you remember?' asked his father. 'You weren't even born when it happened.' The child replied, 'But I was born, Daddy, when I was living before.'

Frances and Len looked at each other and burst into laughter. They tried in vain to explain to their young son that it was impossible for him to remember his grandfather's accident, but no amount of talking could alter Richard's opinion. He assured them that he was the one who had hurt his left hand with the hammer and the 'other big thing' when he was here before.

A few months after this incident the family moved from Surrey to Northampton, which was an entirely new area and one to which little Richard had never been before in his life. Two days after they had arrived at their new home, Richard asked his mother, 'Can we go to York Road today, Mummy?' His mother asked him, 'Where on earth is York Road?' She was still finding her bearings in the new town. Richard replied, 'You know, York Road where I went to when I was living before.' Frances told him, 'You've never been to such a place.' Then, determined to put an end to Richard's stories about having been here before, she took her son out to show him that it was all just a figment of his imagination.

They went down the road and Frances asked the first person they met for directions to York Road, expecting to be told that the person had never heard of such a place. To her amazement the stranger started giving her clear directions of how to get to the place that Frances was sure didn't exist.

When they left the stranger, little Richard turned to his mother and said, 'Why did you ask that man, Mummy? I know how to get there.' By this time Frances was so bewil-

dered that she just let Richard lead her along the road to see
what would happen. The child did not follow the instructions
his mother had been given, however, so fearing that they
might get lost in the new town, Frances remarked to Richard
that she thought he might be taking the wrong route. The
directions dictated that they should turn right at a certain set
of traffic lights. Richard had turned left instead.

'It's O.K., Mummy,' said Richard confidently. 'This is my
short-cut.' A few minutes later, to the astonishment of
Frances, there they stood looking up at the road sign: York
Road.

'Well, where do you want to go to in York Road?' asked
Frances. Her son told her that he wanted to see the old shop
again where he used to buy his cigarettes. 'We wandered up
and down the road several times,' says Frances, but Richard
never found his shop. He hesitated at two or three spots but
then he seemed to rule them out for some reason, saying that
they weren't the same.

Years before Frances's father got married he used to live
and work in Northampton. Frances feels that there must be
some link between her son, her father, and York Road,
although she cannot recall her father having any connections with that particular area. 'At least he never mentioned
the place to me,' she says. 'But of course he could easily
have known the area in his younger days when he lived in
the town. He was a builder and was sent all over the place
on various jobs, so this could explain it. Some of the York
Road area of Northampton has been changed throughout the
years, so that could explain why Richard didn't recognize
his shop.'

Richard told his mother that he knew a big red pub that he
used to go to when he was living before and it was somewhere on a hill going up towards a park, and it was two roads
away from where he used to live. Frances is not entirely sure
of the location of the pub on the hill that Richard referred to.
She is under the impression that when her little boy men-

120

tioned this he was not thinking of York Road but of a different area of Northampton.

When Richard was tiny, he was very attached to his home, and he would get most upset if his parents took him away for the weekend or on a day visit anywhere. As his mother says, 'He would be miserable, unsettled, and a thorough nuisance.'

However, when he was taken to visit Frances's stepmother, he was perfectly happy and contented and as good as gold. Most children love visiting their grandparents but Frances's step-mother was not Richard's grandmother.

Frances says, 'Although Richard does not look like my father he has the same mannerisms and personality. It sounds a bit silly, but I really feel that my father's spirit lives in Richard. My father died in May and Richard was born the following February. He has the same way of expressing himself and he likes the things that my father used to like.'

Richard is continually making statements about when he used to live before, and many of them correspond with events which took place in the life of his grandfather. Len, his father, says, 'He is always so definite about the things that he remembers. It's not as if he has hazy recollections about things, he seems to remember everything so distinctly.'

Len is entirely and utterly convinced that his little boy has lived before. 'I'd stake my life on it,' he says. 'There's a lot of things that might seem strange to us but that doesn't mean that they don't happen. I personally believe that we do come back again for any number of reasons, although I can't pretend to know the ins and outs of it. After listening to Richard I feel sure it happens.'

Richard informed his parents, 'I'm not frightened of dying because it happened to me before. It was O.K.'

His mother says, 'Whenever he recalls an incident or if he relates a story to us, he always phrases it in the same way. He will say this or that thing happened to him when he was living before; not when he was alive before or when he was here before, but quite definitely when he was living before. It's

121

beyond me. I just can't make head nor tail of it. I've heard of odd things like this before but I never thought it could happen in my own family.'

Boy remembers being a ghost
Alexander Dennison, Rochester

A few months after Alexander's second birthday his family moved to Kilburn in London. Because the flat was in such a terrible state and badly needed cleaning, Alexander's aunt Brenda said that she would put the child in his pushchair and take him out for a walk so that Irene his mother could have some peace to get on with the cleaning.

Irene explains, 'I had not long started when Brenda came rushing back into the flat looking as white as a sheet. She told me that she would never take Alexander out again as he had nearly frightened the life out of her. 'When Irene asked her sister what she meant, Brenda told her that she had walked down Willesden Lane by the old graveyard when Alexander had suddenly pointed towards the gravestones and said, 'Look, roses. That's where I was sleeping when I was a real big man.' Brenda got such a fright that she felt the hair on the nape of her neck stand on end.

Brenda then asked Irene if she had ever taken the baby down that road before. Irene explains, 'I didn't even know where she was talking about. We had only just moved into the flat that morning and although I had gone to view it once before, I had just gone straight to the flat and away again. I didn't know anything about the surrounding roads at all.' Irene goes on to say that even on that one occasion when she had gone to Kilburn to view the flat, she hadn't taken Alexander with her. She had left the child with Brenda while she went to Kilburn herself. Irene adds, 'We didn't even have a television so Alexander couldn't have seen any graveyards on any programme and it's definitely not the kind of thing I would ever talk to a two-year-old about.'

Although Irene was puzzled she thought it best to forget the whole incident and so she put it to the back of her mind. However, six months later, Alexander was sitting in the flat having his dinner when he suddenly said to his mother, 'Mummy, you know when I was a real big man, I died.' The same uncomfortable feeling that Irene had experienced when Brenda told her about the graveyard incident swept over her. 'Did you really?' she replied, trying to sound matter-of-fact. He replied, 'Yes. It was when I was lying under the ground that time.' Irene's heart skipped a beat when she heard this. 'What do you mean, darling?' she asked him. He told her that he remembered lying under the ground, and that there were roses on top of the grass.

Irene was starting to get quite frightened by this time but she noticed that her son didn't seem to be the least bit upset. She asked Alexander, 'How did it feel when you were under the ground?' The child chirped up, 'Oh I wasn't bothered because I wasn't hurting any more.' Irene asked him, 'What had been hurting you?' Alexander replied, 'When I was hurt in the war my tummy and legs were all sore, but it was O.K. after I died and they didn't hurt any more then.'

Unable to credit what she had just heard Irene hardly knew what to say. There were so many questions she wanted to ask her small son all at the same time that she didn't quite know where to start. Then she got the feeling that perhaps it would be better not to ask him anything at all but just to let him do the talking first and then she could follow up what he said.

Irene remembers, 'I just sat and looked at him in amazement, waiting to hear what he was going to say next. Instead of saying anything he started tucking into his bowl of custard. After a minute or two I could see that he wasn't going to continue the conversation so I thought I'd better just leave it.'

The following day Alexander was just playing around the flat as usual when Irene felt compelled to give him some kind of gentle hint just to see if he would change his story about having been killed in the war. She asked him, 'You know yesterday you told me that you had hurt your tummy and your legs? How did it happen again?' Straight away Alexander asked, 'Oh, that time when I died?' His mother nodded her head and the child went on to tell her, 'It was in the war.' She asked him, 'What war?' He replied, 'I don't know what war it was, but there was a big bang and noise and I got hurt in my tummy and legs.'

Alexander told his mother that he didn't die straight away but lived for a short time. Then the next thing he knew he was in the ground in the graveyard. 'But how did you know it was a graveyard?' asked Irene. Alexander told her, 'I knew because it was where all the people were sleeping under the ground and there were flowers on top.' Irene said, 'But if you were sleeping, how did you know that there were flowers on top?' The little boy answered, 'I was sleeping but I could see as well. I could see the roses.' Irene laughed and then asked Alexander, 'How could you see if you were sleeping? Didn't you have your eyes shut?' Alexander answered, 'Not my real eyes, Mummy. Only the ones under the ground here sleeping.'

By this time Irene was totally confused and she did not know what to think. She made an attempt to reason with her son by saying, 'Then you weren't really in the ground, were you?' He answered, 'I was in the ground but I could still walk about and see the flowers.' 'That's impossible,' said Irene. 'How could you be in two places at once?' 'You can when you're dead,' came the reply. Irene then said, 'What happened to you after that, then?' Her little boy told her that he just stayed asleep for a long time but he was able to walk around if he wanted to, although he said he felt very tired most of the time and all he wanted to do was to sleep.

Irene asked Alexander, 'Where did you walk to?' He replied, 'It wasn't really like walking, Mummy.' Irene said, 'Do you mean your legs were too sore to walk properly?' The child replied, 'They were all better when I died but I didn't have to walk on them. I was able to move without walking on my feet.' Again Irene asked her little boy where he had moved to and he told her that he had gone to see the flowers and roses on top of the grass and that he remembered going out on to the roadway. Alexander then said, 'That's how I knew the road. It's the road that Aunty Brenda brought me to.'

'Did you do anything else?' asked Irene. Alexander said, 'I used to watch the other people getting put in the ground. Lots of people got killed in the war. I used to look for their flowers on top of the grass.'

Over the following few months little Alexander often mentioned details about being killed. The story gradually emerged that he had been a grown man and that although he had been killed during one of the wars he had not been in the forces. It seems as if he had been killed in an explosion of some description - most probably by a bomb.

When he was first aware of being hurt, Alexander said that he was lying down with bricks over him. He possibly could have been trapped, the numbing weight of the bricks on top of him making him unaware of pain in his legs. 'How long were you under the bricks?' asked Irene. He answered, 'I don't know.' Then she asked him if he remembers being taken up out of the bricks and he told her, 'No, I only remember sleeping after that.' Irene said, 'You fell asleep under the bricks?' At this point there seemed to be some confusion in Alexander's mind. He wasn't sure if he was sleeping under the bricks in the place where he had been struck down or if he was sleeping in the graveyard under the ground. He is in no doubt, however, that he eventually was put under the ground and he seems to have the impression of being there for quite a while.

Then as a little test, just to see if Alexander was going to alter his story, Irene said to him, 'And that was all you can remember?' He immediately piped up, 'No. I told you I remember going out to see the flowers, remember?' Then he added, 'And I went out on to the road as well.'

'Did you see anyone on the road or talk to them?' asked Irene. 'Oh yes,' said Alexander, 'but they didn't listen to me.'

126

Irene asked him why not and he replied, 'They just kept on walking. They didn't want to talk to me.' His mother asked him, 'Did they hear you?' The child answered, 'Oh yes, because I shouted at them, but they still didn't stop to talk to me.' 'What did you shout at them?' asked Irene. 'I told them my legs were better,' he replied. 'Weren't they glad about that?' asked his mother. Alexander just shook his head and said, 'I don't know.'

'What did you do after that?' asked Irene and Alexander replied, 'I just went back to the roses again.' His mother said, 'You mean under the ground?' 'No, I was already under the ground,' he answered. Irene said, 'But you've just told me that you had been out on the road shouting to the people. Now you're saying that you were under the ground all the time. Which is true?' Alexander explained to his mother, 'I was under the ground but that wasn't really me. I was shouting at the people.' 'After you went back to the roses did you go under the ground then?' asked Irene. Alexander replied in a somewhat weary voice, 'I didn't. I knew I was sleeping under the ground but I wanted to stay on top beside the roses.'

Irene recalls, 'He said it in such a tone of voice that he made me feel like a proper idiot not understanding what he was saying. To him it all seemed so logical and he couldn't understand why I was puzzled.'

When Alexander was about three-and-a-half his mother had him out the back in the small garden. She was talking to one of the other flat residents from the same house who shared the garden with her. The subject got round to unusual experiences and Irene just happened to mention to her neighbour some of the things that Alexander had been saying. Irene remembers, 'The woman was listening politely but with disbelief on her face, so feeling a fool I changed the subject.' Since then Irene has never discussed Alexander's memories with anyone. She says, 'It does seem so strange and ridiculous that I don't really blame people for being doubtful, but all I can say is if it happened to them or someone in their own family then they would believe it.'

One day after little Alexander had been playing in the garden he went in to his mother who recalls, 'He was black as the ace of spades, just like a little boy should be.' Irene laughed. 'He looked so happy and contented and I asked him how he was doing.' He answered, 'Fine,' and then he added, 'And if I'm extra good in this life then I'll be given another chance in my next life.' Brenda who was in the flat with Irene at the time said, 'I nearly turned green when I heard him. He was only a tiny nipper and I just couldn't understand how he could know to say a thing like that.'

As Alexander grew older his memories faded out until by the time he started school he remembered nothing at all about his previous life. One day Irene told him about the things he used to say when he was a baby and he got very embarrassed and said that he couldn't remember any of that. The only thing that did linger on in his mind was the feeling that he had been killed in a war.

When he was six, he went up to Irene one day and whispered that he wanted to tell her something. She asked what it was and he said, 'Promise you won't laugh at me, and say I'm silly.' Irene promised but she was intrigued and thought to herself that he was probably going to tell her that he had a girlfriend.

Alexander said to his mother, 'Mummy, I think I died in a war, but I don't know what war.' Irene remembers that all his childish ramblings came back to her. Since that remark Alexander has not mentioned anything else.

Irene wonders if her son really had wandered across Willesden Lane cemetery and if he had tried to communicate with the people hurrying past him on the roadway that day. Every so often she used to walk down that road and she could never resist glancing across at the graveyard and wondering, although she never dared venture in.

128

Girl remembers watching silversmith at work
Mandy Richards, Llandyfyl

When Mandy was two years old her aunt moved from Wales to Norfolk, which was brand new territory for the whole family. After a few weeks of settling in, Mandy's mother Sybal received an invitation to go and visit her sister at the new house, so one bright summer afternoon Mandy set off with her mother and father on the long drive from Wales.

The journey was pleasant and the family stopped for lunch on the way. The roads were not too busy and Mandy's father was able to enjoy the drive. On the outskirts of the town of Harleston, a place completely unknown to the family, Mandy suddenly yelled out excitedly, 'Oh look, Mummy, that's where the old man made all the rings.' The child was pointing to an old derelict shack with a black tarmac roof. Her parents just fobbed the child off thinking that she was just half dreaming, but Mandy persisted, saying, 'I remember watching him through the window.'

Sybal asked her little girl, 'What man, Mandy?' and the child replied, 'The old man with the funny hammer.' Sybal was sure that the child was thinking about some toy hammer or that perhaps she had heard a story about a man with a hammer, so she said, 'Are you thinking of someone from your story books, love?' Mandy shook her head and said, 'No, Mummy. It was a real man. I used to watch him through the window round the back.' Sybal asked her, 'When was this, love?' knowing perfectly well that her daughter had never even been out of Wales before and could not possibly have been to the old shack. Mandy answered, 'When I lived before, and I used to look in the back window.'

Mandy's father started to become interested in the conversation when he heard the child say such a strange thing. He asked his daughter, 'How could you have lived before, Mandy?' and the child told him, 'Oh I remember it. I lived near here and I used to play around the hut with my sister.'

Her parents laughed when they heard this and Sybal said, 'But you don't have a sister, Mandy.' The child replied, 'No, but I did have when I lived before.' Mandy then went on to tell her parents that she remembers having had a sister called Sarah, although she could not remember what her own name had been. Sarah had been a few years older than Mandy and when they used to play around the old shack the bigger girl would lift Mandy up so that she could peep in through the back window. Mandy says, 'I saw an old man with a funny hammer thing. He was bashing away at silver rings and bracelets on a workbench.' She vividly remembers the man's face. He never used to take any notice of her. He had grey hair and a grey bushy moustache, and he wore thin-rimmed spectacles which had very small lenses in them. Mandy remembers that the man wore the glasses perched on the end of his nose as he looked down through them on to his workbench.

Mandy told her parents how the small window at the back of the shed was, as she put it, 'in two halves. The bottom half was cloudy glass that I couldn't see through but the top half was just ordinary glass. That's why Sarah had to lift me up so that I could see in through the top half of the window.' She said that as well as the old man there were two or three other people working in the shed, all ladies, and all doing something to the rings. She thought that one lady was always packing the silverware up into little boxes, then wrapping them up with brown paper.

The man was the clearest in Mandy's memory because he had been working at his bench facing the window. His work seemed to alternate from banging wildly at the pieces of silver with his peculiar-looking hammer, to doing more intricate detailed work, because Mandy described him as sometimes being very serious as if he was concentrating very hard on the item before him on the bench.

She doesn't recall any details about the women or their

clothes or hairstyles but she does remember that the man was all dressed in dark colours. He wore a shirt or jumper of either black or dark navy-blue and over this he had on a large black leather apron. She remembers thinking how strange his hands looked.

Each and every time the family would visit that particular part of the country, Mandy would say the same thing. She always pointed to the same shack and she always said that she had watched the old man making rings when she had lived before.

This had been going on for about a year when Sybal decided that it was about time that she put a stop to what she thought were her little girl's imaginative wanderings. One day when they were driving towards her sister's house she asked her husband to stop the car at the shack so that they could walk around it with Mandy just to prove to her that the back of it was nothing like she had described, and so put the matter out of her head once and for all.

They got out and walked round the back of the old tumbledown shack and sure enough there was the one window at the back in the exact position that Mandy had described. Sybal says, 'It was so old I knew that it probably hadn't been used for years.' The window had been barred across on the outside with thick iron bars which were coated in rust, but behind these, through the thick layers of dust and cobwebs, Sybal could see the old glass window still intact. She gasped when she realized that the lower half of the window was fitted with dull frosted glass, while in the top half there was the ordinary clear variety. Immediately she remembered that little Mandy had described the lower half of the window as cloudy and that she could not see through it. The child was too young to know the term frosted but she had certainly got the description correct.

When they looked into the shed they could see that it was filled up with old junk. Sybal says, 'It looked as if it had been used as a storage shed at one time but everything inside

131

looked so rusty and old I got the impression that the owner had just gone off and forgotten all about the place.'

The shack still stands to this day, just outside Harleston near an old disused railway bridge. Mandy's parents wonder if there ever has been a silversmith who worked in the old shack, but Mandy doesn't wonder, she says she knows there was, because she saw him working with his hammer.

Although Mandy cannot remember anything much about her previous parents she has flashes in her mind that they used to visit a friend's house somewhere near the old shack. It was on these occasions that Mandy and her sister used to watch the old man at work.

Unbeknown to Mandy or Sybal, further research was carried out to see if there has ever been a silversmith who worked in that area. From the census offices in Norwich we received confirmation that in the year 1868 there did indeed exist a silversmith who had his own little business just on the outskirts of Harleston. At that time the area was virtually open country and the way in which isolated houses or huts were documented was by relating them to the nearest railway line. The silversmith, a Mr Michael Mothersole, was believed to have operated from a location very close to where the road was crossed by the railway line by an old iron bridge. This is the precise spot where the old shack still stands to this day.

Girl remembers being a nun
Elspeth Lacey, Newcastle

When Elspeth had only just started to talk at around eighteen months her mother was bathing her one night when she started mumbling away to herself in the bath. Her mother got the impression that the little girl was trying very hard to communicate, but because the child had only just started to put phrases together she was obviously finding it difficult to say exactly what was in her mind.

Her mother asked her to repeat herself and she said quite clearly, 'I'm going to the vows.' Elspeth's mother asked her, 'The vows? Where's the vows?' The child answered, 'You know, the vows up the big hill.' At this point Elspeth's eyes glazed over and she appeared to be in some kind of trance. Her mother Joan says, 'The strange look on her face sent shivers up my spine. She was in a complete daze.'

Elspeth went on to tell her mother that she was on her way up the hill to the vows. There were lots of flowers around her, growing by the side of the footpath. She said, 'We like to pick the flowers for the altar,' Joan asked her little girl where she was going and Elspeth answered, 'I'm going to take my vows with the other girls.' When her mother heard Elspeth phrase the words in that way it began to make sense to her. She asked the little girl, 'What vows are you going to take, Elspeth?' The answer came back, 'I'm not Elspeth now.' Her mother gently asked her who she was and the little girl said, 'I'm Rose, but I'm going to be Sister Teresa Gregory.'

Joan was fascinated by her daughter's words, both at the way she was speaking coherently and at the content of her story. She knew that the child had no knowledge of nuns or vows or anything like that. She says, 'We have no nuns in the family at all, in fact we're not even Catholics. I was dumbfounded when she started talking as if she knew all about being a nun.'

Elspeth then told her mother, 'I've got a long frock on and I'm walking up to the altar. I've got my white frock on.' After that, Elspeth gave a little jump and she looked up at her mother Joan and stared at her. Joan says, 'She looked so startled as if she had suddenly wakened up.' Joan got her little daughter out of the bath and started dressing her for bed. Just as she was snuggling down under her covers with her teddy bear Elspeth said to her mother, 'Do you know that I was an old lady once, Mummy?' Joan asked her what she meant and she answered, 'I always had a long black dress down to the ground and I had a black cloth over my head and I was very very old.' Joan asked her where she was when she was old and Elspeth replied, 'It was when I was here before.'

Joan could see that Elspeth was getting very sleepy so she didn't want her to go on talking much longer. She tried to settle the child down, but Elspeth seemed to be once more in her trance. Joan says, 'She just lay in her bed staring up blankly at the ceiling. Normally she would look at my face when she talked to me, but not this time. She had the same glazed look in her eyes that I had seen when she was in the bath.'

The child said nothing more that night and for a long time there were no other such occurrences. Joan had almost forgotten all about her daughter's story about being old and having had a previous life till one night about two years later when Elspeth was four she was chatting normally to her mother when her eyes suddenly glazed over again and she began to talk.

The child's words came pouring out without any effort or hesitation. She said that she had been a nun and that the convent was in a country area where there were lots of flowers. She remembered when she first went to the convent as a novice and then later took her final vows. As a nun, Elspeth, or Sister Teresa Gregory as she was known, had to do lots of jobs around the convent. She had to milk goats and help cook the food and make cheese. She said that she wasn't allowed to talk very much especially when a certain bell was rung. It was the sign that the nuns were to keep silent no matter what they were doing.

She remembered that she used to say a lot of prayers and that she lived in a tiny cell with only a bed and one or two other pieces of furniture in it. The child described it as cold and she said that she had to get up very early in the morning, sometimes when it was still dark.

Elspeth stopped speaking for a while. Joan did not feel comfortable leaving the child until she was sure that her daughter was completely back to normal and out of the dazed state. Joan says, 'Although she had stopped talking I felt that she was still deep in her trance because her eyes were still quite glassy-looking. I wasn't quite sure what to do. I didn't want to shake her or anything in case she was startled. She seemed very happy and she had such a peaceful expression on her face. I decided that I'd better say something to her to see if that would bring her back to normal.'

'Are you feeling all right?' asked Joan. Elspeth replied, 'Yes.' Joan says, 'When I asked her that, it seemed to set her off again because she went on to tell me how she died.' Elspeth told her mother that she had been praying in her room and she fell down on to the floor. She remembers trying to call out but couldn't. The next thing she knew was that everything went dark.

From out of the darkness, Elspeth woke up to find that some of her friends were with her. They told her that she would be going to stay with them for a while. She said that these friends were also nuns who had died before her. They all had their nuns' habits on but some of them looked younger than she had remembered them. Then Elspeth said that after a while she started to get young again too. She said that she waited with her nuns for a while only; then she went away to live somewhere else. She did not seem to have any memories after this point.

Joan says, 'She was talking like someone who had been hypnotized. I didn't ask her any questions except that one

135

about how she was feeling and she just kept talking all the time, without any prompting from me. I just sat quietly and listened. 'Joan says that when her little girl got to the part where she had left the other nuns to go away to a different place, it was almost as if everything in her mind faded out. It was only then that she caught her mother's eye and Joan realized that Elspeth had started to focus properly again.

Since then there have been no more trances or remarks about being a nun. Elspeth is now a happy playful little seven-year-old girl who loves her school and joins in with all the games in a carefree way. Her mother says, 'Sometimes when I see her tearing around with her little friend's football I find it very hard to imagine her as a nun. Still, her memories seemed very real at the time, and considering how young she was I can't believe that she could have picked it up from anywhere, especially since the first time she mentioned about the vows she was practically a baby, hardly able to talk at all.'

Joan has never told Elspeth what she used to say when she was younger. She feels that her little girl has probably forgotten all about it. Meanwhile Elspeth plays football with her friend from next door. Joan says, 'She doesn't bother much with dolls and girls' toys, she seems much more interested in trying to score goals at football!' Then Joan adds with a laugh, 'She's a right little tomboy.'

Girl remembers pet horse from previous life

Debbie Sellers, Hornsea

Ever since she was a baby, Debbie has always had what her mother Sandra describes as 'an uncanny way with horses'. Her mother could never quite understand this as she herself was always terrified of horses.

One night when Debbie was three years old, her mother put her to bed as usual, but just before the child dropped off to sleep, Sandra heard chuckles of laughter coming from Debbie's bedroom. When her mother went to see what was causing the mirth, Debbie told her, 'Oh I was just thinking about the time when I was riding my horse over fields and I came to a roadway and on the road there was a policeman on a bicycle. I went past him and put my arm out and knocked his hat off. He was very angry but I galloped off quickly and couldn't help laughing.'

Debbie's mother asked her when all this happened, and the child replied, 'Oh when I lived before.' She told her mother, 'We owned lots of horses and I loved them all. Paintbrush was my special horse. He was brown with patches on him.'

Debbie remembers how she used to help her husband in the stables. She described to her mother how to saddle, bridle and groom a horse, although she has never owned or ridden a horse in her life. Debbie tells of how she lived in the country and her husband ran a kind of riding school. She says, 'Lots of children and some adults used to come to ride our horses, and my husband showed them what to do.' Then she added, 'But I knew how to gallop on Paintbrush because he already showed me.' She was responsible for looking after Paintbrush.

When Sandra asked Debbie if she went to school the child replied, 'Oh yes. It was in the village.' She said she liked school and has remembered some of the things she was taught in her previous school. Recently Debbie started school, and when she had been there for a while her teacher gave her some simple spelling to learn. She always got every one of the spellings correct and when Sandra remarked to the child that she had never seen her learning them at home, Debbie replied, 'Why learn what I already know? I've already done all those words a long time ago.'

Although Debbie is aware of having been part of a family in her previous life, she can only recall her husband. She said his name had been something like Davidson. Then she added, 'But maybe it was just David.' She is not clear whether the David is part of the surname or whether it had been her husband's Christian name. She has no recollection of the rest of her family but she seems to think that there were quite a few people involved, although she does not know if they were brothers, sisters or other relatives.

Her main memories centre round the horses. She says, 'I loved it when I gave Paintbrush his dinner. He got it from a big bag of stuff.' Sandra thinks that Debbie's previous family may have been horse breeders because her daughter remembers, 'There were always lots of new baby horses but I didn't get to ride them.'

Debbie remembers the house that she used to live in as being old with big rooms and a very large kitchen. Sandra says, 'It sounds like a very old farmhouse by the way Debbie describes it.' The kitchen seems to stick in the child's mind more than any other part of the house. She says, 'It had a funny black shiny oven that was attached to the fire.' Apparently when the fire was lit the heat would spread to the oven part and in this way the food could be cooked. It must have been rather antiquated because there doesn't seem to have been any gas or electricity. Sometimes pots and kettles were placed on top of the fire, literally amid the burning cinders, and sometimes they would be hung over the flames from some kind of extended hook.

Another thing that Debbie remembers about the kitchen was that it had a large marble slab which was used as a worktop for baking bread. The loaves of bread would then be placed in the black oven to cook. Debbie says, 'I remember the lovely smell of the bread in our kitchen.'

Debbie's father Jim, a very practical kiln manager, is highly intrigued by his little girl's memories. He says, 'Well, she's either got a vivid imagination or else she's lived before.' Then he added with a laugh, 'I wouldn't like to put my money on it either way.'

As for Debbie, her big ambition is to own a horse again. Her father says, 'She's supposed to be saving up to buy one just like Paintbrush, but the way she's going she'll be a pensioner before she makes it. Every time the ice-cream van passes the door she's out like a shot to spend her money. Then she's got to start saving all over again.'

Boy remembers waiting to be reborn
Daniel Jones, Preston

Two-and-a-half year old Daniel is a beautiful brown-eyed dark-haired child with a ready smile. The great love of his life is water. He adores his bath and usually cries when his mother picks him up out of it to dry him off.

On odd occasions when Daniel has been brought to the sea-side he has been entranced by the sight of the sea. His mother Greta remembers the very first time her boy saw the sea at Blackpool. She says, 'I thought his eyes were going to pop out of his head he got so excited. He just couldn't wait to get his swimming trunks on. Although he was excited, I thought that he might be just a bit timid of actually going into the water for the first time, so I told him that I would take his hand and go in with him, but I never got the chance. He was off like a bee as fast as he could go, straight for the water. I ran after him expecting him to stop when he got to the water's edge but instead he ran straight in and started dancing up and down with sheer joy. '

When he was eventually persuaded to come out of the water, Daniel said the strangest thing to his mother who was busy with a towel trying to dry him off. He said, 'I had to go into the water to get born, Mummy.' His mother was so taken up with getting her child dry she didn't pay too much attention to him and just made a casual reply, 'Oh that was nice,' without really thinking about what she was saying.

Daniel then said, 'It wasn't the same as the sea, though. It was a river.' Again Greta answered automatically, saying, 'Oh really? Where was that, love?' Daniel answered, 'It was in Heaven, of course.' Greta's ears started to prick when she heard this, and she asked Daniel, 'What are you on about, Danny?' Her son then said, 'You know, Heaven, where all the little boys and girls live before they get to be born.'

By now Greta was beginning to be interested in this

strange conversation, so she said, 'Well, where is this Heaven then?' The child answered, 'It's where the river was before I was born.' Greta became more and more intrigued as she listened to her son. She asked him, 'How do you know that it was Heaven?' and he replied, 'Well that's the name everybody here gives it.' His mother asked him, 'Is that the name you called it when you were there?' The child replied, 'No.' Greta asked him what he had called it then, and he told her that they didn't call it anything, they just lived there.

As the weeks and months went past, every now and then Daniel would remember more and more details about his life in this other place where he lived before he was born. When he was nearly four he told his mother that there were lots of other children there and they were all good friends. The river flowed through this place and when it was time for any of the children to be born they would be led to the river with all their friends around them and then they would either jump into the water themselves or else someone would push them in.

Daniel remembers very well when it was his turn to be born. He said that he had been told well in advance that he would soon be leaving all his friends for a while because he was to come to earth and that his Mummy and Daddy would be waiting for him. He was told that he would see his friends again when he went back there to live with them all again.

A strange thing that Daniel said was that he knows some of his friends were going to be born at the same time as he was and they all knew that they would meet up with each other while they lived on earth. When his mother asked him if he knew any of these friends Daniel told her that he hadn't met them yet, but he was sure that as soon as he did meet one of them they would know each other straightaway. When Greta asked Daniel if he knew his friends' names he told her that their names would all be different on earth but the little boy was confident that somehow he would know his friends when they eventually met.

Daniel said that when it was his turn to be born he was pushed into the river and that was all he could remember. He went on to tell Greta that when he went into the river, that was the time when he left the other place where he had been living. He told his mother, 'That's when I came to you and Daddy.'

Greta and her husband Ralph can't help wondering if their little boy really does remember living in what we think of as Heaven. They find it so hard to believe that he could have thought up such an involved story. All his statements seemed to be so spontaneous.

Daniel is a well-behaved child who is thoughtful and considerate. Greta says, 'Sometimes I think that he's so much wiser than I am. It's funny, but the way he looks at me sometimes, I feel that there is so much in his eyes that he wants to tell me.'

Girl remembers being hit by previous mother

Mandy Hartley, Maidstone

From the moment she was born Mandy was an alert bright baby, very aware of everything which was going on around her. Her mother Susan says, 'The minute she was born she was handed over to me. I took her in my arms and she not only opened her eyes and focused on me but she actually seemed to look at me and say, "Who are you?" '

During the following few days in hospital Susan was constantly amazed at the reactions of her new-born baby. The infant seemed to understand everything which was being said to her. Her mother remembers, 'She had such a knowing look on her face as if she already knew the whole routine of babyhood back to front.' Susan remembers that when her mother-in-law came to the hospital to see the baby for the first time she took one look at Mandy and said 'You're foxy, you've been on this earth before.'

One day when she was two-and-a-half years old, Mandy got up to some childish mischief in the kitchen. Susan came in to find the child sitting in the middle of the floor covered from head to toe in cream, surrounded by half-a dozen half-eaten cakes from which she had eaten all the cream apart from that which was mashed into her hair and smudged all over her clothes, face and arms. Susan's immediate reaction was to burst into laughter but when the laughter subsided, she thought about the cakes and naturally enough she was rather cross. She attempted to tell the child off and was just about to try to make the little girl understand that stealing cakes was not a very lady-like thing to do, when Mandy, being well aware that her mother was annoyed and sensing that she was going to be told off, chirped up, 'I'm going to tell my mummy of you.'

Susan was stopped in her tracks at the child's words. 'But I am your mummy,' she said. Mandy answered, 'I mean my other mummy.' Her mother asked her what she meant, and Mandy replied, 'My mummy when I was a little girl before.' Susan told her, 'You weren't a little girl before. What on earth are you talking about?' The child replied, 'Oh yes I was, and I had another mummy.'

Susan could see that Mandy was absolutely serious so she asked her, 'Well, why did you leave your other mummy then?' A rather dejected expression crept over the child's face. Then she answered, 'Because she hit me with knives.' Susan was horrified, and she asked her daughter, 'Are you sure? Are you just making all this up, Mandy?' Mandy said, 'She did hit me with knives and then I died.' Mandy looked quite upset by this time so Susan thought it best to change the subject.

Some weeks later when Mandy was in bed she again mentioned her other mummy to Susan. This time the child went on to talk about her death. She said, 'I was very poorly. Then I feel asleep and went very small. I woke up and I was with you and Daddy and then I grew big again, into a big girl.' Susan asked Mandy if she knew what age she was when she was poorly and the child replied, 'I think I was eight.'

Mandy then told her mother that she remembered the time just before she was born. She said, 'I was in your tummy. It was when I woke up again.' She told her mother that it was dark and warm and she could hear outside noises, and that she had heard Susan talking and sometimes shouting.

When Mandy was only two years old, Susan unfortunately had a miscarriage in the tenth week of her pregnancy. Soon afterwards she conceived again and Mandy informed her mother that although the earlier baby had died in her tummy the very same baby had come back to her.

Susan is not certain what to think of her child's remarks . She is very open-minded on the subject of reincarnation and says, 'I can't say for sure whether my little girl really has lived before. Who can really tell? Her memories just seem to come in flashes now and again. There's no way to really prove anything but at the same time when she does get these flashes they come so quickly. She blurts out things without taking time to work anything out in advance.'

The girl has mentioned her other mummy so often that Susan feels there could well be something behind all of Mandy's remarks if it was possible to dig deep enough, although she doesn't wish to have her child hypnotized or anything like that. She says, 'It's the expression on her face more than anything else that is so convincing. There's no doubt in my mind that she believes her memories to be real, so who knows?'

Two-year-old girl remembers being born
Hermione Baker, London

Little Hermione, named after her godmother, a famous actress, has distinct memories of her own birth. She describes it to her mother Anne as being very noisy and tiring. In the child's own baby words, 'When I were born it were very dark and I heard loud noises. I felt very tired.'

Hermione says that before she was born she was with Jesus. She says, 'But He went away. I did not know where He was going and He didn't say.'

She remembers the days and months before her birth when she existed in her mother's womb, and her conscious memory goes back even further than that to a previous life in which two little boys were her special friends.

According to Hermione, the darkness which she experienced during her birth did not exist while she was in her mother's womb waiting to be born, but she does remember the sounds of the outside world penetrating into the womb. She says, 'It were golden and bright, but noisy like chug chug,' and she says that she could hear her mother speaking.

One day while Hermione's actress mother was busy looking over one of her scripts, Hermione suddenly announced, 'I'm in my life.' Her mother was quite amazed. Then the child followed this up with, 'I'm in the whole world.' Anne says that the statements seemed to come out of the blue, and were not preceded by any other conversation. She seemed to be in a state of wonderment and great happiness.

Maps hold a strange fascination for Hermione and she appears to have an inner knowledge of geography. The first time she ever saw a map was in January 1982 when her mother came across an old map of the world which had been folded away in a drawer. In an attempt to keep her daughter amused for a time, Anne thought that she would show the map to Hermione to let the child see what the world really looks like. She spread the map out on the coffee table, but before she had time to say a word, Hermione pointed to North America and said, 'That America. Godmama lives there.' Her godmother does indeed live in New York. Anne then pointed to Kenya on the map and straight away Hermione said, 'That in Africa.' Anne was overwhelmed at this because she had never mentioned the word Africa.

About a month after the map incident, Anne was reading Alice in Wonderland to her daughter. Anne recalls, 'She was listening intently, but I couldn't believe she was really understanding it. After I read, "The caterpillar was smoking a hookah", I asked her if she knew what a hookah was. Very confidently Hermione replied, "I do." ' Somewhat sceptically Anne asked her, 'What is it, then?' Hermione replied, 'It a pipe,' as if she was amazed at her mother's ignorance.

Anne describes herself as an agnostic, and very sceptical about reincarnation but she admits that Hermione's insight into things which belies her age really makes her wonder.

Hermione's father, a solicitor, is open-minded on the subject. He is a practising member of the Anglican Church and like his wife Anne he is not given to assumptions. He does not know quite what to make of Hermione's statements. Anne says that her husband is just not sure what lies behind it all. 'It takes a lot to really convince him about such matters, but in spite of himself, he feels that there is definitely something strange about the way our little girl knows so many things that she has never been taught.'

Normally Anne buys frozen peas, but one day she was passing a greengrocer's shop and she caught sight of some pea-pods. She thought that it might be a good idea to buy some and take them home to Hermione to show her how to do some podding. Anne says, 'It was to give her something to do more than anything else.' To Anne, podding peas seemed like a marvellous change from the never-ending rows of sticky dough messes which little Hermione proudly referred to as 'my cakes ready to go in the oven'.

Anne took the peas out of the bag and was all set to explain to Hermione what they were, as she knew that the child had never seen peas in a pod before, but before she had time to utter a word the child chirped up, 'Oh goody, pea-pods! I haven't done podding for a long time.' Anne knows for a fact that Hermione has never done podding at all.

The child said, 'I need a colander when I do podding.' This tickled her mother because the word colander was total-ly outside the child's vocabulary. 'I had no idea that she had even heard the word, or knew what a colander was used for, but she put her little apron on, rolled up her sleeves and set to work as if she had been doing it all her life. She knew exactly what to do without my having to say a single word.'

One day Hermione was chatting away happily with her mother about some of her friends. She was relating a story about some funny incident that had recently occurred. Anne asked Hermione if she had made friends with any boys. The following is the resulting conversation which took place between Hermione and Anne:

Hermione: (In reply to her mother's question about mak-ing friends with boys) I haven't. I have. Those little boys have already died. Have already died from me.

Anne: Cried?

Hermione: Died.

Anne: Who's died?

Hermione: Those little boys who I had made friends with. Those two boys.

Anne: You made friends with two little boys?

Hermione: And those have already died.

Anne: The friendships died?

Hermione: No.

Anne: No?

Hermione: Those little boys who I did make friends with.

Anne: What's happened to them?

Hermione: Died.

Anne: How did they die?

Hermione: They did fall into the water and a shark did eat them.

Anne: Oh dear! So they won't be coming anymore?

Hermione: No.

Anne: Who told you about this?

Hermione: None of the little boys - none.

Anne: Is that a true story?

Hermione: Mmm.

Anne: Have you seen them since this?

Hermione: Mmm. A shark did come and eat they up and I saw they go in and I didn't fall in.

Anne: Is this when you were swimming?

Hermione: No.

Anne: Oh, I think you're making all this up!

Anne says that she is loathe to question Hermione outright for obvious reasons, but because of the odd flashes of past memories the child experiences, she thought that she would ask a few test questions just to see what her daughter's reaction would be.

The following is an account of the experiment. Anne wonders whether it is all just a delightful babble of nonsense or if there is more to it than that. 'I'm not really sure what to make of it,' says Anne. 'I noticed she seems to have a recurring fascination with sharks, although she has never seen a real one.'

Anne: I don't really believe it but some people think they've lived before. Do you think you have?

Hermione: I do.

Anne: Where did you live?

Hermione: In London.

Anne: When? Now?

Hermione: Long ago.

Anne: What did you wear?

Hermione: Like this. (She was wearing a short white dress.)

Anne: Just the same? or longer?

Hermione: Longer.

Anne: Who were you?

Hermione: I was a lady.

Anne: A lady of Leisure?

Hermione: I was a lady of Pleasure (!)

Anne: Were you married?

Hermione: I was.

Anne: Did you have any children?

Hermione: I did.

Anne: How many?

Hermione I7.

Anne: Did you live in London all the time?

Hermione: In London and Northland. (No great break-through. Northland comes into Noggin the Nog.)

Anne: And what were you in Northland?

Hermione: I was half a man and half a woman and I was on a boat and I was eaten by a shark!

Hermione's mother Anne, a well-known West End actress, is rather non-committal regarding her daughter's memories of far-off lives and sharks. 'Who really knows what it is?' she says.

Hermione is a healthy happy toddler, somewhat chubby and extremely pretty with big blue eyes and fair straight short hair. 'She loves her food,' remarks her mother, 'and she will eat positively anything including our best Stilton cheese. She is a darling little girl and a great delight to us.'

Anne remembers when Hermione was only a year old and she took her into their local post office to buy some stamps. While they were waiting in the queue a perfect stranger walked up to Anne. and pointing to the baby said, 'That one has been here before. Look at her face. She's seen it all.' Anne says, 'I didn't take much notice of it at the time, but so many little incidents make me wonder.'

Life After Death

There are countless cases of people who have given evidence of survival after death; indeed so many that the subject is well catered for in the many volumes of books which adorn the shelves of our public libraries up and down the country. However in the course of our own research into life before birth, several interesting experiences have been brought to our notice which substantiate the case for survival of the personality after physical death.

As our research dealt primarily with children, the case histories dealt with in this chapter also feature babies or young children, and we feel sure that we should include these accounts in this book, not only for their interest value, but because we sincerely believe that the stories will bring some degree of solace to bereaved parents and offer them a hope to cling to that they will eventually be re-united with their children.

Mrs Angela Rigg-Milner, a doctor's wife, is a very sensible, level-headed lady, very down to earth and not given to flights of fancy. One day Angela was driving along the Arterial Road at East Horndon, Southend, when her car was involved in a three-vehicle smash. Five-year-old Samantha, the youngest of Angela's three children, sustained critical head injuries, and three days later the child died.

Angela was inconsolable, and at the time had no religious beliefs. Despite the bitter heartbreak Angela experienced at the time of Samantha's death she refused to take any pills which would have dulled her senses. She knew that somehow or other she was going to have to get through the ordeal by herself, without resorting to drugs or alcohol. She was tortured by feelings of guilt and she kept blaming herself for her daughter's death, telling herself that if she hadn't taken the children out for that car run it might never have happened.

She tried desperately to come to terms with the situation and she made a brave effort to face up to life for the sake of her husband and her other two children. She knew how much they were all suffering already, and she didn't want to add to their unhappiness by having a break-down. Being a doctor's wife, she was well aware of the dangers of depression and she made up her mind to do her best just to keep going in the face of her grief and desolation.

Then an extraordinary thing happened which entirely changed the course of Angela's life. She had been walking through the house one night, just six weeks after Samantha had died, unable to sleep, feeling restless and uneasy. She went back to bed and she noticed that the time was 5. 30 a.m. by the clock on her teamaker. Something made her turn and look towards her dressing table which is incorporated into a unit in the corner of the bedroom. 'There was Samantha, standing in the bedroom watching me,' says Angela. 'She was wearing her favourite pink and-white nightgown.' Angela had not allowed Samantha to wear that particular nightgown very much because it was made of nylon. She knew the nightgown was folded in the drawer in the children's room, but yet there was Samantha wearing it.

Angela says, 'She looked extremely bewildered and lost. I got out of bed and walked down to the end of it and sat down, watching Samantha all the time. She was now only about two-and-a-half feet away from me.'

Then Angela spoke to her daughter. 'Hello, darling,' she said. 'You're not dead at all, are you?' Samantha replied, 'I'm very tired, Mummy.' Angela says, 'I put out my arms and she walked over to me. It was the most unbelievable thing anyone could imagine. She sat on my knee and she was warm and solid and very much alive. I stroked her long silky hair and she felt real in every way, just like any normal child.'

Angela was completely aware that something remarkable was taking place and she made a point of lifting up one of

152

Samantha's arms to make sure that it was real. She says, 'Her arm felt warm and perfectly normal. I touched her body from head to toe and it was every bit as complete and solid as you and me.'

Angela then asked Samantha if she would like to come into bed beside Mummy and Daddy for a cuddle. At this point, Angela called her husband so that he too could see Samantha, but she just couldn't waken him up. She says, 'I was afraid to call him too loudly for fear that the noise or disturbance would make Samantha go. When he didn't wake up I thought I'd better leave him.' She then took Samantha by the hand and walked round the side of the bed and took the child into bed with her.

Angela says, 'She snuggled in to me quite naturally, the way she always had done. Again I stroked her long brown hair as it spread across the pillow, and it felt just as ordinary as ever.'

After a few minutes Samantha said, 'I am tired. I've got to go now, Mummy.' Angela could see that as Samantha said the words she was looking into the corner of the room to the spot where she had first appeared. She says, 'It was as if Samantha was looking at someone, and being told to come back. I could see nothing there at all, but I'm certain that my daughter was following someone's guidance.'

Angela then asked her little girl, 'Will you come back and see Mummy again?' but the child didn't answer. Angela says, 'The next second she just disappeared. I immediately looked at the clock by the bed and it was exactly 5.40 a.m. The whole thing had lasted for ten minutes.'

Angela vividly remembers her feelings at that moment. 'I felt an unbelievable sense of relief that I will never forget. Out of the hell came this incredible peace, with the knowledge that life does exist after death.'

The experience has changed Angela's entire outlook on life. She explains, 'I admit I used to be a very materialistic person and had no real religious beliefs, but since seeing

153

Samantha after she died I now know for sure that life continues. It was inevitable that I should change my opinions drastically.'

Angela now devotes her life to helping other parents of children who have died. She is a member of an organization called 'Compassionate Friends' which was set up by a group of bereaved parents. Members are on call day and night to offer help and sympathy to those in mourning.

A famous American medium once told Angela that she had shared a previous life with Samantha and that the child had been meant to die so that Angela would later be shown the proof of survival after death.

'The relationship was not a parent-child one,' says Angela. 'We were just friends in our previous lives. Seemingly there was a debt owed to me by Samantha in repayment for some good turn which I had done for her. The manner in which this debt was repaid was carefully worked out so that I would be led to change my ideas and opinions, and indeed my whole way of life. Samantha was to be born to me as a daughter, then die and then return, leaving me in no doubt as to the fact that life does continue after death.

'It may seem a harsh way to prove a point,' says Angela, 'but I suppose it was the only way ever to convince someone like me that there is more to life than the materialistic side. I was such a sceptic.'

Angela says that she now thanks Samantha for the experience because she is so much richer in spirit for having gone through the ordeal. She now believes, where before she didn't. She feels that Samantha is always with her and she knows that they can never be truly separated.

Debbie Neesden lost her baby in a cot death when he was only a few months old. For the first week after the child died, his mother's grief was almost unbearable. Then something happened which helped to console her and lighten the weight of her agony.

She explains, 'A week after my baby died, I had a strange dream. A woman appeared seemingly from nowhere with a small bundle in her arms. I could not see her face as it was veiled by light but I knew she was holding my baby boy. I could see that his hair was definitely the same shape round his forehead.' In the dream Debbie went up to the woman, who did not speak but pulled back the shawl and showed Debbie her baby. Debbie asked the woman to give her the baby, and the woman reluctantly agreed. Debbie took the infant, held him tightly and kissed him over and over again.

Debbie says, 'I then asked the woman if I could take the baby away with me, but she shook her head, held out her arms and took my son away from me. At this point I woke up and found myself in tears.'

A month later Debbie had another dream in which she was walking about in a large storeroom which was filled with big crates. She heard a noise, turned round and found herself face-to-face with the same unknown woman who had appeared to her in her previous dream. Debbie remembers, 'Our eyes met and she beckoned me to follow her, which I did, and she led me round the back of some crates, stopped by one, and invited me to look inside. I did so and there lying in the crate was my baby son. He looked a lot older than he was at the time of his death. He looked like a baby of about seven months and he was much bigger than I expected. He recognized me and held out his hands.'

Just when Debbie was about to pick up the baby, the woman shook her head, picked him up herself and started to walk away with him. This upset Debbie so much that she screamed after the woman to stop, but the woman didn't. Debbie then ran after her but she kept darting in and out behind the big crates to avoid her, till Debbie yelled out, 'Why tease me like this? I only want to hold him.' Then the woman disappeared and Debbie woke up feeling extremely distressed.

Several weeks later she had the most interesting dream of

all. She found herself outside a shopping precinct and recognized her pram outside a shop. She went up to the pram, looked inside, and there was her lovely baby lying in the pram chatting to himself. Again he recognized Debbie and smiled up at her. She says, 'He seemed to be roughly the same age as before. The same woman then came out of the shop and she smiled at me. I knew she was the woman from the other two dreams, but there was something more familiar than that about her. I had the feeling that I knew her from somewhere, but I couldn't think who she might be. She was about seventy years old and had white hair. I stroked my baby's head and he cooed at me, and I began to cry. The woman held me to her and told me not to cry because she said that she was looking after him now and that he was very happy with her.'

The woman explained to Debbie that soon these dreams would stop and that she would not see her baby any more, but that everything would be explained to her in her next dream. Debbie accepted this, kissed her baby and then woke up. This time she felt far more relaxed and was not upset or frustrated as she had been the time before. She was just a little perturbed by the fact that her baby had not cried to be with her.

Debbie had the final dream about five months later. She found herself on a grass verge by a shallow stream. There was a bridge over the water, and she saw a woman and a child walking over the bridge and approaching her. The child was a beautiful fair-haired little boy who was holding on to the woman's hand. Debbie remembers that as they came nearer to her, she noticed that the child was very unsteady on his feet, as if he had only just learnt to walk.

Debbie says, 'When they came up close to me I recognized them both. It was my darling baby Lee Michael John, and the woman was my beloved grandmother who had died ten years previously.'

'I grabbed my son, who cuddled me closely,' says Debbie. 'He looked about a year old. He wore ordinary clothes, just like any other small boy would wear in summertime, and chatted away in his own style.'

Debbie's grandmother told her that Lee Michael John was a good child and that he was not meant to have been born to earthly parents, but was meant to be a spirit child. The old lady went on to explain to Debbie that although her heart had been broken it was all for the best, because if the baby hadn't died of a cot death when he did, God would have called him just before his third birthday. Debbie was told that soon she would conceive again and give birth to a female child.

The woman said that Lee Michael John had progressed enough to enter another sphere and that she would be taking him herself. It was explained to Debbie that her dreams were not really ordinary dreams at all but what she was experiencing was astral projection and that in fact she had entered the spirit world while her physical body was asleep.

Debbie was told that she would not see her son again until she passed over into the spirit realms, but her grandmother promised to love the child and teach him all the things that Debbie would have done. Debbie says, 'I nodded and tearfully passed Lee Michael John back to Grandmother. I smothered him with kisses and then Grandmother led him back towards the bridge. I waved to them and they walked over the bridge and out of sight. Strangely enough, I was not tempted to go after them. The next thing I knew I was awake.'

Debbie feels as she looks back on the experience that she is part of some strange plan. She says, 'Lee wasn't like an earth child. He seemed angelic.'

Since the dreams, which have now stopped, Debbie has become pregnant again and is looking forward to the birth of her new baby. She says, 'I feel that everything that has happened has been carefully worked out for my well-being. I am glad I had astral projection and have been greatly comforted by it and I know that there is life after death, and that my son is being well looked after. I only wish that more people could experience such a wonderful thing.'

Mrs Barbara Hoole, a kindly grandmother from Cheltenham was devastated when the joy of her life, her beautiful grand-child Siobhan, died of a cot death at the age of eight months.

Mrs Hoole remembers the horror of the moment when she realized that the baby had died. She says, 'She was put down as usual for her afternoon rest, a happy, seemingly healthy, normal baby, but when her mother went to the cot later and picked her up, the baby just flopped over her arm like a rag doll, for she was dead.'

There was a very special rapport between Mrs Hoole and Siobhan and just previously, the old lady had been seriously ill in hospital. She recalls, 'The family would bring the baby in to see me and put her into my arms. She would gaze at me fixedly, tiny though she was. It was as if she was trying to give me a message. I got the clear impression that she was trying to tell me that I wasn't going to die, as everyone, including the doctors, thought, but that I was going to get bet-ter. She was right, bless her. I did get better. If only I could have gone instead of her.'

'After the baby died, I had a strange recurring dream,' says Mrs Hoole. 'The baby used to come to me as a little barefoot child wearing a floating, short, blue shift. Her hair was short and fluffy and she had such a happy laughing face as she stretched her hands out to me.'

Mrs Hoole feels that the baby is trying to show her that death is not the end. She says, 'The strangest thing is that before the dreams started, I always imagined the child as I last saw her, a small bouncy baby, but each time she appears to me in my dream she is slightly different, as if she is slowly growing up. She is no longer a baby. She died in April, 1980, and it seems that she has since then developed into a toddler and is able to walk, just like a normal two-year-old girl would.'

The above cases have one thing in common, although the cir-cumstances are different, and that is that each one suggests

158

not only that life continues after death, but that there are great efforts being made to bring to us the proof of this fact by various methods: materialization, astral travel or dreams.

PART TWO

HYPNOTIC
REGRESSION

There are many accounts of people who under hypnosis have been regressed to various stages in their lives; in some instances back to the womb and beyond. Often very colourful and dramatic past lives are tapped and events are described in great detail.

In countless cases valuable hypnotherapy can be carried out to help people solve a particular problem such as alcoholism, gambling, smoking, compulsive eating, kleptomania, etc., and even physical illnesses can be cured by using regressive hypnotism to pin-point the origin of the illness, and then forcing the patient to face up to the conditions which originally caused the illness, thus coming to terms with those conditions, leading to a cure or disappearance of the symptoms.

There is no doubt that hypnotherapy plays a useful role in our society today, but this must not be confused with the other type of hypnotic regression which is not concerned with any medical or sociological problems and is performed solely for the purpose of regressing a hypnotized subject back to a real or imagined previous life.

In extremely rare cases, the subject may possibly be retrieving memories of past lives, but the hard evidence for this is almost non-existent. In almost every case investigated there arises at some point a serious insurmountable obstacle to the validity of the claimed previous life.

For example, a man may, under hypnosis, give an elaborate description of life as a Roman centurion with an impressive wealth of detail, but instead of this being the manifestation of a previous life, it could be nothing more than the surfacing of data which had previously been fed through to his brain from long-forgotten experiences in his present life, via a book, a film, a newspaper article, etc. Although this information would be completely forgotten by his conscious mind, it would, nevertheless, be stored in his brain and could be recalled at any time by the hypnotic technique.

In this age of mass communication there are endless opportunities for picking up knowledge, and considering that every single experience, feeling and thought which has ever occurred to us is lodged in our brains, it is not surprising that many long-forgotten experiences can be drawn into the area of consciousness in a misleading manner. Because these experiences appear to be totally new to the conscious mind, they can often give the impression of being incidents from another life.

One very well-known and respected hypnotist who practises regression sums it up by saying, 'If I could have found it out so could my client.' He means, of course, that if evidence exists to verify that a certain incident has occurred in the past, then the very fact that this evidence does exist and can be researched makes it possible, however improbable, that the evidence had, one way or another, consciously or subconsciously, reached the client's brain, and lay there computerized and ready to spring to the fore at the appropriate time, i.e. when the client was under the hypnotic influence. On the other hand, if there is no evidence available to substantiate the subject's story, then how can it be proved at all?

The main question to consider is the order in which the experience and the verification registered in the brain of the client or subject. The answer to this question is the crucial pointer as to whether or not the subject is really remembering a previous existence or merely recalling past incidents from his present life.

Unfortunately the question is not easily answered, due to the fact that we are dealing with subconscious experiences. If, as in extremely isolated cases, the experience or mind picture registered before the subject had any knowledge of a particular incident, either conscious or subconscious, then there is a strong indication that the subject did indeed experience such an incident at some point in his existence and that the experience is lodged in the memory of the subject.

We must also consider the possibility that a subject, knowing that he was to be hypnotized, and not wishing to let the hypnotist down, as it were, invented a plausible story, either deliberately or not. There are many examples in which the subject pre-conditions himself by auto suggestion or a type of self-hypnosis so that when he is then put into the trance by the hypnotist, he is certain to come up with the appropriate response.

The power of suggestion must not be underestimated. There are many instances of people behaving in a totally illogical manner simply because they have been led to believe that this is how they should react.

For example, an experiment was set up where four people known to suffer from hay fever were subjected to the following test. They were blindfolded and told that a small bowl of pollen was being placed under their chins. They were then asked to dip their fingers into the bowl to feel the pollen dust. The subjects did this, but unknown to them, instead of pollen dust they were in fact dipping their fingers into bowls of cornflour. They were then asked to breathe in over the pollen dust. In every case, the breathing produced all the symptoms of hay fever sneezing, irritation of the eyes and nose, etc. After a little time elapsed, the same four subjects were lined up, again blindfolded, and this time they were told that they would be breathing from bowls of cornflour - in fact, bowls filled with pollen. The result was that although each of the four subjects was a known hay fever sufferer, not one single person reacted to the pollen when they had been preconditioned to believe that they were only breathing cornflour.

In the same way, if there is a suggestion, either stated verbally or simply inferred, there is a strong tendency in most subjects to comply with that suggestion, so when a session is set up with a hypnotist with a view to regressing the subject to a previous life, then because the subject may well feel compelled to give the desired and expected results, he will relate all kinds of weird and wonderful experiences. This does not indicate that the subject is being consciously deceitful in any way, it is merely that he has reacted to the suggestion.

It is interesting to note that in stage hypnotism, the subjects are carefully selected by the hypnotist. This may not be made apparent to the audience, especially if he is a skilled showman, but nevertheless he will only work with subjects whom he knows for sure will be responsive to his suggestions.

As far as the audience is concerned, they see a random group of people rush up on to the stage in answer to the hypnotist's request for volunteers. They are indeed exactly what they appear to be - just ordinary members of the public. But once they are on the stage the hypnotist goes into a carefully-planned process of elimination which is presented in such a way as to make the audience think that it is all part of the main act, when in fact it is only a precautionary preliminary to the main event.

Usually the elimination routine will go as follows: The group of people on the stage will be asked to carry out a simple instruction, such as having to clasp their hands over their heads. The hypnotist will then say that on the count of three the volunteers will find it impossible to unclasp their hands. He will then watch closely to see which of the volunteers immediately unclasp their hands and which of them comply with his suggestion and remain with their hands tightly clasped together. At this stage he will recognize any extroverts amongst the volunteers as they will already be putting on a great show of straining and grimacing to give the impression that they are trying desperately to separate their hands.

From this simple demonstration, the hypnotist can spot the best subjects. He will ask the people who unclasped their hands straight away to leave the stage, usually to a round of applause. He may then do a follow-up experiment with the remaining volunteers in order to classify them into further susceptibility categories. While this is being done, the hypnotist will keep up a constant line of patter so that his audience is not aware of the fact that he is still evaluating his subjects.

The stage hypnotist will soon select in his mind his star performers and he will then choose one of these and with the confidence that the subject can't wait to take the spotlight, he will carry out some spectacular trick which will cause the audience to roar with laughter or gasp in awe.

Most of these hypnotic stunts are nothing more than optical illusions - tricks of the trade - whereby a relatively simple feat is trumped up and presented as if it was something incredibly difficult which can only be performed because the subject has been put into a so-called deep hypnotic trance. Normally, the clever showman will try to impress his audience with high-falutin' phraseology, thus lending himself a stamp of authority and credibility.

Perhaps there is something of the showman in all of us, and under hypnosis we are provided with a shield to hide behind in order to protect our true personality and identity, and forget about our inhibitions.

This tendency to perform in a certain way to overshadow deep-seated problems can lead to a variety of complex phobias and psychological conditions. It is in this area that hypnotherapy is especially valuable. One practising hypnotherapist attached to the Institute of Biodynamic Therapy in London had a telephone call from the doctor of a patient who had all the outward symptoms of heart trouble, yet even after extensive tests, and visits to a Harley Street consultant, there was no sign of any malfunctioning of the heart. The patient was an attractive middle-aged woman who had been happily married for twelve years to the same man. She regularly complained of pains across her chest and forearms, and she had what she described as palpitations and heart rhythm problems.

The hypnotherapist relaxed the woman and put her into a trance. He asked her to go back to the first time that she experienced the heart trouble. The woman was able to recall vividly that she had been having dinner with her husband and in the course of general conversation he remarked that he hoped that she had had a nice day, and then he asked her what she had done that afternoon. The woman instantly suffered a heart attack, or what appeared to be a heart attack.

Delving deeper into the matter, the hypnotist then asked the woman to go back to earlier on that afternoon and to tell him what she had been doing. The woman described how she had gone out shopping that afternoon and by chance she happened to meet an old boyfriend, someone she had been very attracted to before she met and married her husband. She only spoke to her ex-flame for a few minutes but with continual encouragement from the hypnotist, the woman admitted that while she was talking to this old friend she started to feel strongly attracted to him. In her mind she had tried to fight against this attraction because it made her feel uneasy and she felt guilty because of her attraction to a man other than her husband.

Later on that evening when the woman's husband asked her what she had done that afternoon, all her feelings of guilt came to the fore, confusing her so much that her only way out was to simulate a heart attack. The tactic worked because the husband got such a shock that he dropped the line of questioning immediately.

Once the trend had been set, the woman was forced to maintain her line of defence by continuing to have these attacks, which were so subtly contrived by her own subconscious efforts that even the woman herself did not know how or why she was having the attacks.

When the hypnotist brought the woman face to face with the underlying motive behind her heart attacks, she was able to come to terms with the whole thing, and of course the attacks ceased.

It remains true that many people have been regressed under hypnosis into what they sincerely believe to be their previous lives. David Stevenson, Senior Lecturer in International Community Health at the Liverpool School of Tropical Medicine, who has worked in Africa as a mission doctor and for the Malawi Government, wrote the foreword to Monica O'Hara's book, New Hope Through Hypnotherapy, in which he states, 'Regression into the memories of previous personalities can also sometimes cure anxieties and disabilities in this life. Fear of water or of heights may be traced to a memory of drowning or falling. Realization that a nightmare or a phobia is due to something past and done with, rather than something likely to happen in the future, can dispel fear.

'Though modern science may tend to dismiss such phenomena as superstition, or ignore them as being inconvenient to the usual scientific picture of the Universe, careful recording of the phenomena and investigation of those memories which can be checked for historical or other accuracy is in fact scientific research. If a sufficient body of this is built up then science will have to accept it and fit it into the normal pattern of belief, much as once upon a time the Establishment had to accept that the world is round and not flat!

'Science and the Church may find that they have much in common, both in restricting acknowledgement of these phenomena and in the need to accept and adapt to their existence once acknowledgement can no longer be denied. Some scientists and churchmen do, of course, already accept that they do exist and that they should be more fully investigated and understood.

'Modification of the materialism of much of our present society and of the short-term views of our politicians might be a useful effect of better understanding. It may be we, ourselves, who shall have to live with the environmental desolation and radioactive waste which we may leave to our grandchildren if we are not careful. That might serve us right, but

169

realization of the possibility could help us to avoid it. In some African societies a newborn child may be referred to as "Grandfather" in the belief that he is indeed his grandfather reborn.

'If we have lived (and died) before, there is less need to fear, or desperately try to postpone, dying again. A greater willingness to talk about death seems helpful to those who have fatal illnesses and to their families and friends.

'It is an irony of our society in these islands that we are now too humanitarian to execute a known murderer but are content to terminate the lives of over 100,000 unborn children a year through abortion. What is the correct balance between the slogans to be seen on walls in Liverpool: "A Woman's Right to Choose" and "A Child's Right to Life"? One might argue that if reincarnation occurs, then abortion, to end an inconvenient pregnancy, merely postpones that individual's return to Earth. But those who support easy abortion tend to do so in the belief that the unborn child's mind is a blank slate on which nothing has yet been written. If it is a being with memories of earlier lives, or with an immortal soul, then that changes the situation.'

In a letter published in the British Medical Association News Review, headed Foetal Memories, Dr Stevenson writes, 'I have sat in on a great many sessions of hypnotic regression with the Liverpool hypnotherapist Joe Keeton in which he has taken people back, under hypnosis, to memories of times before they were born. Many of these people produce vivid and convincing memories of previous personalities . . .

'Some people are totally unwilling to accept these memories as anything other than fantasy. Others take them as evidence for reincarnation. I have tried to trace three doctors, mentioned in these memories, in the Medical Registers in the B.M.A. Library, but have found no trace of them - though I found without difficulty my father and his uncle who were medical practitioners at about the same date as given in the memories.

170

'It may be very difficult to decide whether an adult, under hypnosis, is producing genuine memories or a mixture of memories and fantasies based on forgotten experiences, reading and radio and television programmes, absorbed between childhood and adulthood. Clearer evidence of memory of previous personalities can be found in examining the cases of young children, too young to have done any reading, and often in communities where there is not yet television who produce, soon after they learn to talk, accounts of previous lives as identifiable individuals, usually living near, in both time and space, to their present homes.

'We should not refuse to examine such evidence just because, if memories of previous lives can be demonstrated, the implications for our present systems of belief and action may be considerable. If facts can be demonstrated then we have to adapt to them.'

While hypnotism serves its purpose, and may be one possible method of retrieving memory of previous lives, it is, by its very nature, fraught with doubts, ifs and buts. Also the majority of subjects regressed through hypnotism are adults with a lifetime's store of knowledge and experience to draw upon, thereby supplying sufficient raw material for the reconstruction of a supposed previous life.

Hypnotism has played no part in any of the case histories covered in this book. In each and every case, the child has given spontaneous information of their memories of their previous lives. Without exception, the initial statements of the children have come completely out of the blue without any related foregoing conversation whatever.

PART THREE

MEDICAL AND
RELIGIOUS VIEWS

Medical Views

The main aim of members of the medical profession is to enhance the quality of life on earth by caring for the physical body. One eminent London consultant remembers the advice given to him by his mentor in his student days: 'Just make sure the body is free from the danger of infection and then leave it alone to get on with the work of healing itself.'

There is no denying that a good night's sleep goes a long way towards curing many of our minor ailments. What happens during this period of sleep which causes us to wake up feeling refreshed and cured? What forces have been at work while our bodies have been asleep? Something must have happened to alleviate the aches and pains and discomfort which affected us on retiring the previous night.

One possible explanation could be that the revitalizing repair-work was done by the etheric body, which is the non-material counterpart of the physical body. During sleep, the consciousness blanks out, thus allowing the body to relax completely. Then the etheric body takes over and recharges the flow of vital energy into the cells affected, causing them to make a speedy recovery.

Many people would argue that the cells of the body do this repair-work by themselves. It is a proven fact that the body cells are continually dying and being discarded, and are replaced by new cells which have been forming meanwhile. The question is, what makes this happen? What form of energy activates the birth of a new cell?

Let us look upon the physical body as a type of computer which has been programmed to operate under certain conditions, i.e. when the previously established number of cells are working with perfect efficiency. When a cell withers away and dies due to various causes such as the effects of sun, wind, injury, etc., a new cell automatically replaces the dead cell, as dictated by the programme. This replacement process, however, must be carried out by the exercise of some type of energy, and some directing force must spark off the whole procedure.

If we can accept the idea that a human being is made up of more than just the material body, then many questions can be answered. The etheric, or non-physical, body could be the linking influence between various reincarnations.

Each time a soul becomes incarnate in the flesh, the physical body will be different because it is formed from different parents, but the etheric body, containing the soul, spirit and essence of the personality, remains the same, and it is within this etheric body that impressions affecting us, during re-incarnations on earth, are lodged. The etheric body then passes on these impressions to the physical consciousness, thus giving flashes of scenes and incidents from a previous existence.

This transparent etheric body which permeates the physical contains all the impressions of previous incarnations including a replica of all injuries and damage to previous physical bodies. Some babies are born with evidence of these previous injuries in the form of scars, birthmarks and deformities, as in the case of young Dominic who was born a healthy beautiful baby with a scar on the front of his right thigh. It looks exactly like a stab scar - a raised white line of flesh which remains white when the rest of his body gets tanned. Just before the child's third birthday he was standing up on chair to look at a picture on the wall, and his grandmother who was standing by the chair gently touched the scar, which had never been referred to before. Dominic astonished his grandmother and his mother by saying, 'Man on boat did that with big knife. Lots of blood everywhere, all covered in blood.' When his mother asked him what happened after that, he said, 'Fell in water and got drowned' The child then looked as if he was going to cry, but he went on to say that his name had been Olaf and that his sister had been called Zita. When his mother asked him if he knew Zita now, Dominic replied, 'Yes, she's you, Mummy.'

Dominic has always been terrified of water, and he used to cry so much when his mother was bathing him that she was forced to give it up as a bad job and just sponge him down instead. The scar is still to be seen on the boy's leg and it grows with him.

His mother confirms that Dominic has never ever been on a boat of any description, and that he certainly has never been confronted by a man brandishing a knife. His mother was surprised at the remarks about blood because he had never seen blood before and she didn't think he even knew what blood meant.

It is the non-physical body which continues to exist after death, independent of the physical body which is really only an outer shell which decays as soon as it is separated from the etheric, at death. The etheric body then goes on to exist on a different plane of vibration. These vibrations can be likened to energy waves, but as yet science has not succeeded in locating them. However this need hardly mean that they do not exist. Before radio waves were discovered people would never have believed such a thing was possible; nevertheless the waves were all around us just waiting on someone to declare their existence. The time will surely come when these vibrations will be known to all of us and perhaps then they will become accepted as part of our lives, or more accurately, as part of our after-lives. This would undoubtedly dispel the fear of death which to some people makes living intolerable.

Often inherited memory - or, as it is sometimes referred to, genetic memory - is put forward as an explanation for cases claiming reincarnation.

As an example of how this would work, let us look at the Mandy case history. Mandy's mother was present at the funeral of the first baby who died at the age of five months. The distressed mother almost fell into the grave. This traumatic experience would be strongly imprinted in her mind. When she gave birth to Mandy Number Two her genes were passed on to the new baby influencing the child's physical attributes and tendencies. Could it be possible that the mother's memories and experiences were also passed on to the child via the genes, thus implanting the impressions received by the mother at the graveside incident?

Genetic memory can no doubt play some part in explaining odd behaviour in children, but because it cannot possibly account for all the aspects of the Mandy case, it would be unwise to rely on this as the explanation. It is true that although the silver bracelet was buried with the baby, her mother saw this bracelet and knew that it had been buried in the coffin. That impression could have been transferred from the mother to Mandy Number Two, but what about the yellow fluffy ball? Mandy Number Two remembers this being buried with her, a fact of which her mother was totally unaware. How could a memory be passed on to a child by a parent who never experienced it in the first place?

Another important factor regarding the Mandy case is that any possible genetic influence could only have come from one of her parents, her mother, because the father of the first Mandy was not the father of the second Mandy. Also there re the remarks about Stephen to take into consideration. Here, there is no blood link whatever between the first Mandy and Stephen, but there is a 50% connection between the second Mandy and Stephen, both having the same father. Could the second Mandy's remarks about Stephen come about by either genetic influence, or by some form of telepathy from father to daughter? This may be a possibility, but the words 'He can walk now' would make one question this suggestion. George Seabrook remembered his son as a cripple in a wheelchair who had never been able to walk. The only other explanation could be that deep down in Mr Seabrook's subconscious he was telling himself that his son could walk now, and these thoughts had been telepathically picked up by Mandy.

Dr Peter Fenwick, Neurophysiologist at St Thomas's Hospital, London and Senior Lecturer at the Institute of Psychiatry, feels that in Mandy's case it would be unlikely that inherited memory is the explanation. In his view, it is much more logical to suggest that she heard these or similar statements from the mother and was repeating them. It is, however, a logical possibility that reincarnation is the answer. Dr Fenwick feels that genetic memory is probably ruled out when we remember Mandy's words, 'Why did you cry when I died? Didn't you know I would come back?' Dr Fenwick says, 'This is a very telling statement because it is unlikely to have come from the mother.'

It is significant that most of the cases which come to light are toddlers between the ages of two and three. Could it be that most people are born with certain memories of previous existence imprinted in their minds, and as soon as they can make themselves understood they start to describe people, places, incidents and experiences of their past lives. The majority of parents just fob their children off, thinking that the stories are childish gibberish inspired by vivid imagination, and the stories die a natural death. Possibly by the time speech becomes coherent all memories of life before birth have already faded. In almost every case, by the time the children reach school age all talk of previous life ceases. It could be that because of the increasing demands made upon the child, these pre-birth memories are pushed to the back of the mind and into the subconscious. This would explain the ever-increasing number of cases in which the subconscious reveals a wealth of facts appertaining to previous existence through hypnotic regression. The facts could hardly be revealed if they were not there in the first place.

Dr Fenwick mentioned scientific work which shows that the brain rhythms of babies in the last month before birth show changes which have been interpreted as periods during which they may be dreaming.

This strongly suggests that the unborn child experiences dreams. We may well ask what the baby could be dreaming about, since it has not as yet had any of the experiences of life upon which earthly dreams are founded. Could the unborn baby possibly be dreaming about a previous life in another realm?

Recent evidence shows that the foetus can hear, feel and see in the womb, and this ties in with the many accounts of young children remembering their impressions during their foetal days. Some were aware of extreme darkness, others of golden light; most got the feeling of being wet; and almost all of the reports confirm that being an unborn baby is indeed a noisy business. All kinds of descriptions of noise have been put forward by small children trying to describe what they heard before they were born: splashing, chug-chug, loud talking, and just plain noisy.

The sound factor is one of the most important in connection with the baby's emotional development. Ordinary everyday sounds can filter through to the womb whether it's the shrill ringing of an alarm clock, the sound of a jet plane screaming overhead, or the sounds of conversation. It is interesting to note that in Japan, pregnant women are banned from working in noisy factories because of the risk that the foetus could be adversely affected, and might, in later life, suffer from psychosomatic problems.

The differences reported in connection with what the children remember seeing whilst in the womb could be accounted for by the fact that the foetus does sleep, so during sleep (excluding R.E.M. sleep) they could have experienced the blackness, and during waking moments they could have been aware of light, either golden or just of comparative brightness.

Dr Arthur Guirdham, a psychiatrist from Bath, well known for his work with children suffering from nightmares, is convinced that in many cases, the bad dreams are due to traumatic experiences in previous lives. This explanation can very often account for phobias and odd behaviour in children where the parents cannot trace any significant incident that could possibly be responsible. In many cases, neurotic behaviour was traced back to a previous violent death, such as,a stabbing, drowning, railway accident, etc. These children show a morbid fear of knives, water, trains and so on.

Dr Guirdham also feels that difficult labours can lead to obsessional conditions in adult life - phobias, anxiety, etc. - and he states 'The foetus/child becomes aware of duration too early due to the uterine inertia associated with difficult births.'

The mother's emotional state during pregnancy has far reaching effects on the baby, especially during the first three months. That is the crucial time when all the organs are formed and when the child is most at risk from drugs, alcohol and especially nicotine, which is detrimental to the child's normal progress within the womb.

An unborn child can interpret maternal depression and stress, and reacts to this. When a person becomes depressed, every singlwe cell in the body is part of that depression, and therefore the negative feelings are communicated to the baby who in turn suffers along with the mother.

If the pregnant mother allows herself to fall into a pessimistic frame of mind there is a very real danger that her attitude could start off a chain of events which could lead to actual physical illness. It is a known fact that too much dwelling on sad or morbid thoughts can lead to gall-bladder trouble and liver ailments, which do nothing to the physical or emotional condition of the mother-to-be.

We are what we think, and if we insist on taking a depressive, negative attitude, for whatever reasons, imagined or otherwise, and swamping ourselves in thoughts of misery, we could start off an irreversible process effecting the organs and glands of the body thus preventing normal activity, the outcome of which could range from loss of appetite, lethargy, inability to concentrate or think clearly, immobility, leading to a variety of conditions including severe malnutrition, insanity, coma and even death.

We can see where constant depressive thoughts can lead us, but the opposite is also true. If we think happy thoughts these in turn effect our outlook on life and we begin to see that things are not all bad. Even the darkest tunnel has light at the end of it, although sometimes it cannot be perceived at first glance. Everyone on earth has troubles. How we handle them is dependent upon one thing: attitude of mind.

Therefore, when the foetus is subjected to pleasant and calming influences the baby will respond positively. This fact is substantiated by evidence accumulated by Dr Michele Clements of the City of London Maternity Hospital, who with the help of Yehudi Menuhin, the world-famous violinist, some time ago tested a number of ante-natal patients to see if their unborn babies would respond to music. The babies showed interesting reactions which pointed to the fact that the majority of them favoured the Flute and violin above the other instruments used in the experiment.

Nowadays most mothers-to-be are familiar with ultra-sound scan equipment used to monitor the movements of the foetus on a television screen making it possible to chart the development of the baby. By measuring the head, the expected date of delivery can be verified. If there are any abnormalities discovered, more detailed tests can be carried out whereby some of the fluid surrounding the foetus is drawn off, then analysed by examining the chromosomes to locate conditions such as Downs Syndrome (Mongolism).

This brings us on to the difficult question of abortion, and all the related medical and moral principles. The main moral consideration when dealing with the subject of abortion surely must be to establish the moment when the soul, spirit, life-force, call it what you will, becomes united with the physical foetus. If, as our evidence in the case histories suggests, this life-force and the consciousness which contains the personality, is present not only in the womb, but also before conception, then there is every possibility that it could also be present throughout the entire nine months of pregnancy. Remember, a lifeless foetus can hardly have dreams, yet dream-pattern E.E.G. readings have been recorded in unborn babies.

If this possibility exists, however slight, then perhaps we would do well to review the current law and attitudes regarding abortion.

The laws of life operate in mysterious ways, and we can't hope to understand all of them. Since the regular use of ultrasound equipment in ante-natal clinics, a most inexplicable phenomenon has puzzled doctors and patients alike. It is the case of the dreaded vanishing foetus whereby a mother diagnosed by her scan results as expecting twins, goes back for a further scan only to find to her horror that one of her babies has disappeared without trace.

Dr H. P. Robinson, obstetrician and gynaecologist at the Queen Mother's Hospital, Department of Midwifery, Glasgow University, has been carrying out extensive tests to try to solve the mystery.

One possible explanation is that the tissue of the baby is completely absorbed into the body of the mother. After all, the tissue of a foetus is not that foreign to the mother, so there would not necessarily be any systemic problems such as poisoning, and the other foetus apparently is not physically affected. Whether or not the remaining twin suffers emotionally in later life due to the sudden disappearance of its womb companion is another matter, and in fact one case history shows that a surviving twin grieved throughout childhood for the twin who didn't make it through to birth.

The most distressing cases of vanishing foetus occur when ultra-sound tests have not been carried out through out the pregnancy. A mother could be happy in the knowledge that she has been indisputably diagnosed as bearing twins. As it draws near to her confinement she excitedly makes her preparations for the birth of her two babies, providing two of everything, and she prepares herself psychologically for the great event.

When delivery day arrives, and only one baby is born with no sign of the other twin, the mother is totally devastated. She cannot understand what has happened because if her second twin was not born dead, where could it be? At this stage, when all the post-natal problems are setting in, the mother could start to harbour all kinds of delusions about her missing baby. Who took it? Why? In such circumstances the mother usually takes a long time to adjust herself emotionally.

As in cases of natural abortion, the vanishing foetus is another example of nature's great plan. For some reason the second twin is not meant to be born. We can assume that the souls of these children return whence they came to await the correct moment for them to be born again on earth

When a fluke of nature occurs, such as the vanishing foetus, still birth, etc., perhaps it may be explained by taking into consideration the ever-changing circumstances of the world and everyone in it. Say, for example, that a certain child is due to be born to certain parents, and during the pregnancy, either consciously or subconsciously, the mother has a change of attitude towards the baby which leads to the mother secretly wishing that she did not have to bear the child, then it may be a logical conclusion drawn by Divine Providence that the child would not benefit from being born to that particular mother.

Religious Views

The Protestant church, including Anglican, Presbyterian, Methodist, Baptist, United Reform, Church of Scotland, Pentecostal, Lutheran, Welsh Congregational, Adventist and others, does not generally accept reincarnation. From Lambeth Palace, headquarters of the Church of England, a spokesman for the Archbishop of Canterbury states, 'This is not a subject on which there are any official Christian views. As you are probably aware, a very long time ago the Church threw out any idea of reincarnation. No evidence has since been forthcoming to suggest any reconsideration. If there was forthcoming evidence I have no doubt that it would be considered, but at the moment what evidence there is must be left in the category at least of "not proven". '

The Roman Catholic Church does not accept reincarnation because this is not seen as part of God's revelation. Life on earth is looked upon as a period of decision and choice whereby we choose to follow a life of good or evil. We die once and according to the state of our immortal soul at the time of death, and taking into consideration the choices and decisions taken throughout the lifetime, it goes on to Heaven, Purgatory or Hell. Heaven is to enter the sight of God; Purgatory is a place of purification for souls who die in union with God but still require further preparation before reaching a state worthy of entering Heaven; Hell is the resting place for souls who, during their lives on earth, have cut themselves off from God. It was stated that although it is accepted that Hell exists it is not known if anyone is there or not.

The Church of Christ, Scientist, states that reincarnation has no part in its teaching, although it does believe that in death the spirit continues to exist in a state which is determined by the type of life which was led on earth.

Some Christian Spiritualists accept reincarnation and some do not, although the majority believe that it can and does occur. Their main objective is to prove to the world that life continues after physical death and they hold demonstrations of clairvoyance in most spiritualist churches whereby a medium gives messages from departed people to their relatives, relating personal data which could not be known by the medium, thereby providing evidence that the dead person really still exists and can communicate. They believe that all of us have spirit guides who help us in our everyday lives and who act as go-betweens in contacting deceased relatives and friends.

Mormons do not accept reincarnation but they do believe in life before birth in the form of a pre-mortal spirit existence. They state, 'These spirit beings, the offspring of exalted parents, men and women, appearing in all respects as mortal persons do, excepting only that their spirit bodies are made of a more pure and refined substance than the elements from which mortal bodies are made.'

It is a Mormon belief that since one of the purposes of earthly life is that we should live by faith, the memory of this pre-earth life with the Heavenly Father is generally blotted out. Life is eternal, the spirit of man never dies and the universal re-uniting of spirit and body is promised to all. At physical death, to each of us will come the rewards and punishments earned on earth with eternal progression and happiness the ultimate hope of all.

The Greek Orthodox Church does not accept reincarnation and is of the belief that when a person dies they go to either Heaven or Hell. This is a once only and final destiny. It states that if a soul is damned to Hell then there is no escape from that doom. It terms Hell as a state in which the soul is forced to be turned away from God. Heaven on the other hand is a state whereby the soul is united with God whom in Greek Orthodoxy is called Theos. Whatever has been achieved on earth dictates the route which the soul will take at physical death. Once a person dies that person cannot do anything to help himself but the prayers of people still alive on earth can help the soul of the dead person to progress.

Jehovah's Witnesses do not accept reincarnation but they believe that after death everyone will rise at the final resurrection to be judged, according to the type of life each person has led on earth. This rising up of the dead reunites the departed spirit with the revitalized physical body. Therefore every person will come back as the person they were originally and not as the same spirit clothed in a different physical body, which is of course the accepted idea of reincarnation.

The New Church was founded on the teachings of Emanuel Swedenborg who was born in Sweden in 1688, and died in 1772. It does not support reincarnation, mainly because of the belief that it is not necessary to live more than one life on earth in order to prepare for eternal life. Life is believed to continue after death in what is termed the world of spirits, in which the soul continues its life prior to its final destiny in either Heaven or Hell. The purpose of life in the material world is that the ruling love of a man may be established. Once this is formed for good or evil, then the state of life after death is a state of preparation.

Swedenborg believed that there are with all men, spirits from the unseen world in close association. The spirits who are with us have themselves lived on earth when they were in the body. An explanation of reincarnation is given as the result of these companion spirits communicating from their own memories with the minds of the people they are watching over on earth. In this way, a man will have a recollection of something he has never seen or heard, and he will attribute this to his own personal memory of previous existence.

Buddhists do not accept reincarnation as such, but they do believe in re-birth on earth which to them is something different, involving a process of mind and body interacting throughout the cosmos. In Buddhism there is no God, no soul, no spirit, only living beings concerned with the enlightenment of mind and body, achieved by following the middle way - the path of perfect balance.

Buddhists believe that the body fuels the mind in as much

as it provides the energy upon which the force of the mind feeds, and although the mind is dependent upon the physical body for its vital energy, the charged mind then takes over the role of controller of the material body. However they also believe that the mind can exist without a body.

Buddha did not accept that death brought eternal happiness to some and eternal misery for others. He taught that life and death follow on from one another so that any particular lifetime on earth will be subjected to conditions laid down by ourselves in past lives based on the degree of moral development we attained in that past life, i.e. if a person speaks or acts with an evil mind, unhappiness will follow him, and if a person speaks or acts with a pure mind, happiness will follow him. The body ages, dies and deteriorates but the mind survives death. All things that come into being are the effect of causes and conditions, which themselves act as causes and conditions in turn again, to give rise to other effects, and so it goes on.

The Islamic belief does not include the acceptance of reincarnation. There is only one life on earth and at death the soul is separated from the body and goes on to Heaven or Hell.

Hell is looked upon as a kind of hospital where the soul is treated in order to make it worthy to enter the realms of Heaven. This recuperation period in Hell is fortunately always an intermediary stage and is never under any circumstances an eternal fate or punishment, because God, known as Allah, is all merciful.

In Heaven, and in Hell, the soul is given ample opportunity for learning and advancement and according to how these are embraced and dealt with, the soul gradually progresses in an upward direction towards God, or Allah. If the soul rejects the opportunity for advancement then it stays static in its Hellish plane of existence until such time as there is a change of attitude. Every action and decision is motivated by the free will of the soul.

The Hindu religion, in marked contrast to all the rest, is

entirely based upon the concept of reincarnation, according to Karma - the record of good and evil accumulated during life on earth. Every person comes back to the earth many many times in order to balance their Karma, i.e. work off any outstanding debts owed by the soul. The circumstances into which a person may be born are determined by the condition of that person's Karma before birth. If the person, in a previous life on earth, had been, say, extremely short-tempered and impatient, the balance of that soul could be restored by means of a rebirth on earth into circumstances whereby that soul will learn to be more patient. This could be achieved in various ways - perhaps that person will be destined to choose a wife who is a patient loving person, and from her example the person will learn patience himself.

However, things may not always work out in such an amicable way. It could be that for the guaranteed advancement of the soul, and to ensure that the person really does learn patience, he might be taught the hard way. For example he may be born into a family in which some member is severely handicapped; thus the person will be compelled to exercise patience. Another possibility would be that the person could father a child who turns out to possess the same impatient traits that the person himself displayed in his previous life. By having to deal with such a child, it would become apparent to the father that patience is indeed a virtue.

So in this way, by operating the law of Karma, all misdeeds are atoned for, all unfinished works are completed, all evil thoughts and actions are wiped out by a corresponding good thought and action. The Karma of a person stays with them throughout the continual cycle of births and deaths and is a permanent part of the consciousness or soul. It usually takes many incarnations in the flesh to work off all of our Karmic debts, but when this is completed, and the perfect balance of the soul is attained then there is no need for further reincarnations and the soul has reached the ultimate state of perfection and immortality known as Nirvana.

When a man and woman conceive a child, the type of child which will be born to them will depend upon various factors, that is the Karma of the mother, the father and the child. If, resulting from the Karma built up from their previous lives, the mother and the father are destined to have a saintly child born to them, then when a saintly child is ready to be born, that child will be sent to those particular parents. It can sometimes happen that, again according to an individual's Karmic content, he is re-born as a lion; and a cow could be born as a person. According to the Hindu philosophy the law of Karma applies to every facet of existence, human or not.

Scientologists do accept reincarnation, and believe that what we sow in one life, we reap in another. There is an emphasis on continually trying to improve the spiritual side of life which they believe lives on as an independent force when the physical body dies.

They believe that over the years there has been a steady decline of moral values which has resulted in the formation of certain attitudes, i.e. a leaning towards the materialistic side of life as opposed to the more spiritual outlook. They are concerned with the great increase in neurotic and psychic diseases and they try to offer practical help in this direction by counselling and, when necessary, regression.

Jews believe that when they die their souls go to God via Purgatory where they stay for a time of reflection and possible retribution. Jewish opinions are divided on the question of reincarnation, although their mystic tradition affirmed the doctrine of the transmigration of souls and this was accepted by the Rabbis.

According to Jewish beliefs there is a complete scheme of reward and punishment which can be observed in operation. Louis Jacobs gives an example of this in his book, A Jewish Theology. He states it is the view of the Jewish Kabbalists, 'If good men suffer in a national catastrophe this is because once the decree has gone forth it must embrace all without exception, unless it be that of the man so righteous that he deserves to be saved. But one who is partly to blame, i.e. because he failed to rebuke the others for their misdeeds will perish with them. It is also true that an especially great saint may have the power to save even the wicked. A wicked man may be blessed with prosperity in order that he might serve as an instrument for the fulfilment of God's purpose. He may, for example have a righteous son who will inherit his wealth and use it for good purposes. When a woman miscarries this is because of her own sins and also because the embryo deserves the punishment because of the sins he had committed in a previous existence. This explains too, why innocent children suffer. They are not, in fact, innocent but are guilty of sins committed in a previous incarnation.'

In the same publication Louis Jacobs states, 'What can a modern Jew believe on this whole question of the Hereafter? It depends on which type of modern Jew we mean. Some modern Jews clearly have no use for any doctrine of a Hereafter and, oddly enough, this includes some religious Jews. But it is surely a very curious religious outlook which limits man's opportunities for encountering God to the brief span of this life . . . Can it be believed that God has created only to destroy, that all man's hopes and dreams of a higher life are doomed to frustration? Nor is it much use speaking of individuals living on in their children or in the lives they have influenced, or in their deeds and works. To say that Shakespeare is immortal in the sense that his plays will always be read is not really to speak about the man Shakespeare at all but about his ideas. The quality of this life is quite different if it is seen as a school for eternity as well as being good in itself. Surely the idea that man's deeds have eternal significance is not to be treated lightly as a kind of optional belief or pious opinion. Belief in the Hereafter is deeply rooted in Judaism and to reject it is to impoverish and despiritualize Judaism itself.

'The general tendency among modern Jews who do

believe in an afterlife is to place the stress on the immortality of the soul rather than on the resurrection of the dead.'

As can be seen from the above, very brief, outlines of the various religions, a general theme of birth, death and afterlife runs through all of them. Perhaps an appropriate way to end this chapter on religious attitudes towards reincarnation would be to draw attention to the fact that in the Bible it was suggested that John the Baptist had come in the spirit of Elijah, in other words, that John the Baptist was the reincarnation of Elijah.

It would appear that at the time of the ministry of Jesus on earth, the idea of reincarnation must have been an acceptable one, even amongst His disciples, because when Jesus asked them who they thought He was they gave various answers, all indicating that the idea of a soul of a dead person coming back to earth in a different physical body was not foreign or strange to them. From the fact that the disciples answered Him as they did, it is clear that a belief in reincarnation must have been an everyday part of their lives.

MYSTIC FORCES
– EXTRACTS –
by Peter and Mary Harrison

FOREWORD

Over the past five years or so, since the publication of our book Life Before Birth, we have received a steady flow of correspondence from people all over the country, reporting their stories of the unexplained, unusual or prophetic dreams, apparitions, hauntings, miracles, faith healing, fateful encounters and other inexplicable experiences. Some of the stories are sad, some funny, some, on further probing, can possibly be explained by rational means, some are probably due to wishful thinking.

In this book we are looking at true stories of out-of-the-body experiences (OOBEs). These have been selected from over three thousand case histories of ordinary people in everyday situations finding themselves released from their physical bodies. They float in a state of suspension from where they can look down upon their physical bodies, all the thinking/feeling personality being contained in the released entity, soul, spirit, call it what you will.

In some cases, the people have been in traumatic situations, such as on a hospital operating table or in a car crash, but the vast majority of people report that they had the experience in normal circumstances, without any warning whatsoever. Many of them were so disorientated that they could hardly believe what was happening to them. All of them are adamant that they were most definitely NOT having a dream. Most of them state that they had never heard of out-of-the-body experiences before it happened to them, and it was only afterwards that they started to ask questions in order to find out more.

It appears that the phenomenon is fairly widespread and is not confined to any particular type of person. We have cases from a complete cross section of the public, every creed, colour and social background, and from all age groups. The only common denominator seems to be the hesitancy to speak about the subject, for fear of being ridiculed. Many people are terrified by the experiences, and just as many find profound joy and peace. All of them state that they are not afraid of death because they know that the spirit exists independently of the physical body.

All of the people in this book have experienced spontaneous release, not drug-induced, with the exception of the controlled hospital operation cases. We reject all cases where controlled methods of achieving out-of-the-body experience have been instigated. We are aware that some people practise a formula for achieving OOBEs. We are strongly against such procedures. We believe that if, and when, a person is meant to experience the spirit leaving the body it will happen to them when the time is right.

Peter and Mary Harrison
Easter, 1989

MYSTIC FORCES
– EXTRACTS –

What is an OOBE?	199
Light	207
Vantage Viewpoint	216
Paradise?	227
Strange Forces at Work	232
Animals	246
Music	257
Borderland	262
Timeslips	269
Decision	285
The Silver Cord	292
Coincidence	301
Fate	309
Escape	326
Children	332
Fear of Death Conquered	341
Premonitions	355
Danges of the Occult	359
Psychic Aromas	368
Angels	375
Positive Conculsions	387

WHAT IS AN OOBE?

Oh would some power the giftie gie us
To see ourselves as others see us

ROBERT BURNS

It appears that the gift has been given to us to do just that, 'To see ourselves as others see us'. Thousands of people from all walks of life have been silently experiencing the revelation into life and death which comes from an out-of-the-body experience, in short an OOBE, whereby the 'spirit' leaves the physical body and can view the material person from a different angle. This is not a dream, not a vision, but a stark reality, which has both terrified and exalted the people who have shared the experience. It is not connected with drugs, alcohol or mental instability. It affects people profoundly, as in the case of Mrs. Dickinson of Liverpool, who states:

'I was asleep in bed when suddenly I found myself standing at the top of the stairs. Because my daughter was afraid of the dark, a light on the landing was left on all night. I could see my bare feet as I descended the stairs. When I entered the kitchen I was aware of faint moonlight streaming through the window. I reached out for the light switch which was immediately to my left as I entered the room. I could see my hand touching the switch but the light did not come on. I then realized that I could not feel the switch and my hand somehow or other seemed to melt into the wall behind. I was stunned with the realization that the door behind me was still closed and that I had walked right through it without opening it. This frightened me greatly. I knew I was out of my body. At once I felt myself lifted up to the ceiling and then I seemed to be hurtling through space at great speed in a sort of spiral. I then awoke back in my body.

I tried to convince myself that it was just a dream but I knew that the experience was real and quite different from any dream, and no amount of rationalizing could alter this knowledge. After that night, my whole attitude to life changed. I became aware that this life is just a part of a much wider existence. I also feel sure that it happened in order to prepare me for the events which have occurred since then. I know that with my previous attitude to life and death I would have been unable to cope with the death of my dear husband three years later.'

Our research over the past few years has resulted in an accumulation of overwhelming evidence to support the view that the physical body is but a mere shell, a material organism, the only purpose of which is simply to accommodate the real essence of the person, the spirit, and this same spirit, totally intact with the individual's consciousness and personality, has the power to release itself from the trappings of the material shell and thus allow the person to look down upon his or her physical body from a completely detached and objective viewpoint.

Many people have reported that they have been aware of other entities during out-of-the-body experiences. Sometimes it is just the feeling of a 'presence' and other times the strange unearthly companions are seen clearly or heard, as in the case of Mrs. Alcock of Spalding, Lincs., who remembers:

'I recall leaving my body asleep on the bed and floating

through the bedroom door and downstairs. I stood in the doorway and tried to switch on the light but found that I couldn't. My fingers seemed to come down through the switch. As I turned around I knew that there were two other 'presences' with me and although I did not know who they were, I distinctly heard one say to the other, 'We must get her back.' I felt myself being propelled by two pairs of hands, four lots of fingers, that seemed to support my back as I returned, floating up the stairs. The next thing I knew I was lying in bed back in my body.'

In many instances people recognize and hear the voices of relatives and friends who have died. A significant pattern emerges whereby the deceased relative advises the person to go back. Many people have reported a similar trend where the hands of the dead first beckon, showing that they are happy to rekindle the acquaintance, but then at a certain point in the proceedings they advise that the time is not right, and hold their hands up to stop the wanderer venturing further.

In almost all cases there is a reluctance to return to the physical world and leave the peace which is felt in this twilight dimension. What causes the return is often a sense of uncompleted work, or in the case of parents, they become aware that they are still needed to look after their children, and this compelling urge seems to be the trigger which instantly reverses the course of activitiy, resulting in re-entry to the physical body.

There seems to be some significance in hands being seen. An overwhelming number of people have reported that during their out-of-the-body experiences they have been guided by hands, sometimes belonging to loved ones who have passed on, or often to strangers. In many instances the hands are not connected to any being but are shown clearly and always seem to be visible for a definite purpose which the person understands fully, as in the case of Ted from Luton (*See 'Animals' Chapter 7*). To give examples of this we outline the following cases where hands have been seen to perform actions and to convey definite messages:

One woman who was very ill in hospital remembers first of all lying in bed in great pain after a major operation. She then floated out of her physical body and hovered above her bed, but the main thing that struck her was the fact that she was no longer in pain. She felt relieved, relaxed and quite bemused. Suddenly she felt herself floating towards the end of the hospital ward and then into what seemed to be a long, narrow, dark tunnel. At the end of the tunnel there was a dazzling light which attracted her. She felt she was travelling at great speed and she felt exhilarated and full of joy as she drew nearer and nearer to the light, which got brighter as she approached. She then became aware of hands looming out of the darkness at each side of the tunnel.

Although the hands were not connected to any bodies there were rows and rows of them, and despite the peculiar circumstances she was not in the least afraid. She had a distinct feeling that she recognized the hands, even though she could not actually see their owners. She thought she saw the hands of her long departed grandmother, whom she remembered from her childhood days and she was convinced that she saw her father's hands. He had been dead for several years. There were several pairs of hands which she did not recognize, but from which she could sense a feeling of great love. The hands and fingers seemed to beckon her forward.

Then she was overpowered with emotion when she saw a

pair of tiny baby hands, which seemed to come out of the darkness, appealing for her to approach. She knew in that instant that they were the hands of her dead baby. She longed to dash forward to take hold of the little fingers when she was aware of seeing her father's hands in front of her, but this time they were held with the palms towards her in a gesture which forbade her to go forward. She remembers the dilemma which she felt being halted from rushing towards her baby, but then she became aware of her other three children who were at home awaiting her return from hospital.

Again, her father's hands moved as if trying to push her back along the tunnel. In her mind she was filled with compassion for the three small children who still depended upon her so much. It appears that the moment she experienced this emotion, she had the willpower to reverse the movement, even though she felt great sadness at having to leave the dead baby, of whose presence she was acutely aware. At once she began to move backwards along the tunnel, the light at the far end becoming smaller and smaller until it resembled a pin prick. The next moment she opened her eyes, and she was back in her hospital bed, with pain surging through her.

The vivid memory of floating and moving through the tunnel, the light, the hands, the dead baby, remains fresh and real in her mind today. She knows it happened to her and it was not just a dream. She is convinced that the experience was meant to happen to her to stop her grieving for the dead baby and to apply herself to her earthly life. The main two points that are uppermost in her mind are firstly that she is no longer afraid to die, and secondly, although she always thinks about the dead child, she has a comforting feeling that the baby is being looked after by loving caring friends.

Mr Palmer's Story

Mr. Palmer of Farnborough went to bed as usual one night when he became aware of a buzzing sound that seemed to vibrate through his head. This sound was accompanied by a sinking feeling. He remembers trying to sit up in bed, but became alarmed when he found that he could not move a muscle. He thought that he had become paralysed. Again, he tried to move his arm, but no matter how much he willed himself, he could not move. However, he was able to open his eyes. The bedroom appeared perfectly normal and he could hear the night sounds from the street outside. Suddenly he had a rising feeling, as if he had floated upwards, to about thirty feet. Again he tried to move his limbs but this seemed to make him spin round and round, so he stopped trying to move and remained floating.

At this time he was living in a bed-sit in a large old Victorian house. It entered his head that if he wanted to, he would be able to float anywhere in the house, so it occurred to him that he could travel to the floor above where a certain girl had a room in the house. He remembered working it all out in his mind, and he was aware of having read somewhere that the only thing necessary to be able to travel off to any particular place was to think about that place and it would happen. He thought about the girl's bedroom, and in that split second he found himself standing in the middle of her room. He wanted to turn round towards her bed to look at the sleeping girl but, as he turned, two large hands, not attached to anything, appeared in front of his eyes, preventing him from seeing the girl. He remembers getting the clear message in his head: *'This experience is not meant for spying on people'*. The next thing he knew he was floating back down towards his body.

Mrs. Brown's Story

Mrs. Brown relates the story of how she awoke one night to find her room filled with what she could only describe as swirling mist. She thought this most odd and at once looked across to the window to see if it had been left open. She saw that it was closed, but the curtains were still giving the impression of a breeze coming into the room. She then heard the most wonderful music unlike anything she had ever heard before. She thought at once that one of her sons must have left the radio on in the downstairs room. She raised herself up in the bed to get up and go downstairs to switch off the music when suddenly there before her, hovering in mid-air, she saw the most beautiful pair of hands.

'I was not frightened at all, even though it was a strange thing to see. The hands were absolutely perfect, like those of a ballerina. One of the hands reached forward as if to take my hand to help me up out of bed. Just as I was about to grasp the hand I turned my head back for some reason, and then I became petrified when I saw my sleeping body lying behind me on the bed. At that moment I looked back round. The hands had vanished and I felt myself sliding back down into my physical body. The following morning I awoke and the first thing I did was to go over to check the windows to make sure that they had been properly closed the night before. They were locked. I will never forget the experience. It was short and simple but it has changed my whole outlook on life, because I know I was not dreaming and I really did see the hands and I heard that music.'

THE LIGHT

Mrs Ellis' Story

At 3.00 a.m. David Ellis answered the telephone. 'It's your wife,' said the nurse. 'She's had a relapse. She's failing fast. The doctor wonders if you would like to come into the hospital straight away.'

Mr. Ellis answered in a panic, 'But what about the children?'

'Can't you get a neighbour to keep an eye on them?'

'Yes. Yes. I'll see what I can do. How is she? Is she critical?'

'I think you'd better come in.'

Mr. Ellis telephoned his sister who lived nearby and told her that he'd leave the key outside the back door, under the mat. He got to the hospital, shaking with fright, and rushed to his wife's bedside.

'She's lost a lot of blood,' explained the nurse.

'She'll be OK though. I mean she won't...'

'We're doing everything we can. Would you like a cup of tea?'

'Can I talk to the doctor?'

The nurse nodded sympathetically and left the room.

As he took hold of his wife's hand she opened her eyes and looked up at him. He was sure that she recognized him, although she didn't say anything. It hurt him to see her eyes so full of pain. Slowly they closed and she became still. The room was silent. He glanced over at the heart monitor in horror.

'No! No! Marjorie, come back!' The monitor displayed a long, continuous, straight line.

As Mr. Ellis sobbed over his dead wife, little did he know that he was being watched. As Marjorie had closed her eyes, she had experienced the bewildering feeling of slipping out of her physical body, with all her senses intact.

'One minute I was tortured in pain,' she recalls, 'The next I seemed to be floating upwards until I reached the ceiling, where I remained, hovering. The main thing I kept thinking was, 'I've got no pain now – what a great relief.' After a few seconds I seemed to get used to this floating sensation, then I began to become aware of what had happened. Down below me I could see my body lying on the bed, and I remember feeling horribly confused because I could see my husband crying over me. 'What's wrong with him?' I thought. 'Can't he see me? Doesn't he know I'm all right now?'

Then Marjorie's attention was drawn to the heart monitoring machine by the bedside. She watched the long steady green line. 'It was only when I noticed the line on the machine that I realised what was going on. Just beforehand the machine had been showing a zig-zag pattern. Then it dawned on me that I must be dead, although I could hardly believe it, I felt so well and peaceful.'

Just then the nurse returned with the cup of tea. 'I saw the alarmed look on her face as she rang the emergency bell. Within seconds the room was filled with people all rushing around. First they gave me mouth-to-mouth resuscitation, then a nurse injected a large needle into my chest. I could see clearly what the nurse was doing, and I was bewildered at the fact that I could not feel the pain of the needle. Then they gave me a heart massage, then electric shock treatment. I was amazed as I watched my physical body writhe on the bed then fall back into its state of stillness. Gradually the medical staff left the room. I watched the doctor put his hand on my husband's shoulder and then shake his head.

'I'm all right though', I kept calling to my husband. 'See! I'm up here, I'm fine.' I remember becoming quite upset when he just ignored me. Again I called out desperately trying to make him hear me. He simply bent over, kissed my still white face and walked out of the room.

'I kept wondering why he hadn't answered me. I was shouting as loud as I could.

'Then a nurse and hospital porter entered the room. They lifted my body onto a trolley and placed a sheet over me. I followed the porter as he wheeled the trolley down a long corridor. I floated behind the porter into the hospital mortuary. A wave of shock hit me as I realised what was happening. As I watched my body on the trolley the scene suddenly misted over. The mortuary faded and I felt myself floating along a marble-like passage. At the end of the passage was an extremely bright light – brighter than anything I had ever seen before. I felt myself strongly attracted towards the light and was, at the same time, engulfed in a feeling of warmth and comfort. Then, as if from the midst of this light, there appeared lots of hands stretching out towards me.

'I felt so happy and carefree and I had an overwhelming feeling of being loved. The strange thing was that although there were no bodies or faces connected with the hands, I seemed to know instinctively who they all belonged to. There was my nan, my dad and several other relations and friends, all of whom had been long dead. It was then I noticed them – a pair of tiny perfect hands were beckoning to me. I knew deep in my heart that they were the little hands of my dead baby. I longed to rush over and grasp them. They seemed to be saying, "I love you, I love you" over and over again. I've never felt so loved before or since. I reached out to them as they came nearer and nearer to me.

'I then heard the firm voice of my father telling me, "You can't come yet, you've a lot to do. Your children need you, especially Julie." (Julie is my youngest child.)

'Despite my father's words, I still wanted so much to go forward to the dead baby, even though I was fully aware at the time that I loved all my other children and my husband as well. I struggled with myself for ages, and it seemed to me that I had no strength to turn back. It was then that I heard my nan's voice ringing out in support of my father. She too was trying to persuade me to go back. In an instant I felt a wave of pity for my other children who were depending on me, and my heart went out to my husband, as I remembered his grief-stricken face. In that split-second, like a thunderbolt, I was hurled back into my physical body.

'The first thing that occurred to me was that something was irritating my face – something seemed to be covering it. As I raised my hand to pull away the covering, a piercing scream made me open my eyes. I just caught sight of a young nurse as she fainted down onto the mortuary floor.

'A minute or so later the nurse was peering down at me. I'll never forget the terrified expression on her face. I reached out my hand towards her. I only wanted to comfort her, but she ran screaming from the room.

'After that, the mortuary was filled with doctors and nurses. One young blonde nurse with a sweet face bent over and whispered, "So you've decided to come back!"

Marjorie made a rapid recovery. Soon she was out of hospital back home with her adoring husband and children.

'I shall never forget the love and peace I felt – even now it makes me feel warm all over. I think I became a better person – less selfish, kinder and certainly happier and more contented with this life. I have the inner conviction that there is no need to panic about things now. I just take life as it comes. My dad was right when he told me that my family needed me, especially Julie.'

Jean Wilson's Story

As they left the cinema young Jean Wilson and her best friend Kate made their way towards the local hamburger bar to have a quick bite to eat before they went home.

'What's the matter with you tonight?' asked Jean, noticing that her friend was unusually quiet.

'Oh nothing. It doesn't matter.'

'Come on – what's troubling you?'

'Well,' replied Kate hesitantly, 'Remember that new clerk I told you about?'

'Oh don't tell me you're bothered about him,' quipped Jean. 'Remember what my dad told us – "Men are like buses – Never run after them, another one will be along in a minute." Jean stopped talking when she saw that her friend was not laughing. In a more serious tone she urged Kate to share her problem.

'It's just that he took me out the other night, like I told you.' After a pause, Kate continued: 'Well, I found out today that he's invited Debbie to his friend's birthday party tomorrow night.'

'So?'

'There! I knew you wouldn't understand. Let's just forget it.'

They munched their burgers without further conversation until Jean suggested, 'Why don't we have our own party tomorrow night? We could invite a few people round to our place. I'm sure my mum wouldn't mind.'

Kate looked unimpressed. 'You still don't realise, do you?'

'What's wrong now? I'm only trying to help.'

'It's no use,' answered Kate. 'If I can't go out with Tony, I don't want to go out with anyone at all.'

Kate put down her knife and fork and got up to leave the table. She thanked Jean for trying to help, then added, 'But it's useless.'

Next evening, Jean was at home with her parents. 'I was standing in the kitchen and suddenly began to feel quite ill. First I got very cold and the next moment I felt as if I was burning up, feeling sick and faint. I tried to make my way to the front room to tell my parents that I wasn't feeling well when everything went black and I remember falling to the floor just inside the back door.

'I was quite surprised to hear Kate's voice, and I remember thinking to myself that she must have decided to call round to our house after all. I hoped she wouldn't be too disappointed to find that there was no party. My next recollection was of walking with Kate towards what I can only describe as a vast calm black sea. I then realised that far out across the sea there was an extremely bright light. It became brighter and more dazzling by the second. At first we just stood at the edge of the water and stared at the light. I was overcome by its power.

'I watched Kate slowly wade into the water. She turned back to me and waved for me to follow her. I was beginning to feel afraid. I didn't move. She called out to me to follow her. She kept calling me over and over again. "Come with me. Come with me." For some reason I felt paralysed. My feet would not move. It was as if I was cemented down on to the earth. As I watched Kate wade deeper and deeper into the water I began to feel even more apprehensive, but at the same time there was something about the light that had a strange calming effect. It's just that I seemed to be caught between two directions. I could see Kate moving further away from me and still I could hear her voice crying after me to go with her.

'In a flash, my mind started sending me messages not to follow her, even if I could have moved my feet, although at the same time I seemed to know that if I did choose to follow her no real harm would have come to me. It was a most peculiar feeling. I remember shouting out, "I must go back. I can't come with you. No."

'The next thing I knew, I was wakening up on the couch in the front room, with my worried-looking parents tending to me. I told them nothing of what I had just experienced. The doctor was duly called in and it turned out that I was suffering from food poisoning. The doctor left a prescription for me, advising that I should go straight to bed.

'I dozed off to sleep, but on awakening later that night I was concerned to see my mother's saddened face.

'"What's the matter? What did the doctor tell you? Why are you looking so worried?," I asked.

'"I've just had a phone call from Kate's father," replied my mother grimly. "Kate committed suicide this evening."

Barbara Horrsbury's Story

When Mrs. Barbara Horrsbury was admitted to hospital suffering from a massive haemorrhage, she was placed in a bed and the curtains were pulled around so that she could not see anything else that was going on in the small ward. Suddenly, she slipped out of her body and hovered in mid-air from where she saw another patient being wheeled into a bed opposite hers. She watched from just underneath the ceiling, and peering down, Barbara could see that the patient who had just been brought in was wearing a pink nightgown. She watched a nurse place a vase of daffodils on the patient's locker.

She then found herself in a long dark tunnel which had a bright light at the end of it. The next moment she felt herself being swooshed back along the tunnel and into her body again. Shortly after, the nurse pulled back the curtains which were surrounding her bed and there, sure enough, across the room was the other patient in the pink nightgown, with the vase of daffodils on her locker.

Mrs. Neale's Story

Mrs. Edith Neale also had the feeling of slipping out of her physical body, then travelling down a very long tunnel towards a brilliant light which seemed to illuminate the entire end section of the tunnel.

'I heard the most heavenly music and was filled with great joy and peace. I became aware of someone travelling beside me. I looked across and saw my niece, June. June had been in an accident and was in hospital at the same time, recovering from serious injuries. She smiled and waved to me saying, "Come on in, Auntie Edie, don't be afraid." I heard myself answer, "Not yet, love, I've got a lot of work to do, but I'll be seeing you soon."

'Everything went black after that and I don't remember anything more except being aware that I was safely back in my own bed.

'The next day I was at work as usual when I got a phone call from my distraught sister to tell me that June had suffered a relapse and had died in the middle of the night.

'I never told my sister or anyone else about the tunnel or the light, but on the day of June's funeral, June's brother put his hand on my arm and asked me if I had been in the hospital corridor on the night June had died.

'I told him, no of course I hadn't been there or I would have gone straight into the ward.

'"That's what I thought," answered my nephew, "It's just that before she died June kept saying, 'There's Auntie Edie out there – she can see me.'"

VANTAGE VIEWPOINT

Frances and David's Story

Frances was on holiday in the south of France with her boyfriend Dave. They had gone down to the beach on Dave's motorbike. Frances went into the sea for a swim, leaving Dave on the beach. She was an excellent swimmer and was splashing about in the warm sunshine having a lovely time when, suddenly, she got caught up in a freak wave formation.

'I did not fully realize what was happening and certainly I cannot recall feeling in any real danger of drowning. There was a split-second awareness that something was wrong. The next instant I found, to my amazement, that I was hovering in the air about three or four feet above the waves. Incredible as it may sound, I was suspended in mid air. I looked all around me, then I remember looking back towards the beach where people were just lying on the sand, some under big umbrellas.

'Everything seemed so normal, apart from me, that is. Something immediately below me caught my eye. I realized it was an arm sticking up out of the water. The arm was waving around and then it disappeared below the waves. I kept watching and I saw first the fingers appear back out of the water, then the hand and eventually the whole arm. It was only then, as I watched the arm go under the water again, that I realized the arm belonged to me! The horrible, frightening truth dawned on me. I was watching myself drown!

'I tried to call out to people on the beach. I opened my

mouth but no sound came out. Somehow, I managed to lower myself down towards the spot where I had seen my arm go under the water. I was aware of trying to stretch out my arm but my fingers seemed to melt through the water.

'I couldn't feel any sensation of touching the turbulent water. The more I tried to feel underneath the waves to try and grasp hold of my physical arm, the more it felt like I was just waving my hand through thin air.

'When once more I tried to shout for help I noticed that three young men were running into the water towards me. "At last," I thought, "I've been heard." I could see my boyfriend and some other people standing on the beach looking out to sea. As the young men got nearer to me I started to wave to them. I could see by their special clothes that they were life guards. I called out to them but I felt disappointed that all three of them totally ignored me.

'I watched the life guards fish my body out of the sea and I followed them back on to the beach where they stretched my body down on the sand. One man started to give me the kiss-of-life. I watched as they went through various procedures to try to revive my body which remained deathly still.

'It was at this point that I noticed my boyfriend standing nearby. He was watching the life guards with a ghastly white face. He seemed to be in a state of absolute shock. I heard the life guards tell him that they were not able to bring me round, then I watched him dash away and get on his motorbike. I decided to follow him to see what he was up to.

'I watched Dave start up the engine and take off at speed. He drove very fast, but I remember thinking how easy it was to keep up with him, just by moving through the air above the bike. It was just like flying, only without an aeroplane. I kept going at the same speed as the machine. It was quite an exhilarating feeling, much better than sitting on the pillion. As Dave increased his speed I felt myself speed up automatically. At one point I called to him to look up, but he didn't take any notice of me.

'We came to a sharp bend on the road and I screamed out in horror as the wheels of the motorbike skidded and I watched Dave smash down on to the road. The motorbike slid along for a few yards, then came to a halt by the side banking. I could only stare at Dave, sprawled down on the ground. I was very relieved to see him move, so I knew he was still conscious.

'I hovered around Dave for a while, feeling completely helpless. I kept talking to him, trying to comfort him, but he took no notice of me whatsoever. Then I began to wonder what was happening to my own body back on the beach. No sooner had the thought entered my head than I felt myself speeding back along the road, through the air, towards the beach.'

'When I arrived, I saw one of the life guards pump down on my chest. I noticed that one of the other life guards was kneeling beside my body. The man was crying. I got the impression that he thought I was dead, yet I felt perfectly fine and healthy, with no aches or pains whatsoever. I felt sorry for this man, so I moved up beside him and touched his arm as if to say that I was all right and he needn't worry. I got such a shock though when my hand went right through his skin. I just could not stop my fingers from passing right through his arm.

'I felt puzzled at this stage, and became frustrated at not being able to make my presence felt. I looked down at my washed out body lying lifeless in the sand. The lifeguards had stopped working on me by this time. They were just watching for a few moments, then I heard them start to talk between themselves in lowered tones. I could speak fluent French, so I could understand what they were saying. They all agreed that I was dead and there was nothing they could do for me. They arranged that one of them would stay with my body whilst the others went to their base to inform the police and to report my death to their supervisor.

'Suddenly I was faced with a distinct choice. I knew at that point that it was my last chance to decide whether to stay as I was or whether I should go back to my body. I knew deep down inside me that I did not want to die and as if in a flash I found myself back in my body. I could feel the sand sticking to my back as I felt my weight press down on the ground.

'I opened my eyes and I heard one of the lifeguards cry out to the others telling them that I was back. They came running over towards me, all of them quite excited. They fussed around me for a few minutes and seemed surprised that I was able to pick myself up off the ground and walk away.

'I picked up my belongings from the beach and made my way back to the hotel where I was staying with Dave. I quietly opened the door of our room and entered. I could see Dave standing across the far side of the room beside a mirror. Our eyes met in the mirror, he spun round with a stunned expression and just stared at me in silence.

'It's all right, you can relax, I'm not a ghost,' I reassured him. I walked over to him and kissed his face, which was grazed and bruised. I told him that he really ought to be more careful of that motorbike of his. I told him that I had seen him take that bend like a madman. He stared hard at me and asked me what I was talking about. How could I have seen him? All I could answer was, 'It's a long story.'

Paul Picken's Story
Paul Picken used to work as a bath attendant at a coalmine in the English Midlands. One Saturday night when he was on night duty on his own, he began to feel very sleepy. He made himself a cup of tea to see if that would keep him awake, but still he could hardly keep his eyes open.

'About 2.00 a.m. I lay down on top of a long bunker and started to read a book, but eventually I dozed off to sleep. I felt myself rise up out of my body and on looking down I could see my body stretched out peacefully on the bunker, still holding the book which had fallen onto my chest.

'I felt perfectly natural floating around the room and I remember although I was puzzled at being in two places at once, I had no fear whatsoever. It was if I was in my true state of being as I floated around the room. I was totally aware of what was going on at all times, and thought it interesting that the 'me' floating around was the part that housed all my awareness and consciousness. When I looked down on my body sprawled out on the bunker, I couldn't help feeling how insignificant my physical shell really was. It didn't appear to have any mind of its own, all the thinking power was up in the air with me.

'Within a very short period, I started to feel myself drawn out of the room. I was compelled to follow the instinct which led me towards a ladder. I used this regularly to get up on the roof of the baths. I floated towards it, but when I put my hand out to grasp hold of the sides of the ladder, my hand just went right through the metal and try as I would, I just could not get a grip on the thing. It was then that I realized how silly I'd been and I thought to myself that if I can float upwards, who needs a ladder? The minute that thought came into my head, up I went right on to the roof of the baths.

'Now, unbeknown to anyone else at the colliery, because I was responsible for the safety of all the goods in the baths, I had previously drilled a tiny hole in the roof, so that I could look through this from up above to keep an eye on the locker area directly below without anyone knowing that I was checking.

'For some reason I felt myself drawn towards the section of the roof where this small hole was. I found that I could see down through the floor into the locker area. I was quite surprised to see two men going along the line of lockers and searching all through their fellow workers' belongings. They had either a key or some small gadget which they were sharing to open the doors of the lockers. I recognized both men instantly and I must say that I was surprised. I would never have guessed that they would have done such a thing in a million years.

'I floated back down the ladder, then looked through a window into the room where I could see my body still stretched out on top of the bunker, fast asleep. I approached my body with some trepidation, not quite knowing what to do to get back into myself.

'I stood beside my sleeping body for a while, wondering what I should do. The only thing I could think of was to lie down in the same position on top of the bunker. It must have done the trick although I don't remember anything very clearly about how I managed to merge back into my physical body. I looked at the clock and it was 2.10 a.m. I

221

had only been asleep for about ten minutes. The one overpowering thought in my mind was of the two men I had caught robbing the lockers.

'I immediately made my way to the locker area of the baths and sure enough, there I saw the rows of lockers with some of the doors visibly ajar, where they had been forced open.

'The next morning I felt compelled to go to my boss and report exactly what had happened, although I admit it did take me some courage to find the right words to describe how I managed to catch the thieves red-handed.

'I think my boss thought I was raving mad to start with. I had a feeling though that he began to believe me just a little bit when I freely admitted having allowed myself to fall asleep. You see, that was strictly against all the rules, and both the boss and I knew it. He could see that I was so certain of my facts that I was willing to put my own job on the line.

'The outcome of the story was that the police were called in to investigate the thefts and the two men in question were discovered to have the stolen goods in their keeping. A court hearing was arranged, the men were charged and dismissed from their employment.'

Bill Crocker's Story

It started when Bill heard a loud buzzing sound in his head, then the next thing he knew he was floating in the air in his bedroom. 'I looked down and could see myself and my wife lying in bed. I quickly became accustomed to my new condition and began to feel quite bemused at the sudden realization that I could fly. I was aware of passing straight through my bedroom window and out into the night air. I

222

was able to direct myself so that if I had the desire to turn any particular way or if I wanted to go slower or faster, higher or lower, all I had to do was wish this, and it would happen.

'I directed myself towards a particular area of town but I was surprised to find that the normal modern office block was not there. Instead, in the exact same place, there stood a somewhat shabby tenement building, totally unknown to me. I floated through a door and found myself in a dim corridor which led to a stairway. I floated up the stairway and I remember getting the distinct feeling that I was not in the present time. There was something about the structure of the staircase, the landings and the door designs that gave me the feeling that I was somewhere in the past, although I noticed that there were electric lights on at the time, therefore it cannot have been too far back in the past.

'All at once I met a small boy who came wandering along one of the landings towards me, stopping by the top of the staircase. The child was about five years of age and was quite talkative. I exchanged a few words with the boy and we seemed to be getting on fine. The child wore short trousers and little laced boots.

'There didn't seem anything especially out of the ordinary about him. He struck me as a likeable little chap, with a dirty face and a freckled nose.

'Suddenly one of the landing doors opened and a young woman came out. She took one look at me and started to scream blue murder. At that stage I began to feel alarmed. I could see the terror on her face and that started me off. I felt terrified although I wasn't sure why. I stood there, staring hard at her, then she dashed over towards me, grabbed the little boy off his feet, ran back in through the doorway and slammed the door behind her. The next thing I knew, I was back in bed beside my wife.

'I am convinced that I had a time slip of some description. There was something about the woman's hairstyle and the floral wrap-around apron that suggested the 1940s to me, although I can't be sure.

'I'll never forget the look on that woman's face. I know I'm not the best-looking chap in the world, but she was overdoing it a bit. The funny thing was, though, the child didn't seem to be one bit bothered by my presence. He just gabbed away to me like I was his dad or his uncle, but the woman definitely acted as if she's seen a ghost. When I think about it now, I sometimes wonder if she was right. Maybe she did see me as that. Maybe to her I was a ghost.

'The following day, just out of interest, I walked down to that part of town. The towering office block stood dominating the scene. There were no tenement buildings and no women in wrap-around aprons.'

Derek Scott's Story

It was a sunny afternoon. Derek Scott was travelling down the motorway towards his home in Cardiff when the nightmare happened. Before he knew what was happening, his car was ploughing into a heap of piled up vehicles spread right across the motorway. Derek was taken to the nearest hospital in bad shape, with broken bones, cuts and bruises.

'The doctor gave me some sort of jab, and to tell you the truth, I might have put my experience down to that, if I hadn't seen the proof for myself.

'I was just lying in the bed with the doctor and nurse attending to me. I was in terrible pain and felt like crying out. The next second I found myself hovering up near the ceiling. I just couldn't believe it. Two main things struck me. The first thing was that the pain had vanished and I was feeling really relaxed and light-hearted with not a care in the world. The other thing was that I could see myself lying below on the bed quite clearly. I could see everything, the nurse was fussing around the bed and the doctor was sitting down reading something, I'm not sure what. I looked just like a corpse but I wasn't really bothered. I think I was more tickled than anything.

'After a short time, I got used to the feeling of weightlessness and then I found to my amusement that I could, somehow or other, navigate myself around the room, a small side ward with only my bed in it.

'I could go close up against the ceiling and I got the feeling that I could have gone straight up through it if I had wanted to, but I was more curious about what was happening to my physical body, and I suppose that kept me in the room.

'I noticed that the lighting system was attached not to the ceiling, but to one of the walls. There was a long strip light running almost the entire length of the wall behind the bed. From my bird's eye viewpoint I could see that the light was attached to the wall by a metal structure.

'Above the light, running almost the same length along the wall, I noticed that there was a narrow wooden shelf. Something caught my attention. From just below the ceiling I could look right down behind the light-strip and I could distinctly see that a card had got caught deep down in the space between the light and the wall. For some reason I kept staring at that card. I couldn't make out the picture because of the way it was lying.

225

'There was a kind of swoosh and then I found myself back in the bed with the pain seering through my body once more. The first words I uttered were, 'Nurse, there's a card up there behind that light.' The nurse just smiled patiently and took absolutely no notice of my words. It was only after I repeated myself again and again that she started to take notice. She argued that there was nothing up there and I was just suffering from shock. I insisted that I knew there was a card trapped behind the light. I was told to settle down, then the nurse added that there was no way I could have seen behind that light.

'Even though I was in agony, I was determined to make the nurse listen to me, and again stressed that I did see down behind the light and that I saw a card trapped down there. I told her that I had been hovering up in the air. At that point I nearly lost heart when I saw the look of disbelief on the nurse's face, but I was so sure that I had seen the card I made myself ask her to have a look behind the light fixture.

'Giving me an odd look, and without saying a word, the nurse impatiently pulled a chair across to the wall, stood up on it and tried to see behind the light. I told her to look over to her right a bit. She felt behind the metal attachment and then looked down at me with a stunned expression as she fished out an old yellowed get-well card from behind the light.'

chapter four

PARADISE?

The Simpson Family's Story

The Simpson family were preparing for Christmas. Mum had confided in the eldest boy that, for the benefit of the two younger children who still believed in Santa Claus, Dad was going to dress up as Father Christmas to give them a surprise. There were only two weeks to go and there was a lot to do.

That night Mr Simpson went to visit a friend who was a scout master. The man had promised to lend him a Father Christmas outfit, a relic of the previous year's scout concert. The children were fast asleep in bed when Mrs Simpson answered a ring on her doorbell. She was taken aback to find two policemen standing outside. She invited them in out of the snow.

After the policemen left, Mrs Simpson sat on the end of her bed. 'It felt as if my whole world had fallen apart. How was I going to tell the children there would be no Santa Claus that year. How was I going to tell them their father had just been killed?

'In a state of shock I walked around the house looking at all of the rooms, each filled with memories of my husband. I checked and re-checked the children as they all slept peacefully. I gazed down at their calm, slumbering little faces, dreading the next morning when they would wake up and have to face life without their Dad.

'I walked downstairs to the kitchen to make myself a cup of tea. The first thing I saw as I entered the room was the cluster of fairy-lights on the kitchen table. My husband had

227

been checking the bulbs to make sure they were safe. I remembered the last words he ever spoke to me: "Remember love, don't touch these till I get back, I don't want anything to happen to you."

'I collapsed down on the kitchen chair, tears streaming down my cheeks. I think I was at my lowest ebb at that moment. I felt so bad I didn't know how I would find the strength to carry on living. It was as if nothing mattered anymore. I just sat there for ages, gazing at the walls, then my eye was attracted by some bright red crepe paper. I think that seemed to jolt me back to reality. I had just bought some rolls of brightly coloured paper that afternoon to give to my little girl for her school party. She was going to help the teacher make some fancy hats.

'The thought of the children's party and those coloured hats made me realize that life somehow had to go on. The more I thought about it, the more I knew that all my attention and energy was going to be needed to help the children through the terrible days and weeks that lay ahead.

'I walked back upstairs and got into bed. I didn't even bother to take off my dressing gown. I lay in bed, staring into the darkness until I sobbed myself to sleep. A while later, something made me stir in my sleep. I woke up and got out of bed. I wrapped my dressing gown around myself and walked towards the bottom of the bed.

'I was stopped in my tracks when I saw a little box a short way in front of me. It seemed to be hovering in mid air, surrounded by a strange light. I turned round to see if the bedside lamp was on and I got the fright of my life when I saw myself lying asleep on the bed. I looked down at myself from where I was standing. I felt perfectly real. I even remember pinching myself. That felt real too. I could not understand why there were two of me. I kept watching the other me in the bed. I was so confused.

'I turned back round and I could still see the little box in front of me, with the mysterious light surrounding it. I recognized it this time. It was a little wooden trinket box which had belonged to my husband's mother. That brought everything back to my mind with crashing reality.

'I looked back at my body lying in the big bed and I thought that I must have died in my sleep. I started to float upwards. I couldn't stop myself and when I could not control this drifting, I got really frightened. I could feel my heart beating faster and faster and I got more and more terrified.

'I floated right up to the ceiling. I just seemed to pass right through the plaster and then up through the loft and right up to the roof and outside.

'I became aware of an extremely bright light somewhere above me. I looked towards it and there, standing in a long, white robe, stood my husband. He looked so much younger. He just stood there smiling at me with a happy, relaxed expression on his face. He seemed quite serene and radiant. He stretched out his hand to me. I ran to him and he led me by the hand to the most beautiful place I have ever seen in my life.

'We entered a room which was filled with a warm light. I tried to work our where this light was coming from as there didn't appear to be any shadows. It was nothing like our ordinary sunlight, that seems dull in comparison.

'In the room there were the most exquisite flower arrangements. The shapes and colours of these flowers were beyond anything I had seen before. I doubt if I could have imagined such creations and some were of colours I'd never seen before.

'Suddenly into this room came my husband's parents, who were both dead. They greeted me warmly and spoke to me. When I remarked about the beautiful flowers, my husband told me, "Mum grows them. She has plenty of time now." He then took me over to one side and explained to me, "You remember how Mum always loved to potter about in the garden? This is her latest work." He pointed to some lilies which were just too incredible to explain in ordinary words.

'My husband explained to me that his parents had just come to see me again. They embraced me and both of them left. My husband then told me that I was standing in our own house, the house he was preparing for me. Something outside moved, and made me walk towards the doorway. There outside in the most charming garden was Charlie, our faithful gardener, who had passed away the previous year. I asked my husband what Charlie was doing here. He told me that Charlie was keeping the garden in shape, of course, and then added that the old man's bad knee was all better now.

'My husband told me that Charlie was helping him to get everything ready for when I was to join them, but he assured me that there was no rush. He explained to me that he was praying for me and the children and that they needed me very much. That was why I couldn't stay with him in our new house.

'I felt so comforted by his words, and I knew from then on that there was no need to grieve any more because I could see that he was very much alive and waiting for me.

'The next instant I found myself waking up in my own bed. I felt a deep calm inside, and although I missed his constant presence desperately I knew that one day we would be together again.

'I never told the children about my strange encounter with their father, although on many occasions I was tempted to. Especially that Christmas, when they were crying for their Dad, I longed to tell them, but I felt they were all too young. Their little minds wouldn't have been able to take it. The only thing that pulled me through those bleak days was the knowledge that he was looking after us. That gave me the strength to give the children the help and guidance they needed.'

STRANGE FORCES AT WORK

When a baby cries a visitor to the household will look up anxiously to the young mother, expecting her to immediately dash towards the cot. Sometimes the mother may not exert herself, much to the disdain of the visitor.

"It's all right, Mrs. Jones. I know that cry. There's no problem."

"But don't you need to attend to him?"

"Of course," smiles the young mother calmly. "But it's not urgent, I can tell by the cry."

The mother-child relationship is uniquely telepathic. After all, the tiny baby has not yet learnt coherent speech, and it certainly can't write mum a note, yet the mother seems to know instinctively not only the needs of her child, but also the degree of urgency involved. This can be true even when the parent and offspring are separated by hundreds of miles. The same forces are often at work between twins, husbands and wives, and relations.

Very often when experiments have been set up to try to prove that thoughts really can travel, it has appeared that the results are nothing more than those which would normally be expected under the headings of chance, coincidence, law of averages, statistics, etc. The trouble with such experiments seems to be the aimlessness of the operation. The secret of achieving anything bordering on worthwhile evidence seems to lie in the root cause of the situation, the underlying need for motivation of the power of thought.

In other words, if there happens to be a telephone close at hand, why bother trying to send a message by thought wave to granny down in the West Country. It's a lot less bother just to dial the number.

The most convincing instances of telepathy or thought travel seem to take place when there is no telephone, no other means of communication, and a crucial state arises whereby contact must be made. In these circumstances it appears that our brains have inbuilt radar systems which can send out messages, either consciously or unconsciously, to a given target.

When a pebble is thrown into a pond we see first the splash, on impact, then the ripples on the water. What we do not see is the ripples caused in the air above the pond, but that does not mean that they do not exist.

Hardly anyone has escaped the strangely irritating sensation of *déjà vu*. We look at possible explanations and relate stories of people who have been able to describe in detail places they know they have never before been to. Is it in the genes? Is it the way in which one part of the brain receives and analyses information a fraction of a second faster than the other half, thus giving the impression of familiarity? Are we dipping into a pool of cosmic knowledge?

Nuala's Story

When Nuala Walshe was introduced to a tall, handsome, fair-haired Australian who was visiting her small, remote village in the rustic west of Ireland, she was delighted to meet the newcomer who proved to be like a breath of fresh air to the close-knit community where everyone had known each other from birth. Des, the Australian, who was staying with his relatives about two miles away from Nuala's cottage, formed a friendship with her, which speedily blossomed into what they both thought was love. Nuala had been brought up by her aunt since her mother died when she was only three.

'I was excitedly looking forward to my engagement day. On the great day, Des had been invited by my aunt to have tea. At the tea table, without thinking much about it, I produced a letter from my father who had been living in England for years and who had recently re-married. He had written to congratulate us on our forthcoming marriage and had invited us to England to visit him and his new wife, whom I had never met. I got the shock of my life when Des suddenly snatched the letter out of my hand and, in a fearful rage, he tore it to pieces before my eyes.

'The next moment the most frightening thing happened. Suddenly the room grew icy cold. I felt a strange cold draft behind me, then as I looked over at Des I became absolutely terrified because there, standing behind his chair, was the figure of a young dark-haired man, watching me with a strange, concerned look on his face. I froze with fear, unable to utter a word, hardly daring to breathe. In an instant, the man disappeared.

'I looked across at Des and realized that he had gone deathly white. His eyes were staring into space as if he were looking at something behind my chair. I was still in a state of shock myself, and I couldn't even speak to ask what was wrong. Suddenly he passed out and collapsed down on the floor.

'I was so frightened that I could not move from my chair. My aunt fetched some water for Des, who recovered consciousness. He was mumbling that he had just seen a ghost. He said that a woman had appeared behind my chair and had stared at him. He was able to describe the woman, saying that her hair was piled up on top of her head in a kind of bun. I was still speechless with fright, and didn't dare open my mouth to tell him what I had seen behind his chair.

'Quietly, my aunt went over to the dresser, and from a drawer, she took out a small box. She returned to the table, opened the box and took out a silver locket on a chain. Des told her that was the locket he had seen on the woman's neck. My aunt and I exchanged glances. We both knew that the locket had belonged to my mother. Once more my aunt went to the drawer and returned with an old photograph of my mother which had never before been shown to Des. He looked at it with a terrified expression, and told us it was the same woman. My fiancé had seen the ghost of my mother.

'Des got up to leave. I would normally have seen him off at the door, but I was so upset that my aunt insisted that it would be best if I went straight to bed to calm down, so Des left the cottage by himself. He later told me what happened to him. As he had walked up the long pathway to the gate, he had become aware of the cold atmosphere again, even though it was a beautiful, warm August day, and the sun was shining. As he had gone to open the gate, he stared in horror when he saw the bolt moving on its own, and the gate opening for him, as if bidding him to leave. In a panic, he ran to his car to start the two mile journey to the house of his relatives.

'As he drove away from the cottage, a woman loomed out in front of his car, as if from nowhere. He slammed on his brakes, then he went into a panic as he recognized the woman. It was my dead mother. She was holding out her hand and pointing into the distance, as if trying to tell him to go away.

'Des told me that he started up the car again, and as he

drove forward, my mother floated in front of his car, all the time gesturing to him to go away. By the time he had reached his destination he was sick with fear. He got out of the car, and to his great relief, the woman was nowhere to be seen. He made his way to the gate, where he was stopped in his tracks. Again he saw the gate open by itself. It took him all his courage to enter past the gate, and as he did so, the gate closed behind him of its own accord.

'The next day Des visited me to tell me that the engagement was off because he was certain that my departed mother was trying to frighten him away. Then he told me that he had arranged to travel back to Australia within the next few days.

'To get over the disappointment of my broken engagement, I decided to take my father up on his offer to visit him in England. I was in a rather tearful state when I arrived, but my dad and his new wife Betty gave me a sympathetic welcome. Betty made me feel very much at home straight away, and a bond of friendship was instantly formed between us. Later that evening there was a ring on the doorbell, and as Betty got up to answer it, she remarked that it would probably be her nephew Jim, who was due to call round to see her. I couldn't believe my eyes when Jim entered the room. He was the same young dark-haired man I had seen standing behind Des in my aunt's cottage. I was even more amazed when he smiled at me, his first words being, 'Haven't we met before some place?'

Redwing's Story

Ron Turner, a young British airman in the Second World War, was honourably discharged, having been badly wounded in action. He moved to the West Country with his wife Ellen, where they bought a run-down tea-room which they redecorated themselves, and then subsequently opened to cater for servicemen providing them with good, inexpensive luncheons.

Ellen recalls, 'A crowd of American airmen became regular customers, and two young men in particular became great friends with Ron and I. One of the Americans, called Bill, had shocking red hair and so was nicknamed "Redwing". Although I was happily married to Ron, I was nevertheless attracted to Redwing, and I felt that the feeling was mutual. Redwing always used to whistle "The Girl I Left Behind Me" and he always sat in the same seat.

'One day, after the Americans had been away for several weeks, some of Redwing's friends entered the luncheon room without him. Instantly I knew that something terrible had happened to him. Sure enough, I learned that Redwing had been missing for some time, presumed dead.

'A few years later, after Ron had died, one Easter Sunday afternoon, I was busy working in the kitchen. I had just locked up the luncheon room, when I suddenly heard a familiar whistle coming from the dining area, "The Girl I Left Behind Me". I slowly walked towards the dining area where I could see an American airman sitting alone. I remember the feeling of joy I experienced as I recognized the bright red hair. It was Redwing. He had come back. I started to walk towards him, then I stopped dead in my tracks when I realized that he had suddenly disappeared. I looked everywhere around the tearoom for him, but he was nowhere to be found.

'From that moment I was certain that Redwing was alive and I started to make enquiries, only to find little encouragement. Later that year, one winter's day, I was throwing out some rubbish at the side of the building when I saw a man muffled up in a large scarf, with a huge hat pulled down over his eyes. He was standing at the front door, looking at the "Closed" sign. I called over to him, telling him that I had just closed. He just stood there, staring at me, saying nothing. There was something about him that made me feel sorry for him, so I told him that I could offer him a bowl of soup.

'I opened up the tearoom door, without paying too much attention to him, and I went into the kitchen to prepare the soup. Suddenly, I heard a tune being whistled, "The Girl I Left Behind Me". At first I froze, then I ran out and saw the man from the back. He had taken off his scarf and hat. I would have recognized that red hair anywhere. I called out "Redwing", and he turned round with an impish smile and winked at me.

'We fell into each other's arms, and he told me that he had been in a prisoner-of-war camp for years, after he had been shot down over the North Sea. I asked him if he had ever come back to the tearoom, but he assured me that he had not. Then he told me that at one point he had been so ill that he had nearly died. I asked him if it had been last Easter. Redwing looked at me in astonishment and silently nodded his head.'

Dr. Sturman's Story

One late afternoon when Dr. Sturman had just returned home after his calls which that day had been heavier than normal, because of the multiple ailments which usually hit his patients in the depths of the British winter, he heard a knock at the door.

238

'I opened my door to find a young girl of about 17 years of age standing there. She wore a child's school hat on her head, one made from straw, which was drenched through with the heavy rain. The girl was near to hysterics. She begged me to come urgently to visit her father, who had suddenly taken ill.

'I did not recognize the girl, and soon established that her father was not my patient. I tried to reason with her, advising her to go to her father's own doctor. The girl's persistent sobbing convinced me that I should visit the father to see what I could do.

'I followed the girl along a few streets as she led me to her house. On the way I remember her telling me that she was most concerned for her mother who would be completely forlorn should her father die. Not knowing the extent of her father's illness I answered as sympathetically as I could, and I assured her that I would do what I could to help.

'On the way to the girl's house we passed a workmen's hut on the pavement. I remember that we had to walk past in the gutter as there was a burning brazier on the footpath. As we passed, I glanced into the hut where three workmen were seated. We nodded to them and they acknowledged us.

'When we reached the house, the girl stood back, so I knocked on the door, which was opened by the lady of the house. She was most distressed and was weeping. I explained that I had come to see her husband. The woman led me upstairs, but on the way she tearfully told me that I was too late as her husband had died minutes before.

'I examined the body and confirmed that death had taken place. The woman then asked me how I had known to come to the house. Somewhat surprised at her question I remind-ded her that her own daughter had called to see me and had asked me to visit her father urgently. She was the one who had led me to the house. The woman's face grew deathly white, then she told me that their only daughter had died ten years earlier. She had been coming home from school and was knocked down by a car and killed outright.

'As I walked back to my own home in a somewhat dazed state, I passed the workmen's hut again. I stopped and asked the men inside if they had noticed me only a few minutes earlier when I had passed them with a young girl.

'All three workmen laughed, then one of them explained that they had seen me pass their hut but they had wondered why I had been talking to myself. They had seen only me; there had been no girl with me.'

Denise's Story
One desolate Christmas Eve a young woman, Denise, walked along a quiet street, engrossed in her own thoughts. 'I hesitated to look across towards a toyshop doorway, from where the strains of "Silent Night" were coming. I saw an old tramp, dressed in a tattered military coat, playing his violin. I remember seeing a brightly lit Christmas tree in the shop window, but I had no heart for anything that night.

'I arrived at my mother's home and just managed to summon up enough courage to tell her my news before I broke down in tears. I had just had a visit from a soldier friend of my husband to tell me that my husband, Joe, was missing, presumed dead. Joe had been serving in Northern Ireland. My family rallied round and tried to comfort me, but with little success, although I tried hard to keep up a brave front.

'Although my mother pleaded with me to stay at her

house that night I insisted on going home just in case there might be any more news about Joe. Later that night I was even more melancholy, and I missed my husband desperately. I feared that he must be dead as he would definitely have contacted me for Christmas. I looked at some photographs of Joe in his army uniform. Tearfully I went to bed.

'Later I was awakened by someone tapping at the door. I was frightened, but I got up and went to answer. I peeped through the curtain, and to my joy I saw Joe standing outside the house. I rushed to the door and welcomed him in. I sobbed with relief as we hugged each other. It was then that I noticed that the front of his heavy army coat was soaked with blood. I stared at him in horror and asked him what had happened, then I told him I would call the doctor at once. In a vague, far-off voice, he replied, "It's OK, it's all better now." He kissed me again, and I asked him if he wanted a drink, and again I suggested that I call a doctor. I went to help him off with his coat, but he slowly shook his head, moved towards me and held out his hand. I took his hand and he led me into the bedroom.

'The following morning I awoke and excitedly turned round towards Joe, only to find that his side of the bed was empty. I looked around the room, then I ran to telephone my mother. As I started to dial the number there was a loud knock on the outside door. I could see the outline of a soldier in uniform. My mother answered the telephone. Breathless with excitement I told her briefly on the phone that Joe was all right, but I had to go because he was at the door. I told my mother to hold on saying that he must have lost his key.

'I ran to answer the door, expecting to see Joe, but I was

241

taken aback when I saw his friend, Alan, standing there instead. I asked him into the house. Solemnly he handed me an official letter which I read. I cried out in disbelief, saying that it couldn't be true. Joe couldn't be dead. He was here last night. I told Alan that there must be some mistake. He was sympathetic and told me that I was suffering from shock. He confirmed the contents of the letter, stating quietly that Joe had been killed on Christmas Eve.

'I looked at the telephone receiver, which was still off the hook. I murmured to Alan that my mum was on the line. Alan picked up the receiver and broke the news to my mother.'

Joanna's Story

'As a young nurse, some years ago, I was having a tea-break with my friend, and we were chatting about the new houseman, an extremely good-looking young Scotsman, Dr. Robertson. The young doctors were usually the topic of conversation, and I remember that I was particularly smitten with Dr. Robertson, and I admitted that I was looking forward to my forthcoming night duty, hoping that I would get the opportunity to talk to him and get to know him better.

'A few nights later, in the middle of the night, the ward sister asked me to check a drip which was attached to an elderly male patient, Mr. Taylor, who was in a serious condition in a side room. I did what Sister told me, then I spoke quietly for a while to the patient, who was very emotional and nostalgic. This was not unusual and I had been trained to cope with the situation. He asked me if I had a boyfriend, then he went on to tell me that whatever happened in my life I should always do what I felt was right, no matter what other people might tell me.

'I left the room and walked along the corridor to report back to Sister, but on looking back I caught a glimpse of a nun entering Mr. Taylor's room. I mentioned this to Sister, who remarked that it must be one of the nuns from nearby St. Cecilia's convent. We all knew that the nuns often popped over during the night, especially if any of the patients were near the end. Sister and I then exchanged a few words regarding Mr. Taylor and we mentioned the fact that he never had any visitors. Sister told me that he was a bachelor and he had no relations left in this country, only a sister in Canada.

'Sister then asked me to put the kettle on to make some tea, and to remember to make a cup for Dr. Robertson. Before I had finished making the tea, Dr. Robertson came into the kitchen and we chatted for a few minutes. The doctor had just come from Mr. Taylor's room and, for the sake of conversation, I mentioned that I'd better get the nun a cup of tea as well. He asked me, "What nun?" I presumed she must have left.

'The following night, as I started night duty and the day nurses went off duty, I was told to keep a special eye on Mr. Taylor, so I went along to speak to him. I noticed that he was much weaker than before. Trying to cheer him up, I asked him if his visitor would be coming back to see him. He replied that he had never had a single visitor since he had arrived at the hospital. I assumed that he must have fallen asleep the night before when the nun had visited him. He raved on a little about how he could have had a family if only he'd not listened to others. He then dozed off to sleep and I left the room.

'I was walking along the darkened corridor when something caught the corner of my eye. I looked round just in time to see the nun enter Mr. Taylor's room. I went straight to Sister's office where Dr. Robertson was discussing a patient. I told them that I just wanted to mention that I had just seen the nun go into Mr. Taylor's room again. Dr. Robertson then decided he would go and check Mr. Taylor, and Sister nodded to me to go with him.

'We walked quietly down the long dark corridor until we reached the door of Mr. Taylor's room, from where we could see the nun standing at the end of his bed. At this point she had her back to us. Dr. Robertson gave a quiet cough, then we entered the room. The doctor glanced at Mr. Taylor, who appeared to be asleep, then he turned to the nun. For the first time I saw the nun's face. She was young and very beautiful. Dr. Robertson remarked quietly that Mr. Taylor had settled down all right. The nun smiled very sweetly and said, "I'll look after him now." With these words she turned to leave the room.

'I suddenly screamed out in terror, "She's got no feet!" Dr. Robertson glanced down just in time to see the nun glide out of the room, her long robes almost touching the ground, but not quite. I knew he had seen the same as me. His eyes widened in fear as he realized that I was right, the nun had no feet! I was shaking with fear. Dr. Robertson rushed towards me and put his arms around me to comfort me. We both walked quickly out of the room to have another look at the nun. When we got to the corridor it was completely empty and the nun had disappeared. We immediately went back into the room to check Mr. Taylor, and we found that he was lying in the bed, dead.

'Later, when we were going through Mr. Taylor's locker,

I came across an old poetry book. As I lifted it up, a photograph fell out on to the floor. My heart jumped with fright as I recognized the girl in the photograph. It must have been taken when Mr. Taylor was a young man. He was laughing cheerfully, with his arm round the pretty blonde girl in a flowered summer dress. There was no mistaking her face. It was the nun who had come back for him after all these years. I couldn't help the tears rolling down my cheeks.'

ANIMALS

What is the difference between human beings and animals? As far as their physical bodies are concerned there is no difference other than those arising from culture. The flesh, blood and bones of an animal are comprised of the same atoms and molecules as those of the human body. The structure and assembly of these particles decree the form, shape and species of the resultant living being, the blueprint.

It has been stated by various religions that what makes animals different to human beings is the fact that they have no souls. This would appear to be an over-simplification. Although the animal does not seem to have a soul similar in nature and origin to that of the human being, it does not necessarily follow that there is no soul. In fact, evidence suggests that animals do survive physical death.

Perhaps the differences between animals and humans can be described as follows: human beings have a spirit which, on physical death, rises towards its own natural sphere of existence, depending on the development of the spirit at that point in its evolution towards its optimum state of perfection. Animals, on the other hand, merely move on to their own animalistic realm on physical death.

It appears that animals are especially susceptible to mystic forces. It is well documented that an animal will react in a frightened manner when it is taken to certain locations and, in fact, it is often the reaction of an animal which draws attention to the fact that something odd has occurred at a particular spot. Many old English pubs have rooms where the owner's dog refuses to enter. Often we find that people report feeling a chilled atmosphere in such rooms, even though the central heating is operating at full capacity.

One particular pub in Northamptonshire is, to all appearances, trying to fight against being renovated. The chief architect (working on behalf of a major brewery) reports that since he started work on the site several months ago, every task which would normally be completed without any problems seems to be fraught with difficulties, without any logical reason. They have had a record number of injuries on site, and the morale of the workmen is at an all-time low. The project is under such stress that it is, in fact, in danger of being cancelled. Perhaps it is only coincidence, but this particular pub was used as a shelter for dying soldiers from the battle of Naseby. Rather than allow the men to die on the open field, they were carried in and stretched out in the cellar. All of the men died in that room. And now, over three hundred years later, the present landlord cannot entice his two Alsatian dogs into the cellar under any circumstances, yet the dogs roam freely throughout the rest of the building. Could it be that vibrations from that battle are still felt in the vicinity?

The suffering of the soldiers seems to be lingering on in the vibrations surrounding the pub, and these are picked up by the animals. These forces are so negative that they are not conducive to the type of plan that the brewery is trying to execute for that building.

Another example of an animal reacting to negative vibrations is given by Mrs. Mylak of Daventry who reports that the morning after Halloween she and her dog started their usual morning walk. 'Suddenly, the dog stopped dead

247

in his tracks. His hair stood up, from the top of his head to his tail. The skin on his face was tight, he was scared stiff. I bent down to his level, but could see nothing. I took him home, or rather he took me. Once he had calmed down, I took him again on the same path, and exactly the same thing happened at the same spot. By this time I was glad to go home with him, as I felt as scared as he looked. An hour later he took the path with my husband, and he walked on, perfectly normal.'

Mr. Turner of Kent reports a similar occurrence. He used to take his Alsatian dog on a regular early morning walk. 'It was very dark at the top of the road leading into the field. Every morning four local ladies would meet and go along a path by the field to a nearby school where they were cleaners. This particular morning, as I went into the field, they were walking along the path about thirty yards from me. One was shining her torch and they were chatting to one another when, all of a sudden, the whole field was lit up by the whitest light I have ever seen. It was brighter than daylight. I looked up, expecting to see a flare, but there was nothing in the sky to account for it. I could see the ladies going by, but they did not seem to see the light. They never even looked up, in fact the one with the torch was still shining it on the ground as they went along. My dog had gone down on his belly and was whimpering with fright. This lasted only a few seconds, and then it all went dark. The next day I saw the ladies and asked them about the light, but they had seen nothing. This never happened again, but for a long time afterwards I had a job to get my dog to go into that field.'

Sometimes, although there is no evidence of anything traumatic having occurred in a specific location, phantom animals are sighted, as in the case of a lady from Northamptonshire:

'One Saturday night, around 7.45 p.m. my husband, myself and our son, then aged five, were travelling in the car along the A509 from Wollaston to Bozeat. It had been snowing, just enough to cover the fields and verges with a thin layer. Just as we were approaching a spot called Fullwell Hill we noticed the large silhouette of a dog. I say silhouette as this is how it appeared at the time. It appeared to get closer to the road as it ran and, at one point, a huge shadow seemed to pass through the right side of the car. It all happened so unexpectedly, and we did not think it weird at that moment. We assumed it had got loose from one of the farms and the snow was causing the shadow effect. For a short time we lost sight of it, but suddenly we could make out the dog's figure against the snow as it came from the hedge towards the road a few yards in front of us. My husband braked, but the dog just disappeared as it reached the middle of the road.

'Nothing could have been further from my mind than ghosts until that moment, when I realized that we had seen the phantom dog that I had heard talked about many years before, and that was said to appear at that very spot. Strangely, when the dog came out into the road it appeared a normal size border collie, but it looked like the negative of a film. I could clearly make out the markings and shape, but there was no real substance. If it had been a real live dog our car would have hit it.

'I have since been told by a young man that he has also seen the dog, whilst he was travelling along the same stretch of road on his motorbike.'

A new bypass has recently been built, which covers the

spot where this lady first saw the dog, and it will be interesting to note if any further sightings are made.

Another version of the phantom animal is contained in a report from Ted of Luton, but this time it occurred at the moment of the dog's death.

'Pip was an old dog, suffering very badly from arthritis. Her back legs were stiff, and if she was lying down she would give a low growl and I would have to pick her up and put her on her feet. Eventually things got so bad for her that I decided to have her put down, and took her to the vet.

'I stood her up on the operating table, while the vet prepared the syringe. He took a long time over his preparations to give me time to change my mind. I looked at Pip's face, she looked me straight in the eye, and I felt a real coward for doing this to her, although she was in pain. I had to avert my eyes from her gaze. She seemed to be saying "Why?" to me.

'Within a few seconds the vet had injected her and she died, although there was no change, she just stood there, supported by me. I looked at ther and did not think she was dead. The vet said, "It's OK, she's gone now."

'I moved over to the desk to write out the cheque and the vet turned away to wash his hands. I turned to look at Pip lying on the table, when suddenly I saw what seemed to be a young version of Pip coming from her head. It was just as solid as the corpse, and was lying in the same position. It seemed to glide, and made a right hand turn just before the end of the table, at the point where the vet normally stood. As it moved towards the side of the table I saw a pair of hands in what looked like a monk's brown habit appear to receive it. The dog's head seemed to disappear into an aperture, followed by the strange hands and the rest of the dog's body. I looked back at the table to see Pip still lying there. The whole thing took about four to five seconds.'

An interesting point arises from this story that if animals could speak, perhaps they would report experiencing out-of-body travels, and it would be fascinating to compare their accounts with those of human beings. If animals are connected to the astral world in the same way as humans, i.e. by a cord of some description, then the theory is that as long as the cord remains unsevered, the spiritual body can come back and be reunited with the physical one. When the cord is broken, permanent death takes place.

The healing forces are not exclusive to human beings and can be used to great effect to cure animals. A lady from New Zealand, who was already well known as a dowser, or water diviner, discovered that she could adapt this particular ability for healing both human beings and animals. She became a human conductor and attracted the healing forces towards the patient. She treated a race horse who had hit a hurdle, severly bruising its chest. She was asked to treat it, as a last resort, and it recovered to win again.

Perhaps wishes are granted in the afterlife, as in the case of the gentleman from Kent, who had always wanted to have a dovecote in his garden. His widow reports that, 'I disagreed as being in a built-up area I said we would have complaints from the neighbours about the cooing. After his death my mother stayed with me for a while. Imagine my surprise one day when looking out of the window I saw two white doves in the garden. We had never seen doves in the garden before. I remarked to my mother how thrilled my husband would have been to have seen them. One evening shortly afterwards, I had my bedroom windows open as it was very hot. When I went to close the windows I spotted a white dove sitting on a shelf over the window. I couldn't get it down, so I called my neighbour, who told me that he had seen the dove sitting in my open window all evening. My neighbour had a great deal of trouble in putting the dove out, as it seemed reluctant to go. Before going to bed that night, I went into another bedroom to draw the curtains, and there was the dove, sitting on the outside of the window ledge. I remained in the house another two years, but never saw doves again.'

Perhaps old wives' warnings cannot be laughed off so easily when we hear such tales as the magpies of Chippenham, Wiltshire, which appeared to give a definite warning of impending death. Mrs. Hughes says, 'Our lounge, living room and bedroom windows look out onto our field garden, as we call it. There used to be two magpies which regularly sat on the field fence. One morning one of these magpies woke up my husband and myself by pecking viciously on our bedroom window. The look in its eyes was quite alarming. I knew that tits pecked at the insects on windows, but had never known magpies to do this.

'About an hour later we received a phone call to tell us that my mother-in-law had died. This came as a great shock as although she was in hospital she was expected home the following day, as she had recovered. My husband, who is not at all superstitious says that he had heard this old country tale many times, but had never believed it. This happened two years ago, and although we still have magpies in our garden, they have not pecked at the window since.'

Animals feature in different types of psychic phenomena, including unusual or prophetic dreams and telepathy, There are lots of examples of people being in telepathic communication with their pets. Mrs. Hague relates that she had to go to Africa, and while she was away from home she had asked a kindly neighbour to look after her cat. On her way back from Kenya she had a vivid dream that her cat was being offered a saucer of milk from a stranger. Something about the expression on the cat's face worried her. She suddenly became aware of the fact that this was no ordinary saucer of milk. 'It was as if a voice in my head was telling me that the milk had been poisoned.' Throughout the long journey home she was worried about the cat and could not get it out of her mind.

The most upsetting aspect of the dream was that although she knew that the animal was being offered poisoned milk, she was totally helpless and could do absolutely nothing to prevent her cat from drinking the milk.

As soon as she arrived home she went to her neighbour and was greeted with a sorrowful story. The cat had become unaccountably ill, and the neighbour had taken it to be put down.

It often happens that when a death takes place in a family, the animals of the dead person react in strange ways, possibly because they are more aware of vibrations in the ethereal sphere.

Mrs. Newman of Hampshire experienced this when her mother died suddenly, leaving the entire family grief-stricken. 'My sister and husband, my brother and wife, my daughter, my husband and I were working out mother's papers on the following Tuesday in my house. Suddenly the phone rang. I answered it. A good friend was phoning with her condolences. I chattered away, saying how much this friend had always cheered me up.

253

'Looking across the room, past the family gathered round the table, I saw over the curtains, towards the farthest corner of the room, a bright orange ball. For some reason I watched it without bringing the attention of the family to it. The cat suddenly started to behave very oddly. She rushed to the curtains, then under the table, back to the curtains looking very frightened, eyes wide and ears back. I excused myself from the friend on the phone, mentioning the behaviour of the cat. My husband and I went to the windows to see if anyone was outside. We opened the door, but the cat wouldn't go out.

'Within ten minutes all was calm again. The cat had quietened down and, of course, by then I had forgotten the light, it had vanished. Later, sitting relaxed in the lounge, my brother remarked, "Mum has been here tonight." We all agreed, feeling that she had been to see that we were all all right and once having satisfied herself she went. I discussed this with the vicar, who had heard of similar stories.'

Sometimes, the opposite happens. When the animal dies, the owners report that their pets come back to visit them. These feelings are very strong and cannot easily be talked away. The most common example is the sensation of the animal's fur rubbing against the master's legs. Sometimes, if the animal had a particular cushion upon which it always rested, the bereaved owners would see the cushion incline as if the animal were still sitting there, although usually no visible trace of the animal is reported.

In some cases sounds are perceived, not always in the obvious way, such as a dog's bark or a cat's meow, but in more subtle ways such as the sound of claws scraping on a door in exactly the same way as the pet used to scrape when it was alive. Perhaps the reason for this is that a straightforward bark might not be sufficiently distinctive and, indeed, might be lost to the perception of the owner, especially if there were other dogs in the vicinity. Usually these 'messages' come in such a way as to leave the owner in no doubt whatsoever that their own pet has been trying to make contact by using a method of communication peculiar to that individual pet.

For example, a listener to Birmingham's Radio WM reported that he had lost his dog and immediately bought another one. However, the new dog was very different in its habits to the one which passed over. The dead animal had always scraped on the door in a distinctive manner. It would only give one long scrape. The new dog used to scrape ferociously at the door with a repetitive action, not stopping until the door was opened. On various occasions, the owner distinctly heard the sound of the dead dog's one long scrape on the door.

'At first I didn't think anything of it, assuming that it was my new dog. I suppose I'd been so used to hearing the single long scrape for so many years that I was more or less seasoned to it. One particular night I heard the long solitary scrape sound, I got up to let, as I thought, the new dog in, and I was taken aback when my new dog came running along behind me. It had been inside in the kitchen towards the back of the house, in a completely different direction. I bent down to stroke my new dog and, at that moment, I heard the solitary scrape again. I remember looking at my new dog in amazement, wondering how on earth he could be standing beside me and scraping outside the door at the same time. It was only at that point that it dawned on me that, of course, the long scrape was how my dead dog used to tell me that he wanted to be let into the house. I naturally went the few paces to the door, opened it, but I could see nothing. I smiled to myself at the time, thinking what a rascal my dead dog was, giving me a turn like that. The strange thing is that as soon as I accepted in my heart that the old dog had tried to communicate with me, I never heard his scrape again. It was as if he had made his point and he was now happy to leave it at that.'

MUSIC

One point which keeps arising time and time again during our research of cases of out-of-body experiences is in connection with music. Not just the ordinary sounds of earthly music, but something much more – something that defies description in our earthly vocabulary. Most people end up by using the term 'Heavenly Music'.

The manner in which the music becomes evident to people varies considerably. Sometimes it is heard as a beautiful melody, sometimes there are pure voices heard singing in unknown tongues, sometimes the music is the trigger which switches people into another dimension, or often it is the vehicle whereby the attention is drawn to the fact that something strange is taking place.

A man was in Co. Sligo in Ireland, on holiday from Zimbabwe with his sister and her husband. They were walking across a remote field towards a lone cottage which stood by the shore, when suddenly, as if from out of the sky, a blast of joyful music echoed across the field. There was no sign of anyone else in the area. They both heard it and were afraid. The husband reported:

'It was an unnatural fear, that I have never experienced before and never want to again. I could feel the hairs on the top of my head stand erect. I could see that my wife was terrified, so I told her to pay no heed and just keep walking.'

The music seemed to follow them. They quickened their steps, but still the music seemed to be with them.

They then became aware that the nature of the music changed slightly as if a girl soloist was being featured, a clear, high-pitched, ringing voice singing in a foreign language. As soon as the girl's voice was heard, the woman turned to her husband and said, 'It's Mary!'

Mary had been married to the woman's brother, with whom they were on holiday, but she had died twelve years previously during the birth of their son. She was Dutch. Afraid to tell his brother what had happened for fear of upsetting him, the woman reported the story to the authors the day after she had heard the music, saying that she was worried about her brother. She had the feeling that the music seemed connected with him, as if it were 'calling' him. He was a fit man, in his prime, with three sons on holiday with him, and a daughter back in Africa. Within a week the man was dead. He had suffered a dreadful head injury from a fall, was rushed to hospital and died within hours.

A young boy of 14 skipped school one day. He saw a horse and cart approaching, and thought he would go closer. The horse kicked him, and he fell down, one of the wheels of the cart running over his arm. The next thing he knew, he was hovering above, looking down on his body which was lying on the ground. He became surrounded by a brilliant light and heard the most joyous, high-pitched music. 'It was so beautiful and made such an impression on me that I was unable to speak about it to anyone for years.'

A lady from Norwich reports that, 'One Good Friday I was part of a congregation singing "Sing My Tongue The Glorious Battle". I found I was about a foot in front of myself and a little higher up, and could hear myself singing behind me. When the hymn was finished, and I "fell into place", I felt cold. Of course it is an emotional time, and I was hungry – this may be relevant. I think the anonymous composer knew very well what he was doing! I have been on the edge of being "sent" before and since, but this is the only time I have been right over.'

Another example of church music having an effect comes from Aberdeen, where a lady reports, 'Many years ago, I was standing singing in the church choir, when suddenly my soul (or spirit) left my body. I went floating up past the pulpit but then thought, "What if my body doesn't sit down at the end of the hymn?" So, I willed myself back into my body, with a jerk. I was in perfect health at the time.'

Music can be used as a warning in some instances and often can come to the rescue of vulnerable people who cannot help themselves. A very disturbing story was related by a young girl, who had been brought up in New York, and who was unfortunately a victim of child battering.

The mother used the child as a scapegoat whenever there were problems, and the result was that the child lived in a constant state of fear. On one particular day, while she was suffering physical violence from her mother, suddenly the piano which stood in the corner of the room started to play of its own accord. The tune was distinctive as being the only one played by the child's aunt, who had recently died.

'There was no mistaking the tune, and my mother stopped beating me instantly as we both stared in amazement at the piano. We could definitely see the keys moving up and down, as if they were being depressed by unseen fingers. There is no doubt in either of our minds that my aunt was making her presence felt, and from that day on my mother never mistreated me again and, in fact, we became good friends.'

In some cases the origin of the music is fairly easily

traced, as in the case of a woman who lived in the top flat of an old house with her husband and new baby. She was very fond of music, but did not own a piano.

From time to time she was invited down to the ground floor flat by an elderly lady, whose late husband had been a professional pianist and who had, in fact, played at Carnegie Hall. The man had recently died, and the old lady enjoyed the company of the young woman and her baby.

'One day I tried to play "I'll Find You". Suddenly I felt as if someone was watching me. Then I sensed someone moving my fingers onto the right notes. I was absolutely petrified. The old lady was not in the least perturbed – she simply smiled and said, "That's my husband, trying to teach you."'

When author, George Chaplin, was researching his book on the famous composer, Lawrence Wright, a strange thing happened that he cannot explain. He went to Blackpool to the house of the late composer to interview his house-keeper, in order to get some background information on the man.

The house was called 'Souvenirs' after one of his famous songs 'Among My Souvenirs'. The interview went very well, and as Mr. Chaplin was about to leave, the house-keeper suggested with a laugh that she should give him her rendering of 'Among My Souvenirs' on the old piano, which had belonged to the composer. The author turned on his tape recorder, and the housekeeper played it through. When Mr. Chaplin played it back, he felt that he should have been a little closer to the piano as the recording was not as clear as it might have been. He suggested that the housekeeper play it through again, and that he would try to obtain a better recording. From that moment on, the tape recorder would not function, no matter which buttons he pressed. The housekeeper just laughed, and said, 'Lawrie's up to his tricks again. He wants you to keep the version I have played. Just wait and see – as soon as you leave the house your tape recorder will be fine.' When Mr. Chaplin left 'Souvenirs', he thought he would turn the tape recorder on to see what would happen. Sure enough, it played as normal.

BORDERLAND

There are varying accounts of the scenic surroundings encountered during out-of-the-body excursions. There does seem to be a united opinion that the wandering spirit reaches an area which can be described as a 'Borderland', situated at the demarcation line between the two realms of consciousness. This borderland lies within the area of brilliant light so often encountered, and is always described as being unbelievably tranquil. In fact, most people state quite clearly that they would have preferred to stay with the beneficial effects of the borderland, rather than return to their earthly bodies for all sorts of reasons. The moment the will to return becomes uppermost in their minds, they are instantly drawn back and into their physical bodies.

In some instances people find that they have to put up a tremendous struggle to return to their bodies, always with the terrifying thought that if they do not manage to get back they will be dead. Other people report that they are more or less ordered to go back because the time has not yet come for them to pass over.

While in hospital after a serious accident, Mr. Stephenson of Lincoln floated out of his body. He felt a great freedom and enjoyed the weightlessness as he travelled towards an earthly coloured valley. 'I came to a beautiful silver stream which, although fast flowing, sounded quiet and it had a strange calming effect on me. Across the stream on the far bank was the greenest grass I've ever seen. There was a hill, on top of which stood a huge, solitary tree. Behind the tree was the most brilliant light you could imagine. There is no earthly brilliance to compare it with. Our sun seemed like a dim candle glow in comparison to this wonderful light.

'At this point, I became aware of the voice of my minister, who was praying and calling on God to save me on behalf of my wife and small family. All I could think of at that moment was how much I dearly longed to cross the stream and reach the other side, to the beautiful peace. As much as I tried to approach the edge of the water, something seemed to be holding me back. Again I could hear the minister's voice, pleading for my recovery. I was truly disappointed at the thought of having to leave such beauty and comfort. The third prayer by the minister asked God to remember Mrs. Stephenson and her small family. Something must have clicked when I heard those words, for the next moment I found myself back in my hospital bed. I was quite angry, and I remember snapping at the nurse, asking her whatever was going on; I did not wish ever to come back here – why didn't he (the minister) leave me alone?'

The Sister in charge of the ward came up to Mr. Stephenson and told him quite frankly that there were very grave fears for him ever getting better. He felt so rejuvenated after the experience that he laughed at the idea, and told the Sister that he would be up in a few days. Sure enough, much to the surprise and wonderment of the staff, he was out of bed in three days.

Many people see gates of different kinds, which mark the boundary into the afterlife. A Wirral lass encountered beautiful pearl gates, and she recognized lots of people she knew, who had all died, standing around with open arms as if to welcome her. It was a moving sight, full of all the love that the people could pour down on her.

When a lady of Preston, Lancashire, was taking a casual stroll one day, she felt her spirit body walk out in front of her physical one. 'I stepped into a silent world of filmy mist. I found myself in a dark, damp tunnel and there, far ahead, was a brilliant small light which grew bigger and bigger. I then noticed a white wicker gate, but as I put my hand out to open it I heard a voice telling me to halt. There, before my eyes, I saw my dead father, who was sitting on a marble seat, looking well and young. He said, "You go back and tell your mother that at last I am happy." The garden in which he sat was glorious, with all the flowers one could find.'

Peter Hall, from Cambridge, described what happened to him. 'I cannot remember leaving my body, but I became suddenly aware that I was floating in my room in hospital. I was near the ceiling by the door of the room, and was looking down at myself lying on the bed. I could see all the tubes attached to me and the traction on my legs. I then floated out of the room and found myself walking in a strange place. It was hot sunny weather, and I was walking on sand. Ahead of me I could see a very high wall with no windows in it. I would estimate that it would have been in excess of twenty feet high. The only break in the wall was a pair of large wooden gates. I went straight up to the gates to see if there were any gaps in the wood, so that I could look through them to see what was on the other side. There were no gaps so I started to knock on the gates. Because the wood was so thick I realised that no-one would hear my feeble knocking, so I started pounding on the gate with my fist. Someone from behind the gates called out to me, "Peter, you can't come in – go back where you came from."

I couldn't see anyone so I looked around behind me and I got the shock of my life when I saw myself lying in the hospital bed again, with a doctor leaning over me. The ward sister was by his side. I seemed to gently slide back into my physical body, and when I opened my eyes I saw the doctor's anxious face staring down at me.

'Nothing was said; they turned and walked away, and I stayed where I was. I have never experienced anything like it before or since. It was as if I was dying, and when I was sent back by that voice it was decided that I should live.'

A lady of Armagh, Northern Ireland, came across a wooden gate when she was in labour. She was having a rough time, and she knew that the birth of her child was imminent. 'Just at the last moment, before my son came into the world, I had the feeling of travelling down a very dark, long corridor. I was approaching a bright light, which seemed to be at the far end of the corridor. As I drew nearer to the light I saw the most beautiful garden of golden daffodils. There was an ordinary wooden gate, and I could sense that there was someone standing at this, although I could not actually see anyone. I was not allowed to enter the gate and I could hear someone calling me back. I turned away from the gate very reluctantly, and heard someone calling my name, and then I felt someone's hand touch my face. I opened my eyes to find that it had been the nurse's voice I heard calling my name, and she was soothing my forehead. I have often wondered since what it would have been like to go through that gate, and indeed at the time I had a strong longing to do so. Only for the fact that I had just given birth to my baby son, I didn't.'

Flowers of all descriptions are seen at the Borderland. Ann Barrett from Kent, remembers what happened when she was attending a memorial service in the Crematorium Chapel at Charing in Kent. 'A very dear friend called Marguerite was being cremated. I was alone, but there were many mourners there. I was singing a hymn, and suddenly I wasn't there at all. I was standing in an open doorway looking across a lovely field fringed with trees. It appeared to be high summer, and the grass in the field was a vivid shade of green, lush, about six to nine inches high, and covered in marguerites. I could see every individual flower moving although, of course, there were hundreds and hundreds. Suddenly, breathlessly, I was back in the pew in the chapel, still singing, but we were about four lines of the hymn further on.

'I gave a quick glance round, but all was just the same as I had left it.

'This all happened several years ago, but the beauty, clarity and fresh perfection of every detail has not faded in the slightest. I have always lived in the country, but I have never seen a field like this before or since.'

Another example of an out-of-the-body experience during childbirth comes from Christine of Bedford, who found herself going down a dark tunnel, at the end of which was a light. 'I entered into this light and found myself in a most beautiful area of grass and trees, which was so peaceful and welcoming. The colours were so much more vivid and clear than anything I have seen before. Suddenly, I appeared to be above my body, hovering on the ceiling, watching myself lying on the bed.'

A more elaborate description of the boundary territory comes from Olive Wright of Gateshead, Co. Durham. 'I was being transported at a tremendous speed through mid-air, then I found myself lying on a marble slab inside what looked like a brilliantly lit castle. As I looked up, there was a man wearing a sort of Roman-type clothing. He had a very concerned expression and he started to press down on my stomach. I looked around the room and I could see other men, similarly dressed, attending to other people who were also stretched out on slabs. As these men walked about, I could hear their footsteps echoing through the castle hall or whatever it was. The next thing I was back in my own bed.'

A woman from the north of England sent us the following account of what happened to her departed grandfather over a century ago.

'A miracle of prayer came to me in 1888 when I had the ordeal of seeing my own body and coffin and thanks to the Rev. Thomas Mason of Deptford Church, Sunderland, I am now 72 years and five months, and can still record what I went through in 1888.

'One day I came in from work and lay down on the sofa for a few minutes before dinner. All of a sudden everything went black – as if I was on a train entering a tunnel – and I felt as if I was floating upwards. I saw quite clearly my landlady come in, find me lying there and send for the doctor. He put his instrument on my chest, and actually wrote out my death certificate. The next thing I remember I was back in the tunnel where I was met by a guide, who was exactly in the form of a human being. He said to me, "Look neither to the right nor to the left, but follow me." And he led me on to a point of light I could see in the distance. But I could not restrain my curiosity and looked down on my left, where I saw an immense gulf filled with countless people, among whom I recognized quite clearly pals of mine who had already died.

'Suddenly we emerged on to a wide plain, whose beauty I cannot describe. There were grass and trees and flowers as on earth, but of no earthly loveliness. And from there I saw a city as of alabaster with towers and turrets, and a little door where only one might enter at a time. After prayer we entered, and inside I was at once greeted by my father and mother whom I had never known for they had died when I was very young.

'My guide led me towards the Figure and the crowd parted to make way for us. When we arrived before Him my guide stood aside, and Jesus received me into His arms and blessed me. Then Jesus turned back to my guide and said, "Take him back to earth until his work be done." And the guide took me back to the gate whereby we had entered and left me. Immediately all went dark again.

'I awoke on my bed, all bound up and with my arms crossed on my chest. By the fireside I clearly saw my coffin. The minister, who was beside, me, had seem a small vein throb in my forehead and had sent for the doctor. I then saw them desperately trying to hide the coffin from me – but it was too late.

'When I woke, I am told that I wept for two hours for the beauty I had left.'

TIMESLIPS

In the days before electric light was in common use a man called Frederick lay in bed, reading by the glow of a little candle which flickered on a small table by his bedside. He grew tired, put the candle out, and fell fast asleep. He had the most wonderful dream in which he saw himself as a little boy, running around his parents' home, playing make-believe battles with his toy soldiers. He relived his childhood days, step by step, through his schooling, then remembered how he had felt the first time he'd kissed his sweetheart.

As a young man Frederick was then called to action, and with a stout heart and a prayer he set off to fight in the Napoleonic Wars. No longer did he face tin soldiers; now it was for real. He remembered clearly the look of terror in the eyes of the first man he had ever killed, the man he had been indoctrinated to believe was his enemy. He looked just like any other human being, he did not appear evil or have two heads!

As the fatal blow was struck, the impact affected not only the victim. For years and years the face of that dying man haunted Frederick's mind. He tried hard to make sense of it all.

One day, shortly after he returned home safely from the war, he met a young girl called Florence. She had a sunny disposition and Frederick slowly but surely fell deeply in love with her. He was overjoyed when he learnt that the feeling was mutual. He approached her father and formally asked for her hand in marriage. The happy event took place and the couple went off on their honeymoon to Sorrento on the west coast of Italy.

They were out one afternoon walking and enjoying the sights when Frederick's hat blew off. Florence's instant reaction was to run after it. Just as she reached out, the hat disappeared over the edge of a deep chasm. Frederick's heart missed a beat as he watched his beloved Florence stumble and lose her balance. With every ounce of energy he could muster he threw himself forward and landed bodily on top of Florence's legs, pinning her to the ground. She froze with fear as the entire top half of her body hung over the edge of the fissure. Onlookers came quickly to the rescue and pulled Florence up to safety. Frederick held her in his arms until she stopped shaking.

Shortly after they returned from Italy, Frederick was given a partnership in his uncle's firm, running a small newspaper, and he was able to buy Florence a beautiful house in Richmond, Surrey, near to the banks of the Thames. Life was beautiful and they were deliriously happy. Nothing could be more wonderful, thought Frederick, until Florence came to him, beaming radiantly with the news that she was expecting a baby'

Little Susannah came into the world on a bleak December day, just before Christmas. Frederick always remembered that first Christmas with his new daughter as one of the most wonderful, peaceful times in his life. Other children followed, three sons and another daughter.

The boys were very different in character, but Philip, the middle son, always displayed a marked flair for business. All of the boys were educated at Eton, went on to University and followed different careers. The eldest son went into medicine and became a general practitioner, the youngest became an accountant, and Philip followed in his father's footsteps, helping to run the newspaper.

Frederick's two daughters married and settled down. The youngest girl lived with her husband and son in a comfortable apartment, quite near to him in Richmond. Susannah, the light of his life, had married a lecturer, who had secured an enviable post at Edinburgh University. It saddened his heart the day she moved north of the border, but he always enjoyed the trips to see her. He particularly remembered the family outing to Loch Lomond, the sparkling waters of the loch, the towering majesty of Ben Lomond, the vivid purple of thousands upon thousands of foxgloves and the perfume of the heather.

Florence was his constant companion through the trials and tribulations of his life, for as well as the good times, Frederick had suffered his fair share of problems like everybody else. The most crashing blow came when his creditors united and took legal action, forcing him into bankruptcy and throwing his life into chaos. Only for the devotion and support of Florence and his children, Frederick doubted if he would live through this crippling ordeal.

One day, in the midst of his gloom, he received the news that he had been left a fair sum of money in a will. An aunt on his mother's side had passed away and, to his great surprise, she had remembered him in a most generous way.

That night, for the first time in months, Frederick was able to sleep soundly in his bed. But after falling asleep something made him jump. He opened his eyes to find that he was still holding his book in his hands. He glanced to the side of his bed and in the bright moonlight he could see the thin column of smoke rising from the candle which he had

271

extinguished only *moments* beforehand.

The above story illustrates how time can play tricks with our minds. Because we associate the passing of time with events, we could be in danger of living in a delusion, a total misrepresentation of the true concept of time.

Because we live in the three dimensional world of gross matter, it is almost impossible for our material brains to deal with events which spring from a non-material world of more than three dimensions. If we could free ourselves from thinking of time in the normal way, subject to the tick of the clock, perhaps we could then make sense of the many accounts of people who have suddenly found themselves cast into what they describe as a timeslip.

Mrs. Sally Vinson of Waltham Abbey in Essex had the most strange experience when she travelled through France some years ago with two friends. They were on their way to Morocco, and not having much money they slept in farmhouses rather than hotels.

They came to a small town in the Garonne Valley not far from Toulouse. They would shortly be crossing the border into Spain, so their first thought was to find a bank or a bureau to change their money into Spanish currency. Sally spotted a policeman, ran up to him and explained in her best broken French what her problem was.

'The policeman seemed to understand what I wanted. He pointed towards a rather quaint looking small hotel and told me to enquire at the reception desk, and they should be able to change the money.

'I waved to my two friends and the three of us started to walk towards the hotel, which was across a square of paving stones. The oddest thing happened as we moved towards the hotel. I felt myself hovering about six inches up in the air. I was stunned at how I did not fall over. I didn't know what on earth was happening. I looked at my two friends and instantly I could see by the startled looks on their faces that they too were experiencing something most strange. They also had the sensation floating.

'It was so sudden and unbelievable that I think we were beyond fear, or perhaps we were reacting directly to fear because all three of us started to laugh. When I think about it now it was probably some sort of nervous reaction, although we were not actually aware of feeling afraid. I suppose if I had been on my own I would have been terrified out of my mind, but because the others were sharing the experience it somehow struck us as being hysterically funny because we just couldn't understand what was happening.

'The odd thing was that all three of us were able to communicate between ourselves in the normal way, so we knew that all of us had the feeling of floating. We were tickled by the fact that we did not need to take steps in order to move, we just seemed to glide forwards. The more this went on the more uncontrollable our laughter became. I could feel tears of mirth running down my cheeks. I remember remarking to one of my friends that if anyone was watching us they would think we were lunatics. Even this simple remark seemed to send us into convulsions of giggles. I think we were imagining how we must look to anyone passing by.

'We reached the hotel and entered. No-one was at the reception desk. We all noticed that the decor was very old-fashioned, but that did not strike us as particularly out of the ordinary because lots of little hotels in France have an old world feel to them.

'We rang the bell on the counter, but no-one came to see what we wanted. By this time we had calmed down slightly, but we still had the sensation of floating. I think we were slowly becoming acclimatized to the condition. After waiting a few moments longer, we decided to have a wander around the hotel to see if we could find anyone who could change our money.

'Just adjacent to the end of the counter was a wide staircase. We walked up the stairs, or should I say floated, and when we got to the top we followed a long corridor which had several windows with coloured glass in them. There was a strange bright light in this corridor, much too bright to have come from the windows. I remember thinking that normally stained glass windows only cast a dim glow, even when strong sunlight shines through them, but this was no ordinary light, as it did not appear to come from any particular direction, and I could not see any shadows, the light just seemed to come from nowhere and everywhere.

'As we moved along the corridor, we could see ahead of us now there was a long landing which went off to the left. At the point where the landing branched off there was a huge mirror, which reached right up to the ceiling. As we approached the mirror, we could see the reflection of our corridor. It looked very long, as if it were going on forever. We kept advancing towards this mirror in a very relaxed state of euphoria. I distinctly remember saying the words "Curiouser and curiouser" because the mirror reminded me of Alice in Wonderland. It was only when I heard the sound of my voice that I seemed to snap out of the malaise with a jerk. I screamed at my two friends, "There's no reflection!" We were almost on top of the mirror, yet there was no reflection of our bodies whatsoever.

'The very next instant our reflections flashed on to the surface of the mirror, just as we were about to smash into it. I don't know how we didn't have a terrible accident. My foot must have only been a fraction away from the glass. It was the most weird thing I've ever seen in my life, the way the three reflections suddenly loomed back at us in that flash. My friends said that they both saw it in exactly the same way.

'By this time all the laughter had gone, and we were all quite afraid. We just stood there for a few moments, very shaken. We all had the same thought uppermost in our minds, what would have happened if I had not spoken out loud and broken the spell, or whatever it was. We wondered if we really would have been able to step right back through that mirror and into some other dimension.

'When we realized that we all now had our feet firmly back on the ground, we decided to forget about changing our money. All we wanted to do was to get out of that place as quickly as possible. We then became aware of the fact that everything was perfectly silent. There were no sounds of any description, apart from our own voices. Somehow it was not a natural quiet, but something more eerie. We looked at each other, then all of us started to run back down the corridor.

'I'm not quite sure exactly what happened at this point, but I think we must have passed the entrance to the top of the staircase leading down to the ground floor. Anyway, we came to a room with wide open double doors. We were absolutely petrified when we looked inside and saw five or six very old ladies sitting inside, all doing embroidery. They were all dressed from head to toe in black and each of them wore a black lace bonnet.

'One of the old ladies saw us, then she beckoned to her companions and they all turned and stared at us. Their faces were white with fear and there was terror in their eyes. Whatever it was about me and my friends seemed to scare the wits out of them. Mind you, we were just as terrified ourselves.

'The three of us took off as fast as we could to try to find the way out of the hotel. Eventually we found a different staircase and got out into the street. We were all in a dreadful state of shock. Needless to say, we moved out of the town as fast as we could. That night we were still afraid and nervous of every building, so we decided to sleep out in the open. We were thankful when we crossed the border into Spain. When I think back to that experience I can't help wondering if we were caught up in a time-warp of some description.'

Mrs. Trenchard of Falmouth in Cornwall had a strange experience when one day she floated out of her body. Completely out of the blue, she found herself in a fairly large room which she had never seen before. She could not understand how she got there and had no recollection of a journey.

'There were bare boards on the floor and in the middle of the room there was a smallish rug, rather faded. There was furniture around the sides of the room, rather indistinct, the middle of the room being bare. I looked down at my feet and I was amazed to find myself suddenly wearing roller skates. "This is crazy," I thought to myself, "I don't wear roller skates. I never even wore them as a child, how ridiculous!" However, I then found myself starting to skate up and down the boards and rug.

'My mind was very alert. I said to myself that I will always remember this as everything seemed so real and vivid. The lightness of my body gave me such a lovely feeling, and I smiled as I realized that my bad foot, which had always given me much trouble, was now at perfect ease, despite the fact that I was skating up and down.

'I was intrigued to find that the rug in the middle of the floor did not hamper the skating and in fact there did not seem to be any friction at all, as the skates just glided over the floorboards and rug. I skated backwards and forwards several times, thoroughly enjoying myself, thinking how fantastic it was.

'I have to explain something before I come to the next part of the story; my mother, who was a good pianist, had a Bechstein grand piano. When she grew old and could no longer see well enough to play, the piano was sold to a neighbour who was an acquaintance of mine, but I had never been inside her bungalow.

'From the roadway, this woman's place looked so small that one would have thought that there would be no room for a grand piano inside. Apparently she had a large basement which I did not know existed, since it was below the level of the road.

'Shortly after I had experienced the skating, I was walking past this woman's bungalow, and she happened to be standing at her front door. She called out to me and said, "Thelma, do come in and see your mother's piano. We've had it restored. We spent £80 on it and it looks like new."

'I went in and was shown down to the basement. Immediately my blood ran cold as I recognized the floorboards and the faded rug. It gave me quite a shock. I said,

"What a lovely big room you have." "Yes," she said, "When my grandchildren were small we used to clear the furniture to the side and they used to skate in here."

A lady from Stevenage had a dream that she was alone in a very big rambling house. She knew that she was waiting to let the gas man in to read the meter. At the time she had the dream she was single, but in this dream she was engaged to a young dark-haired man. In reality she knew no such person.

About ten years later, she met a man at a party and became quite attracted to him. There was something vaguely familiar about him, but she could not quite pinpoint exactly what it was or where she might have seen him. They went out together for a few months and soon realized that they had fallen in love. They became engaged and they decided to look for a small flat in Margate on the south coast of Kent, as his family lived down there, although at the time they both lived in London.

On the first flat-hunting session in Margate, they naturally arranged to visit the man's parents as she had not yet been introduced to the family. They were invited to dinner, but when they got to the house they found a note on the narrow window ledge and a key. The note was from the man's mother, informing him that she would be back later, but would he let himself in. Also, would he mind showing the gas man where the meter was, as she had received a card from the gas board, informing her that someone would be calling to check the meter that day.

As soon as she stepped into the house, everything came flooding back to her. It was the exact same house of which she had dreamt all those years before. A further thought then struck her. She turned and looked at her fiancé's face.

Yes! It was the same man! Now everything clicked into place. That's why she felt that there had been something familiar about him on their first meeting.

'I was quite taken aback when I realized that the details were so exact, right down to the business about letting in the gas man. In my dream I never saw the gas man arrive as I woke up before that happened, but I've often wondered if it would have been the same man who, just a few minutes later, knocked on the door and came in to check the meter.

'I truly believe that I was meant to meet my fiance. We have since married and are very happy. We both believe that there must be something in the old saying that marriages are made in Heaven, at least we're sure ours was.'

Some years ago, when she lived in central London, Mary Harrison, the co-author of this book, had a strange dream which took her back in time to the days of Bonnie Prince Charlie and the Battle of Culloden.

'I was in a small boat with Peter and an elderly white haired man whom I'd never seen before. He was dressed in what could only be described as a long navy overall, which was wrapped around him and secured by a belt or cord around the waist. The water was quite shallow and, as the tiny boat drifted towards the side bank, we all got out. There were two tall, thin evergreen trees by the bank and as I stepped out of the boat, to the right, there stood a big mansion house, with a flight of steps leading up to a large front door.

'We all started walking towards the house. Nothing was said at this point. We walked up the stairs and the man opened the door. We entered the house, which was completely unknown to me. I remember thinking how elegant and grand it looked. We walked across a large hall area, and proceeded up a flight of steps. After a few steps my attention became attracted by the bannister. Because the staircase was wide, I somehow or another expected it to be of polished wood. I was quite surprised to see that the handrail was, in fact, covered with what I took to be red and white brocade material. I stopped and looked over at this as it made such a strange impression upon me, making me curious to find out why there should be such an unusual covering over the broad handrail.

'At that point, the elderly man who, with Peter, had been walking a few steps ahead of me up the staircase, came back down to where I was standing. He too looked across at the bannister and said, "You are interested in this, let me show you." With that he took my arm and led me over to inspect the handrail. To my horror, as I moved nearer, I realized that what I thought was a red and white pattern was actually blood stains. When I looked closely I could see that the white part was made up of lots and lots of bandages. It was as if masses of blood-stained bandages had been wrapped around and around the length of the handrail.

'The man could see that I was shocked. He said, "These are the bandages from the Battle of Culloden. If you look closely, you will see the names of the people who were killed, and alongside their names it states the type of weapon which killed them." I studied the material, and I could distinctly see lots of names, written in what looked like faded navy blue ink. The entries appeared on the white section of the cloth, but always alongside a bloodstain. I could not make out what was written, but there were about three or four lines of writing for each different name.

'I remember the overwhelming feeling of sorrow that

280

engulfed me at that moment. I looked up and down the bannister at the dozens and dozens of names. In that one instant I felt the grief of all those families and the pain surrounding each of those faded names.

'The man then pulled me away from the side of the staircase, saying, "Don't look at it too much, we've got to go now." He guided me up the stairs to a landing from which the stairway branched out at either side close to each wall, turning back in the opposite direction, leading up to the next floor. Along this landing against the far wall there was a row of what looked like old fashioned tailor's dummies. Each one was dressed in a different tartan, representing the different clans which fought in the Battle of Culloden. I turned to the left and by the far wall there was an oak panelled door. I stretched out my hand to open this door, but I never found out what was on the other side because at that point I woke up.

'The dream was so clear that I, of course, related it to Peter there and then.. After that there came a stream of coincidences. A few days later I opened a book which I had just got out from the Marylebone Library entitled *The Mask of Time, The Mystery Factor in Timeslip, Precognition and Hindsight*, by Joan Forman (Corgi). I was casually looking down the acknowledgements page, when I suddenly spotted "The Culloden Trust". I was immediately interested to see what this was about. It led me to a particular story in that book which told of how a woman from East Anglia had travelled to Scotland on a coach tour. They reached the battlefield of Culloden on a warm, sunny August afternoon. The crowd got out of the coach and started to eat their sandwiches.

'Suddenly, the sky clouded over and became grey, damp

and misty. The woman could not see any of her companions, but instead she was faced with a solitary hawthorn tree. There were no leaves on the tree but, blowing in the breeze, draped from the branches, she could see long, white, blood-stained bandages. She stared hard at this peculiar sight, then she heard a voice telling her, "These are the bandages from the Battle of Culloden."

'The next instant the tree and the bandages disappeared and the woman could hear the chatter of her friends and one more she felt the warming rays of the sun!'

Mary was struck by this, especially as the words which the woman heard were identical to those which the old man said to her in her dream.

'I had never been to Culloden, not had I any particular link with that part of Scotland. I remembered having been told about the battle at school, and I do admit that in the history lessons there was something about Culloden which always upset me more than any other event. In fact, I remember, as a little girl, trying to hide my face with my hands when the teacher spoke to us about the massacre, so that no-one would see that I was crying. But all of that was years ago, and I had not even given it a thought since then.

'The next thing that happened was a small package was delivered by post. I almost fainted when I opened it to find a brochure with a picture of a huge mansion house on the front and the words "Culloden House". This was within a week of my dream. Because we had been thinking of buying an hotel, we had approached a few agents and by a strange turn of fate, Culloden House, which unbeknown to me had been converted into an hotel, was on the market.

'I'd never seen Culloden House, or even a photograph of it, up to that point. I stared at the mansion, and it looked exactly like the house I'd seen in my dream when I'd stepped out of the boat. I was sure in my mind that it must be the same house, with the flight of stone steps leading up to the front door.

'I opened up the brochure and there were a few small photographs inside which did not really convey much to me.

'Eventually, some time later, I telephoned Culloden House, as I could not get the dream out of my head. By this time, it had been bought by an hotelier. I was somewhat apprehensive when I first spoke to the proprietor on the phone, as I was not at all sure what I was going to say, or what his reaction would be.

'After the initial niceties, I explained that although it was probably going to sound a bit daft, I just wanted to verify what the interior of the house looked like. I told him about the lake and the trees, the outside of the house and the staircase, also how it branched off into two other side flights of stairs, going up by the side walls. He listened patiently and did not laugh. At that point I did not mention anything about the bandages, I simply wished to find our the layout of the house.

'He confirmed that there had been a shallow lake at the front of the house and, in fact, the two tall trees were still there. He told me that the large hallway was correct, also the elaborate staircase, but there the similarity ended because the stairs did not branch out and go up by the side of each wall, as I explained had happened in the dream.

'I thanked him for his information and remarked that it must be a weird coincidence. However, two nights later, I received a telephone call from Culloden House. The owner had been so intrigued by my query that he had gone to his local planning department, and had been allowed to see the plans for when the original old house had been extended.

'"You were right," he told me excitedly. "The original stairs did branch out exactly as you described, but when they extended the property, they partitioned one of the staircases off. Also, the door on the landing did exist."

'It was with mixed feelings that I received this news. It was not exactly a surprise as I seemed to "know" inwardly that these stairs did exist at some time in the past in precisely the same way as I saw them.'

THE DECISION

In almost any account of out-of-the-body travel, the person reports that at some point they are faced with a decision. To many, this was the most important decision of their lives, in fact they feel it was a definite choice between life and death.

Mrs. Radnell of Nottingham was so concerned about her children that she made the conscious decision to try to get back into her body. She says, 'In the summer of 1983 I fell asleep whilst lying on my side on the settee; I had my arms folded at the time. Having slept normally for some time I awoke and found I was drifting into one of my "sleep paralysis" states. I tried not to panic, and thought if I could just move an arm, I would be O.K. But, unfortunately, I had my arms folded and this made it doubly difficult. Just when I thought my arms were unfolding, I found instead that I sort of "peeled" out of my body. The next moment I was standing by the gas fire, which was directly in front of the settee. To describe the terror and panic I felt is impossible; it is something I will never forget.

'I knew my body was back on the settee, but I just didn't dare look. I felt very distressed because I realized that the children would find the body on the settee, would think it was "me" and this would break their hearts. There would be no way of communicating to them, or anyone else, that I was perfectly O.K. I really believed I was dying on the settee, and I was panic stricken. Just as I was thinking, "Oh, no I'm dying", the thought came into my mind, "No, not dying, out of the body," but it was as if another mind had locked into mine and so closely was it overlapping, that grammatical sentences were not necessary. However, I saw no-one nor had I any mystical experience.

'What I did notice was that I could think and feel things at an incredibly fast speed, so that whilst I was wondering who I might see, I could also think, "What do I look like?" "What is the time?" etc. I did notice that I had no concept of time, and had no idea of where the children were. Also, I felt very flat and flimsy and sort of "whole" – by this I mean that I felt I could form arms and legs if I wanted to, because I considered the idea of lifting an "arm" to see what it looked like, but I chickened out!

'I think the biggest impact the experience had on me was to realize that I was exactly the same person as I am in the body, and this pleased and reassured me. I even noticed I could swear if I wanted to (something I do far too much of).

'Another thing I noticed was that I felt vulnerable and unprotected without my "shell" and soon wanted to be back "inside". I remember praying something like, "Oh God, (expletive) I don't want this," and the second I thought this I began travelling backwards towards my physical body. I could feel a tremendous sucking sensation in the region of my "ethereal" cheeks and I travelled back very quickly. In front of me, but not part of me, was a whirling circular shaped object, made of a sort of vapour (I could see the bookcases through it). Soon I was back in the body, jolted upright with a start and feeling very shaken.

'I told my husband what had happened but, like most people, he was sceptical and said I had dreamt it. But to me it was very, very real. I am willing to tell anyone if it can bring comfort to those who think they have "lost" their loved ones, in order to reassure them that we do survive physical death.'

A new-born baby was the incentive for Mrs. Bartlett of Birmingham to return. She remembers floating just below the ceiling in the corner of the room, looking down on the scene below, where medical staff were attending to her physical body. 'I was feeling warm and peaceful, and could see the bright sunlight which attracted me forward. There were soft country sounds and I felt I must be on holiday. I watched the figure on the bed with all the people around her. I then looked down beneath me at the tiny baby in the cot. I felt as if I'd shouted out, "Why that's me down there. I can't leave that baby there – she's mine. I must get back!" The sun faded away and it all went black. Someone was calling my name. When I awoke, it was night, and no-one was there but my sister-in-law, holding a cup to my mouth.

'I was told afterwards that the doctors had worked on me for over two hours and did not expect me to survive.'

Chris Broad of Newcastle has built up an understandable apprehension regarding the medical profession. He has had two out-of-the-body experiences, but he is very glad he made the decision to come back both times.

'The first occasion I was about twelve years old when I was knocked off my pedal cycle by a doctor in a car. I clearly recall being about telegraph pole height and seeing the crowd. At first I did not notice it was me down there but I recognized my cycle and when I saw myself I could not be sure what to do – go up or come down. I was so happy. Then I thought of my family, mother, father, brother, sister, and how upset they would be, so down I came, into my body. It was like putting on a boiler suit! Honestly, I can still feel the sensation of climbing into it. Then, in a flash I was back and on the ground, with all these faces looking down at me, so I got up amid gasps and staggered to my cycle.

'The second occasion was similar. I was thirty-six when I was knocked off my motor-cycle – again by a doctor in a car! Then I thought of my wife and four young children. I was happy up there but I knew I had to get back for their sakes. They needed me and I wanted to see them grow up. So, down I came. Again it was like putting on a boiler suit. I could see the crowd from above and two damaged cars, my crushed motor-cycle and myself in black motor-cycle clothing on the road. I found it amusing when I went down. I thought I will surprise the crowd!

'Both times though, it was a very pleasant and wonderful feeling. I was tempted to go higher because I felt so free and happy – the hurt came when I returned! If I do have another out-of-the-body experience I think I will go higher out of curiosity.

'I am very happy with my life and pleased that I came back. I am trying to avoid any doctors driving cars!'

It was the love of her husband which was the trigger which enabled Mrs. Cumberledge (a first cousin of Enid Blyton) of Eastbourne in Sussex to return. 'One lovely summer's day I had just come home from my work in a dress shop. It was my half-day and I was feeling fed up. I went up to bed and thought, "I wish I could go to sleep and not wake up." Well, I woke up out of my body. I checked the time by tne clock at the side of the bed – nearly 3.45 p.m. I was not frightened or alarmed, but I was concerned, knowing what my thoughts had been. Now I thought while checking the time, "I'm dead!" I thought of what a shock it would be for my husband who would be home around 5.20 p.m. "Well," I thought, "I've got from 3.45 to 5.20 to work out how I'm going to get back." Then I looked at myself lying in bed and thought, "I must get back." Then, back I was. I checked the clock to find that only a few seconds had passed.'

The conviction that she was choking frightened a lady from Toddington, Bedfordshire, back down into her body. 'I floated out of my body and right out through the open window. It was light and I remember quite distinctly that I was "floating" in a sitting or curled up position (perhaps the embryonic position). There were long, thin gardens all divided by tall hedges on either side. I floated up the gardens, having to rise slightly over each hedge. I remember wondering if I put my legs out straight if they would scrape on the hedges – but I never tried it.

'I'd got about ten houses up when I had the most urgent, choking, cold feeling that I had to get back. I felt like I'd come out in a cold sweat. I sped back, bouncing over the fences, rushed through the windows, and no hanging about, shot over to my sleeping body, when I instantly woke up, puffed, heart beating fast – I was quite convinced that if I'd not got there in time, my body would have been dead. It was an incredible sense of relief I'd made it. I didn't want to be shut out."

In his book *Reach for the Sky* (Collins, hardback, 1954; Fontana, paperback, 1969), Paul Brickhill relates how the famous Second World War air ace Group Captain Douglas Bader was faced with a similar decision. He had an odd experience while in hospital after losing his legs in a flying accident. It did not occur to him that he had been dying until after he had made his decision.

Later the young man woke and the pain had gone. He could not feel his body at all, but for some reason his mind was perfectly clear. He lay still, eyes open and head raised on a pillow, looking straight out through the top of the window at a patch of clear blue sky, and into his mind crept a peaceful thought: 'This is pleasant. I've only got to shut my eyes now and lean back and everything's all right.' Warm peace was stealing over him, his eyes closing and his head seeming to sink into the pillow. It did not occur to him that he was dying; only that he was letting go, drifting down and wanting to. In a dreamy haze the mind was shrinking into a soft, deep pinpoint.

Through the slightly open door of the room a woman's disembodied voice slid into the receding clarity: 'Sssh! Don't make so much noise. There's a boy dying in there.'

The words quivered in him like a little electric shock that froze the drifting dream and sparked a sharp thought: 'So that's it. Hell, am I!' Feeling began flickering out through his body like ripples from a pebble tossed in a pool. He stopped letting go and the mind was clearing; the body did not move but the brain began gripping thought and reality. It was the challenge that stirred him...

As he lay thinking, quite clear-headed, the pain came back to his leg. Somehow he did not mind this time; it was almost satisfying because he felt he was normal again and had slipped away from the ethereal spirit that had been floating him to Limbo. Another thought came: 'I mustn't let that happen again. Apparently it wasn't as good as it felt.'

Some instinct told him that he had been dying in that moment. (Ever since then he has been convinced of it, and from that moment has never been frightened of dying. Later this was to have a vital effect on his life).

One of the most peculiar stories of decision making comes from a lady in Nottingham, who reports a weird administration problem in the afterworld.

'I was ill in hospital, just lying in bed, thinking of nothing in particular when I felt a "swoosh" and, to my amazement, I found myself hovering in mid-air above my hospital bed. I felt quite fine apart from being utterly puzzled at the fact that I could see myself lying in bed. I just couldn't understand what was happening to me. The next thing I knew, I was gently moving along the corridor outside the hospital ward. This corridor somehow or other turned into a narrow passage of extremely bright light. I began to feel uneasy at this stage, because I had lost sight of my physical body, and I had an overpowering feeling that I shouldn't really be in this passageway, although at that stage I was unable to stop myself moving forward.

'The end of the tunnel came into view in the form of an archway. I could not see anyone but I sensed that someone was standing there.

'I distinctly heard a woman's voice saying, "Oh, just a moment, we only wanted two. We've got one already and anyway it's not time for you at the moment." Again the woman's voice stated, "We've got one already!" Then the voice added in a most apologetic tone, "Would you mind going back?"

'As soon as I heard her say that, I thought about the hospital ward. I started to feel worried about what the sister would say to me for being away so long. I began to wonder what I would tell them, and then I convinced myself that I was in for a right telling-off for wandering away like that. I don't remember anything at all about what happened next, except waking up in my bed in the early hours of the morning. I could hear a man's voice out in the corridor. He sounded most distressed as he explained to the nurse that he had received an urgent call to come into the hospital because his mother had died.

'I've often wondered to myself if that poor man's mother was the "other" person that the woman at the arch awaited. Somehow they got me instead, but sent me packing as it were!

'Since that experience, I have no fear of death whatsoever, because I've seen what lies ahead and it is truly beautiful.'

THE SILVER CORD

Many poems and songs refer to the Silver Cord, or the Golden Thread or the Cord of Light. Different names have been given to this part of ethereal matter which connects the astral body, which contains the soul, to the physical body.

In most reports of out-of-body travel, people are so disorientated by the different conditions into which they have been hurled that they do not notice anything connecting them with their physical bodies which they can see, either lying on a bed, walking or setting on a chair, etc. It takes some moments for consciousness to become accustomed to the change. The first, and most impressive, perception which the wandering spirit experiences is the feeling of weightlessness. After living for years and years in the heavy material world of gross matter, suddenly the spirit escapes from the restraints of gravity. The result of this is the almost unbelievable feeling that the entire being is as light as a feather, just floating effortlessly.

Most people remember this as a delightful experience, comprised of a strange mixture of exhilaration and peace. The material body is without senses at this point, all the perception and feeling being contained in the released spirit body.

As you can imagine, this sudden change in vibrations, coupled with having to adapt to totally different laws of creation, overpowers the spirit so much that it is not altogether surprising that some factors of this new experience may be overlooked by the awe-struck spirit consciousness.

Nevertheless, some people have observed the connecting cord between their hovering spirit bodies and their physical shells.

A lady of Northampton describes what happened to her husband. 'One night when we were in bed, I woke up. He was holding on to me so tightly that I could hardly breathe. When I asked him what was the matter, he said that he had been "frightened that he couldn't get back". I asked him what on earth he was talking about, then added, "It must have been a dream." He was adamant that it had not been a dream and that he had left his body and was floating around the room in mid-air. He told me that he could see himself but that he was attached to his solid body by a fine thread. He was very afraid.

'He could see the thin thread coming from the part of him that was floating, going towards and connecting with his physical body lying beside me on the bed. He was terrified that the thread might somehow get broken and he was convinced that if that happened then he would never get back into his body. He was sure that he would be dead to this world.

'To be honest, I have to admit that it all sounds totally ridiculous, doesn't it? I've not spoken about it to anyone because they would probably think we were both barmy.'

A somewhat similar story comes from Janet White of Southampton. She remembers that when her daughter was being born, she drifted out of her body and, from high up in the corner of the room, she found herself looking down on the nurses in the delivery room. 'It was a wonderful, strange feeling. I seemed to have a fine thread holding me to my body. I remember being fascinated by this thread, and as I moved, or should I say floated, the thread seemed to stretch with me. It must have been made of an elastic-type material, which could stretch as far as I cared to make it. When I floated down nearer to my body, the thread just shortened accordingly. It was the strangest thing I ever saw in my life. I had all my reasoning powers with me up there and as I looked down upon the scene below, I was perfectly aware of the fact that I was in the process of giving birth. Although I could comprehend this; I did not, for some reason, feel particularly affected. The overpowering thought that seemed to take over my mind completely was the fact that all the horrible pain had gone. I had been lying on that delivery bed in unbearable agony just a few seconds ago, and now look at me. No pain or discomfort whatsoever. In fact, it was the exact opposite, I'd never felt better or more happy in my life.

'I then felt myself being drawn slowly back down towards the bed. As I hovered just a few feet above, I seemed to be able to pass right through the bodies of three nurses who were attending to me. I remember feeling most apologetic for having "bumped into them", and I was expecting them to be a bit annoyed but, to my surprise, they did not react in any way. They completely ignored me as if I didn't exist, and they didn't seem to feel a thing when I was knocking into them on my way back down to my body.

'I could see one of the nurses slapping my face. I was taken aback by this and wondered why she should do such a thing. Then, as if far away in the distance, I heard the words "Come on, come on, it's all over now, come on." The words got louder in my ears and made me open my eyes. I knew that I was now back in my physical body. The nurse was still slapping my face. It was then I heard the cries of a baby. "It's a lovely little girl" the nurse told me, and I fully realized that my baby had just been born.

'A great gush of love washed over me and I couldn't wait to hold my baby. I stretched out for her and the tiny little bundle was placed in my arms. As I looked adoringly down at the little pink face and the mop of golden hair, which was still matted with blood, I remember wondering how I could have felt so indifferently towards her whilst I was out of my body. Maybe it was because at that point I had not actually seen her. All I could do was hug her and look at her in wonderment. At that moment I truly felt that she was worth all the pain and suffering I had just gone through, and I would not have changed it for the world.'

Yet another version of how the cord has been witnessed comes from a lady who had a dream that she awoke in what she thought was a morgue.

'I was lying on a marble slab, but I felt completely fit and well, and I could not understand why I should be there. I'd seen such places in films and I remember thinking that only dead people are brought to places like this. I grew more and more uneasy as my mind started to run riot, and I got frightened in case I should be put in a freezer or sent to a crematorium. I started to call out, but there was no sign of anyone. I then started to panic, calling out as loud as I could, "I'm not dead, I'm not dead." I sat up on the slab and got the shock of my life when I spotted just further along that there was another marble slab and another version of me. It was like looking at a twin, but I never had a twin. I sat up as much as I could to have a better look. I noticed that the other me was quite ashen looking and lay silent and still.

295

'By this time I was in a state of complete confusion. I genuinely thought that the other "me" must really be dead. I called over to the other body, "Merle, are you all right?" It was an odd feeling, because I knew that I was talking to myself, but it became more and more disturbing because the other Merle did not seem to hear me calling and made no response whatsoever.

'In the back of my mind I had a recollection of the old saying that when people start to talk to themseles, that is the first sign of madness. I thought about this and wondered to myself whether or not I really might be going mad. But then I calmed down a bit when I considered that I was still able to think in a clear rational way, surely mad people couldn't do this.

'What I could not come to grips with was the fact that the thinking me, the real me, felt quite natural and alive. What was disrupting my logical mind was this other "me".

'I decided that the only way I would ever find out what was going on would be to take a closer look. I eased myself off the marble slab. This was not difficult to do because I just seemed to glide off with hardly any effort. I stood upright but I don't remember feeling my feet touch the floor. I was so light that I was literally standing on air, ridiculous as this may seem.

'As soon as I stood upright I noticed a long silver cord which connected me with my other body. I don't know how I never spotted it before. Perhaps it was because it appeared to come out of me in the same way as an umbilical cord attaches a baby to its mother.

'I then became aware of the presence of other people in this morgue, although I could not actually see them. I was so concerned about the Merle who was still stretched out motionless on the other slab, so I asked the people who I felt were present, "Is she all right?" They answered me, "Yes, she is all right."

'The answer came as a great relief to me, so I then proceeded to float above the marble slab. I experienced a tremendous uplifting feeling of well-being and I noticed that whenever I chose to move, I did not have to make any effort at all. It sounds quite incredible, but I only had to think of moving to any particular area and off I would float. It was as simple as that.

'The other thing that I found bewildering was that wherever I floated, the cord which connected me with my other body seemed to lengthen itself. It felt as if I could go as far as I like and this cord would still travel with me, stretching as far as it needed to stretch to allow me to move freely to where I wanted to go.

'The reverse also was true. When I moved nearer to the marble slab where my other body lay, the cord automatically reduced its length so that there was not any extra cord lying around which was not required.

'It reminded me of when I used to wind up my wool into balls for knitting. I had a little playful kitten at the time, and it delighted in unravelling the wool from the nearly made up balls. The only difference was that when my kitten drew out long stretches of wool, it would all lie in a jumbled up heap on the floor until I wound it all up again, whereas with this silver cord, it just fed itself back into my body, so that only what was required would be left out.

'I have never felt so much at peace with the world as when I had that dream, if it was only a dream. Sometimes, I wonder!'

A Newtownabbey lady was working as a weaver in a factory. 'It was very noisy, with twelve looms in three rows of four. One of the looms stopped, indicating a broken thread, so I leaned over to tie the thread in. I felt the strange sensation of drifting out of my body and then I floated up to the rafters.

'There was a wisp of silvery smoke between me and my body. I seemed to be travelling towards a light. In my head something said, "Not yet." I came back into my body with such a bang that I hurt by chest. Whilst I was up in the rafters I could not hear the looms. I remember looking around but no-one seemed to notice anything strange. There were no bruises afterwards, and I felt fine, but how I got up to these rafters still baffles me.'

The only experience the authors have had regarding the cord is when Mary had yet another one of her strange dreams.

'I found myself standing in a pleasant place which I did not recognize, but where I felt somehow or another at home. I could hear sounds of laughter and the general noises of people enjoying themselves.

'I was suddenly in the midst of my dead mother, father and aunt. They had bright, shining faces, all looked extremely happy and young. They all gave me the most tremendous welcome as if they were delighted to see me, but there was something of a novel feel to it all. I got the definite feeling that they knew something that I didn't. Being my usual inquisitive self, I asked them why they were all laughing in such a way. I might add that it was not in any way a jeering laughter, but more the type of laugh which one gives when one is faced with a sudden, but pleasant surprise. I suppose it can be compared to the laugh at the end of a joke which has a benevolent twist to the punch-line.

'Anyway, I knew perfectly well that something was taking place which I did not fully understand. It was so natural to be in the company of these beloved people that I was completely at ease, with no real reason to question anything except for the expression on my father's face. He always loved a joke and I recognized the impish twinkle in his eyes.

' "Come on, what are you up to?" I asked him. This question set him off into roars of laughter. My mother and aunt just laughed along with him, then I remember my mother giving my father a kind of familiar warning look, as if to say, "Don't tease her!"

'At that moment something drew my attention to the fact that something was shining behind me. I looked around quickly and saw what looked like a rope of luminous light somehow attached to me.

' "What's that?" I asked them. They stopped laughing and told me, "It's all right." I started to fidget and then tried to grasp this rope to free myself of it. At this point my mother became most alarmed and told me: "Stop pulling it. You need it. Everything is all right." My father put his hand out to stop me from trying to back away from the rope. My mother's words were solemn as she said, "She'll have to go back now!"

'As soon as she said these words I felt an enormous pull from behind as if I had been swooshed right off my feet and into the air. This happened so quickly that I did not even have time to say "Good-bye" to them as I was hurled away without warning.

'I've often thought about what might have happened if

I'd managed to free myself of that cord. I have the strong feeling that although my parents were thrilled to see me again they were, as usual, protecting me by sending me back to my life on this earth, to Peter and the children.'

COINCIDENCE

Have you ever tried to explain a coincidence? It is one of the most difficult tasks to undertake. Maybe there is no explanation which we can grasp with our material conscious brains, but nevertheless there must be an explanation.

It may be that because the experiences cover such a wide range, the explanation lies in more than one source. For example, some experiences may be the result of telepathy, others the manifestation of true extra-sensory perception, some may be down to pure chance, and others may be linked into our fate.

Instances of *déjà vu* have been experienced by most of us, whereby you may enter a room for the first time and immediately you have the strong feeling that you have been there before, in exactly the same circumstances with exactly the same people. Most people will go as far as to state that because the feeling of having done it all before was so unmistakable, they were able to foretell what was going to be said next, and by whom. These feelings do not seem to last for very long, and in all cases, it is impossible to recall when the previous 'visitation' to that particular room occurred.

There are various theories on *déjà vu*. It is thought that one eye takes in information and relays this to the brain slightly faster than the other eye. By the time the comparatively sluggish eye surveys the scene and makes a mental note of it, the work of processing the data has already been completed by the brain on the instructions sent to it by the eye which first viewed the scene. From this, therefore, follows the familiar feeling of having seen it all before. In this case it is not that you have experienced the scene twice, simply that the brain has been given the same message twice, once by each eye.

In some cases this could well be an explanation; however, the argument is eliminated when we hear of cases where people are walking up a street for the first time, but the surroundings are so familiar that they feel they have been there before. They even know what is going to be round the next corner. Now, because human eyes can't see round corners, there must be other factors at play in these cases. Could it be that during these flashes, the unsuspecting people have a flash of intuition whereby their ethereal bodies have been able to view the entire scene from a point above, this information has then been conveyed to the sub-conscious mind, which in turn transfers it to the conscious mind? It is a simple explanation and perfectly logical.

Mrs. Elizabeth Smith from Amersham in Buckinghamshire still cannot explain a coincidence which took place a few years ago, when she was sitting under the dryer at the local hairdresser's, leafing through some magazines and casually exchanging a few words with a woman sitting next to her, who was also having her hair dried. She had never seen this woman before in her life.

As Elizabeth turned the pages of the magazine she saw a photograph of a luxurious bathroom which she and the other woman admired.

'I then said that the grandest bathroom that I had ever encountered had been in an old house in Scotland, and not only were the bathroom fittings of an Edwardian grandeur, but there were tanks of fish in the room. I went on to tell the woman next to me that the house was now owned by my sister-in-law and her husband who is the factor (or estate manager) of a large estate in the north.

'My new-found friend stated that she too had known such a bathroom, and how spendid that one also had been. I explained where "my" house was, near Forres in Morayshire, and she said incredulously that it was precisely the same house about which she had been talking.

'It turned out that she had lived in that house during the war, when the house had been made available to accommodate war service families. She had lived in one of the smaller rooms at the back of the house.

'I don't know what the odds are on such a coincidence might be, extremely high, no doubt. In a sense, however, we both seemed to be approaching the subject by different paths in a logical way towards the incredible dénouement.' Mrs. Smith is a member of the Chesham Bois Women's Institute, but none of the other ladies at her branch can offer her an explanation.

Mr. Chris Smith of Long Eaton, Nottingham, remembers something which happened to him when he was serving with the Military Police, stationed at Edinburgh Castle. His room-mate, also serving with the Military Police, was a local man called Jock Cunningham. 'We had only been sharing the same room for a couple of weeks, but we got on fine and on our time off we used to walk down the Royal Mile to a little pub where we used to have a few drinks and a laugh with some of the locals.

'One night we got acquainted with two girls. We all seemed to spark off great together, so after a few drinks the girl I was with invited us back to her house somewhere on

303

the outskirts of Edinburgh. The four of us got one of those plum coloured corporation buses, and ended up somewhere at the back of beyond.

'After a couple of hours at the house, I could see that Jock was getting on well with his girl, but my girl got drunk and we had a trivial argument. I can't even remember what caused it now. Anyway, I was so cheesed off that I got up and left the house, not knowing from Adam where I was. It was the middle of the night and there was nobody outside in the street at all.

'I just walked and walked, trying to find a main road. At last I came to road signs pointing to Edinburgh, so I started walking along that road. For the first time in my life I thought I'd better try to hitch a lift or I could be walking all night. It was pouring rain at the time, which didn't help matters, and there was little or no traffic on the road.

'Eventually, a white Mercedes, left-hand drive, pulled up and the driver invited me to have a lift. He said that he never ever gives people lifts, but something made him pull up when he saw me. There was no particular reason, he added.

'He asked me where I was going, so I told him "The City Centre." He asked, "Whereabouts?" I told him that I had to get back to Edinburgh Castle. He then said, "Oh, you must be in the Army, what unit?" I replied, "Actually, it's the Military Police." He perked up when I said this and told me, "My son is stationed up there in the Military Police. You might know him, his name is Jock Cunningham."

'I could hardly believe my ears. When I think back on it, I keep pondering on how it could have happened, is this a true coincidence? It is the only time in my life I had ever tried to hitch a lift, Mr. Cunningham did not normally give lifts to people, and Edinburgh is a big city.'

304

A puzzling, but sad, story comes from a man in Luton. 'One Saturday in June I had closed my office and had decided to do some overtime to catch up with the filing and other paperwork. The time was approximately 1.15 p.m. Suddenly, for no reason at all, I fell off my chair. After I got over the initial surprise, I picked myself up off the floor and, of course, the first thing I did was to examine my chair. Everything was intact and I could not see how I had fallen. It was as if some force had knocked me right off the chair. I did not hurt myself unduly, apart from a bruise on the base of the spine, so it was not long before I was back at my desk, working through my papers.

'About half-an-hour later I received a telephone call from my niece who had been visiting us. She sounded petrified on the phone as she asked me to come home immediately. 'What's happened?' I asked. I was told that my little daughter, Sharon, had had a terrible accident, having fallen out of a window, and had been rushed to hospital. I ran from my office in a state of shock, and drove straight to the hospital. As soon as I saw my wife's tragic face I knew the dreadful truth, Sharon was dead. She had died in the ambulance on the way to the hospital. I was completely numb. The days and weeks which followed were like a living nightmare.

'It was a long time before I could bring myself to talk about my daughter, but one night while I was just sitting talking to my wife, something made me ask what time Sharon had fallen. My wife told me that it was exactly 1.15 p.m. because she was just about to serve lunch and she had looked at the clock just as she heard the scream.

'A cold shiver ran through me when I realized that it was precisely at 1.15 p.m. on that same day that I had unaccountably fallen off the chair in my office.

'Several months later on the first anniversary of Sharon's death, my wife and I were sitting quietly at home watching the television and feeling rather low (not unnaturally) when there was an almighty crash, followed by the sound of breaking glass. Sharon's photograph had fallen off the wall. Nobody had been anywhere near the photograph. It was most eerie. To this day I have never been able to understand it.

'We moved house shortly after that because there were too many painful memories there. Since moving nothing out of the ordinary has happened, but I've often thought of what could have caused these events to happen. Could it have been an attempt by my daughter to contact us?'

A gentleman from Wellingborough, Northamptonshire, was serving in the R.A.F. in the Second World War, when he was captured in the Far East. He and a group of fellow prisoners were being transported around the Spice Islands in a ramshackle wooden boat by their Japanese captors to form working parties on the myriad of small islands.

A field gun, with no elevation, was mounted on the bow of the vessel. 'Suddenly we saw something silver, glinting as it flew out of the sun. It was a four-engined aircraft. We knew it was an Allied plane because the Japanese didn't have any four engined planes.

'The Japanese sergeant, who was in charge, ordered the prisoners to wave at the rapidly-approaching aircraft, to show that we were not hostile. Now, this was in September 1944 and we had been prisoners since February 1942. We were clad only in a few rags, we were greatly emaciated and very deeply tanned. We must have appeared very strange to the Allied plane as we waved and cheered.

'The aircraft circled the wooden boat lower and lower,

trying to decide whether we were hostile. In the end, the Japanese gunner lost his nerve and fired the field gun. Of course, he had no hope of hitting the plane because the gun had no elevation.

'The plane flew away, turned and flew back, very low, at great speed, with cannons firing. The result was that the boat disintegrated completely, killing some eight Japanese and twenty prisoners. The survivors were thrown into the shark-infested waters of the Banda Sea, and had to swim for the shore of the nearest island.

'We remained on the island for a few days until a passing Japanese boat picked us up.

'Some years later, I attended a F.E.P.O.W. reunion, and was talking with an old friend of this incident. He told me that he had been drinking in a pub with some friends in Leytonstone, London. They were sitting at a table near to some men who were playing darts. My friend was relating this story, when one of the darts players visibly paled, and came over to their table. He asked if the plane had destroyed the boat near to New Guinea in September 1944. My pal replied that it had, and that he would like to meet the bastard responsible. The darts player slumped into a chair, saying, "Well, mate, you just have! I was the navigator on that flight." He explained that the pilot had not been sure if the boat was hostile, which was why he had been circling. He had just about decided that it was a boat-load of Allied prisoners, and was about to fly off when the Japanese gunner opened fire. Of course, he felt he had no option but to return the fire, with devastating results.'

Equally baffled is Mr. Harrison of Shorwell, Isle of Wight. 'This was a very strange experience of a coincidence which happened some years ago. It is not supernatural, but my wife and I thought it extraordinary.

'We had plans to move from Essex to the Isle of Wight, and because we would be moving to a larger house we needed extra furniture. We approached the firm of Redman & Hales of Hatfield Peverel, explained what we required, and they agreed to make the furniture for us.

'We decided to call to check the progress of the furniture making one day. Mr. Hales showed us an old watch upon which was engraved the words 'North Court, Isle of Wight'. Mr. Hales explained that he remembered me telling him that we were going to the Isle of Wight, and when he had picked the watch up in a sale a few days earlier, he recalled our conversation. That was what made him show me the watch, he just thought we might be interested.

'I replied, saying that I was not interested but amazed because North Court was the exact house which we had just bought. Mr. Hales told me that the watch was one of a verge movement, made by George Body in 1780 and was probably a gift to someone on the estate.'

FATE

The Tube

Deep in my eye I see a hole
I slowly change from man to mole
The more I do the more I find
Those buried questions in my mind.

As in a spiral tube it seems
With blowing wind and hazy beams
Like walking down a lamp lit street
No feelings come from hands or feet.

The tube seems large, it's huge to me
And still so dark, no floor to see
My body's gone – it's locked outside
Still in the tube, down I slide.

I journey on deep down I go
But just where to I still don't know
The whole new world is all around
And still no floor is to be found.

The sides grow wide like in a cave
My fear shows now I must be brave
I've come this far, I must go on
Through shadows, storms and raging sun.

Those sudden lights they hurt my eyes
Like comets lost deep in the skies
All around me doors appear
They look afar but feel so near.

And when I knock or open try
A sudden flash they're gone from eye
What's going on is this a game?
Open up – give me your name.

I move onto another door
Succeed with this I must for sure
Then as before it goes the same
Still no answer still no name.

I look around at every door
They're even on the roof and floor
And at the back I quickly see
There's one half open – swinging free.

I slowly creep up to this door
The buried secret's here for sure
But as I grab this open gate
I quickly feel I hold my fate.

Now what to do I must be sure
A sense of fear comes more and more
What happens if beyond I find
My fate and future in my mind.

Is it right to see this way
Or should it be from day to day
Dreams and hopes would be no more
Best I think is close the door.

And as I close the door up tight
All the others go from sight
I feel I've had a chance to see
What my future is to be.

And as I walk back through the street
All fields, so tidy, good, and sweet
From my visit to a world unknown
Fresh new thoughts and seeds I've sown.

I'm sure it's best never to find
Those hidden secrets in your mind
You never know I might just chance
To come again and take a glance.

Bob Anthony
Woodhall Spa
Lincolnshire

Bob Anthony was inspired to write 'The Tube' just a few
hours after he suffered a heart attack. 'I lay there in bed and
suddenly I saw what I could describe as a tube. I noticed
that my feet were not on the floor any more and I was
travelling or gliding down this tube. It was windy yet my
hair stayed still. At the end of the tube there was a glow of
silvery light. I carried on walking until all of a sudden the
wall of the tube became covered with doors of all sizes.

311

'All of these doors kept opening and shutting apart from one. I reached this one door and I was just about to open it when a sudden fear came over me. I let go quickly and turned round. I honestly felt at that moment that if I had opened that door I would have seen my fate. I wasn't ready for it. I was too afraid. I know it sounds crazy, but I somehow knew it was my fate.

'I can remember how wonderful everything looked on my way back. Although I was still floating, there was now a visible pavement and there were trees, fields, and a fantastic bright blue sky. I observed my physical body as nothing more than an empty shell. In fact I still strongly feel that I exist in two parts, and that my material body is only here to keep the real part of me serviced and maintained.

'As I opened my eyes I saw a scrap of paper by my bed, and I instantly started to write the poem "The Tube". Now I have trouble trying to write a simple letter, let alone a poem. It took under fifteen minutes. I didn't plan it – it just seemed to flow out of the pen and on to the paper.'

Some things in life just seem to click into place without any effort whatsoever, yet when trying to instigate other events, no matter how much trouble we go to, the desired end result never happens. Could it be that some events are mapped out by fate and that certain people are fated to meet on this earth?

People might argue that if we have free will, how then can we believe in fate? Perhaps the answer lies in a mixture of the two. There are certain signposts marking our way along the pathway of life, in the form of events to be experienced, lessons to be learnt, tasks to be handled and people to be encountered, decisions to be made. Precisely how we deal with these signposts rests with us and our free will.

Nevertheless, some things just seem to happen out of the blue which change the natural course of events in a person's life in an inexplicable way. A gentleman of Letchworth, Hertfordshire, experienced something whilst serving in the Royal Auxilliary Air Force, Fighter Squadron.

'I was working as an aero-engine fitter at the time with my friend, who was an airframe rigger. We were feeling a bit low because we had recently lost our pilot, who had had a fatal crash in a Spitfire. Our new pilot was the best friend of the one who had been killed, and we were allocated to him as his ground crew. We had been re-equipped on the Squadron with new jet fighters, and one particular weekend the whole Squadron was on a big air defence exercise based away from our home airfield. However, my pal and myself were ordered to stay at base to re-fuel and service our new pilot's plane, while he was on a short leave as his wife had just had a baby. He had been permitted to fly back to see her and the baby briefly, then return, in a couple of hours, to the exercise area.

'Our pilot taxied in and stopped the engines. He got out and asked us to re-fuel with full tanks and check over the plane to have it ready to fly again in about an hour. He went off, telling us that the Form 700A was in the cockpit, under the parachute, in the seat. This was the special log book into which we had to enter all the servicing details and how much fuel we had put in.

'We carried out the re-fuelling and did the other between-flight checks as did the electricians, armourers and instrument mechanics, but when we came to sign up for all these little jobs, the log book was nowhere to be found. The Flight Sergeant was very angry about this, because to lose a log book in the Air Force was as bad as losing your birth certificate or passport.

'We searched every nook and cranny. We even took the parachute to pieces, then we took the complete seat out of the cockpit. As a last desperate resort, I felt that we should check the camera-gun bay which was over the nose-wheel. I took off the cowling panel and, to my surprise and great concern, there, wedged in the undercarriage retracting mechanism I found a one-pound hammer. The implication of this was that it would have been quite possible during the next flight, when some violent tactical manoeuvres were to be carried out, that the hammer would have jammed the nose-wheel in the up position – and on this type of aircraft it would have caused a particularly dangerous type of crash-landing for the pilot.

'I removed the hammer, put the front end together, and we put the seat and parachute back in the cockpit and resolved to tell the "Chiefy" that we had utterly failed to find the log book. At that moment the wireless mechanic came up to do his check. He leaned forward into the cockpit, picked up the missing log book, which was on the top of the seat which had just been refitted. "Is this what you chaps are looking for?"

'We were all stunned! The book just seemed to materialize out of thin air. Did our old first pilot have something to do with looking after his pal who was due to fly off in the plane? Had we spotted the book in the first place, I would never have found that hammer. I know what I think.'

During the Second World War, a young soldier from Newcastle was sent to Bournemouth on a mechanical course for three months.

'I had just been married for over a year and I remember I

314

distinctly had the feeling that all was not right at home, and that if I could only get up to Newcastle everything would be all right. I had the overpowering feeling to get back home as quickly as I could, but being in the forces it was absolutely out of the question.

'That night I went to sleep in my bunk as usual. I felt myself coming out of my body and rising up. I looked down and saw myself on the bed, and I realized that although my body was there, I was not part of it or, if you like, my spirit was not there.

'I remember the thought that came to me. It occurred to me that if I went to Newcastle, which I knew I could have done easily, would I be able to return to myself? The fear that I would not be able to get back to my physical body cancelled out the will to travel north, then I found that I was returning to my body. I was completely conscious of my re-entry. I just seemed to merge or blend into myself.

'Needless to say, I did not mention any of this the next day. Can you imagine the response I would have got from a barrack-room full of soldiers?

'When I returned to Newcastle, I learned the awful truth. My wife had, in fact, been having an affair with another man. Our marriage was dissolved, but I can't help wondering sometimes what would have happened had I had the courage to make that trip to Newcastle to check up on things. Perhaps we were fated to split up, who knows? All I remember is the intensity in my mind to get home to save the situation.

'It's funny when I look back on those days. I'm sure my life would have followed a totally different course. I have been happy in the way things turned out and I can't help feeling that it was meant to happen the way it did.'

A short example of fate can be illustrated by the story of a young girl, who for obvious reasons wishes to remain anonymous. She had just moved into a top-storey flat with her boyfriend of several months, much against the wishes of her parents. One morning, they had a blazing row, and the boy stormed out. She drank a full bottle of brandy and devoured a bottle of aspirins as well as some packets of flu-powder. The flat was three flights up, over a small parade of shops. The cocktail of brandy and aspirins acted on her system very quickly. All her thoughts blackened to despair. Her attention wandered to the window.

In a split second she ran to the window, pushed it up and took a nose dive straight out. As she fell head first, the heavy window clattered back down and pinned her by the ankles. She was held by her feet, and could not move up or down. She screamed and screamed and screamed. A passer-by rushed to the back of the building, broke into the flat and saved her life.

Had the window come back down a fraction later, or had she been a fraction quicker diving out, she probably would not have been alive today. Was this fate?

A young lady called Shirley from Dorset had just become engaged, and was sent on a training course to Birmingham by her company. She had only been in the city for a few days when she passed an old tramp in the street. She just glanced casually in his direction, while hurrying past him. Their eyes met.

'Something magical happened in that moment. As soon as our eyes met we both knew that we were in love. It's the craziest thing in the world, and if anyone else had told me that this had happened to them I'd think they were completely mad. There was an unbelievable fascination

316

and attraction between us, yet were total strangers, apart from the fact that he was a filthy vagrant, the kind of person people cross the street to avoid.

'We kept staring into each other's eyes. I felt as if I was rooted to the spot. I couldn't move and I couldn't look away; nor did he. After what seemed like an eternity, he spoke to me. His voice was gentle. He smiled, and as he did I realized that he was not as old as he had first appeared to be. I think the wild beard and moustache, and his straggling hair, gave a false impression – but it was his eyes that held me spellbound.

'We fell head over heels in love, and had a sizzling affair. I was very apprehensive about my engagement, but every time I thought about my fiancé back in Dorset, I kept hearing a voice in my head telling me that everything would turn out all right. No matter how things looked at that moment, everything would work out and that I was not to worry.

'After two weeks, I received a message to go to the local hospital. When I got there I was told that the tramp had collapsed with a brain tumour, and he had died just before I arrived at the hospital. My phone number was in his pocket – I was the only contact he had in the world.'

Although she was devastated at the news, she knew in her heart that she had been fated to meet the tramp in the very short time he had left on this earth. She also had the overwhelming feeling that her relationship with him had been designed in order to help her overcome something – something which would affect her in her own future although, at the time, she had no idea of what that 'something' would be. She put her marriage off, although she remained good friends with her fiancé.

317

Four years after the death of the tramp, Shirley was given the news that she herself had a tumour and she was suffering from terminal cancer. Instead of the expected reaction of grief and despair, she found that she possessed an inner strength and determination to fight. She knew then deep within her soul, that her tramp was helping her through and her own illness was what she had been aware of four years beforehand.

She made a complete recovery, married her fiancé and has been happy with him, although she feels, beyond doubt that someday she will be re-united with her romantic tramp.

Many people claim that they fell in love at first sight, despite the levelling remarks of their friends who suggest that to talk about love at first sight is fanciful nonsense, and could not possibly happen. All kinds of explanations and theories are presented in an attempt to disprove the claim.

However, even the most cynical adversaries admit that there is such a thing as attraction at first sight, but love? Never! Others argue that it is all accountable in retrospect, and that because the couple eventually grew to love each other they became tricked into believing that their first feelings for each other were nothing less than true love.

There is evidence to show that claims of love at first sight may not necessarily be the idyllic ramblings of star-struck infatuated fools, but that this can, and does, happen. Sexual sensibility operates on energy at molecular level, which means that impulses are sent to the brain at very high speed – in fact, thousands of times faster than ordinary signals are transmitted by the mind. Therefore, people receive sexually-related messages in record speed because they by-pass the logical mind, which is far too slow to deal with such perceptions.

It is perfectly feasible that within a few moments of two people meeting for the first time, thousands upon thousands of messages are relayed between them at split-second speed, and experts say that the information relayed could be sufficient for the two people to weigh up everything there is to know about each other in a single instant.

The feeling of recognition when meeting certain people for the first time could be explained by the idea of collective consciousness, or group souls, whereby people tend to cling to their own kind.

A sympathetic bond connects the members of the group, and compels them to seek each other in whatever realm of existence they happen to find themselves.

Over two hundred years ago, a young girl called Jean Armour jilted her husband-to-be Robert Wilson, and wed another Robert – Robert Burns, a struggling tenant farmer, who was to become a household name throughout the world as Scotland's national bard. Now, another piece of history has been made – the Armours and the Wilsons have finally got together when their descendants, Karen Armour and John Wilson, recently married in the old town of Ayr. Karen is related to the bard's wife, Jean Armour, and John is a direct descendant of Robert Wilson, the 'Gallant Weaver', jilted by 'Bonnie Jean' and immortalized in song by Burns two centuries ago.

Karen admitted, 'John and I might never have got together if it hadn't been for our strange family histories. I have distant family connections with Jean Armour and John is the great, great, great, great grandson of Robert Wilson, the man Jean should have married if Burns hadn't "bowled her over".'

The couple met at a dance and John told Karen that he

was researching his family history, and was writing a book about the Wilson clan. He recalls, 'I knew quite a lot about the broken romance between Robert Wilson and Jean Armour, who had been his childhood sweetheart before the poet had come into her life. When Karen told me her surname, and that she was related to Jean Armour, you could have knocked me over with a feather.'

Karen added, 'I think Burns had a romantic soul. I believe he would approve thoroughly of two young people getting married and fulfilling the destiny that was planned for Jean and Robert Wilson so many years ago.'

There must have been a very special kind of love between Robert Burns and Jean Armour. That is the only explanation for her sticking by the side of her poet husband through thick, and mainly thin. She was the mainstay of his adult life and the woman he always returned to. In Edinburgh, his new-found glittering society told the poet that his Ayrshire roots were holding him back. They said he should abandon the Scots tongue and write in 'proper' English, but it was Jean who gave him the safe anchor, who bore his children and who nursed him devotedly through his last long illness, to the end.

John Wilson is doubtful if he will ever be able to express his love as beautifully as Burns did, but he proposes that a new line should be included in the wedding vow - 'And I will love thee still my dear, till a' the seas gang dry.'

One evening, Carol Reynolds walked into a smart hotel lounge bar with her boyfriend, and she immediately caught the eye of the young man who was tinkling away on a baby-grand piano. Her heart skipped a beat as she instantly recognized the handsome features but, try as she would, she could not place his name. The pianist smiled and waved across to her, then she instinctively walked over to him and told him how lovely it was to see him again. He replied unhesitatingly, 'Yes, it's been a long time, hasn't it?'

At this point, Carol's boyfriend interrupted the conversation by ushering her away from the pianist to a quiet corner of the bar. After a few moments Carol began to feel acutely embarrassed, saying to her boyfriend that she felt she had made a terrrible blunder, and that she must have mistaken the pianist for someone else. The feeling was so strong that she was compelled to approach the pianist and make her apologies to him. However, when she once found herself face to face with this stranger, she became even more convinced that she was not mistaken, and that deep down she knew him very well. Before she could utter a word to him, her breath was taken away by his remark, 'I suppose I should apologise for mistaking you, but I could have sworn that we knew each other.'

During the following months Carol and Tom, the pianist, became closer and closer, and when he asked her to marry him she accepted eagerly. They became engaged and a few weeks before the wedding she was invited to visit Tom's parents, who lived three hundred miles away, for the first time.

As they waited on the crowded platform for the train, Carol suddenly remembered that she had left her handbag in the Ladies' room. In a panic, she ran back to retrieve it, without taking time to explain to Tom what had happened. When she returned to the platform, she was just in time to see the train pulling out of the station, and to her horror, there was no sign of her fiancé anywhere. She stared in shock as the last carriage chugged further and further away from her, taking with it her whole world.

321

The painful days and months turned into years as Carol tried desperately to put Tom out of her mind. Eventually, she met a kindly, considerate man who proposed to her and she accepted, thinking that marriage would free her from the torture of her unrequited love. Although she was extremely fond of her husband, she learnt that the deep underlying pain was not erased as she had hoped, but it was becoming easier to live with. She had three children, and after a reasonably happy twenty-six years of marriage, her husband died. Four years later, encouraged by her family, Carol joined a pen-friend club.

One morning she was slightly bemused when she opened a letter from a new pen-friend, a widower with two sons, who signed himself Tom Patterson. She smiled sadly at the coincidence of receiving a letter from someone with the exact same name as her beloved pianist.

After a few more letters had been exchanged, the amazing truth dawned on Carol. Her new pen-friend was the same man who had broken her heart when he jilted her so many years previously, but because Carol had naturally been writing to him in her married name, he did not realize that she was the same person.

On answering a knock at her front door one day, Carol was surprised and shaken to find herself face-to-face with her ex-fiancé, who stood sheepishly holding a bunch of red roses. He had decided to introduce himself to his pen-friend. The astounded look on Tom's face told Carol that he instantly recognized her. His dark hair was greying at the temples, but apart from that he had changed little over the years. When his clear blue eyes gave her that old, familiar, special look, her heart melted.

They sat down to talk and Tom told Carol that he could

never understand how she had jilted him without warning, that day at the station.

'But you were the one who jilted me,' exclaimed Carol. They found themselves laughing at how silly they both had been, but then the laughter faded when they realized that their whole lives could have been so different, had it not been for that one misunderstanding. Each of them had been too hurt to contact the other to seek any explanation.

There is a happy ending to this story. Two months ago Carol and Tom became engaged to be married, and they are absolutely convinced that they were always meant to be together. 'It's as if we have always loved each other,' says Carol. 'Although we've both been married to other people, somehow we always knew that we were made for each other.'

Tom, a mature, practical man admits, 'I know it sounds ridiculous, but I feel I've known Carol since time began. It's the only way I can explain it.'

Bob of Oxford, a shy, rather awkward young man in his late teens, always found it very hard to attract girlfriends. 'I'm not much good at small talk,' he explains, 'And when it comes to chatting a girl up, I just get tongue-tied and embarrassed.' He worked as a junior accountant for a big company, and was dedicated to making a successful career, so after a few blind dates which had been arranged by his friend went disastrously wrong, he more or less resigned himself to the life of a bachelor.

One night, after he had been asleep for some time, something made him open his eyes. He became aware of a bright light in the corner of his bedroom. 'When I saw it first I was so puzzled I didn't know what to think. I wasn't afraid so much as bewildered. I could not take my eyes off this oblong-shaped, orange-coloured light which seemed to hover about a foot above the floor. As I gazed at it I began to realize that it was not just a light, but that I was looking at three forms. I suppose my eyes were gradually becoming adjusted to the terrific brightness, for at first I was just too dazzled to distinguish anything.'

The forms became more and more clear as Bob stared in disbelief. In the middle, there stood a woman in her late thirties with short, dark curly hair in a rather ordinary dress, wearing dark coloured spectacles. On her right side there stood a boy of about ten, and on her left a little girl of about seven or eight. All three of them were staring intently at Bob, who admits, 'I didn't recognize any of them, and I remember wondering why they were there and what they had to do with me. Funny though, when I think about it, there was no sense of fear. I didn't feel threatened in any way, just mystified, if that's the right word.'

All of a sudden, from out of the silence, Bob heard a strange voice announce to him, 'These are your wife and children.'

'I felt thunderstruck,' recalls Bob. 'I remember thinking to myself that it must be some kind of weird joke. The woman was years and years older than me, and she appeared more like a mother than a wife. The next second everything vanished and I was left staring at the bedroom wall. I remember looking at the clock, and it was past three in the morning. It certainly wasn't a dream as I was wide awake. I even got out of bed and went downstairs to the kitchen to make myself a cup of tea.'

Bob's life continued as usual and nothing remarkable happened, until one day over two years later when he literally bumped into a girl on the stairs at work. She was a new secretary who had just started the previous day. Bob turned to apologise to the girl, and the moment his eyes met hers, he heard a voice repeating in his head 'This is the girl – this is the girl.' He was totally confused by this voice because the young girl called Susan was a glamorous blonde and looked nothing like the woman who had been shown to him – no spectacles, much younger, even different coloured hair.

Within the next few weeks, Bob found that he was able to talk to Susan very naturally without the usual self-conscious feeling which he normally got with girls. She was vivacious, pretty, good fun to be with and, most of all, she made him feel at ease. They started dating and, after a short courtship, they agreed to get married.

All of this happened over twenty years ago, but the incredible thing is that today Susan looks exactly like the woman in Bob's vision. She now wears glasses – with thick dark rims, she has allowed her hair to go back to its natural colour – dark brown, and she has put on some weight since her children have been born – yes! – two children, ten year old Michael and little Julie who is nearly eight.

'It is so unbelievable when I look at Sue and the kids,' says Bob. 'Their faces are exactly the same as I was shown them all those years ago. I could understand it if I had known someone who looked like the woman in the apparition but, at that time, I knew nobody like her at all. It really is uncanny how things work out.'

ESCAPE

The release of the spirit from the physical body frees the wandering soul from the natural limitations and restrictions of being trapped in the body. People have likened it to a prisoner being set free from solitary confinement. All the hampering conditions of flesh, blood and bone have no longer any effect on the spirit. One of the main differences which people constantly remark upon is that when they are out of their material bodies they feel no pain whatsoever, yet that is not because 'feeling' is not experienced. On the contrary, they report that they felt 'wonderful', 'happy', 'exuberant' and a string of positive conditions.

It is interesting to note that, apart from fear as a result of the initial shock of finding themselves out of their bodies, very few people have reported anything other than a feeling of extreme well-being.

Because human beings feel pain as a direct result of messages relayed to the brain, due to a change in our physical tissue, then it follows that when we are not clothed in our material bodies we cannot be subject to these conditions which brought about the change. It also follows, therefore, that it is impossible to feel pain once the spirit has separated from the body.

Some human beings seem to have a built-in safety mechanism whereby, under certain conditions when they are in severe pain, an escape is engineered by the spirit slipping out of the body. Many women have reported that this happened to them during childbirth. It is documented that some prisoners-of-war had the same release when life became unbearable in the cells.

A woman from Tamworth in Staffordshire was informed by her doctor that she had a cancerous tumour. 'The pain was getting more and more intense, and I was really struggling to get on top of it. Last year things became unbearable, the pain was absolutely unbelievable. On many occasions I used to drift out of my body when I just couldn't stand it any more. I would sit on the other side of me, and I was able to see how ill I looked. To be quite honest, I sort of knew I was facing death. It was as if I could no longer stand the pain in my body, and during those moments I had taken a little time out of it.

'I didn't dare tell anyone about this, as I am certain I would have been sent to the madhouse. All I'm saying is that I knew that I was able to escape from the brunt of that pain when it all got too much for me. It is now a year after my chemotherapy, and I am doing quite well.'

Angus Dudley of Bedfordshire remembers how he had a narrow escape when, as a boy, he had been out playing with his friends. 'It was one moonlit night, shortly after Christmas when the ice on the village pond was two feet thick. It had snowed on top of our slides, so we chopped a hole in the ice and spread water over the snow, so that it would freeze over and give us a smooth surface.

'Later around 9.00 p.m., I went back to the pond with my friend, John, and as the water had not yet restored the surface sufficiently to make a reasonable slide, we thought up a new game. We took a stick each and started to play putting, by using a piece of ice instead of a ball. We took turns in getting the piece of ice into the hole which we had dug previously.

'When we ran out of pieces of ice, I squatted at the side of the hole to pick some out and I fell headlong into the hole. I remember sinking into the icy pond, slipping down and down, with columns of green water rushing past my eyes. Then I started to float back up to the surface, but instead of remaining there, to my surprise, I kept floating right up out of the pond and into the air, lying face down on nothing. When I was about ten feet up I watched my friend put his arm into the hole in an attempt to find me. He was peering down into the dark water, fishing around with his hand and, at the same time, trying to prevent himself from toppling into the water. I could see him struggling, then he put his other arm into the water. I saw that he had got hold of something which, I then realized, was my hair. He pulled frantically at the hair until he managed to drag my head above the surface of the water.

'I drifted down to give him a hand, yelling for him to try to get a hold of my shoulders, but he took no notice of me. I shouted louder and tried to grasp at my sodden clothing, but I found that my hands could not form a proper grip on my jacket. The next thing I could feel the freezing water all around me. I opened my eyes and found that only my head was above the water, and I could see the dark elm trees on the bank of the pond, silhouetted against the sky. The cold was excruciating, so I started screaming loudly then, with John holding my collar, I managed to climb out of the hole. I ran home and dried off, and I did not even catch a cold.'

When Mr. Paul Bright of Warley in the West Midlands was a small boy, living with his parents, he was constantly the victim of bully tactics by a boy called Stan, who was three years older, a bit taller and heavier.

'One day Stan had been playing at my house and, as

usual, he started to bully me. He had pinned me to the floor and was literally strangling me. I was terrified because his grip was so strong on my throat that I could not even shout for help. The next thing I knew I was floating near the ceiling.

'I remember looking out of the window as I was bemused at being able to see out from so high up in the air. However, instead of the normal sights which I should have been able to see outside the window, I could only see a cloud like a fog and there were no sounds whatsoever. At this time I did not realize that I had left my body. It was only when I turned and looked down that I guessed that something odd was happening, because I could clearly see Stan, with his hands still pressing on my neck. He and my own body seemed to be in the distance, although we were all in the same room.

'I felt as if I were extremely small, although I was quite happy with the situation and was not in the least afraid. I turned my attention back to the window, then I thought that I'd better investigate this cloud of fog, so I tried to move closer to the window to have a better look. I was stopped from moving to the window by what felt like heavy hands on my shoulders, preventing me from moving. No matter how hard I tried to wriggle free from this grip, I could not shake myself away from it. It was as if the hands were turning me round to make me look at how Stan was strangling me. I did not want to watch, but the hands kept turning me, so that I was forced to look down instead of going towards the window, which I still wanted to do. I was completely indifferent to what was happening to my physical body.

'I then realized that the hands which I could feel pressing on my shoulders were trying to push me back down into my body. I struggled even more to get away, and towards the window. I could now see Stan slapping my face, I had passed out on the floor, and I think he had started to panic. At that moment I felt the mysterious hands give me an almighty push, which sent me rushing towards the floor and into my own body.

'A draining sensation swept over me, which started at the top of my head and crept all over my body. I could hear Stan asking me if I was all right. I told him what had happened but he just laughed at me and left. I told my two cousins about it and they also laughed at me, so I did not mention it again.

'When I was in my twenties I read an article in the paper about people having OOBEs, and it was only then that I recognized the similarities, and realized that that was what I'd had all those years ago, When I think of it, I find myself shaking slightly, or shivering as if I were cold. It all seems so vivid, unlike other ordinary memories which tend to become a bit hazy.'

A distraught battered wife found escape from the clutches of her irate husband's hands by slipping out of her body. 'My husband regarded me as a chattel to vent his frustrations on. One day, when the children were toddlers, they had been playing with his tube of toothpaste. This infuriated him so much that he came storming into the kitchen, roaring at the top of his voice. He had a dreadful expression on his face and I honestly thought he was going to kill me.

'He rushed straight up to me and put his hands around my throat. I was absolutely terrified, but then fear was my main emotion at that time in my life. I said, "Lord, help me," then immediately I was up on the ceiling looking

330

down. I was at perfect peace and could see both of us standing by the stove, his hands still round my neck. The feeling of freedom from fear was such a relief that I truly did not mind whether I went back or not.

'I watched from above as my husband relaxed his grip on me, then I felt myself floating back down into my body. I was never afraid of him again, as I was not now afraid of dying and to kill me would be the worst thing he could do to me.

'I was a battered wife for ten years. I put up with it purely so as not to disrupt the children's lives when they were so young. After we divorced he married someone else in the village, but by all acounts he is not too happy with his lot (as ye sow, so shall ye reap). He wanted to come back to me shortly after he left, but he would not undertake not to hit us all, so I couldn't have him back.

'I wonder if other people who have left their bodies feel, as I do, that death is nothing to fear.'

CHILDREN

It is accepted that some young children are acutely perceptive, particularly before school age. Perhaps this is because
their minds are not overbusy with the demands of organized learning, therefore they are more receptive to incoming
influences, the lines of communication being comparatively
clear.

Many children can give elaborate details of memories of
what seem to be previous lives, in places totally unknown to
them, and in words beyond their normal limits of vocabulary. In our book entitled *The Children That Time Forgot*
(Sinclair) we document cases of this phenomenon.

One little girl remembers her previous existence as a boy
who lived in a remote Yorkshire village over one hundred
years ago; another child remembers stark details of her
funeral when she had previously died as a child of only five
months old; yet another child recalls what happened when
he drowned after falling over the side of a sailing boat; a girl
remembers being one of the child victims in the Tay Bridge
Disaster, when a Pullman train plunged into the black, icy
waters of the River Tay in Scotland.

There are countless reports of children having seen
ghosts, very often the ghosts in question being other
children. There is a distinct lack of fear on the part of most
of these children, and they accept what they see as being
perfectly natural. We have all heard of some child who has
an invisible 'friend'. This friend is normally referred to in
affectionate terms. No doubt, some children are living in a
world of make-believe in which the invisible friend fits

perfectly. However, there are often cases not as easily explained, whereby there really does seem to be more in it than meets the eye.

A lady from Oxford moved into an old house with her husband and little boy of three years of age. 'The house was always cold. At first we thought that there must be something wrong with the central heating system. We had that checked and we were assured that there was no problem with it. However, even when the radiators were hot, the rooms for some unaccountable reason remained cold. I just couldn't understand it, so I just put it down to the fact that because the house was old, perhaps there was damp in the walls, which our surveyor must have missed or overlooked.

'Then the noises started, all kinds of thuds and thumps, but we could never find any reason for these. I used to watch my little boy like a hawk, wondering if he was getting up to mischief but several times I heard the noises upstairs while my little boy was downstairs with me, my husband was out at work and I was certain that there was no-one else in the house. I noticed that the noises, sometimes like footsteps or running feet, seemed to be restricted to certain areas – the stairway, landing and my child's bedroom. Sometimes I would hear a dragging sound as if something was being pulled across the floor of my little David's bedroom.

'It got so bad that I could hardly stand it. My imagination ran riot and I became convinced that we had either rats or bats in the rafters. We got in a specialist company to go over the entire house. We even had the floorboards removed in all rooms, including David's room, but there was nothing to be found.

'Still the noises continued. They began to sound like

footsteps on the bare floorboards. This just didn't make any sense at all because the entire house was carpeted wall-to-wall, including the stairs. One day, from upstairs, I distinctly heard a child calling out "Mummy". I, of course, assumed that it was David calling me, but I knew that he was out playing in the back garden. I could see him from where I was standing. He was playing up and down the garden path with a little red truck, which had a rope attached to it. As I watched him, again I heard the word "Mummy", and it definitely came from upstairs.

'I rushed up as fast as I could, thinking that some neighbouring child must have somehow wandered into the house. I passed no-one on the stairs, and when I got to the top there was absolutely no-one there. I searched every single bedroom, the bathroom, and I even looked in the linen cupboard on the landing, I was so certain that there was a child in the house.

'I began to wonder if my nerves were playing me up. After all the strange noises, perhaps I was beginning to imagine things.

'Several nights later, in fact at precisely 2.30 in the morning, I was awakend by a voice calling "Mummy". I naturally got out of bed to go and check on David. To my surprise I found him sitting up in bed, wide awake with all his toys around him. I remember saying to him, "What are you doing with your toys at this hour?" He beamed up at me. "I've been playing with John." I tucked him in and didn't think too much more about it until a few days later when I went to my next door neighbour's house.

'I didn't know her very well because we had only recently moved to that area. There happend to be a photograph album on the neighbour's table. She saw me glancing down

334

at the album and she invited me to have a look through it. Now, if there is something I hate doing, that is looking at other people's photographs, especially those of strangers. However, just to make conversation, I turned over a few pages of the album while my neighbour put the kettle on to make us some coffee.

'One photograph struck me as rather odd. It was of a child in a pram, but what drew my attention to it was that the child looked far too big to be in a pram. He was a boy of about five years of age and would have been on the large side, even for a push chair, let along a proper pram built for small babies.

'As I was looking at this photograph, my neighbour came over to me. I didn't like to say anything, but took it for granted that the child must be a relative of the woman. She smiled and said, "I suppose you know about him." I shook my head, then she went on to say, "They used to put him in that pram because he would get so tired. You see, he had cancer." Still assuming that she was speaking of her own relative I asked who the child was. She answered, "Oh, it's little John who used to live in your house. He died in there when he was only five." A cold chill went through me at her words, and everything started to make sense.'

Stephen Worthington remembers an experience he had when he was only five years old. 'Sudden and unexpected though it was I will never ever forget it. It happened late one winter's night on my fifth birthday. I had been playing with my toys on the upstairs landing, when a model car slipped out of my grasp, tumbling down the stairs. I leaned over the top of the stairs, watching in horror as my favourite car lay smashed to bits at the bottom of the staircase. I leaned over a bit further to get a better view and I slipped. I realized my mistake but it was too late. I fell over and bounced down every one of those steps.

'I reached the bottom, badly shaken, but not hurt and felt myself drift off into a deep sleep. After what seemed like a few passing moments I felt myself out of my physical body, hovering at a distance of about two feet, then floating back up the stairs until I reached the landing at the top. By some strange force I was gently placed down onto the landing with the delicacy of a feather floating down onto a velvet cushion.

'I felt completely weightless and as I looked down the stairs at my own corpse I noticed that I was wearing a little white jacket, trousers, tie, shirt, socks and shoes. I just stared at myself at the bottom of the stairs for a few moments, trying to comprehend what had happened.

'Then I jumped in the air and found myself floating towards the attic. I kept moving in that direction until I willed myself down again.

'Soon afterwards I saw my mother and my aunt enter the downstairs hallway from the living room. They saw me lying unconscious, and rushed towards my body to pick me up. The next thing to happen made my heart freeze; my aunt sighed, brushed away a tear and said, "Oh my God, he's dead!" At this my mother started crying uncontrollably, both of them weeping over my lifeless body.

'At this point, my father and uncle rushed into the hallway to see what was going on. They found the two women crying over my body. My uncle consoled my mother and my aunt, while my father examined my body to see what had happened. I then watched him carry me into the living room.

'I got a bit fed up watching them, so I wandered along the upstairs landing into my grandparents' bedroom and passed a tall, floor-mounted mirror. I thought I'd better check my appearance in the mirror to see if the fall had made any cuts or bruises on my face. To my confusion, the mirror reflected back absolutely nothing, even though I was standing right in front of it. I blinked, pinched myself, stared and even made silly faces to see what would happen, but still there was no reflection.

'I moved back out onto the landing and looked down the long forbidding staircase, and in a burst of enthusiasm I jumped from the very top of the stairs and arched myself into a diving position, then proceeded to fly down the stairs. I was just like Superman!

'For the next few moments, I can only say that the feeling I experienced was extremely beautiful and memorable. After flying at an even, gentle speed, I finally reached the bottom, then I felt myself re-enter my own body. The next thing I knew I was wide awake, sitting on the sofa in the living room, surrounded by the grown-ups.

'They asked me how I managed to fall down the stairs. I was too confused to answer, because I wasn't sure if they meant: how did I fall down the stairs or how did I fly down the stairs? Everyone around me was in a most joyful frame of mind due to my sudden recovery. Today, eighteen years after the event, my parents still remember it and are still baffled at how I made such a rapid recovery. As far as they were concerned I was dead and my father found when he had checked my body there was no trace of heart-beat or pulse.

'I know it was real and not a dream, and it is an experience I shall never forget, nor, I think, will my parents.'

Mrs. Rosina Drury of Dunstable told us her moving story of the child she lost. 'Shortly after our little son was born we were given the terrible news that he had cancer in his eyes and that he was almost blind. It was a dreadful shock to my husband and me. The little boy, whom we had named Paul, was admitted to hospital and went through the gruelling ordeal of having one of his eyes removed in a desperate attempt to save his life. Sadly, my little boy did not make it through the operation and died in the hospital.

'Our other child was only two-and-a-half years old, and she could not understand where he had gone. She kept running to fetch his nappy and powder, saying that she wanted to help me change him as she had always done. She kept asking me to let her cuddle him.

'I could not bring myself to tell her that Paul had died. One day I got her ready to take her out. At that time we lived in a ground floor flat in Leinster Gardens, Bayswater, in London. The sun was shining in through the kitchen window. Suddenly, she pulled at my skirt saying, "Mummy, Mummy look." I did not take a lot of notice as I was cleaning round the sink. Again she pulled at my skirt and said, "Mummy, look, there's Pauly!" I couldn't believe what I was hearing, so I looked down at her instantly and there she was, looking and pointing to the sky.

'I looked up, but could not see anything. I put my arms around her and said, "Where is Pauly?" She was adamant that she could see her little brother. She kept pointing to the sky. I asked her what he was like and she said, "He's not as big as me. He is standing by a big goldy gate. It is all shining and he had got all golden curls just like me. Look, there he is." For the life of me I couldn't see him, but I am convinced that she must have seen something. The thing was we had hardly spoken about him, it was too painful.'

When Mr. James Harbottle of Wallsend, Tyne-and-Wear, was only four years old he was rushed to the Fever Hospital on the Burnfield. He was placed in a bed near the window in a serious condition, suffering from the multiple effects of diphtheria and scarlet fever, further complicated by bronchitis. Both of his parents kept a bedside vigil, and it was feared that the end was near.

'I remember lying quite peacefully. I must have been oblivious to everyone in the room as it seemed silent and empty to me. I was occasionally aware of seeing a nurse hovering around the bed. I remember clearly, however, when I started to drift out of my body. I just drifted in the air around the room, then I went towards the window. At first I thought that I'd better be careful not to crash into the window, which I could see was closed. To my amazement, I found myself floating right through the panes of glass and out into the garden.

'There was a pathway and as I moved along I saw a tall man with a long beard. He held out his hand to me and although I did not know him, I moved towards him. I was not afraid, nor was I particularly curious, I suppose I just went because he beckoned to me. He then lifted me up in his arms. When I looked back through the window into the hospital room I saw that both my mother and father were crying. This upset me very much, and I just wanted to rush back to them to comfort them.

'The man did not say a word, but I could see him watching my parents. He seemed to understand so he opened his arms and let me drift back through the window towards them. When I was back inside the room I looked out and saw that he was still standing there. He raised his arm and waved to me. I remember waving back at him, then the next sensation was of waking up in my physical body, gazing up at my parents. They seemed pleased to see me, and kept hugging me.

'I seemed to get better quite quickly after that and soon my parents were wheeling me home in a borrowed push-chair. It was the first time I had ever been in a push-chair, so I was quite pleased with myself. I was taken to visit my granny who welcomed me with more hugs.

'Whether it was the spirit of a man or God who held me, I cannot judge. I've since heard it said that when young children die, the spirits of their dead ancestors look after them. Certainly after my own experience I know that children need have no fears.'

FEAR OF DEATH CONQUERED

Eternal Life

There was no secret key, we scarcely felt
Our final passage through the closing door;
Our only pain was knowing people knelt
Wishing their world of doubt on us once more;
They loved our shadows, and the sun was gone,
They have no eyes to see how we remain.
Nor can we point them to a peaceful dawn
Where blindness sees, and sorrow smiles again.
We have discarded names, waves in a sea
We move to other shores, being as one,
Beyond our fear we find a unity:
As one life ends, another has begun.
We are no longer casualties of clocks,
Death gave us life: we know no paradox.

Frank McDonald

On sifting through the thousands of out-of-body cases, one
overpowering conclusion keeps coming to light again and
again. It does not explain what causes astral projection but
it does point to the effect such experiences have on almost
every person on their return to their physical bodies, they
no longer fear death.

Mrs. Dorothy Bush of Abington, Pennsylvania, USA,
feels that she has completely got over the fear of the

unknown, from which almost all of us suffer, since she had an unforgettable experience just before her second child was born.

'I had a fainting spell in the examination room of the hospital, and the doctor felt that it would be best to perform a Caesarian section. While lying on the operating table and having a conversation with the anaesthetist, I felt as though I was going to faint again. I told her this and she gave me some oxygen, which did not help. The last thing I remember was her yelling to the doctor to hurry, that my blood pressure was falling.

'I then found myself in this beautiful place. I knew it was Heaven: so peace-filled, so beautiful, and such beautiful music and beautiful flowers. Although I could see no-one, someone started to talk to me, saying, "Dottie, I am leaving you on Earth for a purpose; no-one will know what you are going through". He proceeded to make known to me *all things*.

'I felt, as he talked to me, "Why did he choose me to reveal all things to?" And then I thought that since he did, now that I have had this convincing experience, I can be of help to others by helping them to understand. Then I thought about his words, "No-one will know what you are going through." I wondered then if this meant that upon returning to Earth I would not remember what was revealed to me. I was most conscious of this fact and I remember going over, in my mind, what I had just been shown, so that I would remember it all.

'When he finished talking to me I felt myself floating away from that beautiful place to a dirty, ugly one, so great was the contrast between Heaven and Earth. I did not want to return, although he said that I must. I then felt myself back in my body on the operating table.

342

'My doctor told me that resuscitation measures had been required because of apnoea and hypoxia, which translates, I understand, as cessation of breathing and lack of oxygen in the brain. I then felt the doctor putting tape across the bandage on my stomach but I could not open my eyes. Someone was saying The Lord's Prayer, and when they said "Amen" I opened my eyes as though I had just had a nap.

'I was taken back to my room, and told my husband and Mom that no-one would know what I had just gone through. I said I would not complain again about anything. Although my resolve faded with time, I did eventually become more patient with everyone and everything. I always had believed that there was life after death, but having been there and returned, I certainly found out for sure.

'That night, as I lay on my bed, I tried to remember what had been revealed to me, but I was unable to. I knew deep in my heart that I had been shown wonderful things. I have never been able to remember the revelation, but the experience remains vivid and convincing as when it occurred.

'I have gone through some testing and trials in recent years, but I know that they are lessons which must be learned here on Earth. I find myself led to certain places, or drawn to certain experiences at times, and I look upon life in a completely different way since I had my experience. The helping of others and the love that we should have at all times for others, this is what we are here for. It is a great frustration to see others running about with self-centred attitudes and activities that are such a waste of their lives. What I am trying to say is that seeing so much unthinking selfishness in the world just makes my heart ache.

'I have met others who have had the benefit of the near-death experience and they too long to share with everyone the lesson of this higher consciousness and love. I have no fear of death. I actually look forward to going home when God calls, for I know "the best is yet to come".'

Another lady who, like Dottie, was giving birth when she slipped out of her body, Mrs. Jean Norman from Aberdeen in Scotland, says, 'The baby was very overdue, and the doctor was worried about the birth. He gave strict instructions that he was to be called in immediately after I went into labour, since I was having the baby at home. However, my labour was such that the nurse did not dare leave me, even to telephone the doctor, so my husband had to help her.

'After a very difficult time, my baby boy arrived almost dead because the umbilical cord was wrapped so tightly round his little neck. At the moment of birth I found myself floating up to the ceiling. I looked down at my body on the bed, and I could see the nurse shaking me and slapping my face. My husband just stood silently staring at me and the baby who was lying on the bed with me.

'I felt as light as a feather, with no pain whatsoever, such a contrast to the terrible agony I had suffered while I was in my body. I had a wonderful feeling of happiness, and I knew that I needn't ever go back, it was as if I had a choice. I thought to myself that it was so peaceful where I was that it was much nicer to stay there. Then I looked down at the three figures below, and I felt such pity for them. In an instant I was back in my body.

'When the doctor arrived, the nurse told him that she thought she had lost me as I had died just as the baby was being born. I felt no fear of death as I am quite sure we only pass through a door. Previous to that experience I was as scared of death and dying as most people are.'

A date in the beyond was what brought Mrs. Phyllis Wilkinson of Bolton, Lancashire, the conviction that death is nothing to fear.

'I had not been widowed very long when one night I thought I had woken up. It was in my mind that I had made an arrangement to see my husband, although I was fully aware of the fact that he was dead. I felt my spirit (or whatever it was) rise up and leave my body, feeling sure I was on my way to see him. I might add at this point that I am not religious.

'I hovered for a while close to the ceiling, and looked down at my physical body in the bed. I noticed the exact position I (or should I say "it") was lying in. I then remembered that I had to meet my husband outside my old school, so I just floated through the closed window without even hurting myself. It was as if I was flying over the rooftops until I arrived at the outside of the school. Seconds later I saw my husband coming towards me. My mind was clear and I was able to think in perfectly logical terms. As soon as I saw him, I thought that I would have to treat this situation with great care because although I knew he was dead, the exuberant way in which he came rushing towards me told me that he must not realize that he has died, so I would have to choose my words carefully so as not to alarm him.

'We started to walk along, chatting happily, but after a short time, he kept saying that he was cold, so I knew it was time for him to go. I then found myself back in my bedroom, to see my physical body still in the exact position it had been in before I'd left. I just slid into it. It was like sliding into a glove. I then said to myself, "I'm going to wake up now" and did just that.

'I have not told many people about what happened because I think that they would scoff and say it had just been a dream. If it was, it was the most vivid dream I have ever had. In fact, it was a shattering experience which I will never forget. The one sure thing is that I know I will see my husband again, and I have no fear whatsoever of what lies ahead as I am convinced that we all meet up with our departed loved ones.'

For a family man in Belfast, the horror of horrors happened one day when he was shot in an assassination attempt. When his unconscious bleeding body was found he was rushed to hospital and straight into the operating theatre. He regained consciousness and screamed out in pain. He asked to be given something to ease the pain, but was told that he could not have anything until it was decided what was to be done. 'They were worried because I had just had lunch and they had to be careful about what they gave me, so at that point I had been given no drugs whatsoever.

'Suddenly I became aware of someone standing by the side of my bed. I turned my head but could see no-one, but I still had the overpowering feeling that someone was there beside me, a male supreme being. I heard the words, "I'm in charge, everything's O.K. There is nothing to worry about." The moment I heard those words I felt all the fear just leave my body. I could distinctly feel as if a wet blanket was slowly being drawn off my body, I could actually sense the drawing out of the fear from me. I never would have believed it could happen like that. I felt the close proximity of this being and felt engulfed with peace beyond belief. I knew that I would recover and that everything would be fine.

'My attitude to death has changed greatly since then, because I now know that we are never left on our own at any time. There are beautiful good people there who help us through and who are filled with love.'

A lady from Belfast, Trudie Watson, returned home after an enjoyable holiday in the Isle of Man. She felt a bit off colour and did not take too much notice of this. But things deteriorated fast and Trudie found herself in the Fever Hospital, completely paralysed with polio. Being a brave young lady of 25, she asked the doctor to level with her, and asked him what were the chances of her recovery. The doctor could see that she really wanted the truth, so he informed her that she had 24 hours to live!

That night she woke up in the hospital. Being completely paralysed she had been placed in a cot on her back, and the nurses had firmly tucked the bed-clothes in all round. She could only move her eyes, but her brain was completely alert and active as normal.

Suddenly she found that she could sit up in the cot. She thought that this was strange, and then she wondered if perhaps the medical staff had got her records mixed up with someone else's. Then she remembered the dreadful pain in which she had been, and the fact that she had only been able to move her eyes. She became confused because there she was, sitting up in the cot, with every trace of pain gone, and yet she was supposed to be paralysed. She then felt herself move up and away from the cot.

'I just kept floating lightly, like a feather, up and up, until I was about nine feet off the ground. I found myself lying on a black wooden plinth, just like a door without a handle on it. I remember observing that because the wood was so black it must be ebony. I looked down and startled myself when I saw my still body lying in the cot, still all tucked in the way the nurses had left me.

'The plinth, with me lying on it, started to move towards the door. I was not in the least bit afraid. As I got to the door, I heard the cry of a young child. I knew this was not my child's cry, but it immediately reminded me of my own little boy who was only two. The second I thought of my small son I was right back in that useless body again, tucked up tightly in the cot.

'I recovered fairly quickly after that because I had the intense will to survive to look after my child. The doctor told me that I had been drifting in and out of heart failure while I was in the cot. Even though it was a dreadful illness I would not have missed it for the world because I now have not the slightest fear of dying when my time actually comes. So much for the 24 hours to live! I feel as fit as a fiddle and am still going strong.'

A Birmingham gentleman, relates how he was going through an unpleasant emotional period with his lady-friend. 'As I sat in my chair, trying to sort out in my mind the reasons for her unreasonable and unpredictable behaviour (which was the cause of my anxiety), I was unknowingly staring at the wall (fixated). There were long gaps in between my thoughts (one might say daydreaming, where the mind wanders off doing its own thing) and it was during one of these blank spaces that I could actually feel the life force flowing into my body, and as my body filled with this spirit, I became consciously aware of a feeling of peace (well being). I was completely alone, yet something hit me very hard on the back of the neck; I believe it was then that my eyes closed and I experienced a pleasant sensation of "sinking down". A voice occasionally called my name (Derek) and whenever I repeated my name silently to myself, I enjoyed further pleasant sensations of "sinking down". Another two strong hits on the back of my neck each sent me deeper and deeper within myself. I think the sensation of being hit was probably the procedure for releasing my inner body because I found myself floating just below the ceiling and looking down at my physical body sitting in the chair. I could actually move around to different parts of the room and look at myself from different angles. I could move in or out of my body at will, I had no fear, because it was a natural feeling. I felt perfectly free and happy with not a care.

'I instinctively knew that my inner self (or spirit) was indestructible, so when I heard a bus in the street below, I flew through the closed window and, knowing that nothing could harm me, lay in its path; the bus passed over me easily and I quickly returned to my body. The speed with which I could move was fantastic; I remember being quite pre-occupied with speed at the time and the next thing I knew, I was shooting from my body through the top of my head, and powering my way through the ceiling and the flat above. I did not think about my body sitting in the chair and felt rather sorry at leaving it, but this was only momentary. I went through the roof and continued at terrific speed in an upward direction.

'There was a mist which suddenly parted to reveal a place

where colours were transformed by an unusual quality of light, where the sun, stars and planets appeared bold, stark and real, but for me the feeling was of peace, light and love.

'I remained there with my arms outstretched, looking towards the sun, and noticed that my whole body was shimmering in the light. I had no hands, face or feet, and with my arms outstretched, I appeared to be like the "Cross of Peace".

'This place has many names, but none of them quite apt: Christians call it Heaven, Buddhists call it Nirvana and Red Indians call it the Happy Hunting Ground, but whatever it's called cannot reveal its subtle nature. Mystics say it is pure bliss, infinite love and all-embracing unity.

'My out-of-the body experience changed my life considerably, and I am now no longer afraid to die.'

A shorter account of how she overcame her fear of death comes from Mrs. Hall, again of Birmingham. 'It happened shortly after my father died. I was very upset because I had always felt that he had not received attention early enough.

'Anyway, I saw myself lying in bed. I had somehow or other released my true self from my physical body. I started to float down a long dark tunnel which was growing brighter and brighter. I stopped about half way along and, in a brilliant light, I saw my father, sitting in his wheelchair. He smiled broadly, waved to me and put his thumb up as if to say that he was O.K. I turned and started to travel back down the tunnel.

'I know this sounds ridiculous, but I will always believe it. My father convinced me that death is nothing to worry about.'

A sad story comes from Carl, a blind man of 23 years of age, who rang in response to one of our radio phone-in programmes to tell of his experience. It convinced him that death is nothing to worry about.

'I am blind and gay, and had been living with another young man who was also blind. My friend was dying. He had brittle bones. We both knew the score and we tried to be philosophical about it. One day I had the sensation that I was flying, and for some reason I got the impression that he was in New York. I was still blind and could see nothing, but because I could "feel" the high buildings I came to the conclusion that I must be in New York. I'd never been to New York before, in fact I'd never been out of England. I had the distinct impression that my friend was with me.

'I don't pretend to know how this happened, and I would not know where to begin to explain it. I only know it happened. I have often thought about it, and ever since it happened the panic everyone feels about dying just left me. Sometimes I even wish that I could be taken away to be with my friend again, because I depended on him so much in every way. I suppose we depended upon each other. I am certain that we will be together again in the afterworld.

In the *New York Times* of Tuesday, 28 October 1986, the following article was published, entitled 'Near-Death Experiences Illuminate Dying Itself'.

The mystery of death haunts the living, but real understanding of it has always proved elusive. But researchers say new studies of people who have come close to death and show it may be less painful, less frightening and more peaceful than it is generally conceived to be.

These conjectures are derived from near-death experiences of people who came close to death or were revived from a state of clinical death, usually after a painful accident or illness.

According to Kenneth Ring, a professor of psychology at the University of Connecticut, people undergo a 'brief but powerful thrust into a higher state of consciousness' when they are near death. Many people who reach this state describe their experiences in vivid detail. Many report the feeling of travelling through dark tunnels towards a bright light; a few report floating above fields of yellow flowers.

'One definite finding of the research is the diminishing fear of death from those who have had these experiences,' said Karl Osis, former executive director of research in Manhattan and an author of a book on near-death experiences.

Dr. Osis and other researchers say people who have had such experiences may help relatives or friends to face death.

Near-death experiences vary in length and intensity, but follow roughly the same pattern. People who undergo them report feeling abrupt separation from their bodies and looking down upon themselves. Their pain dissolves, they say, and they are overwhelmed by an inexpressible peace and contentedness.

Many say they enter a tunnel of darkness and move towards a brilliant white light that emits warmth and love, and they are flooded with knowledge beyond their ordinary capabilities, so that they discern the pattern or meaning of life.

A Gallup poll reported that 8 million people have had near-death experiences and found that no relationship existed between the experiences and a person's religious or cultural background. Studies have shown that children have these experiences.

John Migliaccio, a New York business executive for a publishing and consulting firm, had a near-death experience in 1968 when he almost drowned off New Jersey. While swimming towards the shore, he became over-tired and said he felt himself leave his body and hang 500 feet in the air, 'like being in two places at one time'. He kept on swimming as he felt he was actually watching himself in the struggle to survive.

After reaching the shore and blacking out, 'I just let go', Mr. Migliacci said. 'I went straight into this blackness, travelling what seemed like a million miles a second. I went up into this great void. The only way I can describe it is that I was part of everything in the universe. Everything fit together and made sense to me.'

The experience changed his attitude towards death, he said. 'A year before, my grandmother died and I went hysterical.' But when his grandfather died a year later, 'I felt inappropriate, everyone was upset but me.'

According to Bruce Greyson, an associate professor of psychiatry at the University of Connecticut, and editor of the *Journal of Near-Death Studies*, no physiological or psychological theory explains near-death experiences.

Some scientists have suggested that the dying secrete endorphins, hormones that act on the central nervous system to reduce pain and which are otherwise associated with 'runner's high'. Endorphins cause effects comparable to those of morphine and may cause hallucinatory experiences.

But people who have these experiences deny that they were simply hallucinations. 'It was a real experience,' Mr Migliaccio said.

While experts say near-death experiences have been recorded for centuries, only in the past decade have they begun to gain credibility in scientific circles.

Leading the research is the International Association of Near-Death Studies, which Dr. Ring and several other researchers founded five years ago, and which is based at the University of Connecticut.

According to Dr. Ring, near-death experiences are a catalyst for spiritual development, the individuals seem to become more self-confident, less materialistic and more giving of themselves. People who have these experiences often believe they have escaped death to fulfil a special mission in this life.

Such was the case of Virgina Sendor of Hempstead. Mrs. Sendor had a near-death experience in 1960 when suffering from uremia. 'I knew I came back for a reason,' she said, 'but I had no idea what the reason was.'

But in the late 1970s she began working with terminally-ill patients and their families. By 1983 she realized it was her mission to open a hospice on Long Island. So Mrs. Sendor founded Long Island Foundation for Hospice Care and Research Inc., which provides a range of counselling and support services to patients and their families.

'I know now this is what I'm supposed to be doing,' said Mrs. Sendor.

Researchers say those who have near-death experiences can share their views of death to comfort others.

Geraldine Divito of Mt. Laurel, N.J., had a near-death experience in 1978 when she had an allergic reaction to medication. Two years later, her husband was diagnosed as having pancreatic cancer. He died three years later. Mrs. Divito believes that she helped ease the pain that her husband would otherwise have suffered.

'I know there was nothing to fear,' she said. 'I had that little glimpse into the life-after death.'

PREMONITIONS

We received many reports from people who have had flashes of events which, by our reckoning of time, were scheduled to take place in the future. Some of these events were quite trivial but some have come in the form of definite advance warning of catastrophe. The people who experience such premonitions feel most frustrated because even if they could pin-point the origin of the catastrophe they feel they would not be believed.

A Coventry man, Mr. Pemberton, had a lucky streak one day. 'It started with a stretching feeling, being drawn out of myself, so to speak. I found myself arriving in a hall and hovering above some people who were about to draw some tote numbers. I watched from above as they turned the barrel and drew out the winning numbers, number six followed by number nine. The numbers were written on ping pong balls. I felt like an all-seeing eye and was surprised they could not see me. I was drawn back into my body, woke up and promptly made a note of the numbers six and nine. For some reason the number forty-two kept ringing in my head. This confused me as I had not seen that number during my escapade in the hall.

'Anyway, later that week when it came to selecting numbers for our tote I played my hunch and told the collector that I would bet on those numbers. I had never been lucky in the tote before so I did not give the matter any further thought.

'A few days later my friend Arty Harper, my confidant at the time and the only person on this earth that I had told about my strange experience, came rushing up to me, eyes all alight, saying, "You'll never guess, the numbers nine and six have won, and there were forty-two winners." It was a very small pay-out that week, but to me the money came second as something more valuable came out of it. By the way, I checked with the collector to ask exactly how our work tote was drawn as I'd never really been that interested in it before. I was told that the numbers were all on ping pong balls and they were picked out of a barrel.

'I think I have been very lucky to have experienced this insight or whatever it was. I know that I am not unique as I have heard of many people who have had similar experiences. I never got any more 'tips' after that, anyway I'm not really a gambling man.'

Mrs. Thelma Trenchard of Falmouth in Cornwall had a premonition when she was staying at her mother's home 'Ivy Cliff' near Falmouth, although her own home, at that time, was in Oxford. 'It was just a quick flash in a dream in which I saw our two youngest children, Colin and Nesta, out on the river in our small boat. I saw Colin bump his head on something.

'That was all there was to it, but when I woke up in the morning, just as my mother's housekeeper was coming into the room with a cup of early morning tea, my hand was shaking so much that I could hardly hold the cup. Although the rest of the dream had been vague, my sense of danger was alerted and I was overcome with a feeling of fear for the children.

'I suppose it felt worse because I was so far away from my husband and children, who were all at home in Oxford. I had been called down to 'Ivy Cliff' to attend to some of my mother's business. I telephoned my husband straightaway, but he put my mind at rest saying that the children were fine and that there was nothing to worry about.

'The following day I received an urgent telephone call from my husband, who was very upset. He explained that there had been an accident, but the children were safe. It had happened after my husband had set off for work that morning. Nesta, Colin and their friend had decided to take our boat out on a backwater of the Thames. Colin had bumped his head on a low bridge. They lost an oar overboard and broke the outboard motor. They had been in grave danger of being swept down a weir which was in full spate below them. Luckily there were other boats on the river and several people came to their rescue, and they were pulled to the safety of the bank.'

Scores and scores of people have reported the Lockerbie plane disaster days before it happened. Some of them felt so strongly about it that they tried to contact the officials of various airlines, but of course without more concrete evidence they were not taken seriously.

Deep in the Welsh vallies there lies the little village of Aberfan, which will forever be remembered because of the terrible tragedy which wiped out almost all of the tight-knit community's children. A landslide caused the local school to be buried under tons of earth and slag from the nearby mines.

Mrs. Williams, a young mother from the North of England, was most disturbed when she had a vivid dream of a landslide in a village area. In the dream she saw a gravestone, on which was marked the name 'Anne Williams'. She was most distressed as this was her daughter's name. She was filled with a terrible sense of foreboding, and was sure that something was going to happen to her little girl.

357

A few days later, she was sitting at home watching television, when the News was broadcast of the disaster. It was reported that the schoolteacher was also killed. Her name was Anne Williams.

DANGERS OF THE OCCULT

All of the experiences described in this book are of a spontaneous nature. At no time did any of the people mentioned take part in any form of psychic formula or ritual in order to release themselves from their physical bodies; nor did they consume any drugs, apart from the cases under medical supervision in hospital.

The dangers of involving yourself in the occult cannot be overestimated. To experience true spiritual perception is one thing, but to purposely set out indiscriminately to seek involvement in the paranormal, by whatever means happen to be at your disposal, is asking for trouble.

Let there be no doubt about the point we are making here. Avoid all involvement in *ouija boards, fortune telling, tarot cards,* and especially any form of magic whether black or white. Although these things may have a degree of novel fun about them, they are extremely damaging to the spirit, because their origins spring from Satanic influences.

Some people might argue that these practices must be all right because they work. How many times have we heard people swear by this or that clairvoyant, often to the degree that no important decisions are made without first consulting the clairvoyant.

From our research, we can state that for the most part it does not work. Most of the so-called clairvoyants utter inconsequential drivel, made up as they go along, mostly based on their acute observations of the unsuspecting person who has parted with his or her money. The clairvoyant is often little more than a pseudo-psychologist, playing with people's emotions and abusing their vulnerability. Within seconds of meeting your run-of-the-mill fortune teller, she will have weighed you up, taking into account your appearance, your accent, your stance and deportment, the texture of your hands and the rings on your fingers, if any, the expression on your face, your general attitude. After a few key questions, which most people react to even if they don't realize it, she has her clues to progress further down the road of deceit. Even if you purposely do not react to her initial questions, this, in itself, tells her a lot about you.

We unearthed a training school for clairvoyants on the south coast, and they unwittingly admitted to us that the entire reading is done by nothing less than trickery, in as much as the questions are framed in such a way as to guarantee feedback (however subtle) from the subject.

After one or two visits to such people, or after one or two sessions with the ouija board, it takes only the minutest degree of success to warrant more and more involvement. This does not even sound logical, and in fact it isn't. Logic has nothing whatsoever to do with it, such is the charismatic effect that sudden power has on most innocent individuals. Every tiny succcess is magnified in the mind beyond all recognition.

Just think of this. How many people have told you that they have dabbled in the occult in some way or another, either by visiting a clairvoyant or by taking part in a seance? They probably told you excitedly about the one main factor which 'came true'. Did they ever mention all the other hundreds of factors which did not come true? Most probably not! That is because the negative factors die a natural death in the mind, whereas the one thing that 'came true' dominates the mind in a totally exaggerated manner, thus giving a distorted sense of importance to that one success, blotting out the hard fact of all the other failures.

This strange deviation from the normal workings of the mind is caused by our inner need to believe in something more than that which we can see with our physical eyes. The problem is that in dabbling with the occult, we are tapping into the wrong source – the negative source – rather than the positive source from which true enlightenment flows.

Everything can be reduced to simplicity. Things are either good or bad; positive or negative; for or against; beneficial or detrimental. Even the grey areas which would initially seem to fall between these firm borderlines can be analysed down to fit into one category or the other. There is really no need to complicate things by assumptions which cloud any particular issue. Therefore, it follows that the occult must also fall into place like everything else in creation – it is either good or bad, positive or negative.

The questions then arise, how can we tell for sure? How do we know whether the occult is good or bad? The answer to these questions can be found by examining the evidence. Without exception, people who embrace the occult (usually either for fun, to start with, or as a last desperate resort to find peace and happiness and reassurance in their lives) do not truly find what they are looking for. They still have to face the same old problems, but added to this is the burden of fresh worries, which often lead to a general sense of hopelessness and disappointment with life in general. In extreme cases people become suicidal.

If you have been dabbling in the occult, ask yourself honestly, have you recognized any of the following tell-tale signs creeping into your life: excess anxiety and fear;

emotional instability; severe depression; an overpowering feeling that life has become almost too difficult to cope with; overindulgence in food and drink; profound feelings of inadequacy and failure; inability to get on with other people. Are you consumed with feelings of self-pity? Is there discord within your own family? Is there the threat of a break-down in your marriage, or symptoms of nervous disorder? Do you feel utter frustration in everything you attempt, leading to neurotic tendencies?

If you are affected by any of the above conditions it could well be that you are suffering from some form of Satanic oppression, either physically, mentally, spiritually or on a psychic level. Because of your wilful involvement in the occult, you have exposed your soul to demonic power and invited evil and negative influences to enter, causing total havoc in your life.

Remember, Satan exists. He is real. He can, and does, influence unsuspecting souls, very often by the most subtle, undetectable means. He is the essence of deceit, and only after you have been well and truly conned will you waken up to the fact that nothing beneficial has come your way since your involvement in the occult.

However, there is hope! Even if you feel you are suffering from any of the aforementioned afflictions, all is not lost. In the time it takes to blink your eye, you can transform your whole life. It only takes a fraction of a second for a thought to enter your conscious mind and relay its message to your brain. The thought which you must introduce to your brain is this: 'I totally and wholeheartedly renounce all evil and negative influences and forbid them to affect me in any way whatsoever.' There! The deed is done! You have freed yourself from Satanic influences.

The overpowering point to grasp is this: by the laws of creation, it is a fundamental fact that evil is secondary to good. Therefore, an evil thought or influence can never, under any circumstances, dominate a pure positive thought or a good influence. Negative thoughts and influences can only have an effect when they meet up with their own kind. Remember, like attracts like!

From this, it is easy to see how a snowball effect occurs by one negative influence feeding upon another, and growing in intensity until the force of negativity attacks the negatively-inclined person with soul destroying vengeance. This can be illustrated by mob violence at football matches. The forces which originate in evil are allowed to run riot, inciting violent feelings to manifest themselves. The excuse is a game of football. How pathetic!

Evil is often cloaked in the most clever disguises, such as in organized cult groups and, in some cases, even orthodox religion. How many misguided souls have set out to fight wars, deluding themselves that they were fighting for their religion? Surely this is a contradiction in terms. Any religion worth its salt should surely preach love. If it does not, something, somewhere is amiss!

Once you have made the conscious decision to reject all evil influences from your life, you have overcome the first, and most difficult hurdle. You have recognized the problem. The next step is to take the necessary action to prevent any further Satanic evil forces from affecting you. This, you may find, will take courage, but remember that good thoughts *always* win over evil, therefore do not lose heart. The reason for needing extra courage at this stage is that Satan and his followers do not give up easily. As soon as they feel they are being opposed you will become aware of the following sensations: you will begin to have second thoughts about your recent decision to exclude all negative influences from your life. This is the typical procedure for undermining your own confidence in your ability to shake off the negative forces. Deal with this as follows: repeat your resolution to forbid all evil and negative influences to enter your life. Even if you are faint-hearted at the prospect of repeating this, do it anyway.

For once in your life be firm with yourself. You will be hesitant because you will start to feel silly about the whole thing. You will have to deal with thoughts giving you the false impression that you are running away with your own imagination. One way or another the doubts will surely creep in. Please recognize these doubts for what they really are. It is a sure fire sign that you have started to upset the Satanic applecart. You are on a winning streak, so stick with it. Show Satan who's boss. Defy him and repeat again that you totally denounce him and all he stands for. As long as you adhere to your good, positive thoughts, he can't touch you.

By now, you will feel a lot lighter in spirit. Positive influences are starting to break though. You can test whether you are on the right track by observing the following: you will now be smiling and even laughing, something you have not done for years. You will really score in the spiritual stakes if you laugh at him and his devious little tricks. You are now mightier than him by far. You can look down on him. He loathes to be ridiculed so why don't you treat him with the contempt the creep deserves?

At this stage, something wonderful will happen to you – something that no amount of money can ever buy: the fear will leave you and it will be replaced by true peace of mind. You will start to feel happier, you will be contented within. You know you are on top of things. The problems that of late have worn you down will gradually disappear. This will come about because your own attitude will have changed. You will be able to see things clearly, as they really are, instead of living in a dazed world of wishful thinking. You will become less self-centred. You will start to make correct decisions. Your judgement will no longer be impaired by negative influences. You will have courage. Your health will improve. You will look radiant and your eyes will shine from the light within your soul. Your relationships with other people will bring you joy. All doubts and feelings of inadequacy will vanish. Life will be beautiful and worth living. You will feel your spirit soar within you and praise God to be alive.

By now you will have created a protective shield of goodness around you that it will be impossible for any evil influences to penetrate through this to your spirit. You have won!

A fascinating development will be apparent at this point. You will now be able to look back on the times when you had dabbled in the occult, and you will see it for what it really was – a complete and utter waste of time and energy. You will see clearly the connection between your past problems and your involvement in the occult.

The next step to take is to ensure that you do not relax your defences and slip back to your old ways. Destroy all occult literature (if you have not already done this), including all occult tools, charms, medallions, instruction manuals, and all associated objects: everything, plus all the contact phone numbers, names and addresses, should be burned. This act, in itself, will further strengthen your protective shield.

All forms of witchcraft, in particular, must not only be avoided but positively rejected, be it presented to you as white, black or anything else. Make no mistake here – it is all Satanic, it is all of evil origin and can only lead you to unimaginable pain and suffering.

The hoard of so-called white witches will be up in arms upon reading this. Their argument will be that they do not practise all the dreadful things black witches involve themselves in. The white witches, in some ways, are more dangerous than their black counterparts, because they have developed deceit to a fine art. They will lure unsuspecting people into their midst by raving on about how they are only interested in nature, herbs, flowers, how they want to save the trees, etc. Don't we all love the flowers. The trouble is that they will not give you the complete picture. They use an incredible soft sell approach, but once they have you under the influence of evil, the rest of the sordid story emerges.

Up and down the country, in the suburbs and back alleys of quiet little England, the most grotesque, repulsive practices are going on. In the book *Witchcraft Conspiracy*, (Sinclair) the extent of this horrific situation is clearly shown. The problem cannot be underestimated. The evil must be stopped! We must unite in positive prayer to God, the only source of good, to bring about an overpowering force into the hearts and souls of each and every person who is, has been, or is contemplating involvement in witchcraft of any description. Evil will only prevail as long as good decent people do nothing.

If you have never before in your life stood up to be

counted, now is your time. There is something positive which can be done to eliminate such Satanic horror from our earth, and every thinking responsible person must do it.

We do not ask for money. We do not ask for anything. We beg you simply to consciously state the following: 'I wholeheartedly reject all Satanic influences from my own life and from the lives of all people living on the earth.'

With such a defence mechanism the witches, in their egotistical craving for power over others, will be wiped out. It truly is as simple and as instantly effective as that. Can you afford not to try it?

For any unfortunate readers who find themselves trapped because they have become involved in witchcraft and are too afraid to try to break free, there is also hope for you. Please have the courage to call a halt to your involvement. Chances are, if you face up to things and explain to your spouse, your parents, or whoever, they may well be sympathetic to your cause. Most decent people will see your need for help. You may well be in for a pleasant surprise. After all, what could be worse than your present Satanic imprisonment?

To employers, spouses, parents, teachers, social workers, medical staff and, indeed, to all people in whatever walk of life, please recognize this appalling problem and if you know of, or are faced with, anyone who is trying to escape from the clutches of witchcraft, for God's sake be sympathetic.

PSYCHIC AROMAS

It often happens that people become aware of a presence in a room, not by seeing any person or entity, but by recognizing a scent which reminds them unmistakably of one particular person.

One man from Lincolnshire can always tell when a family crisis is about to occur as he always gets a strong smell of tobacco, the blend which his beloved late uncle always smoked.

"It never fails, every single time I get the tobacco scent something traumatic happens. It is always something highly personal and closely related to the immediate family. It is as if he is trying to warn me. He always succeeds in alerting my attention, but the only trouble is I can never quite work out exactly what is going to happen. The tobacco aroma has come five times already. The first two or three times I did not pay much heed to it, although I was acutely aware that it was the exact same smell as old Uncle Bert's pipe. Then, when events started to follow the scent, usually within two or three days, I started to wonder about it. When it happened the fourth time I remember thinking, "Here we go again, I wonder what it will be this time." I got myself into quite a state because there was no way that I dare tell any of my family, for fear of frightening them. Each time the youngsters went out on their bikes I found myself growing anxious about them, and when my wife was shopping with the car I was like a nervous wreck. That particular time, in fact, my wife did have a spot of trouble with the car, but thankfully it was nothing too serious –

someone knocked the bumper. I had mentioned to her before she'd left to take special care and not to take any chances. I suppose if I had not been aware of Uncle Bert's warning I might not have cautioned her in the way that I did, and who knows?

"It's a blessing in disguise, I suppose, but I can't help feeling that old Bert is trying to take care of us in the same way as he did when he lived with us."

Pipe tobacco lingered in a London flat even though Mrs. Watton, who had just taken up residence there, did not smoke. She scrubbed and cleaned, disinfected, polished and scoured but the pipe tobacco persisted.

"It was as if it kept coming in intermittent waves. I used to open all the windows but no matter what I did the tobacco smell was always there.

"I found out that the former tenant was an elderly man who had died in the flat, but at that time I knew nothing about him. One night I woke up suddenly and I distinctly noticed the room was very cold and, as usual, there was the strong smell of pipe tobacco. I then heard the front door bang, so I got up and went to look out of the window but I could not see anyone outside or on the pavement. The same thing happened again on two other nights at 1.00 am. The upstairs tenant was a retired nurse and when I told her about the tobacco smell and the front door banging, she told me that she had helped to look after the old man, and she said that he always smoked a pipe. She advised me to contact a priest, which I did. He came to the flat. I did not see exactly what he did, but from that moment the tobacco smell vanished and I have had no problems since."

Yet another story of tobacco aroma comes from a lady in Hyde in Cheshire. "Way back in 1957 my father died suddenly from a heart condition. He lived with us and I worked at the same firm along with him. When we had office picnics, about three times a year, he always came along with us. He was always last out and he would stand in the hallway, light up a cigar and then, when everyone was out, he would lock the door.

"A few weeks after he died, we were going to the Lake District on one of our office picnics. I was standing in the hallway with some of my colleagues. Suddenly I got a whiff of cigar smoke. I looked around quickly to see who had just lit up but, to my surprise, no-one was smoking anything. One of my friends was staring at me intensely, but said nothing. Later on I questioned the friend, asking why he had given me such a peculiar look while we had been standing in the hallway. He replied, "To be perfectly honest, I could swear that I could smell cigar smoke." I smiled, partly with relief and admitted, "So could I."

The same thing happened on three other picnic days, all in the hallway, just before we were about to lock up the offices. It was just as if my father was somehow reminding us to be sure to lock up before we left for our outing."

A bereaved husband was given consolation by the sweet smell of perfume. He was living in a state of numbness just a few days after his wife's death. "She was lying in a Chapel of Rest in Sevenoaks. I had arranged to visit my brother some miles from my home. I duly drove from my home to his, and as I passed through Sevenoaks the air was filled with the scent of perfume. I used no scented preparations myself. I do not use any scented materials in my car, my wife hardly ever used perfume, and certainly not recently, and I had not given anyone a lift around that time. The aroma only lasted for seconds, and it was not until I was passing out of

370

Sevenoaks that I realised that the scent arose at almost the exact time I had passed the Chapel of Rest where my wife was lying. I have a very keen sense of smell, but retracing my journey I cannot think of where the smell came from.

"My wife and I were very close. In addition to the normal man and wife relationship we were great friends, and I can't help wondering whether that once, because of our closeness, there was a brief attempt at contact."

A Lancashire lady believes that her dead husband has attempted to communicate with her and prove himself as a mystic medic.

"After my dear husband died quite suddenly, I felt him so near to me at times. Once when I was ill with Asian flu I suddenly became aware that my pre-fab was smelling of Friars Balsam. Now, Harry, my husband, had been a firm believer that this cured all colds and flu. I did not have any of it at home at all since I'd never bothered to buy any since his death, but nevertheless the whole place reeked of it.

"My son came home and remarked that I had been very heavy-handed with the old "FB", but I protested, telling him that I did not have a drop of it in the house. "But Mum," he persisted, "The whole place stinks of it." I found myself smiling sadly at my son and reminding him, "You know, Roger, your Dad was such a believer in old "FB". The smell lingered for three days and nights and then went as suddenly as it came. I do think maybe Harry was trying to let me know that he was still caring for me, even though he had passed over."

Great Yarmouth is a thriving, happy seaside resort, with all the fun and amusement one associates with a holiday town. The last thing we would expect to encounter in such a place would be a ghost. A woman from Norwich had a strange experience when she went there.

"I had just moved to Great Yarmouth after my marriage breakdown, and after several weeks I was allocated a council maisonette on Ordnance Road. As I was moving in, a young man who lived a few doors down said, "Hello, are you moving in? I hope you know that place is haunted." Taking this as a childish prank I ignored it. I installed my son's bed in a small room at the top of the stairs.

"At about 11.00 pm I went to bed. About 11.30 pm the bathroom door began to open and close, slowly at first but then faster and faster, and louder and louder. Thinking that I must have left a window open and a draught was causing the disturbance, I got up to investigate. There were no windows open and try as I might, I could not make the door creak as it had been doing. I went back to bed and I started to nod off to sleep.

"Again I heard the sound of the bathroom door opening and closing furiously. Again I got up, but as soon as I approached the bathroom, the noise stopped and the door was still. I went back to bed and just as I was almost asleep, the same thing happened again. By this time I was so exhausted after having just moved in that I just hadn't the energy to get up again, so I fell asleep.

"A few days later, my son and I went to stay with a friend for a week. When I came back I was greeted by a very unhappy neighbour who had two small children. She complained strongly to me about all the noise we had been making in the flat, banging and moving furniture about all the time. I explained to her that we had been away for the entire week, so it could not possibly have been us.

"The next day the flat was full of the smell of roast beef

emanating from the kitchen. That night, about 11.30 pm, I was reading in bed and I heard shuffling at the bottom of the stairs. To my horror, someone appeared to be walking, almost dragging themselves, slowly up the stairs. I leapt out of bed and ran to the landing, expecting to find a burglar or a drunk. The stairs were empty, but the laboured breathing continued as did the sound of the stairs creaking as someone invisible walked up them. When the noise reached the top of the stairs it stopped.

"This performance was repeated about three times a week for about a month. One night my son, who was 8 years old at the time, came screaming into my room and told me, "Someone's just kissed me and tried to pull the bedcovers over my face." I went into his little room and there was a loud buzzing noise (like a bee), not coming from any place in particular. Needless to say, I moved his bed into my room and we lay awake, listening to breathing, shuffling and buzzing the whole night.

"About a month or so later, I was talking to an elderly gentleman, and in conversation he happened to ask me where I lived. When I told him, he looked amazed and said, "I know it well. I used to court a lady who lived there, but she's dead now." The lady in question had been called Jane Cowper, and had suffered from a very bad heart. She had been taken to hospital to have a heart valve replacement.

"The small room which was my son's bedroom had often been occupied by her two nieces, whom she invariably put to bed and kissed goodnight. Now apparently her operation had not been successful and, one day, while she was cooking Sunday dinner (roast beef) she mentioned to one of the neighbours that she felt ill. The neighbour sent for the doctor and Jane went back home, and managed to pull herself slowly up the stairs. She reached the small bedroom and died there before the doctor arrived. The date of her death was 29th July. The haunting started about 20th June and reached a climax on the date of her death, then slowly faded away at the end of August.

"Every year after that, on the anniversary of her death, I used to move my son out of his small bedroom and into mine. I used to lie awake listening to repeats of Jane Cowper's last journey up the stairs and into the small bedroom.

"I did a little research into the previous tenants (none of whom stayed too long) and I discovered that many of them had heard Jane. One of them had requested a transfer because Jane had materialised in front of her little girl who had occupied the small bedroom."

ANGELS

When we think of Angels we visualise perfect beings with beautiful faces and butterfly wings, and we usually associate them with sweet heavenly music.

This visualisation of angels may not be far from truth as many people have reported seeing creatures which fit our pre-conceived notion of how angels look, as Mrs. Fawcett of Yorkshire will confirm, although the angel she feels she saw had no wings.

She woke up one morning as usual, put on her dressing gown and hair net. "I felt as though I were walking round in slow motion. I felt awake but everything seemed hazy. I could see people but they couldn't seem to see me. I kept thinking I must go back to bed and wake up, but I couldn't. I could see my daughter asleep in bed but I couldn't get back in, so I walked round again. Then I was in this strange house, there was a pile of records and a man was looking through them. There was a book mixed in with them, the man pulled it out and asked who had put it there. It was a thin book, blue or grey in colour, with the word "Who" written on the cover.

"There was a table in the middle of the room, with a tablecloth on it. In the centre of the table was a jug which seemed to be full of cider. I couldn't understand what was going on. I went back upstairs but, no matter how hard I tried, I just couldn't get back into bed. Then I was walking in a white mist. The building I saw was also a brilliant white. I saw two long white steps on which sat a young girl, who had long fair hair with a parting in the middle. I walked up to her and asked her if I was dead. She smiled and shook her head. I was crying and she put her arms around me. I felt very cold when she did this and started shivering. I'm sure she said something about "Rusty" and that two came over but one didn't make it. Then I woke up feeling cold, although I was still covered up in bed with my daughter asleep at the side of me. It took me ages to get warm again."

Looking back on her experience, Mrs. Fawcett remembers, "When I was crying it was not because I was frightened, it was because I thought I was dead and I didn't want to be – not just yet, anyhow. All I can say about the girl is that she looked serene, very pale complexion, long straight fair hair with a parting down the middle, no fringe. She wore a white dress, no sleeves, and it had a low round neckline. I couldn't see the bottom part of her because of the mist rising from the ground, what with the steps being white plus the building behind her, which I could just make out – being white also everything seemed to mingle with each other. She just looked at me and smiled as if to say "Don't be afraid". I've never seen the girl since, to my knowledge. I don't know who or what "Rusty" is. When she said something about two coming over but only one made it, perhaps I was one of the two, I just don't know. Having said that, she gave me this message, although she didn't speak the words like we do. She just sat smiling, but I got the message just the same and she seemed to know what I was feeling. The worst thing was the terrible cold I felt when she put her arms around me. I'll never forget that. I liked the girl – she must have been in her early twenties, and she looked as though she hadn't a care in the world, serene is the only word for her."

When Mrs. Green of Derbyshire was about to give birth

to her son she had the most wonderful encounter with – not just one – but six angels.

"I had an extremely long and painful labour. However two hours before he was born I suddenly felt as though I were leaving my body and floating up the the ceiling, where I turned and looked down on my body. I could see everything going on – a tortured body and the staff all helping – one particular sister bent over me to sponge me down and the back of her hair parted to show a tiny curl.

"The next thing that happened was my body turned upwards and what was the ceiling parted and became the most beautiful blue sky with floating white clouds. My body started to rise and either side of me were three angels – the music and atmosphere were so beautiful and peaceful and I wanted to go. Somewhere in the background a voice said, "We're not going to get this baby in time". This must have made some impact on me as the voice got louder and louder – the angels and the blue sky floated away and I was back on the labour table. Somehow I got the strength to carry on and my son was born.

"The following day the sister who had sponged me down came to see me. My experience came back to me so I dropped something on the floor and she picked it up – yes, her hair parted and there was the little curl. I was very frightened and thought I was losing my mind, so I said nothing, not even to my husband.

"A few months went by and this experience was constantly in my mind, so I told my husband who reassured me I wasn't losing my mind. I also spoke to a friend about it. She seemed to have heard about this sort of thing and said when you're close to death you sometimes get experiences like this. I have had operations since and been very poorly but have never experienced this again. It still stands out very vividly in my mind and every time I hear anything about this sort of thing both my husband and I think back to that time."

On recapping upon her meeting with the angels, Mrs. Green recalls that they were positioned three on either side of her, one above the other with herself in the middle. "They were dressed in long white Grecian style gowns, their hair a golden colour. Everything seemed to be gold and white apart from the blue sky. As I floated upwards towards the sky I was being drawn slowly upward by a golden rope. There was sweet gentle music in the background – no talking – just an aura of peace and gentleness. When the sister's voice penetrated my brain that the baby might be born dead her voice got louder and louder until I screamed "NO". At that moment the angels started to float away from me higher and higher until everything faded away and I found myself back on the labour table – the ceiling was intact just as though nothing had happened.

"I feel the experience made me strong enough to carry on through the excruciatingly painful birth. It was as if I was given a rest from the pain, as if to catch my breath, but the impression left on me after my flight with the angels was so strong that it completely changed my whole life. I seemed to be filled with the joy of life and when, shortly after my return to the labour table, my baby son was born well and healthy my feeling of joy surpassed everything.

"The only sad thing about the whole episode was that the sister with the kiss curl on the nape of her neck died shortly afterwards while still only a very young woman."

There is a recognized hierarchy of angels which range from the mighty archangels, the chief one being Michael

378

down through the seraphim; cherubim; principalities; authorities; powers; thrones; might and dominion (Colossians 1:16; Romans 8:37). There is some confusion amongst theologians as to the thrones, might and dominions, principalities (sometimes referred to as princes) and authorities. There are some who say that these are really all belonging to the same group and vary only according to the amount of power delegated to each of the types within the same group.

There is agreement, however, regarding the upper realms of angelic identification. The Archangel Michael is looked upon as being the highest of all angels. The name "Michael" means "Like Unto God". The feast of Michael is celebrated on 29th September as Michaelmas Day, and in 1950 Pope Pius XII declared St. Michael the Archangel to be the patron of policemen. Going back to the Old Testament, it was Michael whom God sent to protect Moses in his task of leading the children of Israel out of Egypt and into the Promised Land.

It is believed that in the last mighty battle between the forces of good and evil, Michael with his legions of angels will clash head-on with Lucifer (the fallen archangel) and his satanic followers. According to the scriptures, Michael will be victorious over Lucifer, hell will tremble and Heaven will rejoice and celebrate. It is Michael who will accompany Jesus at his second Coming and with a mighty booming voice he will awaken the dead – "For the Lord Himself shall descend from Heaven with a shout, with the voice of the archangel . . . and the dead in Christ shall rise first." (Thessalonians 4:16).

Gabriel is sometimes referred to as an archangel, but some say he is a unique personage of angelic substance who acts as the messenger of God. The name "Gabriel" in Hebrew means "The Mighty Hero".

It was the angel Gabriel who appeared to the Virgin Mary and announced to her that she was to become the mother of Jesus. It is not hard to imagine how a young girl would be most startled when suddenly being confronted by the awesome sight of Gabriel in all his splendour as he declared to her, "Do not be afraid Mary; for thou has found favour with God. And, behold, thou shalt conceive in thy womb, and bring forth a Son, and shalt call His name Jesus . . . And He shall reign over the house of Jacob for ever; and of His Kingdom there shall be no end". (Luke 1:30-33). Mary's answer was simple and to the point, "Behold the handmaid of the Lord, be it done unto me according to thy word." (Luke 1:38).

When Zacharias was in the temple the angel Gabriel appeared to him to tell him that his wife Elizabeth was to give birth to a son who was to act as a forerunner of the Messiah, preparing the way of the Lord. Zacharias questioned this for the fact that Elizabeth was advanced in years and well past child-bearing age. "And Zacharias said to the angel, "How shall I know this for certain? For I am an old man, and my wife is advanced in years." And the angel answered and said to him, "I am Gabriel, who stands in the presence of God: and I have been sent to speak to you, and to bring you this good news. And behold, you shall be silent and unable to speak until the day when these things take place, because you did not believe my words, which shall be fulfilled in their proper time." (Luke 1:18,19,20). Because of his doubt, Zacharias was struck dumb. It came to pass that Elizabeth did indeed give birth to a baby boy (John the Baptist) and it was only after the birth of the baby that

Zacharias' speech was returned to him. The first appearance by Gabriel took place when Daniel was in prayer, "And behold, standing before me was one who looked like a man. And I heard the voice of a man between the banks of the Ulai, and he called out and said, "Gabriel, give this man an understanding of the vision." (Daniel 8: 15,16). Gabriel went on to explain to Daniel the events which would take place at the end of time.

The seraphim are primarily concerned with love and are constantly glorifying God, being situated above the divine throne. In Chapter 6 of the Book of Isaiah we are given a description of the seraphim . . . "Each having six wings; with two he covered his face, and with two he covered his feet, and with two he flew. And one called out to another and said, "Holy, Holy, Holy, is the Lord of Hosts, the whole earth is full of his glory."

Next in importance come the cherubim. In the book of Ezekiel, Chapter 10 it states, "Then I looked, and behold, in the expanse that was over the heads of the cherubim something like a sapphire stone, in appearance resembling a throne, appeared above them. And he spoke to the man clothed in linen and said, "Enter between the whirling wheels under the cherubim, and fill your hands with coals of fire from between the cherubim and scatter them over the city. And he entered in my sight."

"Now the cherubim were standing on the right side of the temple when the man entered, and the cloud filled the inner court. Then the glory of the Lord went up from the cherub to the threshold of the temple, and the temple was filled with the brightness of the glory of the Lord. Moreover, the sound of the wings of the cherubim was heard as far as the outer court, like the voice of God Almighty when He speaks."

"And it came about when He commanded the man clothed in linen, saying, "Take fire from between the whirling wheels, from between the cherubim". He entered and stood beside a wheel. Then the cherub stretched out his hand from between the cherubim to the fire which was between the cherubim, took some and put it into the hands of the one clothed in linen, who took it and went out. And the cherubim appeared to have the form of a man's hand under their wings. Then I looked, and behold, four wheels beside the cherubim, one wheel beside each cherub, and the appearance of the wheels was like the gleam of a tarshish stone."

"And as for their appearance, all four of them had the same likeness, as if one wheel were within another wheel. And when they moved they went in any of their four directions without turning as they went: but they followed in the direction which they faced. And their whole body, their backs, their hands, their wings, and the wheels were full of eyes all around, the wheels belonging to all four of them. The wheels were called in my hearing, the whirling wheels. And each one had four faces. The first face was the face of a cherub, the second face was the face of a man, the third the face of a lion and the fourth the face of an eagle."

"Then the cherubim rose up. They are the living beings that I saw by the river Chebar. Now when the cherubim moved, the wheels would go beside them: also when the cherubim lifed up their wings to rise from the ground, the wheels would not turn from beside them. When the cherubim stood still, the wheels would stand still; and when they rose up, the wheels would rise with them. for the spirit of the living beings was in them."

"Then the glory of the Lord departed from the threshold

of the temple and stood over the cherubim. When the cherubim departed, they lifted their wings and rose up from the earth in my sight with the wheels beside them; and they stood still at the entrance of the east gate of the Lord's house. And the glory of the God of Israel hovered over them."

"These were the living beings that I saw beneath the God of Israel by the river Chebar; so I knew that they were cherubim. Each one had four faces and each one four wings, and beneath their wings was the form of human hands. As for the likeness of their faces, they were the same faces whose appearance I had seen by the river Chebar. Each one went straight ahead." (Ezekiel 10: 1-22).

The cherubim were called upon in the garden of Eden to guard the way to the tree of life. (Genesis 3:24). In the Book of Psalms confirmation is given that the cherubim are seated beneath the throne of God . . . "Oh give ear, Shepherd of Israel, Thou who dost lead Joseph like a flock; Thou who art enthroned above the cherubim, shine forth." (Psalms 80:1), and again, "The Lord reigns, let the peoples tremble; he is enthroned above the cherubim, let the earth shake." (Psalms 99:1).

A man from Merseyside, Mr. Phillips, had a glimpse of angels and their singing is something he will remember vividly for the rest of his life. It came about one day when he was walking up the road, minding his own business, and he met Mrs. Rogerson. Now Mrs. Rogerson was an unmistakable character, being elderly and eccentric she always pushed a baby's pram in which she kept bundles of plastic bags, filled with her world-worn possessions. She was a sparky individual and always stopped to share a joke with Mr. Phillips.

He remembers their last meeting clearly. He had been impressed at how well she looked. "I knew she had not been too well, but when I met her she looked the picture of health. I had been a bit down in the dumps and she seemed to sense this. She asked me what was troubling me. Before I had the chance to reply I found myself suddenly whisked to a different sphere. I was trembling with fright at first as I couldn't make out what was happening. I was totally and fully conscious all the time because I distinctly remember thinking to myself that I had somehow been transported from my road to another plane of existence above human understanding. I don't know exactly how I got there, I only know that it was instantaneous. I still had Mrs. Rogerson's question in my mind but I found that I was unable to answer her. My eyes, mind and heart were overcome by the sight of countless angels. It would be impossible to say how many. The most memorable thing about them was their singing which was indescribably beautiful. Such was the intense feeling of happiness that I could hardly catch my breath. The next moment I was standing in the pathway again. I looked round but Mrs. Rogerson had gone.

"This all happened at exactly 3.00 pm as I was on my way to collect my younger sister from school. You can imagine my astonishment when, on reaching the school, I heard the news that Mrs. Rogerson had been found dead in her house at 12 noon that day. I don't know what kind of an effort it was on her part to take me to the next world in this manner, but I will always treasure the experience."

Angels do not always arrive with serene faces playing harps, as Catherine of Co. Armagh will verify. She was out shopping one day and found herself in an area where the local punks congregated. She felt threatened as she walked along and tried not to look at any of the menacing youths who were calling over to her.

"Because I ignored them they started to shout obscenities at me. I was very frightened but tried not to show it. My heart started to thump when I realised they were following me, about six of them. I quickened my pace but within a few seconds I was surrounded. one of them reached out to grab my handbag, but before he got hold of it, another punk rushed forward from behind me and took a swing at the mugger, knocking him to the ground.

"By the way the gang of thugs reacted, I could tell that the youth who had come to my rescue must have been from a rival gang, but to me he could have been one of them since he was dressed in a black studded leather jacket and trousers, and he had a bright pink Mohican hairstyle which stood on end about six inches into blue spikes.

"I was so thankful for his intervention and when the others saw that he meant business they all ran away. I turned to the youth who faced me and gave me the most dazzling smile. I opened my mouth to say "thank you" and he vanished in front of my eyes! I just stood there with my mouth open in utter amazement.

"When I thought about it afterwards once I'd had a chance to get over the shock, I realized that God works in strange ways indeed. He sent me help in the most appropriate way possible to meet the punks on their own level. Ever since that day, I've never again thought of angels as being somewhat soppy insipid creatures, not the way that one delivered his left hook."

An old well-loved hymn to the guardian angels:

> Dear angel ever at my side
> How loving must thou be
> To leave your home in Heaven to guide
> A sinful soul like me

These must be the most comforting and reassuring words that anyone could ever say to a child.

How many times to we feel aware of the positive and wise protection of our own guardian angels? Everyone at some time or other has had that narrow escape, or the distinct impression that something or someone was trying to divert a planned course of action, only to find out later, that had we followed the inner voice's suggestion we would have been better off. In some cases where the silent instruction has been acted upon, serious and even fatal accidents have been avoided. In most of these cases the persons concerned feel that they have been guided out of trouble.

We have all be allocated a guardian angel, as we see from the Book of Psalms, 91:11, "For He will give His angels charge concerning you, to guard you in all your ways. They will bear you up in their hands, lest you strike your foot against a stone."

POSITIVE CONCLUSIONS

Doctors now accept that the human mind can overcome even the most dreadful illnesses. Most cancerous cells can be eliminated by the natural immune systems of the body, but only if the mind allows these defences to work properly. It appears that the 'rogue cell' once thought to be the culprit is not, in itself, the cause of the illness.

The attitude of the person affected plays a dynamic role in recovery. Positive thoughts enlighten the spirit and allow the body to function in a way which is beneficial to the person as a whole. Negative thoughts dampen the spirit and cause disorder in the body mechanisms, including the immune system.

You can use the forces of your mind to assist you with any supposedly unsolvable problem. Just tell your subconscious mind what you wish to achieve and ask it to find the answer. Then forget about it altogether and relax. Lo and behold, a little while later, the answer will pop into your conscious mind and you will think to yourself 'Now why didn't I think of that before.'

Positive loving thoughts create an atmosphere of friendliness and wellbeing. This sets up a chain-reaction of goodwill. Ninety-five people would not have died at Hillsborough in Sheffield on that fateful Saturday if there had been goodwill instead of chaos. Why did people have to die to create the subsequent wonderful scene of camaraderie between Liverpool and Everton fans? Why couldn't it have always been like that?

Most other spectator sports seem to attract people who

share the true spirit of sportsmanship. No trouble at baseball, cricket or rugby games. What is it about the mentality of the minority of football supporters that causes them to spread such havoc?

It only takes a tiny spark of love and goodwill to ignite the imagination of an entire nation to support such good causes as The Great Ormond Street Wishing Well Appeal; Comic Relief and Amnesty International. If we all take an active step to consciously think positive thoughts, the domino effect this would have on mankind would bring stunning changes and untold happiness.

Spinechiller

by
Peter and Mary Harrison

INTRODUCTION

SPINECHILLER is a unique collection of true, authentic ghost stories, the experiences of ordinary people from all over the country, also some from overseas.

The stories have been collected over many years, mainly as a result of radio phone-in programmes where listeners have responded, in writing and over the air, to Mary's request for unexplained experiences. One of the most influential sources of material has been the regular MYSTERIES PHONE-IN with Pete Murray on LBC (London Talkback Radio). Mary has been the psychic researcher on this programme for over three years and has received a wealth of intriguing stories from listeners.

It is interesting to note that within the vast weekly mailbag a high percentage of letters start with the words: "Now I don't believe in ghosts, but . . .." Then the writer goes on to tell his or her ghost story! This shows that although people are often hesitant to divulge their experiences for fear of being ridiculed, the effect of what has occurred in their lives has been so overwhelming that they feel compelled to share their stories with others. Most of the stories in the book have been first time encounters and the people have gone to great lengths to emphasize that they have not dabbled in the occult.

PETER & MARY HARRISON

SPINECHILLER
– EXTRACTS –

The South of England   391

The North of England   472

Overseas   524

THE SOUTH OF ENGLAND

LUTON, the industrial town set in the heart of the Chilterns, is the home of Gary Eldridge whose story began when he left school at the age of 16 in 1974.

'I did not know what I wanted to do for a living but after answering a few advertisements I went for an interview for a job as a trainee baker. The bakery was in Salisbury Road in the older part of the town. The owner lived in a flat above the bakehouse and there was a shop at the front of the premises from which the sales were conducted. The baker was married and had five children. Even at my tender age when I first met the man I had a feeling that all was not quite right. I could not put my finger on it and looking back I suppose he might be described as being mildly eccentric.

'Anyway, the job consisted of learning the bakery trade which I was looking forward to and I was offered a reasonable pay packet, mainly because of the unsociable hours that had to be worked; 3.30 a.m. until the work was finished from Monday to Thursday and on Fridays I had to work from 11.00 p.m. until 9.30 a.m.

'I was shown around the bakehouse which consisted of a medium sized room in which wedding and birthday cakes were made; down some old wooden steps into the old kitchen which had been turned into the frying room; the main bakehouse which had two large mixers and two very large old fashioned wooden benches and two ancient provers.

'So my first morning of work arrived and off I went slightly apprehensive as any young boy would be on his first day at a job. At that time the business was being run just by Colin the baker and his wife who ran the shop. I was shown some of the things that I was expected to do.

'On that very first day Colin called me over and asked me something that I will always remember simply because it seemed so strange at the time. He asked me if I scared easily! I said, "No". Nothing more was said which made me wonder even more.

'After I had worked there for about six months, one morning I was just getting on with my chores as usual. I had grown to enjoy the job very much and I was fond of the owner and his wife. I remember I was dividing dough into two pound lumps ready for proving. After a while at the job I'd found that I did not need to keep putting the knife down to add bits of dough to the lump to ensure that the specified weight was maintained. Anyway on this occasion I stuck my knife into the dough to add a small piece to the lump on the scales. I only turned around for a matter of seconds but when I turned back the knife had been moved away out of my reach.

'At the time, although I was puzzled, it never really occurred to me to say anything to Colin as to me it was insignificant. However when the same kept happening about four or five times that week I thought that I'd better mention it to Colin.

'I will always remember the look on his face. His mouth opened and he said, "Oh no. Here we go again." He then surprised me by telling me that if I wanted to leave he would understand. I assured him that I was very happy in the job and I was sorry that I'd even mentioned the incident to him as I did not want to cause a fuss over nothing. No more was said and although I probed him to tell me why he seemed so concerned he refused to say a single word on the matter.

'Shortly after that I was in the bakehouse on my own. I needed to go into the loft to collect a sack of flour. I had done this many times before so it was just part of the normal proceedings. I was in the loft picking up the sack of flour when the only window in the room slammed shut with such a force that one of the glass panes smashed to smithereens. I felt all the hairs on the back of my neck stand up. It had suddenly turned freezing cold. I kept thinking that the loft was always the warmest place in the whole building, the temperature kept at approx. 30° C, so I could not understand why the atmosphere had gone frigid. It was a scorching sunny day so even though the window was broken no cold could have come from outside.

'Something told me to get down the stairs as quickly as I could so I grabbed the big bag of flour and charged down the steps. Halfway down, a box of wafers came toppling down on me making me lose my balance and trip over. The flour bag burst and I found myself almost smothering in clouds of flour.

'I went up to Colin's flat to report what had happened. He saw that I'd had a fright and I was covered in flour so he immediately told me to go home and get changed and that I could take the rest of the day off. I washed my face and hands and brushed down my clothes as best I could, and then I thought I'd better just call back to the bakeroom where Colin was to tell him that I was off home.

'I heard terrible shouting as I approached the bakehouse and when I entered I found Colin on the floor shouting and cursing at something which seemed to be holding him down. When he saw me he shouted over at me to get out

393

quickly but there was no way that I could have left him like that. I made myself walk over towards him. It crossed my mind that perhaps he was having some kind of fit. I was not quite sure what to do so I reached down to grab his arms to try to help him up on to his feet.

'As I reached out for his arms I again felt a blast of cold air and again, unaccountably, I felt the hairs on the back of my neck rise up. Try as I would I could not grasp his arms even though they were only inches away from me. Something solid, but invisible, was preventing me like a barrier. We were both in a state of terror and felt completely helpless. It was as if we were battling with a tremendous unseen force.

'I don't know if Colin had experienced anything like that before but he suddenly seemed to get the upper hand and he roared – and I mean really bellowed at this thing to go away (although his language was somewhat stronger!) The thing, whatever it was, seemed to get the message because suddenly whatever barrier had been preventing me from grabbing Colin's arms had gone. I helped him up off the floor and I noticed that the icy feeling had also gone and the room temperature was back to normal.

'Although everything was back to normal we were both very shaken up and he was flinching as if he was in physical pain. He rolled up the sleeve of his shirt and I was appalled to see three large scratch marks on his arm. They were not bleeding but raised up like weals and they looked extremely painful. I knew that I couldn't have made those marks on his arm as by the time I was able to grasp hold of him he was already starting to get up himself so all I did was to take a hold of his right arm, more to steady him than anything. The marks were on his other arm. (I have given this incident much thought over the years since then and I have always come to the same conclusion: there is no way that he could have made those marks himself.)

'I went home and had the rest of that day off as was arranged. The following morning I reported for work as usual. Each of our baking racks consisted of about 25 heavy steel trays full of bread tins. I had filled up one of the trays with the tins when for no reason that I could think of, the tins started to move around by themselves. They moved only a few inches but the peculiar thing was that they had moved in all different directions so it's not as if the tray was on a slant or anything like that. As I walked out to the retarder room I heard a few loud clicks. By the time I got to the room all the retarder doors were wide open.

'Being a practical person I was getting a bit sick of all the nonsense that appeared to be going on and this was the last straw. I stomped over to the retarders, slammed the doors shut and in my mind I kept repeating Colin's words of the previous day when he had suggested that the entity should "go away". Only I didn't just suggest, I downright ordered the thing to depart from us.

'Just as I turned round from the retarders, out of the corner of my eye something grey caught my attention. I looked round and at the entrance by the doorway there was a cloud of greyish smoke hanging in mid air. I looked hard at this and slowly the sting of coldness permeated the room. I quickly lost my spirit of bravado and started to feel the fear creeping over me.

'In a panic I ran straight for the door thinking that I could maybe just barge through and get out of that place. As I braced myself to pass through the cloud of smoke I suddenly was hurled straight back into the small room with such force that I actually hit the back wall opposite the doorway. I was stunned. Not daring to move again I stood leaning against the wall staring at the smoke. It started to swirl around, at first quite slowly then as it gathered momentum it was moving in a furious circular motion.

'It seemed to work itself into a spiral then it promptly shot upwards and in a flash it was out of sight. I gave a heavy sigh of relief but still did not move – just in case. A bit gingerly I walked across towards the open door and went out of that room never to return.

'I reluctantly left the bakery as I had come to the end of my tether. I remained friends with Colin for a couple of years after I left until he also decided that the time had come to move on.

'One day he had been working in the outhouse by one of the retarders and he also was confronted by the grey cloud of smoke. I had never told him the exact details of what had happened to me in that room because at the time I was only interested in leaving with the minimum of fuss – also I did not want to worry Colin unduly.

'Like me, he saw the smoke in the open doorway. He also tried to get out and he felt himself catapulted back. He had started verbalizing at the smoke in his characteristic vocabulary but this did nothing to help his situation. He heard the sound of mocking laughter, quietly at first, but then it grew louder and louder until he thought that his eardrums would burst. It was harsh and malicious and really terrifying. As he watched, the smoke started swirling again and formed itself into a spiral but instead of just moving upwards and away as it had done when I had seen it, it turned on its side and shot into the room towards him. He buried his face in his hands and cowered down in the corner all the time hearing this fearsome outlandish laughter. He could also hear a swishing sound as this spiral kept swooping around the room.

'With all the courage he could muster he got up on his feet and when the spiral was in the opposite corner he ran out of the room and across the yard. He looked over his shoulder just in time to see the column of swirling smoke whizz upwards towards the sky, the laughter fading as the entity eventually evaporated.'

∞

JOAN Read, a lady from Lewisham, was carrying out a photographic survey of Deptford in South London in 1962 and she had decided to work on Deptford High Street. "Despite the cloud, the light was still good enough to get the detail that I needed. As I worked steadily along the street, the sun came out and the breeze died down.

'By the time I reached St. Paul's churchyard, I was very hot and one of my cameras needed reloading. I mingled through the crowds that always crammed the street on a Saturday, and then I remembered that Saturday was the only morning that I would be able to get into St Nicholas' church. The vicar had explained to me that other than for services the gates would only be opened for about a couple of hours while the flower lady was busy inside.

'I decided that it would be nice to go into the cool church where I could take my coat off and reload the camera then take some interior shots. Five minutes or so later I arrived at the church gates which were surmounted on either side by the figures of Adam and Eve which had looked down on generations of parishioners.

'The gates were unlocked so I went into the churchyard where the air was very hot and still. I made my way to the main doors of the church but found them locked, yet I could hear the organ being played inside. I thought that perhaps the organist was practising, so hoping that he would not mind me sitting in the church I walked round to the vestry door. I was thankful to find that it was slightly ajar. I pushed the door open and walked inside, finding the vestry empty. There was another door on the far wall which obviously led into the main church.

'It was quiet. The music had stopped. I then heard the sound of a door banging loudly in front of me. I wondered if the organist was just leaving, in which case he or she would hardly want to see me hanging around. I paused where I was in the vestry but I heard nothing more. I gently pushed the door to the church open and went inside. There was a lady busy arranging flowers on a small table behind the pews near the door.

'I said that I hoped I would not be disturbing her and I explained that the vicar had invited me to take some photographs of the church. She said that she would not be disturbed and that I was just to carry on as if she wasn't there. She said that she was usually there on her own at that time on a Saturday morning.

'I took my coat off, folded it and reloaded my camera. The church had been badly damaged during the war, but the restoration work had been extremely well done, using many pieces of masonary from the old building. I admired the Grinling Gibbons carving "The Valley of the Dry Bones", which then, in 1962, was not covered by protective glass as it is today.

'The church is a very old one, originally built on

Deptford Green in Saxon times. It was rebuilt in the 12th century and consisted of a chancel, nave and two aisles. In 1630 it was repaired and considerably enlarged. In 1697, due to a big increase in the population, the whole church was pulled down, with the exception of the tower, and rebuilt to a larger scale. The architect did his work so badly that the church had to be fully repaired in 1716. Other repairs followed and during the First World War it was closed for three years. It was bombed in the Second World War and restored in 1958. From early in the 12th century the church tower, with its beacon, guided ships round that bend of the River Thames. This association with seafarers led to the annual gathering on Trinity Monday of the Corporation of Trinity House.

'Just to make conversation I asked the flower lady if she played the organ as well, mentioning that I'd heard the music as I'd walked along the path outside. She looked puzzled as she told me that I must have been mistaken. She had not played the organ and certainly no one else had been in the church as she had been there on her own.

I did not say anything because I was so surprised. The music was so loud that she couldn't have avoided hearing it and it definitely was organ music coming from inside the church. She however was so adamant that there had been no music that I just didn't know what to think but I knew that I had heard it loud and clear.

'This incident made me start to wonder so much that I thought I'd better mention it to the vicar. Not wishing to make too much of it I started by asking him general questions about the church then I just asked casually about the organ. He told me that the original organ had been a 'Father Smith' built in 1697, but this had been destroyed by fire and rebuilt by Hunter in 1868. Further damage was done which was repaired by Bevington in 1876. When the restoration of the church took place in 1958 a new organ was built by N.P. Mander, installed and then decorated with the gilt carvings from the original organ casing.

'He told me something else that really made me think. He said that the day before, he had been busy supervising the reburying of bones which had been left out from the last time that the two large crypt chambers had been tidied up.

'He then went on to tell me that during the last war, a gang set up a workshop in the crypt to steal lead. The coffins were opened, the occupants tipped out and the lead cut up for removal. Later, when the rebuilding of the bombed church commenced, mountains of human remains were found in various stages of decomposition. The corpses had been covered with plenty of lime and left beneath the pews. Perhaps one of the poor wandering souls was an organist. It gave me the shivers to think that only I had heard that music.'

∞

BRENDA Whincup of Shropshire married in January 1961. Her husband is a northerner who at that time was serving in the Metropolitan Police and he wanted to transfer back up north.

'It meant that I was going to have to leave my mother, my one living relative, all alone. However she was only 52 at the time and said that she would consider moving north to live with us if my husband got his transfer.

'We moved north as planned, but my mother remained in London with promises of joining us very soon. Came that

Christmas though, she was still down south so we went down to London to spend the holiday with her. She couldn't come to us as she worked in a local hospital, in catering, and was working an early shift on Christmas Day.

'Our journey south on Christmas Eve, in our old car, was slow and grinding and we did not arrive until very late in the evening. My husband wanted to be up early the next morning to drive my mother to work – they thought the world of each other. She however would not hear of him getting up early after such a long gruelling drive so she insisted that he should have a rest the following morning and I agreed with her. My plan was to be up early myself and walk with her to her place of work.

'She was not pleased to see me up and ready to go out early the following morning and said that she wanted me to have a rest. I argued that I needed cigarettes and so we reached a compromise. I would keep her company part of the way to where there was a vending machine from where I'd let her continue on her own and I would return home with my cigarettes.

'We left the house so early that it was still dark. There was a glorious golden moon and the stars were sharp and bright. We walked hand in hand like a couple of excited children singing carols along the road. When we reached the vending machine, as promised, I let my mother go on alone and watched her go out of sight.

'I did not return to the house by the way we'd come. By taking a right hand turn I could go home by walking around the block which I did listening to my own footsteps echoing loud and lonely. Reaching the end of this road and taking another right hand turn, the last 200 yards to the corner of our road stretched before me.

'Here, with such a short way to go, everything seemed to wind down and go into slow motion. I'd never experienced anything like that ever before and I was most confused and somewhat alarmed. I remember very slowly almost floating up in the air between my steps as I moved along the left hand pavement. Then, from my right, on the other side of the road, the shape of a woman appeared from between a row of parked cars. I was certain that no one had turned into the road from the other end and there had been no sound of any door opening or any cars. She was just all at once there, crossing over towards me.

'My first impulse was to laugh. I had done a lot of amateur drama and here seemed to be someone over-playing a part. She was tall, well-built, wearing a coat so unfashionably long that it was almost down to her ankles. She was leaning heavily on a stick and sort of lumbered forward. Suddenly it was no longer funny and I became aware of the first feelings of fear sweeping over me

'As I moved on she came right up to me face to face. She asked me if I had a cigarette. With my new unopened packet burning a hole in my pocket, I said "No" and tried to hurry past but the slow motion was holding me back. Try as I would I could not move my feet at normal speed. She called after me, "Do you know how late it is?" I turned around and there was no one there. I found that I was walking at normal speed, in fact slightly faster than my usual pace.

'All over the Christmas period the incident was upper-most in my thoughts and I felt very worried by it. I felt an overwhelming guilt about my own meanness in refusing to give that woman a cigarette. I could have spared one easily. I hadn't even offered her a kind word. My actions worried me and I also had a nagging feeling at the back of my mind that I should have recognized this woman. I felt that I should know who she was yet at the same time I knew that I'd never seen her before.

'In the New Year, as other matters took over, I forgot about the incident. We discovered that my mother was seriously ill. She did, at last, come north to live with us for what turned out to be the last few months of her life.

'It was after my mother's death, when we were sorting out her things, that we came across some old photographs. There was one of me as a small girl taken in a garden, where I was standing beside my maternal grandmother who had been dead for some 20-odd years. She had been a big woman, and sturdily built. In the picture she wore a coat which came almost down to her ankles and she was leaning heavily on a stick.

'With great pain, I recognized her as the woman I'd met that last Christmas morning when, I believe, she had tried to warn me just how late it was and how little time I had left with my mother.'

∞

PETER Knights of Wisbech, Cambridgeshire, purchased a run-down property with a business partner in 1971. It was a corner shop with three floors and a cellar. It was situated in London's Fulham Road. 'The idea was to renovate the property and then let it out as flats and a lock-up shop.

'In order to keep the costs down I decided to do most of the interior decorating myself. At that time I was living in Surrey and in order to avoid the double journey each day I would often sleep on the premises in one of the bedrooms on the second floor which I had made habitable.

'I was wakened up one morning at 2.00 a.m. by the sound of glass breaking. My first thought was that a car must have crashed on the main road outside the shop. I looked out of the window onto the road below. The street lights remained on all night and I could see that there was no sign of any accident.

'I then thought that it must have been a passing drunk who had smashed the window of the shop, so I went down to the ground floor with some trepidation. The previous occupiers of the shop had been newsagents and confectioners and they had gone out of business and had done a moonlight flit leaving all the shop fittings, and display stands, behind them. These were all still in the shop as I had not got round to starting the renovations on the ground floor.

'There was a half glazed door leading into the back of the shop so I peered through this to take an initial look at the damage which I was sure must have been done to the large plate glass shop window.

'I was immediately aware that something was different about the shop. Instead of the outline of the counters and newspaper racks, greetings cards display stands, etc., I saw along one wall a number of tall mirrors with basins in front of them and a row of old-fashioned barbers chairs. An old fashioned gas fitting hung from the ceiling and there was a smell of cheap perfume.

'A figure was sitting slumped forward in the chair farthest from me. There were slivers of broken glass all around the place. My first reaction was that a drunken yob had broken into the shop and fallen asleep in the chair. The different appearance of the shop had somehow not completely registered in my brain.

'I quietly opened the door and reached for the light switch, getting ready to run if the figure sprang up at me. I turned on the light. The shop was instantly back as it should have been with the old counters, display stands etc. all in place. No mirrors on the wall, no basins or barbers chairs and no slumped figure. Nor was there any sign of any attempted break-in or any splinters of broken glass anywhere.

'The next morning I visited a nearby hardware store to make a few purchases. It was a traditional old type of shop which had been in the same hands for several generations. I told the elderly proprietor about my experience the previous night. He said that his father had once told him that at the early part of the century my shop had been a barbers, and the owner, returning from the First World War in 1918, had found that his wife had been unfaithful to him. He had gone straight down into the shop and cut his throat with one of his razors. His body had slumped forward smashing one of the wall mirrors as it did so. The time of his death was reported to have been around 2.00 a.m. I shivered as I returned to the shop resolving never to stay overnight in that flat again.'

∞

IN the late 1920s Verity Blake won a scholarship to a grammar school in South London. 'It has never been fashionable to actually like school but I have always cherished happy memories of mine – although I cannot say that I was one of its brighter lights.

'On leaving school I joined the Old Girls' Association. I was most active in the drama section the founder of which was an old teacher whom we all called Miss Dorothy. Seeing that I was keen, she took me under her wing. It was a joke between us that she had left school in the year of my birth.

'The play we were working on was *Viceroy Sarah* based on the relationship of Queen Anne and Sarah, Duchess of Marlborough. I had the part of the eldest Marlborough daughter, and Dorothy played Prince George, the Queen's consort. One tiny cameo remains with me. As the prince, Dorothy took leave of the two ladies announcing that 'he' would take a little nap. "And stay out of the pantry" was Queen Anne's reply. Putting his head round the curtain the prince answered with immense dignity: "I may have my little peculiarities, Annie, but I do not sleep in the pantry." This line always brought the house down.

'The war came and Dorothy went to the Midlands and I did not see her for many years. The end of the war found me with a husband and a family of little daughters, whose care precluded Old Girls' membership so I let my subscription lapse.

'Some years later, when the girls were growing up and becoming reliable, I did temporary secretarial work for an agency in London. One day I met another ex-schoolfellow with whom I had corresponded over the years. She told me that the school Christmas reunion was soon to be held so I decided to go along for old time's sake.

'The first person I saw in the well-remembered school hall was Dorothy. She came forward to welcome me and she introduced me to the school's new headmistress. There were several members of staff whom I had known in my schooldays – most of them long since retired but they all still came along to the reunions. They all remembered me and were glad to see me. I decided to renew my subscription and to attend meetings and functions whenever possible.

'In time, I was voted onto the committee and later I became the secretary for my own age group, so I saw Dorothy more often. She had been retired for several years and lived in a pleasant flat in South London. She used to have open house to her own ex-pupils. Now and then I would telephone her and arrange an evening together. By this time, we had moved to Surrey and all but one of our girls were married. Gradually I realized that Dorothy was looking older and more frail. After all she was into her seventies, but her interest in people was as keen as ever.

'On our Christmas reunions, refreshments were provided and served by committee members. On one such occasion Dorothy and I were dispensing tea and coffee from the refectory. We reminisced about the old Drama Section, which had never been revived since the war. Slyly I quoted: "I may have my little peculiarities, Annie, but I do not sleep in the pantry." Dorothy beamed with pleasure. "Fancy you remembering that, after all these years," she said, and I could see that she was touched.

'The next year, I was discussing herbs and herbal emollients and remedies with the botany mistress, who invited me to the staff table for refreshments. I followed her up to the top table instead of taking my food at the committee table where I generally sat. I could see Dorothy sitting alone at one end of it. I waved and she lifted her hand and smiled, but she looked far from being well.

'Refreshments over, it fell to me to collect money for the school's charity. Rattling my box at my fellow-committee members, I asked: "Where's Dorothy? I thought she looked rather ill."

'There was a shocked silence – then someone said: "Didn't you know? Dorothy died last Easter."

∞

JEREMY of Frome in Somerset used to live on a council estate in 1963. One of his school friends, Gareth Lewis, lived in Styles Avenue which bordered the grounds of an old house called Easthill House.

'The house had been derelict for a number of years and I understand that it had been requisitioned in the war by the army for the use of officers (Americans, I think). An old caretaker lived nearby in the early 1960s. Easthill House was uninhabited but stood in a lovely setting surrounded by trees. In the grounds there was a lodge, and strangely, a mortuary. In the bad weather of 1963, Gareth and I were playing, as we often did, in the grounds. That was a winter of extremely heavy snow that stayed until March or April.

'I must, at this point, mention that we were only ten years old at the time and when an old ambulance appeared on the drive outside the mortuary our only concern was to hide behind a hedge from where we had a clear view of the happenings.

'The ambulance looked new but old fashioned and had a red cross on the side of it. Gareth and I had been chased many times by the caretaker but we were prepared to risk this as we were so curious to watch, whilst hidden from view.

'The driver and his mate got out of the ambulance and went to the back of it, opened up the back doors and

408

brought out a body on a stretcher. They went into the mortuary and came out again several minutes later without the body but carrying the empty stretcher. They both got back into the ambulance. Suddenly it disappeared.

'Gareth and I were shocked but finally plucked up enough courage to creep over to the mortuary, some 30 yards away. The snow showed no tyre marks and in actual fact the snow was about two feet thick, sufficient enough to deter most vehicles. The only prints in the snow that day were the ones we made as we dashed home in terror.'

∞

REG of Peacehaven in Sussex got the sad news one day from his wife that her friend's husband had suddenly died at the wheel of his car at the age of 42.

'The following evening my wife and myself called to the lady's home to see if we could help in any way. We had been there on only one other occasion when I had met her husband for the first time. When I met him he seemed rather reserved and his wife explained to us later that he was not keen on having visitors in the house.

'On the evening after he had died, his widow was understandably still in state of shock. After about half-an-hour I had to go outside to fetch something from my car. I let myself out by the front door which opened very easily, but on my return, after only a few minutes, if that, I found the door very hard to push open. It was as if someone was behind the door trying to force it closed on me.

'I was just about to ring the doorbell when the door swung wide open, as if of its own accord. No one was behind the door when I stepped into the house. I did not say anything at that stage as I did not want to distress the lady needlessly.

'We stayed in the house for about an hour and in that time I had the constant feeling that the dead husband was trying to tell me something. It was like someone talking to me from another room. I knew I was being addressed but I just could not make out what the message was.

'On returning home, approximately eight miles away, I suddenly said to my wife to telephone the lady and ask her to pull back the corners of her fitted carpet in the dining room as there would be some money there. My wife was most hesitant to do such a thing in case her friend might feel that it was some kind of practical joke. I had no idea why I had asked her to do this but the feeling was so strong that I was convinced that she should make the telephone call. She did so very reluctantly, and held on whilst the widow turned up the corners of the living room carpet only to find that there was nothing there. My wife was most apologetic to her friend, and what she said to me will remain undisclosed.

'For some days after this I still kept getting that voice in my head over and over again instructing me to make the lady look under the carpet again, and there was something about a blue book to do with the Royal Navy. None of this made any sense to me whatsoever and after my wife being told by the woman that there was nothing under the carpet I thought that I'd better keep my thoughts to myself.

'About five weeks later the lady had to call in some workmen to her house to carry out some repairs. They pulled back the dining room carpet to get underneath the floorboards, and there, just a bit further in from where the lady had first looked, was a large envelope with £200 in it.

'On thinking back to the time I had tried to re-enter that

woman's house, I can't help thinking that the lady's husband had not realized that he was dead as it had happened so suddenly. I feel that he was still around the house that day and he looked upon me as an intruder trying to enter his home.'

∞

MR. Rudland, a Sussex man, like all grandfathers, thinks the world of his first little grandchild, Kirsty. 'When our daughter used to come to visit us when Kirsty was a baby we would put the little one in her carry-cot and put this on the lounge floor or sometimes in one of the bedrooms.

'When Kirsty was about four months old we noticed that after a while she would get very excited and her eyes seemed to be following something around the room. At first we thought that she was just interested in the new surroundings but even when she was left in the dark she would sometimes just stare at one spot without blinking but her arms and legs would be thrashing around in great jubilation. She would then suddenly stop as if someone had left the room, but after looking around the room she would start again, this time laughing and becoming very excited.

'Just before Kirsty's first birthday I was sitting in the lounge with her as she tried to climb up on my lap. She suddenly turned round and started to giggle. She stretched out her arms towards the other side of the room. As I looked up and tried to stop her from falling over, there, on the other side of the room about ten feet away from us, was an elderly man with a kind smiling face.

'Before I could call my wife and daughter he just faded away. When I looked down at Kirsty she was looking at me but pointing to the spot where the man had been standing. At that stage she had not started to speak but I can't help thinking that she had her own means of communication unknown to the adult world.'

∞

JACK Read of Lewisham, South London, remembers when London was still enduring the nightly bombing raids in late 1940. He had come home for a week's leave from his ship.

'I arrived at Kings Cross station many hours late, the train having been delayed by air-raids. I made my way to the underground. What a sight met my eyes! The platforms were crowded with sleeping figures spending the night down there, safely but most uncomfortably. Yet, despite all of the inconvenience, there was little grumbling, just the good old Cockney humour and a hope that their homes would still be standing in the morning.

'When the "all-clear" sounded, I made my way to London Bridge station where I was lucky to catch a train straight away to Forest Hill. Shortly after leaving the station at Forest Hill to walk home, the air-raid warning sounded. It didn't seem long before I heard the drone of enemy planes overhead.

'I became aware of some footsteps just behind me and then I heard a voice call out, "Hello Jack." It was pitch black and I couldn't make out who was calling to me. I then heard the words, "Don't say you've forgotten me – it's Marjorie."

412

'I peered into the darkness and recognized her. She was one of the sisters of my best friend. We passed a few words of general conversation until we arrived at the swimming baths where Marjorie left to cross over the road to her home in the street opposite. However, just before she left me, she made me promise that I would go home the long way round by the old pub called The Woodman and not up Thorpewood Avenue as I normally would have done.

'On reaching the start of Thorpewood Avenue I was in two minds about which way to go, but there was something about Marjorie's insistent manner that made me carry on via The Woodman.

'Some minutes later the sound of a plane's engines grew louder. Here it comes, I thought. Suddenly there were three thundering crunching sounds followed by a violent explosion which made the ground shake under my feet. The explosion was in the immediate vicinity so I started running towards my home to see if the house was still safe.

'I was relieved to see that there was no damage in our street but within minutes the whole area was in a frenzy of activity. Thorpewood Avenue had come under direct fire and three bombs had fallen across the road wrecking nearly all of the houses. My mind immediately flashed to Marjorie and how she had made me promise not to walk up that road. I would most definitely been hit had I gone that way.

'A devastating thought then shot through my mind and I just rushed straight out of our house without taking the time to say a word to anyone. Marjorie lived on one of the small streets branching off from Thorpewood Avenue.

'I raced all the way down the road past the uproar of rescue vehicles and the hundreds of people who were milling around outside, some of them screaming, some very badly injured and some in a complete state of shock. I got to Marjorie's road and to my horror I saw that the whole area – her small street plus a similar one – was demolished.

'I just stood there staring, not quite taking it all in. That was my first night back home after being away on active service for the best part of a year and I was still getting aclimatized to the real effects of war in our ordinary communities.

'I was the only person standing in that devastated road. It then occurred to me that although the houses had been obliterated, everything seemed to have been tidied up in a rough sort of way, but I still couldn't understand why there were no rescue teams bothering to attend to the area.

'While I was still standing there in a dazed condition, a couple of young lads walked by. I asked them if they had seen what had happened. They told me that a land mine had fallen on Marjorie's small road of just ten houses in the middle of the night some weeks previously. Marjorie and all of her family had been killed.'

∞

PATRICIA Ambler of Marlborough in Wiltshire sat one day with her mother in a pleasant room by a large open window. 'It was during the very unhappy early period of the Second World War. Norway had fallen and news from all fronts was discouraging. A large liner had just been sunk carrying hundreds of children to safe keeping in America. We had just heard about this earlier in the day.

'My mother had a few sisters and although great affection certainly existed between them, the distance separating their homes was such that it prevented much in the way of visiting. I always regretted this as I would have welcomed the intervention of my aunts to help me look after my mother. My father, who had always been so full of vigour, and who always knew how to handle every situation, had died suddenly the year before.

'The strain of just trying to survive in those days was beginning to tell on both of us and we had been arguing quite a lot. This particular day I had been trying to read a book but my mother just kept interrupting me constantly. On looking back I can now see that it was her way of telling me that she was feeling insecure and needed attention.

'Suddenly there was silence. After a few moments I looked over at my mother who was sitting bolt upright on her chair, staring into space. She then pointed over and said, "It's Lally. What's she doing here?" I looked all around the room but I could see no one. My aunt Lally was mother's sister.

'The next moment my mother turned a ghastly shade of white and collapsed back in her chair. I thought she was going to faint. All she kept saying was "She's gone. Lally's gone. She's gone." After a few minutes when her colour had slowly returned she told me that she had just seen Lally in the middle of our room, then she had suddenly vanished.

'My mother was a thorough realist and she would not speak further about what she saw. Slightly embarrassed, she fobbed off the incident by saying that she must have been imagining things.

'Early the following morning one of mother's other sisters telephoned us. Lally had been a passenger in a ship called the Simon Bolivar. It had been torpedoed the day before. She had been killed with her children.'

FOR ten years Frank used to be the landlord of the Star public house in a certain Hertfordshire village. 'It had been a fairly busy summer night and I made my usual check on the premises before retiring to bed. On my left was the fireplace with its usual quota of cigarette ends and empty crisp packets which I decided I would clear up the following morning.

'The front wall was at right angles to the fireplace wall and contained the front window, and at the far end, the front door and porch. The serving counter was about six or seven feet long and curled round onto the back wall where there was a small window. That window, with its four panes of glass, was very handy for my customers to look through and watch their children sipping soft drinks and eating crisps in the conservatory type lean-to. The ladies' room was at the far end of the lean-to. I had already switched off the lights but I could still see quite clearly as a very bright moon illuminated the room. I turned to leave the bar, closing the sliding door behind me, turned right and went up the stairs to bed.

'I woke up in the middle of the night in answer to a call of nature. As was my habit, I looked at my wrist watch to check the time. It was only 3.00 a.m. All of the toilets were on the ground floor so I got out of bed and made my way downstairs, thinking to myself that I would just slip into the ladies' room since that was less of a walk. On my way back upstairs I was walking through the conservatory and came to the little window. I just casually glanced towards it and for a few seconds I was rooted to the spot. I'd seen a glimpse of someone in the main bar. My first thought was that burglars had entered the building. I approached the window to get a better look.

416

'Something was dreadfully wrong. The bar looked very different. An almost white solid table stretched for most of the distance between the front and back walls and around it were seated about a dozen or so figures. They were all dressed in a similar fashion with very wide lapelled coats of grey, some with grey or dark blue edging. All of them looked happy and were drinking from large earthenware tankards.

'Some of these figures wore three-cornered shaped hats and I noticed that on a small table in the corner there were more of these hats. Far away in the background I could hear music and singing although I could not see anyone playing a musical instrument. The music sounded as if it was being played on a lute or some such stringed instrument. The figures at the long table were swaying with the music.

'Bizarre as it seems, I was not in the least bit afraid at the time. In fact I was rather annoyed that these people were in my pub drinking without my permission. I walked straight over to the sliding door all set to have a confrontation and walked into the bar. It was empty.

'I must have stood in that room for a good five minutes trying to think of a logical explanation for what I had just seen. I scrutinized every part of the room almost refusing to believe what had happened. Everything was normal, just as I had left it before I had gone to bed. Not knowing what to make of it all I went back out of the room and closed the sliding door behind me.

'I put my foot on the first stair to go back to the bedroom then hesitated. Just to keep myself sane I went back to the little window to have one more look to convince myself that this really hadn't happened to me. Somehow or other I must have misread the scene.

'I pressed my face against the cold glass window pane and

looked through into the bar. They were back! My heart almost leapt out of my body when I saw them. Their faces were quite clear, the tankards, the hats, the long white table, and I could even hear the distant music. They were people, not illusions. Two or three of the men had unbuttoned their coats and then I noticed that amongst them sat a buxom looking lady. All of them had long hair, some tied into a sort of pigtail style at the back. The tankards were quite large and some of the contents had spilled onto the table, which, apart from these stains, looked to be habitually scrubbed white.

'It suddenly struck me that although my face was pressed very close to the window, not one of the revellers had seen me. I stepped sideways away from the window and quietly moved again to the sliding bar door and this time, very gently and as silently as possible, I eased it open. The bar was again empty.

'For ages I stared into that moonlit bar trying to see something of what I had seen through the window but there was nothing unusual there. Leaving the door open this time I quickly moved back to the window. There they were again – the people swaying to the music and quaffing their ale around the white table. I gazed for a few more seconds, and realizing that my door opening and window watching could go on for the rest of the night, I left the window, closed the door on the empty bar, and went to bed, a rather frightened and confused man.

'My wife was fast asleep so I did not wake her. I now regret this as a witness on that night would have been a great consolation to me. I just lay in bed wide awake for the rest of that night bewildered by what I had seen. Being the landlord of a public house I realized that it would be futile to try to explain what had happened to anyone because they would invariably assume that I must have had a bit too much to drink. Only another publican would understand that serving behind a bar on a busy night, single handed, means a minimum of drinks for the barman. I myself knew however that I had only had one pint of my mildest ale. I resolved that I would tell no one about the night's encounters and thus I would retain my reputation for being a sensible, sober landlord of the Star. In common with most people, I do not enjoy being ridiculed.

'It was three or four months later that my wife and I went out for an evening with friends for a meal in a restaurant 50 miles away from the Star. Towards the end of the meal our friend mentioned that he had been reading a book about ghosts in old houses. Because they were long standing friends and I knew that they would not scoff spitefully, I mentioned what I had seen that night in the bar.

'My story provoked a fair amount of laughter from our friends. My wife however, was not so amused. This was the first time that she'd heard of the night merry-makers and she kept giving me knowing looks except I didn't know what the knowing looks were meant to mean.

'On our way home in the car she admitted to me that she too had, as she put it, felt funny things, when she had been alone in the pub. She had once seen a pocket of dense mist on the landing and upstairs passage on a bright clear evening. She had never mentioned it to me as she just didn't think that I would believe her. She added that our two pub dogs had backed away trembling with fright from this mist, which vanished a few seconds later.

'About five or six months later, on a Saturday, I had to go to London for an association meeting. I left my wife to open up the pub for the evening trade and to await the arrival of our barmaid. My wife had been busying herself dusting around the bar when two women entered. One was about 65 and the other about 20 years younger. Both of them were dressed in the quiet, rather old fashioned way, of country folk. My wife bade them a cheery good-evening as they sat down and they replied to her in like vein. They asked her for a fruit juice each which she got them. They explained to her that they were not really drinkers but that they had called into the Star out of curiosity.

'It came out that the older one had lived in the Star many years ago, in fact she had spent her childhood and teenage years there. She told my wife all about the various tenancy changes she had seen and the little alterations that had been made since her father's days. A short time after her marriage, she and her new husband moved north because of his work. She had only come back on a few occasions to relatives' weddings and funerals. Then, without any preamble, she asked my wife, "Have you seen or heard the ghosts around here?"

'Being on the cautious side my wife replied that she had not seen any ghosts but she'd heard some funny noises. The woman looked straight at my wife as if weighing her up, probably trying to establish whether my wife would ridicule her, and subsequently went on to tell her story: It seems that all those years ago there had not been a convservatory behind the bar, and the little four paned window had looked out onto the street. The woman had returned from a very late party and had to get into the building by the back door. As she had passed the little window she'd got the impression that something was not quite right. She stopped and looked into the bar through the window. She went on

420

to describe in explicit detail the exact scene which I myself had witnessed.'

∞

MRS. Seddon from Hertfordshire was on holiday in Devon with her husband about eight years ago. They stayed near the famous Buckfast Abbey.

'We are interested in old churches and so one evening we decided to walk over to Buckfastleigh Parish Church which is very ancient. When we arrived the light was just beginning to fail but we decided to go in anyway.

'The entrance door was made of heavy wood and it required some force to open it. When we entered, the door creaked noisily and when we closed it it slammed shut with a resounding thud. We walked down the right hand side of the church and proceeded towards the altar. As we walked down the length of the building we saw a man walking away from the altar on the opposite side to ourselves. He was dressed in trousers and a woollen jumper. We noticed that he had a bad limp and was using a walking stick. We spoke to him across the building but he took no notice of us and continued to walk past us.

'We reached the altar and both noticed that it had gone extremely cold. I was actually shivering. We turned to walk back and immediately noticed that the man, who had been there only a few moments earlier, was no longer to be seen.

'He couldn't have gone out through the door or we would most certainly have heard him depart what with the creaking and banging of that door. We decided that there must be another exit. There was another door towards the bell tower but that was padlocked. There was no other way out except by the way that we had come in. We tried the door but it was impossible to open or close it without making a great deal of noise.

'We found out later that there used to be a robber roaming Dartmoor with two savage dogs. He was eventually caught and hanged and his dogs were destroyed but initially he was not buried on consecrated ground. It was not until much later that his remains were buried in the Buckfastleigh church graveyard. The ghost of that robber can still be seen roaming in search of his dogs.'

∞

R. HAYTER of Dorset had been working on the Wiltshire Downs in a large sloping field one hot summer's day. 'I had gone there with two friends to help clear ragwort from the field.

'We each had a supply of dustbin bags and set to work. The others had moved into the middle of the field in the hollow of the Down and I worked along the outer raised bank. It was very pleasant in the sunshine just pulling away at the ragwort and not thinking about anything in particular, and filling my dustbin liner with the fruits of my labour.

'I had ambled out of sight of the others and was just putting a handful into the sack when I happened to look up. I saw a man, a soldier or a traveller, sitting under an old thorn tree. He was hunched up with his knees pulled up to his chin. He was dressed in a wine coloured cloak which was wrapped around him tightly. Sticking out from under the cloak was a pair of soft leather boots. On his head was a leather helmet with flaps on it. He looked very dejected and forlorn.

'Beside the man, tied to the thorn tree, was a black mule. It had a soft leather harness on it and a cloth saddle. There were two large soft looking bags tied on either side of the saddle. The mule had its back hunched. What really frightened me about the whole scene was that it was pouring rain over the man and the mule but the rest of the field was bathed in brilliant sunshine. I wiped my eyes to make sure that they were not playing tricks on me, but the man and the animal were still there. The mule streamed with the rain and the man was trying to shelter under the tree, yet I could feel the hot sun burning into my skin.

'I ran, leaving the sack which I had been working with, to find my friends. They remarked that I looked as if I had had a fright, but not wishing to tell them what I had seen, I just remarked that I was a bit worried because I thought that I had lost them.'

∞

MR. E.A. Mead of Gloucestershire was employed as a chain examiner some years ago in a large railway works. 'We formed a gang of about a dozen men and one evening when we were about to go home, one of our mates said that he would not be coming in to work the following day because he would be celebrating the day that he made the best decision of his life.

'Naturally curious we asked him what he meant. Taffy replied, "The day I decided to join the British Army." He went on to say that although he had joined up exactly 30 years ago he felt just the same as he had done on that day – just as fit and the same weight.

'The next day, as expected, Taffy was absent. He did not

come into work on the following day either, nor the day after that. The next day, however, he returned and as he walked down the middle of the workshop all the lads began to send him up, banging their hammers on steel plates and calling out "Taffy you drunken old man" (or words to that effect).

'He had his usual lop-sided grin on his face and yelled over at the micky-takers, "It's grand to be dead." They roared back accusing him of having been stewing in drink the whole week and they jested about the hangover that he must have had. He did not respond to this banter but just walked over to the office to report to the boss, opened the door and went in, closing it behind him.

'After some time when there was no sign of Taffy coming back out of the office the shop steward remarked that the boss must be giving him a right going over so he suggested that he would go in on some other pretext to get Taffy out. The shop steward went into the office but was surprised to see that the boss was just sitting there on his own quietly working away as usual.

'When the boss was asked where Taffy had gone he assumed that the shop steward had been referring to the recent absence of Taffy from work. The steward said that Taffy was back and everyone had seen him walk into the office. There was no other way in or out of that office and the boss swore that he had not set eyes on Taffy since before his absence.

'Later that afternoon the boss received a message to say that Taffy had died in his bed several nights previously.'

∞

A LUTON man, Robert Judge, was walking his dog one

424

morning in late July 1983. 'It was usual for me to walk the dog over the open land at the back of my home as it is a lovely walk with trees, flowers and wild life.

'I left my home at 6.00 a.m. and after walking for about a mile I sat down on the grass to roll a cigarette. As I was doing so, two magpies flew down in front of us about 40 yards away, fighting over some scrap or other which one of them had been carrying. My dog decided to go over and settle the dispute but I grabbed hold of his collar to prevent him.

'As my dog and I were watching the antics of the birds, I noticed a woman immediately to my right, walking from a narrow trackway between the hedgerows. My initial reaction was to wonder what on earth she was doing walking along in such a deserted place at that hour of the morning. I remember thinking that I would not want my wife doing such a foolish thing.

'As she emerged from the bushes into the open, the magpies took fright and flew off, although she appeared not to have noticed them. She was looking down all the time I was observing her so I thought perhaps she had lost something earlier and was retracing her steps to search for it. She then stopped and stood staring down at one particular spot.

'I got a perfectly clear view of her and saw that she was about 5ft 6ins tall, very slim with a roundish face and light brown hair which was quite long. She wore a pink cardigan with long sleeves, a white blouse with the collar turned out over the cardigan, and a pale blue pleated skirt which reached to just below her knees. She had a crepe bandage over her left ankle and I also noticed what looked like a green stain on the skirt on the left side which I first thought

425

was paint but then thought that perhaps it could be a grass stain.

'At this point my dog, who had been watching her, started to whine and to become very agitated. This was not a bit like his normal character so I was patting him and talking to him just to try to calm him down a bit. I remember my words; "Don't be daft, she's not going to hurt you, whatever's the matter with you?" Looking back over at the woman I started to feel sorry for her and I thought that I'd better go over to see if I could help her in any way. I stood up and was about to walk across to her, at the same time beckoning to my dog to follow me, but he would not move, and just continued to whimper. I tugged on his lead and he took one reluctant step forward and then pulled back. He normally runs to greet people wagging his tale as he enjoys being made a fuss of.

'Leaving my dog where he was, I approached the woman and stood about five or six feet away from her, and as I got closer I could smell her perfume. I asked her if she had lost something. I stood there waiting for her to answer but she just ignored me completely and kept looking down at the ground. I wondered if she might be deaf or if she had some mental illness. By this time I had started to feel uneasy about the situation and decided to leave her to it.

'I was just about to turn away to return to my dog when to my astonishment she completely disappeared just as quick as you would flick a light switch off. There was absolutely no way I will ever understand that, as there was nowhere she could have gone and anyway it happened so fast – one second she was standing there looking down at the ground and the next she was gone, and besides I had not taken my eyes off her, even for a moment. I looked over at my dog. He was still where I had left him so I called to him but he refused to come to heel. He was always the most obedient animal to me but it was obvious that he was frightened out of his wits.

'I stepped over a pace or two to where the woman had been standing to see if there was anything on the ground at that spot. All I could see was vegetation, then something blue caught my eye. I stooped down to get a closer look and there in the long grass was a hair-slide made in the fashion of a bow. I picked it up to examine it and noticed that the clip part had become rusty so I figured that it must have been lying there for some time.

'I moved away from that spot to again call my dog to come to me. Although I was calling him all the time he would not budge until I walked about 20 feet or so away from where the woman had been standing. He then raced up to me and jumped up to greet me nearly knocking me over in the process. I threw the hair-slide for him to retrieve and he ran after it, tail wagging. When he reached the object however, he hesitated, then backed off and came running back to me minus the hair-slide. Now I'd had that dog for 12 years and being a labrador he liked nothing better than retrieving objects that I would throw for him. Never once in all the time I'd had him had he refused to bring back any article I had ever thrown for him.

'I kept thinking about that woman and wondering if I had seen what people call ghosts, but she was as solid as I was and I genuinely thought that I had been talking to a real person. I then remembered that when I had picked up the hair-slide from where the woman had been standing, I had felt extremely cold. At the time I hadn't given too

427

much importance to this as I was more interested in seeing what the blue object was.

'Just to satisfy my own curiosity I walked back to that same spot again and sure enough, at the precise spot where she had been standing, it was still freezing cold. Could it be my imagination, I wondered, so I stepped away from that spot and the air was distinctly warmer. Again I moved to the spot where the hair-slide had been and again I could feel the drastic change of temperature, so much so that it sent a shiver all though me.'

∞

MR. Pengilly of Southampton remembers a story which his late father had related to him. 'My father was born in the Whitechurch area of Hampshire in the late 1800s. When he was in his teens he used to deliver groceries for his father's shop to all of the houses in the vicinity and he became friends with a man called Joe Lloyd.

'Joe lived in the old mill in Whitechurch which is mentioned in the Domesday Book. It seems that many years previously an abnormal child had been born to the miller. In those days this was looked upon as a terrible disgrace and so the practice was that such children would be hidden from public view. The miller and his wife, being ignorant and illiterate, were so swayed by the terror of public ridicule that they pretended that their child had died. The poor child in fact had been locked away in chains in a dark shed and treated like an animal. Food and water was delivered daily, then the door to the shed would be slammed shut and the child would be left in darkness until the following day's rations were delivered. Not once was that child ever allowed out in the sunshine or to meet another living soul.

'Eventually the child was found by a passer-by who had heard screaming and the rattling of chains coming from the shed, but the little boy was in such a neglected state that although he was taken to the shelter of the local vicar's house, he died within a short time.

'One day Joe Lloyd's wife was sitting alone in the parlour when she suddenly heard a violent clanging sound followed by a pathetic wail. She jumped up and searched all over her home and then ran outside to inspect the outbuildings and gardens but there was nothing to be seen. She was just about to go back into the house when she heard it again. It seemed to be coming from somewhere in the back garden. She ran round to the back of the building but there was no one there. She then heard very faint sobbing which only lasted a few seconds.

'She walked around the back garden and noticed that when she passed the corner at the far left end, the air was quite chilled. As she turned to walk back to the house she heard the clanking of chains. She got a severe shock as the sound seemed to come from right under her feet and she even felt the ground vibrate with the noise. She heard the stifled sobbing but did not stay to investigate further being almost frightened to death, but ran back into the house and locked all of the doors and windows. When Joe returned he had to shout and thump on the door before she would open it, he found her in a state of terror.

'Joe got the whole story out of her and it was only after he started asking a few questions around the locality that he learnt the story of the chained up child. Because of the nervous condition of his wife he called in the local vicar to bless the house and the grounds and since then there have been no further disturbances.'

∞

VERA, a Surrey lady, went to bed one night as usual. 'I was in perfectly good health and was not worrying about anything. In fact it was just an ordinary run-of-the-mill night. Something woke me up. I sat bolt upright in bed wondering what had disturbed me. I looked instinctively towards my bedside clock and was quite surprised to find that I could see what the time was without putting the light on. The reason that I noticed this was that I was fully aware that my clock was not luminous.

'I was about to get out of bed to walk over and switch the light on when I found that the room was growing lighter of its own accord. Within a few seconds it was like broad daylight yet I could see that the time on the clock was just after 3.00 a.m. I then noticed that my mother was standing by one of the two windows in my bedroom. I instantly thought that she must have felt unwell in the middle of the night and had come down to tell me although I could not understand why she was fully dressed and not in her nightclothes.

'Just as I was about to call over to her I thought that she looked unusually tall. I opened my mouth to ask her if she was all right and found that I could not speak. I was not afraid or anything but for some reason I could not move a muscle in my body. I just sat there staring. Then I did begin to feel frightened, thinking that I was having a stroke. At that moment the woman turned round to face me and I saw to my utter horror that she was me.'

430

WHEN Muriel Stevens of Eastbourne in Sussex was on holiday in Devon she was invited to a party. 'We were asked to leave our coats in a bedroom. As I left the room another woman entered who was a stranger to me. I was half way down the stairs when I heard a scream. Several of us rushed back and we saw the woman standing with her hands outstretched as if she was touching something.

'It was some moments before she was able to speak. She said that she had seen her father in that bedroom and she was most upset because she knew that he was gravely ill. She explained that he had been standing in his dressing gown and he appeared to be very wet.

'We later found out that the woman's father had been in great pain with a terminal illness. Not being able to endure the situation any longer he had drowned himself in a stream at the bottom of his garden.'

∞

MRS. Hathaway of Somerset lived for years in a large Georgian property with her husband and two teenage daughters. It is now divided into two shops with living accommodation above. 'One winter morning my husband and I were unpacking pottery at the bottom of the staircase which spiralled up two floors to a kitchen and lounge on the first floor and bedrooms on the top floor.

'We were very busy and engrossed in what we were doing when suddenly I remembered that I hadn't switched the oven on for dinner. I ran up the stairs and as I reached the bend which led to the corridor which ran between the kitchen and the lounge, I was stopped in my tracks by a man staring down at me.

'My first thought was that we had an intruder who must have come in through the kitchen door somehow although I couldn't see how. As I stood there trying to sort things out in my mind, he disappeared from the head down. He was wearing heavy tweed trousers with turn-ups at the bottom of the legs.

'I ran back down the stairs to my husband and breathlessly told him what I had seen. He told me then that he had also seen a man in the very same place but had not mentioned this to me for fear of frightening me. My mind then went back to two times when I had been working in the kitchen and had felt that someone was looking over my shoulder, but when I had turned round I had been most surprised to find nobody there.

'A few weeks later I was speaking to an elderly lady from our village who told me that there had been two grown up sons living in our house at one time about the turn of the century and that one of them had died by falling down the stairs.

'Nothing would put it out of my head that the man I saw looking down at me was the person who pushed that other poor man to his death.'

∞

A LADY from Kent reports that when she was doing a teacher training course in Bristol she had the most unusual dream. 'I am not an over-imaginative or superstitious person nor am I highly strung. I am a graduate teacher of modern languages, married with three children and am a practising Christian.

'One night I dreamt about a fellow-linguist from Oxford. I had had no contact with him for a couple of years or so, therefore there was no particular reason for me to suddenly dream about him. His French wife, whom I had never met, was also featured in the dream. The very next morning a letter arrived from them informing me that their first child had just been born.

'One other such thing happened in the first year of my own marriage. My husband, who commuted from near Sevenoaks to London, had a peculiar dream about eating glass from a broken light tube. No breakages or such had taken place. That morning, when he got on the train, he sat on some sharp glass that some vandal had left wedged, concealed between the cushions. He suffered deep cuts and had to be stitched up at a local hospital.'

∞

MR. Tony Stokes of Bristol tells about the time in 1973 when he had just moved house. 'The house we had been living in was a semi-detached, three bedroomed property only about four years old. The reason we decided to move was that my wife wanted to live in a small village and the house in question was beautifully situated in the heart of an idyllic little village.

'We had been living in the new house for about a month when one evening all of the family were in the living room watching television and I thought that I heard the sound of laughter coming from upstairs. I assumed that my ears were playing tricks on me or perhaps it was in the background on the television. About a minute or so later I heard the laughter again and this time I was sure that it had come from upstairs in the house. I then heard the chatter of children, again as if it was coming from one of the bedrooms on the first floor.

'Without saying anything to the family, I got up, turned the television sound down and walked out of the room to the foot of the stairs. All the time I could hear the chatter and laughter coming from upstairs. By now my wife and children were all curious as to what was going on so I asked them if any of them could hear anything. None of them could. I went back into the living room thinking perhaps that I must have imagined it after all.

'No sooner had we all settled back down to watch the television when I again heard the excited chatter. I can only describe it as that because I could not distinguish any of the words and the children sounded as if they were talking quite fast in an animated way. Again I asked everyone present if they had heard anything but they all said that they hadn't. I then turned the television off, deciding to investigate, and promptly left the room and proceeded up the stairs.

'As I walked up the stairs it began to feel warmer but the voices had stopped. When I reached the top of the stairs I found that the landing was quite warm. I put this down to warm air rising from below and did not give it another thought. As I could no longer hear any unusual sounds I went back downstairs. By now I had become a good-humoured joke with the children who took great delight in teasing me with remarks like "Dad's been on the bottle," and "Dad's gone senile."

'We lived in that house until October of the same year

434

and I heard the chattering and laughter of children almost every single night for those nine months, but neither my wife nor any of my children ever heard a thing unusual. In the early days, or should I say nights, of hearing the voices, I would get up and go upstairs to investigate but always the result was the same. The voices would stop as I climbed the stairs and it always got warmer the higher I climbed.

'I felt no fear at any time during the whole of those nine months, just a naive curiosity. Gradually I got to ignoring the sounds until eventually I more or less accepted things as they were. I think that had one of the other members of the family said that they had heard the chattering I may well have been less than brave.

'I must at this point say that the young couple living next door had no children nor did any children stay there at any period during the nine months, so the voices could not be put down to that. I must also point out that I never once heard the sounds or felt the warmth when I was in bed at night.

'My wife, who was a trained nurse, eventually got herself a night job caring for the elderly in a rest home. In the evenings when she would be working, I would put the children to bed, tell them each a story and see that they were all well, and tucked in for the night. As I have mentioned, I had grown to accept the chatter and got used to the fact that no one else could hear it, so I was not expecting what happened next.

'I had seen the children to bed as usual, my wife was out working at the old folks home and I decided that it was time I went to bed. The bedroom I occupied was just at the top of the stairs to the left. Three of the children, Tony, Karen and Catherine, were in the long bedroom to the right of the

435

stairs, and Neil was in the small bedroom next to mine. When I went to bed I always left the door slightly ajar just in case one or other of the children should get up in the middle of the night, and as I am a fairly light sleeper it would not take too much noise to waken me.

'I had gone to bed at about 11.00 p.m. and had dozed off lying on my right side facing towards the door. For some unknown reason I opened my eyes and there, standing beside my bed, was a small boy with fair curly hair dressed in a long white nightgown, clutching in his right hand a brass candle holder with a burning candle in it. Within a matter of no more than ten seconds I saw him move away toward the door and leave the bedroom.

'My first thought was that it must have been Neil as he was the only one of our children with fair curly hair, although I could not understand where he'd got the candle from or why he should need it. I called quietly, "Neil, are you alright?" There was no reply so I got out of bed and went into his room to see what was the matter with him. I found him in his bed fast asleep just as I had tucked him in earlier. I then went into the long bedroom just to see if any of the other children had been up but they too were all fast asleep and tucked in just as I had left them.

'I went back to bed puzzled and as I lay down I thought about what I had seen. It then struck me that none of our children wore or even possessed a long white nightgown, neither did we own a brass candlestick, nor were there any candles in the house. The most startling thing in my mind at that moment was that I recalled that the figure of the little boy had not opened the bedroom door wide enough to go out, but had simply gone through it. Although I had left the door ajar, it was no more than about five inches open so no

436

one could have got in or out of my bedroom without opening the door properly.

'The next day I did not tell the children what I had seen and I did not tell my wife for some time after. When I eventually did tell her I felt that she did not believe me – in fact there were times when I had began to doubt my own sanity. It would be about September when I saw the child, about a month before we left and during the whole of those last few weeks I never again saw the boy although the voices continued.

'It was 10.30 on a Friday morning in October and the children were all at school. In fact the cul-de-sac was very quiet and there were no children anywhere to be seen. Our neighbours had both gone off to work and I was busy loading the hired van with our possessions.

'I had loaded some packing cases and had just brought the fridge out of the kitchen onto the path outside the house. As I lifted the fridge up to put it into the van I heard, from behind me, the most pitiful cry of a child calling "Mummy, Mummy." I put the fridge back down on the ground and turned around quickly to see who was crying looking directly at the windows of the long bedroom in the house as the cry seemed to come from that direction. I saw nothing. I turned to my wife who was standing near the garage and asked her if she had heard anything. She said, "No, what do you mean?"

'I explained about hearing the child's cry but then, feeling a bit foolish, I turned back to lift the fridge into the van. I then went back into the house and walked upstairs and into the now empty long bedroom which had been occupied by our three children. I just stood there in the middle of the room looking around me. I don't know what I was expecting to see or hear, but nothing happened so I went back outside to continue loading the van.

'When I was lifting the washing machine into the van, again I heard the terrible plaintive cry of a child coming from the same direction as before, calling in a sorrowful voice, "Mummy, Mummy." I turned as quick as a flash but could see nothing. Again I asked my wife if she had heard anything, but again she replied that she had not. Completely convinced that someone was in the house, I rushed up the stairs into the long bedroom but there was nothing there. This time I checked all the other rooms of the house, upstairs and down, but there was nothing to be seen.

'By this time the van was almost loaded with just a few odds and ends still to be put in and then we would be on our way to our new home after picking up the children from school. My wife was standing by the doorway as I was loading the last box into the van. Once more I heard that loud heart-rending cry, "Mummy, Mummy." This time I did not look up at the windows nor did I go into the house, I just looked at Marion my wife and I knew by the look on her face that she too had heard it this time.

'We quickly packed the couple of carrier bags, locked the house door and left. Some months later when we were settled into our new home I did tell my eldest daughter Karen about the cries I had heard on the day we had moved out of our previous house. She made some enquiries with a friend of hers who had lived in that village all of her life.

'She was told that there had been on old farm house on the site of our previous house. There had been a terrible fire and the farm house had been burnt to the ground and three children had been trapped in the top rooms and had died in the flames.'

438

MR. Young used to be a cycling enthusiast and belonged to a cycling club in Southend. His club used to run time trials whereby a race was set on open roads, limited to 120 riders who started at one-minute intervals. The distances were set at 25, 30, 50 and 100 miles and the time was clocked both on the distance out to a certain point, and then the return journey to the club. The riders who covered the distances in the fastest time would be the winner of that section.

'On a bright sunny Sunday morning in July 1953 I was riding in a 25 mile event on the Southend Arterial Road which was Course E.3, at that time reputed to be the fastest course in the country, being along a dual carriageway over very flat land. The first rider had set off at 6.00 that morning.

'The race starting point was about two miles east of Gallows Corner. The course ran for about five miles and then came to a roundabout at a pub called The Halfway House. A further two and a half miles on the straight road led to another roundabout at a pub called The Fortune of War. After the second roundabout there was quite a steep hill to go down, then onwards for about another five miles to a check point where each rider's number was taken by the marshal on duty. After this the competitors turned back and reversed the journey.

'I started off as number 10, but since number 9 was a non-starter, I had a two minute gap in front of me. The aim was to catch up with the rider in front and keep well ahead of the rider behind. It was a beautiful morning and in those days at that early hour there was hardly a single vehicle on the road. I was cycling along as happy as a sand boy, looking back over my shoulder every now and then just to check if any other rider was catching up on me, but there was not a soul in sight.

'As I got near to the turn marshal at the half-way point of the race, I took another long look back but there was nobody in sight and both ways the road was absolutely empty. I checked in with the marshal, turned around and was on my way back. I had only gone about a couple of hundred yards when a rider overtook me. He was a tallish fellow with all the proper racing kit and a properly equipped bike. He was wearing long white socks which reached his knees. These caught my eye as everyone else wore ankle socks at that time. The rest of his clothes were grey. No word was passed between us but I remember thinking it strange that he had crept up on me so quickly and I had not heard the slightest sound of his wheels on the road. Even as he passed there was complete silence.

'The rider progressed for about 60 yards or so in front of me and then maintained a steady pace, keeping always the same distance between us. I kept wondering where he could have come from because just a few moments earlier I had an unobstructed view of the entire roadway for miles and miles and there certainly was no rider approaching from any direction. I pedalled faster but noticed that each time I made a little ground on him he also progressed by the same distance, so that no matter how I tried he was always the exact same distance ahead of me.

'By this time I was really bewildered because he had not looked back at me even once so I could not fathom how he knew when I was gaining ground on him. He stayed just ahead of me for the entire five miles back to The Fortune of War pub. He went round the roundabout then up the hill and over the top. Within the next moment or so I too was going over the brow of the hill. I nearly fell off my bike with the shock of finding the road ahead of me completely empty. Except for the few moments when he went out of my sight as he went over the top of the hill I had not taken my eyes off him. He had vanished, bike and all. He could not have nipped into a hedge or anything because the grass verges were much too wide for him to have got out of sight in time, and on that part of the road it was so straight and open that I could look ahead and see almost to the next roundabout. The entire length of road was deserted.

'I found out later that rider number ll who was supposed to start one minute after me did not turn up; therefore there was a two minute gap behind me as well as in front of me. That explains why I could not see any other rider on that stretch of road to and from the check point, except, that is, for the one who did the disappearing trick. When I thought about it afterwards, the greyness of his gear together with the total silence made me shiver. I gave up my membership of the club after that.'

∞

MR. BLETSOE of Hemel Hempstead in Hertfordshire is a widower who remembers that shortly after his wife had died various members of the family had mentioned that they could smell her powder, despite the fact that no one else used that particular brand. It happened at intervals at the most unexpected times and in the most unlikely places, for instance when the Sunday lunch was being cooked in the kitchen and no one in the house was wearing any

441

powder at all. It was even noticed in some of the houses of the other members of the family as well.

'I had a dog at the time and each night I used to take him for a walk past the cemetery gates which are quite near to my house. He always went past without any trouble whatsoever, but one night he refused to pass the gates. No matter what I said or did there was absolutely no way that I could entice him to take even one step.

'At that same time, my son who lives close by happened to be coming up the hill from the other direction. When he reached me his face was grey looking and he was quivering with fright. Just as he had approached the cemetery gates from the other side, he had seen a young girl sitting on the wall against a very thick hedge. He thought nothing of this except for the fact that he thought she had chosen a rather odd place to sit. However as he drew near to her and was just about to pass her he watched her body begin to fade into the hedge until she had vanished.'

∞

YET another story involving a dog comes from Mr. Trueman from Salisbury in Wiltshire. 'Lassie was a German shepherd bitch that I had owned since 1969. She was a very sensitive and gentle creature and had come to me as a rescue when she was about 15 months old. We rapidly became extremely fond of one another. She loved people and other dogs, was a great credit to her often maligned breed, and she provided me with enormous pleasure and endless interest in the canine species all the time she was with me.

'It was part of my daily routine, no matter what the weather, to take Lassie on a reasonably long walk prior to retiring for the night. One night at around 11.00 p.m. we were walking along the Southampton Road out of Salisbury, which was a fairly well lit road. There was a ferocious wind blowing and it was lashing rain.

'Our route on this occasion took us to the end of the commercial buildings on the outskirts of Salisbury, across a narrow bridge, so narrow in fact that no footpath existed on either side of the road. From there we turned off left into a track known as Piggy Lane, an unlit lane that curved round to the left and eventually led us back to the Shady Bower area where I lived.

'On this particular night we had just stepped into the road to cross the narrow bridge when, just ahead of us, I saw a large white horse carrying on its back a young girl of no more than 10 or 11 years of age. She had very long blond hair which streamed out in the wind and rain. The horse turned into Piggy Lane just before we did and I could clearly hear the hoofbeats ahead of us. Then suddenly the hoofbeats stopped. Lassie had always been fascinated by horses so she eagerly walked with me into the lane where I expected to encounter the animal with its rider. When we turned into the lane there was no sign of anything and there was no other means of escape from that narrow passageway.

'It was only then that it dawned on me that at this hour of the night and with the weather being as dreadful as it was, it would be most irregular for such a young girl to be riding alone in the darkness in such a desolated place. Lassie and I walked up and down that stretch of lane looking and listening but there was nothing there.'

∞

NANCY of Swindon remembers one morning during the

last war when she was walking to work. 'It was around 8.30 a.m. and I was walking along a street near to where I live which was lined with very old houses.

'A little old lady came out of the doorway of one of these old houses, walked up the garden path and was about to cross the pavement in front of me. She was wearing a peculiar looking tall black hat. Being polite I stood still to let her pass. She walked into the middle of the road then completely vanished.

'Over the years I've thought about that old lady many many times and the only conclusion I could come to was that behind the house which she had come out of was a complex of very old stone built cottages which had been built in the part of Swindon which had been open fields at the time that the Great Western Railway came to the town. The arrival of the railway attracted a lot of Welsh unemployed people to Swindon to work for G.W.R. The stone houses had been built to accommodate these workers and in fact they all had Welsh stoves in them so that the tenants would feel at home. The little old lady I saw wearing the tall black hat could have been one of the Welsh tenants from all those years ago.'

∞

MR. BRETT, a very down-to-earth Londoner, moved into his house in 1953 and has been living there ever since with his wife and two sons.

'As usual after moving into the new area I was eager to set the large back garden to rights. It had been neglected for some time so I started the first week by clearing the weeds, etc. Eventually, after installing the greenhouse and generally

444

tidying the garden up, it was not looking too bad but as time went on I noticed that the front garden did not respond to my efforts in the same way.

'I tested the soil and it seemed to be of the same quality as that of the back garden. I had great difficulty in getting anything to grow there despite trying various types of fertilisers, top dressings and giving it a lot of care and attention.

'Our two boys occupied the same bedroom for a number of years when they were small. Their bedroom door opened on to the head of the stairs where there is a bend and some wide treads. The nightly routine at that time was that the two youngsters were sent to bed in the evening and allowed to look at their picture books and play for about half-an-hour or so then I would call up to them "teeth time" which was the cue for them to get up, go to the bathroom, and then settle down in their beds ready for me to tuck them in.

'One winter evening in 1961 when I had gone up to see them in their beds the boys told me that they had seen a lady sitting at the top of the stairs watching them as they had gone into the bathroom. They had never ever said anything like that before so I asked them what this lady was like, not sure if it could have been their minds playing tricks on them but both of them were adamant that they had seen her and that she was all in grey. I did not wish to put any ideas into their minds so I let the matter rest at that point but over the next week I asked them very casually at different times when I was speaking to them separately what the woman had been like. Both of the boys seemed certain that the only clear thing about the woman was her face, especially her eyes, and that the rest of her was just a greyish form. Both of the boys remarked at how sad she had looked. The thing that intrigued me most about the whole thing was that neither of the kids seemed to be in the least bit put out by this woman. They both emphasized the fact that she was really sad looking.

'I presume that they never saw the woman again as they never mentioned it to me but there was a nagging feeling at the back of my mind. Neither my wife nor myself had ever seen or heard anything but there was something so convincing in the simple direct way that the children had told me about seeing the woman that I felt compelled to make some enquiries.

'I found out that the site of our house was first built on about 1929. The original house received a direct hit from a bomb on 11 October 1940 and the occupants, a husband, wife and two daughters aged seven and five were all killed. The house had been rebuilt after the war.

'My blood ran cold when I learnt that in the total confusion and devastation caused by the blast which damaged the entire street, the bodies of the two small girls had been laid out in the front garden, covered with a tarpaulin and forgotten about for a couple of days.'

∞

ANN ADAMS of Crowborough, East Sussex, used to work in a residential home for old people in Sanderstead in Surrey.

'I was sitting in the lounge feeding one resident and as I looked across the room I saw a figure standing behind one of the other residents. It was a lady dressed in a bright red dress which had a very full skirt which seemed to billow out. Across her breast was a greyish band like a sash which had

446

what looked like a touch of golden thread running through it which made the sash shine in the sunlight. Her hair was in a bun and I recognized the style of her dress as being Victorian.

'The next instant there was nobody behind the chair at all but the old man who had been sitting there died a few days later. Twice after that I saw the very same woman in the long red dress stand behind chairs of the residents and each time within a few days the person died.'

∞

PATRICIA SLARK of Eltham, London was evacuated during the war – about 1940 – to Hartest in Suffolk with her baby brother, young aunt, mother and grandparents.

'I was only 9 at the time and my aunt was only 15. We had all been sent to a very old large manor house which had fallen into disrepair. An elderly couple owned the house and only part of the building was habitable so we all had to make the most of things. My grandparents had one room and my mother, brother, aunt and I shared another huge bedroom with two large beds in it.

'Set in one wall there was a very deep cupboard secured by a large heavy lock – this was a metal ring type which fastened onto a fitment on the cupboard door something like a padlock. The headboard of the bed which I shared with my aunt was pushed flush back against the door of the cupboard. The first night we slept in that house we were awakened by the sound of the large lock banging on the back of our bed headboard and we found that the cupboard door was ajar. It was then that we discovered that it opened inwards so we reckoned that the cupboard must be big

447

enough to walk into. However, at that time in the middle of the night we did not feel like investigating much further. My mother fastened the lock back again and we all went back to sleep.

'The following night the exact same thing happened. We were quite frightened this time because we knew that the lock had been securely fastened and just before we had gone to sleep my mother checked it to make sure that it could not open and waken us up again. Once more my mother had to get out of bed and fix the lock back in place. By this time we were beginning to get a bit frightened so the following night we swapped beds so that my mother and my baby brother slept in the one where the lock was. On that night the very same thing happened and we were all wakened by the large metal ring clanging back and forward against the head-board.

'The following morning my mother reported the clanging lock to the woman of the house who just refused to believe her, saying that the cupboard in question had not been used for years and years since that lock had been put on the door. No one had even opened the door as the cupboard was no longer required.

'The woman explained that when the house had been originally built over 300 years ago, that cupboard had been built in a particular shape for a very special reason. When any of the family had died they had been placed in their coffins and then left in the cupboard until the funeral – it was a type of chapel of rest.'

∞

MRS. SMITH of Polegate, Sussex, went to bed one night as

usual and woke up in the middle of the night to find a shadowy figure walking round the bed. She was so surprised that next morning, although she remembered waking up and seeing the figure, she convinced herself that it couldn't have really happened therefore it must have been a vivid dream and thought no more about it.

'Quite a time after this incident I again found myself wakened up in the middle of the night but this time there was a man bending over the bed looking down at me. I was absolutely terrified and quickly turned away but he then shook me very hard as if he was trying to get my attention. Then to my horror he took a hold of my head to try to turn me round so that I would be looking at him. Although I was nearly frightened to death I managed to reach out my hand to switch the bedside lamp on. The second the light came on the man disappeared. I sat up in bed trembling. Then my mind went back to the time I had seen the shadowy figure. I realized that it was almost the end of April, a year after I had seen the shadow.

'This April I was again wakened up and saw a light – a sort of glowing candle – with a figure in front of it. I just lay staring at this thing until it vanished. I have since found out that an old man lived here before us and he died in our bedroom in a fire.'

∞

EDDIE of Brighton, Sussex, was brought up solely by his mother after his father died when he was only two years old.

'In January of 1958 when I was eight years of age I was seriously ill with whooping cough over a three week period. I did not respond to medical treatment so the doctor had advised my mother to take me to the beach for the day as the freezing cold sea air might be the only hope of clearing my lungs.

'After spending the day in a shelter on the sea front my mother put me to bed at about five in the evening. There was a roaring coal fire which warmed my bedroom but I was feeling very weak from lack of sleep as well as the effects of the illness and I was crying non-stop. My mother had come into the room to comfort me several times throughout the evening but there was nothing that she could do to help me.

'She had just left me with a promise that she would be back in again to see me in a little while. It was then that my father appeared. He walked in through the door, came to my bedside and put his hand on my shoulder and said, "Don't cry son, you'll feel better soon." He gave me a gentle pat then left the room.

'I called my mother straight away and told her what had happened. I was not frightened or upset by it but more excited over the experience. My mother claimed that it was a dream no matter how many times I told her over and over again that I had not been able to go to sleep and I had been wide awake when I saw him.

'To this day I know that I saw him and felt his touch and I know that I was wide awake at the time. The whooping cough improved from that night onwards and was soon completely gone. Both the doctor and my mother said that the cold sea air had worked but I think that I reached the turning point in life that night between the living and the dead and I am convinced that my father saw me back to the living.'

∞

DAVID RITCHIE of Ashford in Kent used to be an airman

serving with 54 Squadron at RAF Stradishall in Suffolk. 'I had been posted after training and my wife and baby son were still living at my father's house in Ashford.

'After making an appointment I went to see a lady with a view to renting her cottage near the airfield so that my wife and son could join me.

'On meeting the woman and her somewhat older, and unfortunately sick husband, I was shown over the property. As I was leaving she explained that they were moving back to their original home in the Midlands for the sake of her husband's health. When I spoke to the man he said that he was disappointed at not meeting my wife and son.

'By arrangement on the following Monday my family and I moved into the cottage. During the night I was suddenly awakened by my wife who was very frightened. She told me that someone else was in our bedroom. I sat bolt upright, not knowing really what to do because sure enough, standing in our bedroom at the bottom of our bed, was the sick husband.

'He just looked at us. For a few seconds I thought that we must have moved in on the wrong date, but as I was thinking of something to say which would sound reasonable he suddenly vaporized and was gone. My wife and I just dived under the bedclothes.

'Within a few days we received a letter from the landlady to say that the trip to the Midlands had been too much for her husband and that he had died on the Monday. He saw my wife and child after all!'

∞

MRS. CLAYDEN of Southend on Sea, Essex, remembers

when, at the age of 13, she went with her sister to live with her eldest married sister in a very large house. Her sister and brother-in-law were caretakers for the local hospital authority who owned the property.

'This building had been a private school before the war started but at the outbreak of war it had been taken over by the army to house the troops.

'Before and during the two months we stayed with my sister in that house, my brother-in-law had been working night shift at the hospital, so my sister was often alone in this massive house until the time we went to stay with them and again after we left.

'Most of the building was unoccupied except for a few rooms. The room they used as a lounge was very large with a high ceiling and French windows leading out onto a verandah at the side of the house. When it had been a school, this room had been the headmaster's study. At the very beginning of the war the headmaster had been standing out on the verandah and was killed by shrapnel.

'Outside this room to the left were double doors leading to the unoccupied front of the building where nobody ventured. These doors were often found open by my sister who kept locking them but they kept opening again. I was sleeping in the lounge on a put-u-up bed over by the French windows and my sister was in a camp bed in the same room.

'One night we were wakened by the rattling of the door knob. Instinctively we seemed to know that no mortal person was causing this disruption. Our little terrier dog who used to sleep in the corner of the room was positively whimpering with fear. This little dog was hated by the dustman and was the bane of the postman's life, yet here he was, whining in terror.

'I was shivering under the sheets and neither of us would dare to get out of bed to turn on the light because the switch was close to the door which was rattling. Then my sister started to say the Lord's Prayer and after a while the rattling stopped and the dog came over to be stroked. He was quivering with fear.

'My brother-in-law checked the whole building over the next day but everything was secure and just as normal. He said that it could not have been an intruder as there was no sign whatsoever of any break-in. We looked out on the balcony and there was a posy of primroses there. To this day I'll never know where they came from but I can't help wondering if someone somewhere was remembering that schoolmaster who met his death on that verandah.'

∞

JOHN HORSEWOOD of Chatham in Kent used to enjoy hiking when he was a younger man. 'I set out towards Whitestable one day and, realizing that I would not reach the town until very late, I decided to book myself into a small inn and make a bright and early start the following day.

'I found a quaint little pub which had rooms vacant so after a good supper I settled down to sleep. I was wakened up in the middle of the night and as I looked towards the window of the bedroom the complete form of a fully grown man just walked right through the glass window and into my room.

'I was ever so alarmed especially as I knew that the bedroom was on the first floor. I just lay in the bed staring at this fellow who was dressed in an army uniform. It was quite dark but I could see him clearly and I noticed then that it was a German uniform. He had his head bent and he just walked up and down the room muttering away to himself in what I can only imagine must have been German. He had a very bad limp and as he paced up and down he had to drag one of his feet along the floor. I couldn't understand what he was saying but he seemed to be repeating himself over and over again.

'I was so petrified by this man who never once looked in my direction that I did not dare to even move and there was no way that I could bring myself to try to get out of that bed to switch on the light. I never took my eyes off him but I did not say anything to him as I thought that if I spoke it would make him notice me.

'Up and down that room he walked for over an hour by which time I was almost at my wits' end wondering what on earth I should do to get rid of him without attracting any attention to myself.

'I suddenly remembered about my Bible. I always used to sleep with The New Testament under my pillow. I said a prayer first because I was so wary about making any move which might make him turn and look at me. The moment I started to recite the prayer I saw the man move quickly backwards towards the window. It was if someone or something like a magnet was pulling him out of the room backwards. He went straight out through the glass window and that was the last I saw of him.'

∞

MRS. BRICKELL from Blandford Forum relates the story told to her, when she was a child, by her mother: 'My late father was born deaf and dumb. When he and my late mother were courting, they would walk out together in the town. My mother had taken the trouble to learn sign language so that she could communicate with my father.

'When there was no moon they used to keep to the main part of the town so that they could converse on their fingers by the light of the streets or near brightly lit shop windows. When there was a bright moon they would venture beyond the outskirts of the town into the open countryside.

'On such a bright moonlit night they were walking along a lonely country road when suddenly a tall man about eight foot in height loomed up before them on the pathway out of nowhere. He wore a most unusual tall hat. They were both so startled that they just froze to the spot clinging onto each other.

'The man then walked right out into the middle of the road and turned to face them. My father, being deaf, heard nothing but saw the man quite clearly. My mother, however, heard the man say, in a most odd way with a gap after each word: "I – don't – think – we – will – go – this – way – tonight." The man then turned and walked straight through the hedge just melting into the leaves in a swirl of vapour and was gone.

'My parents turned and ran all the way home. When they had recovered their breath they told my grandparents what they had seen and heard. My grandfather said that years ago on that road at the section described by my parents, a sailor and a soldier had a bitter fight with each other and the soldier was killed.'

∞

JEAN MARKS who lives near Yeovil in Somerset used to live

in a 400 year old thatched cottage. 'My younger son, aged two-and-a-half, wakened up, at the same time, in the early hours of the morning for several days on the trot. I would hear him happily laughing and chattering away.

'Bleary-eyed, I would grope my way into his room to quieten him down. Each time I asked him what he was laughing at he always answered that he had been talking to the lady who had come to ask him about his toys. He was very much into combine harvesters and farm vehicles at that time. More just to humour him than anything else I asked him what this lady was like. He replied that she looked like Christopher's teachers.

'Now Christopher is his older brother and at that time attended a convent school and was taught by nuns. I asked my youngest son where the lady went and in a most matter of fact voice he told me that she had gone into the wardrobe. This stood in the corner of his room.

'He never mentioned seeing any lady after that but when the day came for us to leave that house, my mother-in-law had come to help with the move. All of the house had been cleared of furniture and the rooms were completely bare and only the two of us were left in the house to do the last minute clearing up. We were both standing in the kitchen when we heard heavy stomping footsteps move across the room where my youngest son had slept. When they reached the corner area they stopped. Mum-in-law and I just scampered out the front door as fast as we could and drove off never to return to that place. Although I must add that there was no real sense of anything menacing about the property, in fact the house had a happy atmosphere about it, nevertheless we both got the shivers when we heard those footsteps.'

CYRIL ANGEL from Yeovil in Somerset remembers New Year's Eve 1962. 'We had not long moved into our new house in St. James Close and there were a few friends in to celebrate the New Year with us. The bells rang in the New Year and after the noisy well-wishing had subdued we all settled down to watch television.

'All at once the loud thumping of army-type boots could be heard passing down by the side of our house and past the side door. We all heard this at once and wondered if there might be some disturbance or street fight outside so we all rushed out to see what was going on.

'It had been snowing quite heavily all that day and as soon as we went outside we could see that fresh snow had fallen during the evening leaving a smooth surface of about two or three inches. We looked all around the house but there was not one footprint in sight apart from the fresh prints we were making as we searched. The weighty thuds which we all heard could not be accounted for. We then got torches and looked around the back garden to see if there might be prints there but we found none. I later learned that the field in which the houses were built had once been used as a short cut for soldiers walking back to Flouderstone Camp from the Yeovil area.'

∞

ANOTHER story comes from the Shady Bower area of Salisbury. Mr. Simons was out walking with his dog Jasper and they were making their way towards The Hollow which is nothing more than a narrow footpath heavily overgrown with bushes and trees.

'On this particular night, as we reached the start of the footpath, Jasper showed a marked reluctance to leave the lighted street and enter the darkened path. So much so, in fact, that he actually lay down on the ground and firmly refused to budge which was most uncharacteristic of the dog.

'I persisted, however, until eventually Jasper plodded unwillingly behind me for several hundred yards and then he lay down on the ground again. This time no amount of persuasion on my part could get him to move further. At this point I clearly observed on the footpath ahead of us, the figure of a nun, standing quite still in the gloom and looking straight towards us.

'Jasper was clearly petrified but I felt little sense of alarm, mainly, I think, because I was so concerned for my dog and I was doing my best to comfort him. When I next looked up, after only taking my eyes away for a split second, the figure was gone. I had no alternative but to allow Jasper to have his own way and therefore retraced my footsteps to the beginning of the path.

'For months after that, this footpath was taboo and I could not get Jasper to enter it. One night I played a trick on the dog and took him by another route to the far end of The Hollow thinking that we would not know the difference, but the moment we set foot on the actual lane itself he lay down on the ground whining and refused point blank to move.'

∞

ERIC JAMES from Irthlingborough, Northants, happened

to find himself killing time in London in the early hours of a December morning in 1949. 'I was on my way from St. Pancras to Covent Garden hoping to make some purchases at the market which started at 6.00 a.m. and then catch the 8.00 a.m. train back to Wellingborough, the nearest main line station to where I live.

'I made my first call for a cup of tea at one of the all night stalls they had in those days. Just a few old timers were hanging around the stall when a man approached it. He loitered about for a few seconds then he asked if anyone could spare him a cup of tea. Since no one else around looked like volunteering, I handed the man some coins to pay for his tea. He was a tall man, about six feet, unshaven, dressed in an army great coat.

'I drank my own tea and turned to move off when the unshaven man asked me if I would mind if he accompanied me part of my way. I nodded in agreement and the bloke walked along beside me. He did not mention where he was going and I had not said anything about where I was going however he seemed quite happy just tagging along.

'Very little was said until, on reaching the cross roads at Russell Square, he thanked me very kindly for the company and said that he might meet again sometime and thanked me for the tea. I made the usual noises assuring him that it was no trouble.

'He still had not told me where he was bound so out of curiosity I watched him walk into the middle of the road then he simply vanished before my eyes.'

'I've often wondered who this person could have been. I had always believed that ghosts couldn't eat or speak but I know that I shared a cuppa with the one I met.'

∞

DURING the war, Mrs. Betty Cordell of Rayleigh in Essex was evacuated to the village of Offord Cluny in Huntingdonshire. While she was living there she became friendly with an airman called Paul.

'I had agreed to meet Paul the following week on the river bridge near the railway station. I looked forward eagerly to our meeting and when the time came I got myself ready and went to the appointed place. It was a lovely warm sunny summer evening and I remember cycling along in my sleeveless pink print dress full of the joys of life.

'I waited and waited but there was no sign of him. I felt very disappointed as this was most unlike Paul. I was just about to leave the bridge when he suddenly appeared behind me. I was so delighted to see him that I moved towards him but I stopped in my tracks when I saw that he looked absolutely ghastly.

'Paul did not move towards me which I thought was unusual. Instead he said, "Sorry I can't meet you tonight." He then disappeared and I found myself standing on the bridge alone weeping, my emotions in complete turmoil. I walked over and looked from the bridge in every direction but there was no sign of him anywhere.

'With a thumping heart I got on my bike and rode down the short way to the railway crossing. I asked the man in the signal box if he had seen a young airman go past through the gates. The signalman said that he had not noticed the man come by, but he then added, "Do you mean the man you were speaking to on the bridge?" He said he had noticed the man with me on the bridge but did not see where he had gone to.

'The next day the news went round the village that some of our planes had not returned from raids and Paul had been killed in his plane two nights previously.'

∞

A NORTHANTS lady, Mrs. Tomezak, remembers the story told to her by her old friend. 'My friend had to go to view a property which was up for sale called the Round House. Because it was a type of museum there were several people around the building when she arrived.

'She bent down to stroke a cat which had edged up against her and was rubbing against her legs as cats sometimes do. She noticed that one or two people were giving her odd looks but she thought nothing more of it and continued to make a fuss of the cat which was still by her legs. One person actually walked over to her to ask her if she was feeling all right. Quite taken aback she replied, "Of course, why wouldn't I be? I'm only stroking the cat."

'One elderly gentleman then walked over to my friend and whispered, "There is no cat!" She told him not to be silly, of course there is a cat, then looking down, she saw that the cat had gone. She felt icy cold all over. She was visibly shaken, so much so that they had to bring a cup of tea to her to try to revive her.

'Another old gentleman caught her up in the garden and told her that he quite believed her, as he remembered an

461

old lady who used to live there when he was a child and she had kept a houseful of cats.'

∞

MRS. WESTERN of Sidcup, Kent, remembers when her children were small her little son and daughter used to play happily together in the long passage on the ground floor which ran along to the bottom of the stairway.

'I looked along the passage to the end where the children were just to check that they were O.K. and I suddenly saw, at the foot of the stairs, a strange woman dressed in a hat and coat. I was shocked and wondered how she could have got into the house without me hearing her. I ran towards the children and quickly pushed them into the front room and the dog ran in with them.

'I stayed in the passage and walked towards the woman talking to her, asking what she wanted. I looked down at her feet but I could not see them as they were shrouded in mist. This startled me beyond words then I looked at her face which had an appallingly sad expression on it.

'I got very frightened and ran into the front room after the children. We stayed in that room until it was time for the schools to come out and my eldest child, who had come back from school, knocked on the door. I peeped my head round the door of the front room looking up and down the passage but thankfully the woman had gone. I let the oldest child in but all the time kept nervously looking around me.

'In the evening I told my husband what had happened. He asked me what the woman had looked like. I described her hat and coat and, as much as I could, her face and hair. He went very quiet- not the reaction I had expected – and then he told me that he thought that I had seen his dead mother.

'I must explain that she had died long before I met my husband and the few photographs we had of her had been taken in her youth. It was my description of the hat and coat that convinced him because seemingly it fitted exactly the clothes that she had worn quite a lot just prior to her death. My husband felt that these were the clothes that she would feel he would best remember her in. She had died at the age of 32 from blood poisoning leaving her husband to bring up a young family of four children.'

∞

A LADY from Kent was working in a baker's shop with two assistants when the most weird thing happened: 'The windows in the shop had three glass shelves, about five feet in height, on which we displayed bread and cakes. I looked over at the window and I was stunned to see a large loaf of our bread hovering about six feet in the air above the glass shelves in the window.

'I looked at the two assistants who were also staring in disbelief at this loaf of bread dangling in mid air. Suddenly, as if some invisible hand had let go of the loaf, it crashed down onto the display below. A customer came running in from the street to tell us that she had seen the loaf from outside the shop window. She was quite terrified but she calmed down a bit when the three of us told her that we had seen it too. We wondered if it had been my late husband who was always in the shop letting us know that he was still around. He was six feet three inches tall and he could have easily held the bread up at the level we saw it. One lady assistant was extremely worried by the event.

'One evening the shop filled up with the smell of disinfectant. It seemed to be the same smell which had been in the hospital ward where my husband had died. We were just about to lock up the shop so I knew that the time was a minute or so to 5.00 p.m. The telephone rang and I answered it to be told the news that my son had been involved in a serious accident and was fighting for his life in hospital. By the time I put the telephone receiver down the disinfectant smell had vanished.'

∞

MRS. JOAN CALMADY HAMLYN of Okehampton, Devon, has a story which goes back to the first decade of the century: 'Before my father-in-law was married, he was occupying rooms in the bachelor wing of the house and his bedroom overlooked the stableyard. One night he was awakened by the growls of his terrier which slept at the end of his bed.

'He heard the sound of a carriage and four turning in through the gates at the end of the drive. He got out of bed and looked out of the window into the stableyard which was bathed in moonlight. He heard the coach and team approaching up the drive and swirl round the corner into the yard, pass underneath his window and go on round the corner of the coachhouse and fade away into the distance. He saw not a thing.

'It came to light sometime afterwards that a woman servant had been working in the kitchen when the figure of an old time coachman materialized in front of her eyes, stood there for a few seconds and then vanished just as quickly.'

∞

WHEN Cathy Doig of Rochester decided to have an early night for a change something happened which she will always remember: 'I was 18 at the time and I got into bed and settled down. My parents were sitting downstairs watching television and there was no one else in the house.

'As I lay quietly in my bed I became aware of breathing to the right hand side of the bed. I lay and listened for what seemed like ages but I was so petrified I lost track of the time completely. The breathing seemed fairly rhythmical but ever so often it would stop for about five seconds and then a deep breath would come followed by the normal breathing pattern again, and there was the sound of an occasional heavy sign.

'I plucked up courage and shouted loudly for my father who came running up the stairs quickly and put my bedroom light on as he entered the room. I recounted what I had heard and we sat quietly listening but the breathing had stopped.

'The following day my father checked with our next door neighbours who assured us that they had not been in bed at that time. In any case I knew that the breathing had been in my room right beside me. Sadly it turned out that at the time I had heard the laboured breathing my grandmother who lived 70 miles away was dying.'

∞

MRS. WHITE of Eastbourne lives with her husband and two

little girls in a small flat above some garages. 'The property was originally built in 1923 as stables, then in 1940 two flats were built above the stables which were at the same time converted into garages. Our flat therefore was situated where the original hay loft had been.

'One night we were in bed reading when we heard footsteps running across the front room. They stopped outside our bedroom so we naturally thought that it must be one of the girls. I called out, "Lisa – Kelly" but no one came into our room. I got up to find out what they were up to and was surprised to find that there was nobody by our door despite the fact that we had not heard the footsteps retreat. I went straight to the girls' bedroom to find that they were both fast asleep in their bunk beds.

'Shortly after that I was working one evening on the late shift and my husband attended to the girl's nightly routine. He had bathed them and told them that they were allowed to play for a little while before he put them to bed.

'While the girls were playing in the front room, my husband went into the bathroom to have a wash. He left the door open so that he could hear that the children were all right. He looked into the bathroom mirror and caught sight of a small girl running past into our bedroom. He immediately shouted out, "Lisa, Kelly, you know you are not allowed in the big bedroom." As he spoke he walked out of the bathroom to see that both of our girls were still in the living room on the floor playing with some toys.

'Very puzzled he walked into our bedroom and there in the corner stood a small girl dressed in white with long blond hair. He looked at her, completely bewildered. The child just stood there looking equally confused then she disappeared.'

MR. LATTER, a Londoner, and ex-Barnardo boy, worked in a famous hospital in West London. 'I was deputy head porter and once on night shift I was asked to take an oxygen cylinder to the private patients' wing. As I walked along the dimly lit corridor a sister passed me in strange clothing. She wore a long brown uniform which reached her ankles and had a dark blue belt around her waist. She had lace frills at her wrists and on her head she wore a huge white frilled hat.

'I said "Good evening" to her and she said "Good evening" back. She then proceeded to walk straight through the wall. I got the fright of my life and quickly delivered the oxygen which I thought for a moment I would need myself. I went immediately to the night sister and told her what I had seen. She quite casually told me not to worry – it was only the hospital ghost.

'Years and years ago a sister at the hospital had had an unhappy love affair with one of the doctors. She had taken an overdose of drugs and was found dead in one of the side rooms off that corridor where I had seen the vision.'

∞

ESSE from Doncaster remembers clearly the time back in 1946 when his mother and sister-in-law (his youngest brother's wife) were travelling in a train from London to visit his brother who was in hospital in Chatham in Kent.

'Eventually their compartment emptied except for themselves and another lady who was a complete stranger to them. She approached them and said, "I'm glad we are on our own for I have been wanting to talk to you." Then to my mother she said, "You are going to see your son who is dangerously ill. He will have a major operation soon and will only be given a 50/50 chance of recovery but he will recover, and although he will have future set-backs, he will live for a good many years yet."

'My mother and sister-in-law were so completely astonished at the stranger's words that neither of them was able to utter a word. The lady went on to tell them, "At present he is only allowed to have fluids and fresh fruit which he is getting." (At that time fresh fruit was in the way of peaches which were still in short supply but which were kindly sent by my eldest brother who lived in London.) The woman went on to tell my mother, "Don't worry; things look black right now but your son will eventually pull through."

'When my mother got her breath back after the shock of hearing what was the Gospel truth from someone she had never set eyes on before, she asked the lady how she knew all this. The lady replied simply, "Your mother told me."

'My mother's mother died in 1925. My brother had a serious operation to have a greatly enlarged and diseased spleen removed. He had several later haemorrhages which resulted in a further serious and complicated operation. From that date in May 1946 he lived a further 33 years.'

∞

A SHORT story comes from Margaret from Hampshire: 'I was going to an evening class at our local secondary modern school, and being early, I arrived before the school was properly opened and lit. Therefore I decided that I'd better try to get into the building by some way other than the usual entrance.

'The corridor was rather dimly lit and I was sauntering along when I felt a restraining hand on my shoulder. I hesitated and slowly put my foot out for the next step. I found that I was at the top of a small flight of three steps, then there was a small landing and another three steps leading up to the corridor again.

'I felt quite shaken for if I had not been prevented from just walking at my normal pace by that invisible hand, I would have surely fallen down the steps flat on my face and there was no one readily at hand who could have come to my assistance. I suppose I'll never know who saved me that night but all the same I'd like to say a big thank you.'

∞

DOROTHY from Coulsdon in Surrey lived in Victoria, British Columbia, when she was a small child. 'My great-grandparents on my mother's side were living at the Manor House in Buckden, Huntingdonshire, after my great-grandfather had retired from service in the Indian Army.

'When I was quite young my parents brought my elder sister and myself over to England from British Columbia to be introduced to the family, making the Manor House our headquarters. Whilst staying there I complained each morning to my mother that she had wakened me up in the middle of the night by sitting on my bed. She told me that she had done no such thing and put it down to the fact that I was sleeping in a strange bed.

'One morning I was playing about in the rose garden on my own when a woman came over to me and sat down on a garden bench and watched me playing. I did not pay much heed to her as by this time I was used to seeing new people. However I did notice two things about this woman. She was wearing a long cloak which went right down to the ground and she was crying. I thought it odd to have such a heavy cloak on since it was the middle of summer and very warm.

'The following day I was again playing in the rose garden but this time my sister was with me. Again I saw the lady who came from more or less the same direction (up the garden path from the summer house) and again she sat herself on the same bench, and again she was crying. I watched her for a moment and then just went on playing with my sister without saying anything.

'I remember we were playing with a ball. It was a special favourite of mine because it was extra bouncy and would bounce on the lawn. My sister threw the ball to me for me to catch it but I missed it and it went whizzing past me towards the bench where the lady was sitting. I started to giggle and called out to my sister, "I hope it didn't hit the lady." My sister asked me, "What lady?"

'I turned round quickly towards the bench but the lady had gone. She had been sitting there just a second beforehand. I remember feeling so confused that I just went on playing with my sister without making any more reference to the woman.

'One late afternoon I was walking up a narrow stairway at the back section of the house. The stairs led to a long corridor which had several small bedrooms off to each side. This part of the house was known as the children's wing. I loved to go up there because one of the rooms had a great collection of children's picture books and old toys.

'As I walked along the corridor I saw the same lady

coming towards me. She was still wearing her long heavy dark blue cloak but what really attracted my attention was the fact that she was still crying. I couldn't hear any sobs but she had the most sorrowful looking face that I'd ever seen and she kept putting her hands up to her face in the same way that she had done when I saw her sitting on the garden bench. I did not like to say anything, seeing that she was a grown-up, so I just went into the bedroom where the toys were and shut the door.

'After our return to Victoria my great-grandfather decided to have the floor-boards on the stairs and landing taken up in the children's wing. They had become quite creaky with age so he planned to have the area re-laid. During the proceedings the workmen discovered a small storage area the end of the corridor which had been boarded over. No one in the family had ever realized that it had existed because it was behind oak panelling but extended underneath the corridor floor-boards. The workmen had been checking for plumbing piping when they had noticed it.

'Great-grandfather instructed the workmen to take down the panels to check the exact size of the storage area in the hope that it could be put into use. When the outer wood was removed, the workmen found the skeleton of a baby wrapped up in cloth.'

THE NORTH OF ENGLAND

BUD FLANNIGAN, the well loved entertainer, ruled for years as the 'King' at the Victoria Palace where he had the audiences either screeching with laughter at his antics with the Crazy Gang or singing their hearts along to his tuneful melodies like "Underneath The Arches", "Hometown" and "Strolling" which he performed with Chesney Allen, the other half of the great Flannigan & Allen duo.

Years before Bud became a household name he used to work the old music hall circuit up and down the country. One such trek took him over the hills in the north of England to Lancaster where he always stayed in the same theatrical digs. Here, like all the other travelling entertainers of the day, he was welcomed by Sadie the landlady and her husband Bert as if he was a long lost son returned home. She adapted her catering arrangements to make sure that there was always a hot meal on the table at ll.30p.m. as Bud and his colleagues got home after the final performance of the night. Sadie enjoyed the chit-chat which would go on to the early hours as the entertainers told their funny stories. Every now and then they'd burst into song or play her a tune on the old upright piano she kept in the dining room.

When Bud Flannigan found stardom he never forgot the gracious lady who had opened up her home to him when he had been a struggling young comic. Every Christmas he sent her a lovely present and any time he was in the area he would pop in to say hello and have a cup of tea.

The fame of good theatrical landladies travels fast

around the show circuit so when Bud's sister and her husband were on tour around the north with a travelling company they remembered the address that Bud had given them. They were subsequently welcomed to Sadie's guest house with their small son John and the other members of the cast.

John was only seven years of age at the time but he remembers those days vividly. 'All the world was new to me, and being the only child in the company I remember everyone being really kind and nice to me. We met a lot of people as we travelled around the theatres staying in different theatrical boarding houses.

'We arrived at the digs in Lancaster and as usual we soon got acquainted with the other people who were booked into the house. That was when I first met old Teddy and his wife Martha; they were two watercress peddlars. Teddy had a limp and used to walk around the streets carrying a huge wicker basket on his back. He was a wonderful, kind old man and he used to sometimes take me out on his rounds with him – carrying me in the wicker basket. Martha, who smoked a clay pipe, would walk along beside us all the time telling me jokes. I only realize now, on looking back, what a peculiar sight we must have been as no one could have seen me in the basket but I expect they might have wondered at the yells of childish laughter that would come from the basket in response to Martha's brilliant sense of humour. I became very close to the two of them and looked upon them as uncle and aunty.

'I used to sleep in a tiny attic room at the top of the house. The electricity supply had not been extended to the attic so there were two small oil lamps to light my bedroom which had only a small skylight window and was therefore fairly dark even in the day time. When it was time for bed my mother used to walk up the narrow stairs with me, holding a lighted candle to take us up the last flight to the bedroom.

'One night we were going up to my room as usual when one of the other guests started speaking to my mother on the first landing. I was used to climbing the stairs so I took the candle and continued up on my own. As I got to the top landing on the third floor I was surprised to see the light of another candle. There right outside the door to my little room I saw an old lady. She was just standing there, but then she started to knock on my bedroom door. As she moved, the slight draft made the flame from her candle wave back and forth, lighting up her face. I could see that she was wearing a brown beret and had silvery hair. She looked as if she was worried about something. I ran up to her and asked if I could help her telling her that I knew how to open the door. (There was a trick in the way the handle had to be turned.) She looked down at me but said nothing. I put my hand out to grasp the door handle but she was in the way and she did not move. Again I asked if I could help her, and asked if she was trying to get into my room. She completely ignored me and continued to knock on the door. I then thought that maybe she was deaf and hadn't heard me telling her that I knew how to open the door so I yelled out quite loudly: "Let me show you." She did not even look down at me but again started to knock on my door. This just didn't make sense to me and her silence was really beginning to frighten me.

'While she was still knocking on the door she looked down at me so I knew that she had seen me. She still did not say anything but I noticed that her eyes were full of tears. She then turned her face away from me and started knocking on the door again. I suddenly became terrified and I turned and ran back down the stairs so fast that my own candle flame went out. I didn't stop running till I got to the door of the living room at the bottom of the stairs on the ground floor where I was met by old Teddy. He caught me up in his arms and whirled me around as was his usual manner of greeting.

'As much as I was full of fear I told Teddy that an old lady was trying to get into my room and that she had frightened me. He listened, and then asked me who she was. I told him I didn't know, that she wouldn't speak to me but she was wearing a brown beret. He put me down and rushed up the stairs as fast as his limp would allow. I just sat myself down on the bottom stair until he came back down. He was as white as a sheet. He took me up in his arms and carried me into the living room where my parents were talking to some of the others. He took my mother aside and handed me over to her.

'They questioned me about the lady with the candle and I told them exactly what I had seen, describing her to the best of my ability. It turned out that the only person who always wore a brown beret was Sadie the landlady. She had been dead for three days.'

∞

THE northern holiday resort of Whitby is situated on Cleveland's North Sea coast and has a lovely little harbour. Captain James Cook, the famous explorer, lived in the town as a young man. It was there that his ship "The Endeavour" was built, in which he set out in 1768 to voyage to Australia and New Zealand. His house in Grape Lane is marked by a plaque.

Whitby holds many memories for Eileen Smith who

visited the town for the first time a few years ago. She had arranged to go on holiday with her sister, but not having enough money to go abroad, they thought that it would be nice to see something of the north of England.

'We stayed in a big old house which had been converted into holiday flats, and from the start I had a strange feeling of having been there before, although I knew this was impossible as it was my very first visit to that part of the country. Somehow I seemed to know my way around the house, and on first entering the room I was to share with my sister, I had a most peculiar feeling which I could not understand.

'It was the usual sort of room you find in holiday flats – twin beds, a wash basin, a modern bedroom suite. But as I crossed the threshold I seemed to see, for a mere fraction of a second, a room which was entirely different! Not a bedroom at all, but a sitting room, dark and rather over-crowded, with heavy looking old fashioned furniture. On one wall there was a huge oval shaped mirror in an ornate gilt frame. The impression lasted no more than a moment, then I saw the room as it really was.

'Although I was shaken and bewildered I said nothing to anybody about the experience but during the first night in that room I awoke for some unknown reason. Moonlight was streaming in at the window and at first I thought that my sister was up and moving about the room. With a chilled feeling of pure terror I saw simultaneously that my sister was fast asleep in the other bed. Over by the wall where I had seen the gilt-framed mirror there was the figure of a young woman. She wore a long flowing skirt, a high-necked blouse and a silken shawl. She was half-turned, looking at me over her shoulder.

'The most horrifying thing about this woman was that she had my face! I was looking at another version of myself – or my absolute double. Feature by feature we were identical, even to the hairstyle - long hair drawn smoothly back behind the ears and tied with a ribbon. It was the briefest of encounters, yet so clear and vivid that I could note every detail of face and clothing before she simply disappeared. I lay, rigid with fear, afraid to move, afraid even to close my eyes for fear of opening them to again witness the return of the figure but nothing happened and I eventually fell asleep.

'Throughout our stay in Whitby I had a feeling of apprehension whenever I entered that room, wondering if I would see it again transformed to an old-fashioned sitting room. I was dreading the thought of seeing that girl again, however I saw nothing more and had no further disturbed nights. The weather was fine all week until the very last day of our holiday when it rained heavily. More for shelter than from any desire for culture, my sister and I went into the local museum and art gallery.

'There in the second room of the art gallery I saw it – just a small picture in a corner behind the door – a painting of the room I had glimpsed. There was the dark old-fashioned furniture, the gilt-framed mirror, and yes, the young woman. She was dressed in the same flowing skirt, high-necked blouse and silken shawl, half-turned and looking over her shoulder. She stood in front of the mirror and was therefore portrayed as a double image. She was exactly like me.

'With my flesh crawling I stood and stared at it for such a long time that my sister, who had moved off to another room, came back to see what was holding my interest. I asked her if the painting reminded her of anyone. After a brief scrutiny my sister said, "Goodness, I think she looks astonishingly like you."

'We sought information but as the pictures in the gallery were changed frequently, especially during the summer months, there was no catalogue nor any reference book which could be consulted, and the young part-time worker at the reception desk had no knowledge of the source or origin of any of the paintings.

'We could not decipher the artist's signature but the picture had a title. It was called, simply "ELIZABETH". Elizabeth is my middle name!'

∞

THE Lake District is a well known beauty spot which lies among the Cumbrian mountains in the north west of England. The longest lake is Windermere and the most popular touring centre is the town of Keswick. There are countless scenic walks across the highest mountain passes in England, some of which are over 2,000 ft.

At the southern end of the village of Grasmere can be found Dove Cottage which was the home of the poet William Wordsworth from 1799 to 1808. Near to the house there is a museum which contains the original manuscripts and other memorabilia of the poet. Wordsworth also resided at Rydal Mount by the picturesque Rydal Water in the shadow of Rydal Fell. He was buried in St Oswald's churchyard in Grasmere in 1850.

Nan lives in the shadow of Crossfell or "Fiends Fell" as the mountain is known by the locals. In olden days, before the pass road over to Alston was made, a "corpse track" led

478

over the summit of the mountain to link the parishioners of the Eden Valley and the North & South Tyne Valleys. Near a place called Little Durfell, a large stone bothy was built to allow the mourners to rest the coffins. Sometimes in mid-winter the weary travellers were forced to spend the night in the building for fear of being smothered in snow drifts. One wild night during a violent thunderstorm the bothy was hit by lightning and an entire funeral procession sheltering there perished in the fire.

For years afterwards shepherds and hill walkers could sometimes hear the dying screams of the mourners echo across the still air, and so to rid the ill-fated mountain of its restless spirits it was blessed by a bishop and a wooden cross was erected on the summit. This has long since gone but the name remains – Crossfell.

Nan describes herself as 'a very down to earth kind of person, I am not given to believing all the old myths and stories, but all the same I had a peculiar thing happen to me when I was walking on the summit some years ago.

'There had been a heavy snowfall but it was a beautiful clear crisp day with a deep blue sky, so I thought I would take a wander up the track to the top of the mountain. There was no one in sight and I could see for miles and miles. The snow covered the track ahead of me for about a hundred yards or so, pristine and untrampled but then two lines of footprints appeared. These led all the way up to the summit then completely disappeared into thin air.

'I turned round to come back down by the same route and found only my own tracks and those of my two dogs. There was no wind or snowdrift that could have covered up the other footprints. When I reached the last plateau on the descent I paused once more to admire the wonderful view and I noticed that my dogs were both staring back up the mountain. They were growling and the hairs were standing up on their necks.

'As I looked back up to the left of the track I saw four tall figures dressed in black. I was too far away to see their faces but I could tell that they were watching me and the dogs. They all stood perfectly still. Then a slight mist drifted over the mountain-top and suddenly a fierce wind started to blow. The next moment the figures were gone, the mist had cleared, the wind had stopped and it was a bright sunny day again.'

∞

LONG before Leeds and Bradford became the centre of the clothing trade, Wakefield was the most important cloth manufacturing area in Yorkshire. Although the clatter of the mills can no longer be heard, Wakefield's splendid Georgian houses still stand proud and strong as a relic to the prosperity of the past.

Nesta from Wakefield was sitting before her fireplace in one such Georgian house in January of 1980. 'I was reading a very nice book about a ballerina's life. It was a happy book, nothing about ghosts or anything scary. My brother who had called in for a cup of tea had just left to go to his own home and there was no one in the house except myself.

'Suddenly I thought that I'd heard my bedroom door open then I heard a gentle swishing sound coming down the open staircase. The stairs came down to the right of the lounge where there was a small hallway. I was too frightened to look around behind me towards the open door so I just sat motionless staring into the fire.

480

'Then out of the corner of my eye I saw a lady come into the lounge and move into the centre of the room. I forced myself to turn round and there she was in full view just a few feet away from me. I can describe every detail of her dress – it was grey stiff silk, with a very tight bodice and a full skirt which reached down to her ankles. There was embroidery on the neck and cuffs.

'She stood behind my late husband's chair – the one that my brother had only just vacated a short time before. She put her hands on the back of the chair and then she slowly melted away. The next day she came again at about the same time but this time I was not so afraid. I watched her glide over to the same chair. Then I remember I so much wished that she could somehow or other bring my husband back to me. Suddenly he appeared but he was not looking my way. He did not look ghostly, in fact he looked quite young and I was surprised to see that he was dressed in a long white gown.

'I then realized that he was looking at the wall behind me. I turned to see what he was looking at and suddenly my daughter (who is very much alive) came through the wall. My husband held out his arms and she went into them and they both slowly disappeared. The woman in the long dress had also vanished.

'I was worried that something had happened to Kath, my daughter, so I immediately telephoned her to find out if she was alright. I was relieved when she answered the phone herself and assured me that she was fine. When I asked her not to drive too fast she wondered what had prompted me to say such a thing as she was not in the habit of driving fast. Although I did not wish to alarm her I felt that I had to tell her that I'd just seen her father. I did not mention anything about the woman.

'She told me, "Oh Mum, don't worry, he comes to the foot of my bed many a time and he holds out his arms to me. I always say that I am not ready to join him yet. He is always dressed in a long white gown."

'I wondered how my daughter could have known about the long white gown because I had not mentioned a word about this to her or to anyone else.

'One afternoon, shortly after that, my brother came to visit me. He was sitting in my late husband's chair and I was in the kitchen making a cup of tea but I could see through the wall-hatch into the lounge. I was just looking towards my brother when the grey outline of a woman's long dress seemed to loom out of the thin air. The figure gradually became clearer and I recognized her as the same lady I had seen in the room before. She bent over the chair and put her arms around my brother's neck. I was shocked as I couldn't imagine what on earth my brother was going to say finding such a strange creature bending over him.

'I'll never ever know what he thought because I never discussed it with him then and that was the last time I saw my brother alive.'

∞

THE Wirral peninsula juts out into the Irish sea north west of Chester, the old Roman city north of the Dee. In the year AD 79 the Romans established their camp to fortify themselves against the savage tribes of Wales. Many Roman remains can still be seen in the Grosvenor museum and all around the city; its ancient heritage is evident in the excellently preserved ramparts and the spectacular amphi-theatre which lies near Newgate.

Mrs Browne, a Wirral lady, recalls the story told to her by her late mother Flo who had left school at the age of 13 to follow her sister Lucy into service as a housemaid.

'In the year 1917 when my mother was just 17, she worked in a large house on the Wirral with Lucy. One evening Lucy asked Flo if she would like to go to the pictures with her and a friend. Flo was not really keen on the idea as she had a great deal of ironing to get through so she declined the offer and decided to stay in to finish her chores.

'It never really worried her to be left on her own in the house. The owners were away and there were no other servants around so she was able to get on with her work without any interruptions. In those days the irons were heated on the kitchen stove and regular changes of irons were needed as they soon became cold in use. Flo was ironing in a room across the hall from the kitchen with its stove and so she was able to run back and forth across the hall fetching irons to and from the hot stove.

'On one such trip she could not put the light on in the hall because she had a hot iron in each hand. It was then, as she came out of the doorway into the hall that she came face to face with a man floating in mid-air. His arms and legs were outstretched and his eyes were staring straight ahead. His hair was combed back flat to his head. He was dressed in a night shirt which reached down to his feet. It was all very plain to see and very real.

'Flo felt as if she was frozen to the spot, still holding an iron in each hand. As she stood there, the figure floated past her, turned and went up the stairway and out of sight.

'She was so afraid that she dropped the iron and ran as fast as she could down to the lodge where the gardener and his wife lived. By the time her sister Lucy had returned from the pictures, Flo was in such a terrible state that the gardener's wife insisted she stay at the lodge with them until the following morning.

'The next day Lucy took Flo back home. When their mother saw the shocked condition Flo was in she immediately called for the doctor. The doctor said that the girl had suffered a severe shock and he advised that she be kept quiet with plenty of rest.

'Flo never went back to that place again. Her mother went to the house a few days later to explain to the owners what had happened. The lady of the house had only just returned from her holiday and upon hearing the story did not show the slightest surprise. She said that she knew the house was haunted and that she herself had seen things on occasions but she had never guessed that anyone else had seen anything.

'The lady explained that a man had been murdered in one of the bedrooms some time back. Flo had often told Lucy, long before that terrifying night, that whenever she was in the Blue Room, as they called it, she always felt uncomfortable and cold. She was always glad to finish her chores in that room and get out. She never felt this way in any other room in the house, only that bedroom. Could this have been the room where the murder had taken place?

'As a result of her experience Flo had a nervous breakdown and was away from work for quite some time. She could never forget that house and that terrible evening. The memory of that experience stayed with her until the day she died.'

∞

IN the year 1934 Florence lived with her parents in a remote

484

stone house between Keighley and Bingley in the heart of the Yorkshire moors.

'My father kept pigs and their sty was about three quarters of a mile from our house. One night he went to feed the pigs as usual, taking with him a bucket of prepared food and his faithful springer spaniel. As we lived in such a lonely place it was my mother's custom to lock the door when alone in the house at night. My father was not long gone when my mother was terrified by the noise of the dog whining and scratching at the front door. She came upstairs and lifted me out of my warm bed and wrapped me in a blanket so that I could sit with her on the stairs listening to the whimpering dog. Although she was too afraid to open the door she kept trying to assure me that everything was fine and that daddy would be home soon.

'I was only five at the time but I remember every detail as if it was yesterday. After about half an hour we heard my father's footsteps and his knock on the door. My mother opened the door to let him into the house and the dog rushed into the kitchen and dashed straight under the sideboard to hide.

'My father explained that as he had turned from one lane to another he had heard footsteps. He felt that he was being followed so he sent the dog back to see who it was with the instruction "Get it Sam." Sam had obediently run towards the noise but then stopped in his tracks and started to whine loudly before taking off in the direction of our house.

'Unnerved, my father decided to go ahead and to feed the pigs, but again he heard the footsteps following him. He pushed open the large gate at the entrance to the sty area and waited. The footsteps continued and went past him down the lane. As the sound of the steps passed him he went stone cold. He saw nothing but he heard and felt a presence and he knew that something uncanny was going on to have frightened Sam off. My father was a big sturdy quarryman, very fit and strong, but he never again fed the pigs in the dark.

'In 1947 in a public house in Keighley my father met a man who had been walking his dogs one night from Bingley to Keighley and he told an almost identical story. That man had not heard of my father's experience and had never even met him before. It appears that Hainworth Shay Lane is still a haunted no-go area late at night.'

∞

ROBIN BALL used to teach at a boys school in Doncaster in 1962: 'There were 18 of the boys whose homes were outside the town and who used to board at the school from Mondays to Thursdays. I was required to have charge of them at night, together with a younger colleague and a matron.

'It was very noticeable that once it turned dark in the evenings the headmaster liked to get away to his own house. Only little by little did we come to learn why. While I was still fairly new, I was puzzled by boys in their dormitories calling out "Goodnight George". When I asked them what it was all about they told me that George was the school's ghost who walked up and down the stairs at night. All they could tell me about him was that he was middle-aged and wore a tweed suit.

'The boys were not frightened of him in the least. Eventually both my younger colleague, Stephen, and the matron had encounters with George. Stephen was a hardy

Cumbrian and the last sort of person to be afraid of ghosts, I would have thought, but he was visibly shaken after seeing George disappear through a wall. I only saw him once on a flight of stairs above me. I took him for an intruder and I rushed up the staircase only to find the place deserted. There was absolutely nowhere that he could have hidden himself.

'The headmaster was a little tyrant who used to cane the boys savagely on occasions. He seemed to live just for the power which he exerted over others. However, during the winter months when it turned dark early, if he came back for a snap inspection, expecting to catch a boy misbe-having, the boys always knew how to get rid of him: "Sir, George went upstairs five minutes ago," they would say; "He should be coming back down again fairly soon." Although the boys were not frightened of George, the headmaster was clearly scared out of his wits at the very thought of him.

'During the summer term the headmaster felt free to stay for the evening meal one night. He had taken more wine than I think he realized and he told us that when he had only just started in the school as a young man, one of the other teachers had hanged himself in the cellars where the boys hung up their coats and caps. From that moment on the ghost of that teacher had appeared on the staircase. As the school was in an old Georgian house, the boys had christened him "George".

'Apparently George had died with a serious grudge against our headmaster, who at the time of the suicide lived in the school with his wife. It appeared that the headmaster had made life unbearable for this teacher and had some sort of hold over him which made it difficult for the man to find another job. He was eventually to take out his revenge, as night after night the headmaster and his wife would wake up to find the ghost of the dead teacher standing over them. On some nights the bedclothes had been thrown off them. This was the reason that he resided outside the school grounds.

'I was not surprised to find that the boys were not afraid of George for he obviously bore no child any ill will – he would not have been a normal teacher if he had.

'Our school, and other schools in the South Yorkshire area, were owned by the headmaster's very rich brother, an unscrupulous businessman. The headmaster had only limited powers when it came to the school's finances. His brother, who was totally unqualified as a teacher, found the headmaster a suitable man to govern that part of his kingdom in that the latter had a good university degree and proper teaching qualifications. So under the headmaster the school had gained a reputation for succeeding with boys aged seven to thirteen. The headmaster allowed for no failures.

'For a time the businessman brother had been the headmaster of a school in Sheffield which he owned. But, after knocking out the front teeth of a boy in his charge in a fit of rage, he had been taken to court by the boy's parents and dealt with appropriately by the law. After that his only interest in the schools he owned was in financial gain for himself. At least his brother, our headmaster, would ensure a good reputation for his school at Doncaster and his successor in Sheffield ran that school on much the same lines – scholastic success above all else.

'Eventually the headmaster and his wife found residence inside the boys' school in Doncaster no longer tolerable because of the hauntings by George. As salaried teachers they depended upon the rich brother as they had nobody else to turn to. The businessman reasoned that if he could make good profits out of boys' education in Doncaster, why should he not do the same with girls. The headmaster's wife was a qualified teacher and suitable as a headmistress. So the businessman brother bought a large house in the wealthiest suburb of Doncaster and converted it into classrooms with the necessary additions for a girls' non-residential school. He made the garden into playing facilities and allowed our headmaster and his wife to stay in a flat within the school buildings.

'From all that I saw, the headmaster's wife was perfectly competent and her school had a good name. It was only 1 ½ miles away from the boys' school where I worked, fairly near to the town centre, so the headmaster could get to us in his car in a matter of minutes. Of course his brother took all of the profits out of both schools for himself and he refused to release our headmaster from his contract with our school and made it clear that he would not be of assistance if any references were ever asked of him to enable the headmaster to leave his employment.

'When the cat's away the mice will play and so each night when the headmaster got into his car and drove off towards the girls' school, our boys heaved a huge sigh of relief. Not only the boys, I might add but Stephen, matron and I were also glad to see the back of him. It was only after he would leave the building that we could ever relax and be our normal selves. Under such a tyrant we became a very close knit family. The matron was the widow of a teacher and being the oldest amongst us she was our natural leader. Boys of that age need plenty of love, care and attention, even tough South Yorkshire ones, we all agreed, so when the headmaster was not there they were allowed to be themselves and were not punished for every minor infringement. We treated them as younger relatives rather than pupils under severe discipline as was the case when the headmaster was there.

'In the winter of 1962-63 it was so cold that a bathroom froze up and the temperature in the dormitories fell well below freezing. We allowed the boys to take hot water bottles to bed and gave them cups of hot cocoa before they went to bed. We paid for this ourselves but the headmaster accused us of stealing the cocoa from the kitchen. He stated that the boys should grow up tough and that we were spoiling them with such considerations. George must have agreed with us as every one of us got the distinct feeling that he was happy about how we were trying to help the boys.

'Although the headmaster used to drink, he opposed the drinking of any form of alcohol by members of the staff. Being in charge of boys at night time certainly made spending any time in a pub an impossibility. However, Stephen, the matron and I felt no sense of guilt in having the odd small bottle of lager or cider and in no way did it place any serious restraint on our abilities. We had a cupboard with a key (which the headmaster did not have) in which we kept our meagre supply. When one of us went out to dispose of the empty bottles and replenish our stocks (always after dark) we would call it disposal operations to keep the boys ignorant, but this proved to be totally in vain. If you live closely with boys of that age they soon discover or deduce the truth.

'They knew all too well that the headmaster considered our drinking beer or cider in much the same way as if they themselves had been doing anything naughty. We used to watch out of the staff room window in case the headmaster's car would appear. The boys in their dormitories did the same thing and we would all warn one another if the head was in sight.

'One evening Stephen, the matron and I were in the staff sitting room marking the boys' written work and preparing the next day's lessons, when the headmaster arrived unnoticed by us – but not by the boys. We were surprised when 12 year old Richard burst into our room saying, "Quick there's no time to lose. Get all of those bottles and glasses out of sight, open the window, and Mr Ball, smoke one of your smelly French cigarettes, the head is here."

'In less than a minute all that the child had suggested had been done. The head arrived and demanded to know what young Richard was doing in the staff sitting room. The matron answered, saying that Richard had come to her with a headache. The headmaster said that he would give Richard a tablet, but Richard knew how to get rid of him. He told the headmaster that George had been very active all night. He had been spotted on the stairs, in the dormitories and all over the place. The headmaster turned as white as a sheet then drove away within a minute.

'I couldn't help feeling that although George could not speak to the boys he had used his own means to communicate with them, and, to a lesser extent, with us. It seemed as if he wanted to unite all of us against that cruel headmaster and his ruthless brother. In that, he succeeded. The atmosphere inside that school was an unhappy one and one which I will never forget. The boys gave it the only brightness and relief from the depression which existed. Without them, we adults would have been suicidal ourselves.'

∞

THE small industrial town of St. Helens is situated north east of Liverpool, the main port on Merseyside. Norman has lived there all of his life and he can verify, 'Yes, there is some very nice countryside in the industrial north!

'About two-and-a-half miles from where I live lies a hamlet which is skirted by a stretch of lush woodlands. In a hollowed-out section of this area can be found mysterious caverns.

'Some of the old timers remember seeing the remains of an old chimney, an engine house and a well around the caverns. From time to time enterprising explorers would arm themselves with torches and boxes of sandwiches and delve down into the depths to try to uncover what lay beneath. Many visitors have ventured past the entrance but at the awesome sight of dozens and dozens of caves and twisting narrow passageways they quickly emerged with a sense of relief at once more seeing daylight. One journalist trudged for two miles underground and came across an intricate arrangement of walled-up passages. One of these had a gap just big enough to enter. He crawled along on his hands and knees for some yards until he found that this path opened out into a maze of smaller tracks and a labyrinth of caves so complex that he did not dare to venture further for fear of getting lost forever.

'However, one nearby opening, being the largest, caught his eye and he noticed that the entrance had been smoothed over for some reason, making this particular cave stand out from the rest even in the dim light of his torch. He braced himself and entered. His breath was almost taken away when he found himself in a kind of church complete with pillared arches and smooth walls. At one end of this church-like place a flight of steps led up to a gallery and an altar. There was an overwhelming sense of pending doom about the place, the silence was not peaceful but of a threatening nature. Although the cave looked exactly like the interior of a church there was something wrong – something he could not come to grips with. His immediate reaction was to run as fast as he could, out through the gap at the walled-up section and towards the long winding tunnel. By the time he had travelled the two miles to reach the exit he was in a state of near-collapse and counted himself lucky to be still alive.

'The last man to have officially worked in the caverns was a fellow called Bill Rigby. It is on record that he had explored the caverns in 1865 when he was a boy of nine. He had begun his working life there four years later when the caverns were owned by a Mr. Charles Howarth, nick-named "Yorkshire Charlie". Over 40 men were employed in the caverns, cutting out huge slabs of stone which were then transported by local farmers to the various building contractors.

'Bill remembered a deep shaft going down two layers of caverns beneath the ones which the journalist had encountered. This section had been filled in when the quarrying work had been completed there in 1870. Could the church have been built for the underground workers of that day or had it a more sinister sacrificial purpose? Judging by the atmosphere in that particular cave it would seem that the latter was nearer the truth. There was no sense

493

of positive good vibrations which one would normally find in any bona fide church.

'Throughout the years there have been many dramatic incidents at the caverns. In 1960 and again in 1977 boys from the neighbouring localities of St. Helens and Billinge had gone on exploratory outings to the caverns and they had become hopelessly lost. After their non-appearance rescue parties were sent down to search for the youngsters and their guides. During the 1977 operation photographers went down much deeper than anyone had ever explored before. They emerged with impressive shots of stalagmite and stalactite formations.

'It is believed that the caverns are haunted by cavaliers who were chased down there by Oliver Cromwell and did not get out alive. In 1650 there were no such things as torches (other than live flames) and the cavaliers had no chance in the spider's web of passages. Several people have reported hearing moaning sounds in the caves from which they got the impression that men were dying.

'A few years ago a group of potholers from St. Helens Technical College spent nearly eight hours exploring the caves. Someone was posted outside the main entrance to keep a watch for them and to look after the gear and change of clothing. When the potholers eventually came staggering out of the caves the blood was drained from their faces and their hands were trembling uncontrollably. They were so petrified that not one of them would utter a single word about what had happened underground, and to this day, they have all kept their frightening secret.

'About ten years ago when I was at the caverns someone there told me about a weird and gruesome happening. Apparently a scout master and his pack went deep into the caves but when they came out some time later, they discovered that two of the scouts were missing. They retraced their steps back into the complicated cave system. Eventually they found one of the boys hanging dead from a stalactite with a rope around his neck and with both his legs missing.

'They then heard a chewing sound and deep in a dark corner of the cave they found a kind of dwarf with a large head chewing the body of the other scout.'

∞

HELENE of Stretford, Manchester, became seriously ill with diphtheria when she was not quite five years of age. 'High fever raged and the nights were especially bad for me,' she recalls. 'It was during these nights that the old nurse used to come to see me.

'She would sit herself at the side of my bed and her lovely cool hands eased my congested chest and aching limbs with their soft stroking. Her voice was very low and had a curious and unfamiliar accent. Later, much later, she would tell me that she had to go and I would beg her to take me with her but she always replied that I could not follow her just then and I would have to bide where I was. She always promised me that she would be waiting for me at her home and that one day I would meet her there.

'Then she would rise from her chair and leave, moving very quietly, and I would follow her with my eyes, taking in every detail of her appearance: very straight-backed, small head with thick white hair, black blouse and skirt.

'She always came during the hours of the night, never in the day time and to my greatest vexation, nobody could ever produce her for me however much I pleaded with the day and night staff to fetch her to my bedside.

'I recovered and my questions about the old nurse ceased after my mother had explained to me that one often imagined things during a high fever which might not necessarily be there. Trusting my mother implicitly I accepted this but the memory lingered and I was often grateful that the figment of my feverish imagination had been such a pleasant one.

'When my dear mother passed away it fell to me to take charge of her papers. She had always been a most methodical and tidy person so everything was carefully sorted and annotated in her neat handwriting.

'Amongst her treasured photographs I found something which startled me. It was a picture of my old mysterious nurse who had come to me all those years earlier. I picked it up and saw that on the back my my mother had written: "My Grandmother, aged about 65 years. Photo given me by my friend Lizbeth in 1957. So glad she found it, no other exists."

'I was stunned and sat motionless for a while. There was no possible doubt that this was the woman who had sat at my bedside and helped nurse me back to health. I had never ever seen this photograph before. I even telephoned my mother's old friend Lizbeth to check and she confirmed that she herself had only found it in 1957 amongst some old papers belonging to her own parents who were great friends with my late great-grandmother.

'Somehow the fear of death which I had always felt acutely suddenly left me as I remembered her words – that she would be waiting for me at her home and one day I would meet her there.'

IN the year 1950, Ben, a resident of Marton in Middlesbrough, Cleveland, was contemplating a big step. He was thinking of giving up his safe regular job to start up in business on his own selling tiled fireplace surrounds. He did not tell anyone about his tentative plans.

'We were living at that time in a terrace house, two up and two down. We had no children and I had only £10 in the bank. Starting any business would have been a dicey step but with virtually no capital it was almost an impossibility. But I reckoned that I would be able to arrange initial supplies on a monthly credit basis.

'One evening my wife had gone up to bed and I had checked all the downstairs doors and windows to make sure they were locked. I lit my last cigarette of the day and just stood in the middle of the living room with my back to the dying embers of the fire. I was thinking about a little corner shop which I had considered renting and I remember coming to the conclusion that the particular shop in question would hardly be spacious enough to display the various designs of fireplaces. I did not have the agent's details so I was trying to recall the exact address and street number, but for the life of me I could not remember what the proper postal address was.

'My cigarette was down to the last quarter inch when something drew my attention to the open door which led to the hallway and the stairs. A rough looking woman walked right into my living room and seated herself on the nearest dining chair with her hands resting on the table. I was so taken aback at the cool way she just came into the room I could not utter a word. I wondered if she could be a vagrant from the street, but then I remembered that I had definitely locked the doors. She was obviously harmless and I was in such a confused state I just stood there watching her. I was just as bemused by her attire as by her sudden appearance from nowhere. Her hair was dark and straggly and her features were gaunt. Some sort of woollen jumper was held together at her throat by an ordinary safety pin. Her skirt was hidden under an apron which seemed to be made from an old sack, fringed at the hemline.

'She turned her face to me but she did not raise her eyes as she spoke. In a low gravelly voice she told me: "Take one A." I had no idea what on earth she meant. I glanced down to flick my cigarette which had burnt my fingers. I only averted my gaze for a fraction of a second but when I looked back she had gone.

'Next day I found that the little shop which I had been thinking about was No. 1A. I took it and I am glad to say that from that moment on my fortunes changed for the better.

'I often wondered who that lady was, where she had come from, how she knew my thoughts, and where she went to. Nineteen years passed and in 1969, when my wife was a Commandant in a world-wide voluntary organization I was elected to become her dogsbody because she did not drive.

'My brief, each September, was to drive my wife and another lady to their annual conference at a Yorkshire seaside resort. Most other members went by bus, particularly a huge young woman with arms like tree trunks. She suffered because Marks & Spencers never had any clothes large enough for her and she had to wear men's shoes.

'On one occasion I had dutifully deposited my wife and her friend at the conference hotel when I noticed that the bus had managed to convey the extremely large lady safely to the venue. I had a snack, took a photograph and departed after promising to return two days later.

'Before I had left the outskirts of the town a terrible unaccountable feeling hit me. Although I was in perfect health at the time my whole body ached and a throbbing headache racked my senses. Thinking that maybe I was suffering from car fumes I wound down the window, but that made no difference. I still felt a melancholy wave engulf me.

'I don't know what happened next because I suddenly realized that I was driving through the market town of Helmsley. I was terrified – I had driven 30 miles in what seemed like just a few seconds. The body aches had gone but I still had the splitting headache, and a roaring sound almost deafened me. I drove for about two miles until I felt that my head was going to burst so I pulled into a lay-by and got out of the car.

'I stood looking over the wide span of scenery taking in gulps of fresh air in an attempt to clear my head. I could see for miles across a vast stretch of land with isolated farmhouses dotted along the valley. An arrow pointed to public conveniences which were hidden from view about a 100 yards inside the pine woods which covered the top of the moorland. I walked down the gritted roadway towards the conveniences which were clean and cool.

'I emerged and there, beneath the nearby trees, stood the old vagrant lady. She wore her tattered jumper and apron which advertised somebody's sugar. She had not aged and this time she looked directly at me – eye to eye contact. Her gaze did nothing for my headache, except I momentarily forgot it. In that same low gravelly voice she said, "Go back." The next instant she had vanished. I stood there wondering what she meant exactly. Go back to where? To the toilets? To the car? Completely flummoxed I made my way back to the car and started to drive home. The headache started to ease as I drove.

'Two days later I was back at the conference hotel. When I drove my wife and her friend back home they seemed cautiously subdued. When we arrived home I got the full story. Moments after I had left them at the hotel they had drifted towards a room which had a bar. The extremely huge lady had landed a playful thump on my wife's shoulder blades, knocking her out cold. It seems that there is a junction of nerves at one point and a blow to that precise spot can almost kill. My wife had found herself seated on a chair at the hotel doorway, crying uncontrollably and had spent most of the following days in bed feeling unwell. The unexpected blow had triggered off an illness which eventually led to my wife's death.

'I was in deep grief trying to find some kind of explanation for what had happened. I remember discussing everything with an aged uncle and I found myself pouring my heart out to him. He told me about the time when my farmer grandfather had been killed in an accident.

'My uncle had been loading hay onto a farm cart and grandfather was working on top. An insect had stung the horse making the animal jerk forward in the shafts. Grandfather fell off and suffered a broken back. As a very small boy I remembered being present when my grandfather was brought into the house on a hurdle. My uncle then said that he had been struggling trying to lift my heavy grandfather onto the hurdle when he became quite annoyed at a woman who just stood close by staring at him. "She was no help to me at all, and even when I called over to her to go and fetch help she just stared right through me. I was so concerned at getting your grandfather moved without causing him extra pain that I just ignored her. She was raving on in a cracking old voice trying to tell me something but I was so confounded that I just snarled back at her telling her to mind her own business. She was wearing an old jumper that had seen better days and she had an old apron affair wrapped round her, made out of a sugar sack or something like that. The next thing there was nothing there. She had disappeared.'

∞

A BRISTOL man used to live in the north of England. 'I am a third generation railwayman,' he says. 'I use that word to distinguish between people who are real railwaymen and those who merely work on the railway. My grandfather was in the carriage works at Crewe after he left the army and all my uncles, except one who died early, were in the loco works along with my father. I followed him in 1939 and spent a long happy working life on the railway. I am currently interested in a couple of restoration projects.

'Once in 1951 I was riding an Austerity 2-8-0 freight engine over the Pennines finishing at Farnley Shed around 5.20 a.m. This was in February and it was therefore dark. I washed and walked along the track to Farnley Junction Station (which is no longer there) to wait for the 5.50 a.m. from Leeds due to arrive at Farnley at 6.00 a.m. to go on to Stalybridge, Stockport and then home.

'It was freezing with an east wind blowing that would cut you in half. The station gas lights were lit and I waited on the westbound platform. I was just standing looking over at the other platform where I saw a man standing under a lamp reading a newspaper. Although the lamp was fairly dim there was reflected light from the frozen snow on the platform so I could see him quite clearly. I was anxious to get home after a long night on the footplate. (I was not footplate staff but was on the engine observing the effect of new balance weights on the coupled wheels.)

'I did notice however that the man was wearing a top coat and trilby hat. Because he was the space of two running lines away and there was only the gas light, I can't say what paper he was reading but I assumed that it must have been the newspaper of that day. I say this because shops opened earlier then than they do now and in the latter stages of the trip from Mirfield I had seen shops with lights on.

'My train approached and just as it slowed down at the platform I saw the man across on the other platform turn and walk straight towards the track. I'll never forget the wave of panic that shot through me as I was certain that he would go over the edge of the platform in front of the engine. I roared over to him to stop. I did not take my eyes off him as I watched him move over the edge of the platform, then he was gone in a whirl of mist which drifted up and merged with the steam from the engine.'

∞

ROBERT CHAPMAN of Preston in Lancs used to be a church warden in 1972 at St Helen's Church, Garstang.

'I had a plan of the location of every grave in the

churchyard, also a list of them so I knew them all well. There were two which I always wondered about. One was a flat slab with a legend: "Leonard Foster, 1632" engraved on it. The other, a few yards away, was a shaped slab, upright, which bore the legend: "Elizabeth Foster died 17th October 1632". I knew that they had both died of the plague in 1632 for they were so entered in the register for that period and they were in fact father and daughter. I was well aware that having grave markers in 1632 meant that they must have been persons of some importance.

'One night, for no particular reason, the two tombstones came into my mind. Although it was 10.30 p.m. I took down the printed copy of the register for the years 1597 to 1686 and located the page on which the Foster entries had been made.

'At that precise moment the telephone rang and I answered it. A voice asked me, "Bob, do you believe in ghosts?" I instantly recognized the voice as belonging to a local farmer's wife. I answered, "Well, on Sundays I swear that I believe in the visible and the invisible...." She went on to tell me that her husband now believed in ghosts because he had just seen one that evening in the field. I remember reminding her that it was getting late but I asked if it would be convenient for me to visit them the following day at around 4.30 p.m. when I could hear the whole story.

'I arrived at the farmhouse on the dot of time as arranged. The farmer explained that the previous evening he had been spraying the young corn by tractor, moving up and down the field in sweeps the width of his boom. Moving parallel to a stream bordering the field he had noticed a figure walking in the same direction as he was travelling but on the far side of the stream. He of course assumed that it must be a local taking an evening walk. On his return sweep the figure had moved along and as the farmer was now travelling in the opposite direction he was able to take a closer look. He began to wonder who it could be, eliminating in his mind all of the locals who were well known to him.

'The large hat of the stranger made the farmer wonder as he had never seen such a hat on anyone before. Also the type of boots he was wearing seemed a bit unusual. As the farmer passed by, he watched the figure cross the stream where there was no means of crossing, and enter the field which was being sprayed. The figure had passed beyond the sweep he was making on the return, so the farmer turned the tractor in a circle to see better and to his horror he saw the spray boom pass right through the figure of the man. The next second the man was nowhere to be seen.

'I was shown the field, and I witnessed the tractor wheel marks in the young corn and the circular sweep which the farmer had taken to enable him to take a closer look at the figure. I asked the farmer to describe the clothes the stranger had been wearing. From what I was told they appeared to be of the type worn in the early 17th century. I requested that if the farmer ever saw the figure again that he would inform me.

'A week later he telephoned me to say that he had seen "it" again in mid-afternoon in a wood and he had been able to see the face. The clothing worn was exactly the same as he had seen previously. He told me that he had been talking to a lady in the village who knew nothing about what he had seen but who had reported that she had seen a figure similar in description on the site of a former coach path in the village.

'After a bit of searching through the old parish books

504

and a few visits to the local library I found out that the coach path runs directly across the land upon which the house of Leonard Foster once stood.'

∞

A WOMAN from Doncaster fondly remembers her late father as 'a very down-to-earth kind of man, certainly not given to fanciful notions.

'Some years ago he had been out on a shooting trip. Coming back in his van along a country lane which had hedges on either side and fields beyond, he glanced to the right to see a car coming straight across the field. It was not quite dusk and he had to pull up sharply, jolting to a stop just as the other car came straight through the hedge. It moved across the road in front of him and then evaporated into the opposite hedge and vanished into the field.

'For some reason my father always associated that experience with some kind of warning, or preparation. He'd had the strangest feeling when he saw the phantom car that it was meant to be taking him on some kind of journey. Although it did not make a lot of sense to him at the time, he seemed to feel that it was in some way significant.

'Shortly after this event I had the most weird dream. I'll always remember it because of its strange content, so unlike any other dream I have ever had. I was in a cemetery walking along with my mother trying desperately to find a way out. On one side of the path there was a larger than life white owl sitting on a tombstone. The moon was shining and as I looked at the owl, wondering if it could be alive, it blinked.

'We passed by the owl hoping that the path would lead to

the way out but I was horrified to find that the exit was blocked by several grey wolves who were snarling at us, their eyes gleaming with menace. On turning back round to retrace our footsteps there were more wolves blocking every pathway. I woke up the next morning with every detail of the dream vivid in my mind but I did not mention it to anyone as I did not feel that there was any reason to do so – after all it was only a dream.

'Very shortly after that my father was out on another shooting and fishing trip. This time it was at Howden near Goole. He stopped his van to speak to a farmer because he wanted to buy a sack of potatoes. The farmer's van was parked up ahead of him. They talked for a minute or two then a lorry approached up the narrow road. The farmer had been looking ahead and had seen the lorry coming. He called to my father to mind his back, but his warning came too late. My father was knocked into the farmer's driving mirror then he slumped down on the road unconscious. He died the following day never having regained consciousness.

'A few days later my sister, brother and I were looking at some of father's belongings; a lovely ivory chess set, a microscope and a three dimensional viewer which, it was unanimously agreed, I was to keep, together with a pack of little picture slides which went with the viewer. I had never seen these before and in fact I was not even aware that my father had owned such a thing.

'Eager to have a look through the viewer, I placed the first slide in position. I thought it rather odd when it turned out to be a picture of a graveyard. I quickly pulled the slide out and inserted the next one from the pack. I nearly died when I found myself looking at the very same large white owl which I had seen in my dream. It was sitting on a tombstone.'

∞

HULL, on the north side of the Humber, is Britain's third largest sea port after London and Liverpool. It was originally known as Wuke-upon-Hull until King Edward l bought it and re-named it Kingston-upon-Hull. It was in the Humberside area that the Vikings invaded Britain in the l0th Century.

Some years ago Barbara Bayes was employed as a "Mrs. Mop" for a company in Albion Street, Hull. 'A large Victorian house had been converted into offices and I always thought what a lovely private house it must have been in its glory with sweeping oak stairways and high ornate ceilings and doors.

'There were a few private flats on the upper part of the building and I had to collect the key from the ground floor office to gain access to the second floor flat. This flat still retained a lot of its original beauty even with the mod cons installed. The cleaning of the flat was simple. The problem was with the door.

'For some reason it would close just when I was on the point of re-entering, armed with pails and brushes, or worse, when the latch was down and the key was on the inside. It wasn't as if it was swinging closed naturally, it was more of a slam as if someone was slamming the door in a bit of a temper. It had happened time after time, even once when I put a pail down to keep it open while I went to collect some cleaning materials from the little storeroom on the ground floor. I'd heard the slam from downstairs but even though I heard it I thought at the back of my mind that it must have been from some other door as it could not possibly be the first floor flat. But I was wrong. When I got back upstairs sure enough the door was shut fast. However, a pass key was kept in the office downstairs so although the closing of the door was an inconvenience it was nothing too drastic.

'One day I had arranged to meet a pal of mine to do some shopping in the town. She called into the downstairs office to wait until I had finished work as she had arrived a bit too early. I heard her voice drifting up the stairway but I just continued to vacuum the carpets with my back to the entrance door of the flat.

'I felt two hard taps on my left shoulder. Turning the machine off, I said, "Joan, you did give me a start. I won't be long, but don't sneak up again like that." I turned as I spoke and realized that I was speaking to an empty room. I walked over to the door and called out, "Have you just come up, Joan?" Joan answered me from the ground floor office saying that she had never left there. After handing in the key I again asked her if she had played a trick on me but she clearly did not know what I was on about, so I dropped the subject. But I thought that I'd better double check to find out if there was anyone on the third floor. I opened the top flat with the pass key but found it completely empty as it had been for months, awaiting new tenants.

'The following day I was polishing the stairway between the second and third floors. I distinctly heard footsteps going up the stairway just above me towards the third floor. I looked up but could see no one. I even called out but there was no reply. It was only then it dawned on me that no one had passed me on the stairway which was the only method of reaching the top floor, and in any case the flat on the top floor was still vacant.

'Within a few minutes I heard the footsteps again. They were quite soft to start with and sounded as if they were walking across the floor of the top flat. To my horror they got louder and sounded as if they were at the top of the stairway. They were coming down the stairs towards me. I broke out in a cold sweat as I felt completely trapped. To make matters worse they were now running. I was peering up the stairs but could see nothing at all. The next moment an icy cold wave went through me as the sound of the footsteps went right past where I was standing. It was as if a freezing draft had just whizzed past. I heard the footsteps run straight into the flat on the second floor and I nearly fainted when I heard the violent slam of the flat door.

'I was so terrified that I was rooted to the spot, not daring to go back down the stairs in case I would meet anything as I passed the second floor flat. I'm not sure how long I stood there but I felt nauseated and I was trembling like a leaf. After what seemed like ages of silence I tried to muster up enough courage to make myself walk back down those stairs. Slowly I tip-toed down, keeping as far away from the second floor flat door as I could. As soon as I got past that door I galloped down the rest of the stairs two at a time until I got to the offices on the ground floor where I grabbed my coat and ran from the building.

'I rang up my employer later that day to tell him that I would not be returning to work. I must say that he did not sound too surprised then he admitted that no char had ever stayed to work in that building for more than a few weeks. I had been there longer than anyone and I'd only been employed for just over a month.

'This got me wondering, for although there was no way that I ever wanted to enter that building again, I was curious as to what was really going on there. I made some enquiries in the library and around the locals and I found out that many years ago a young girl had lived in the house and had fallen in love with a young man whom her parents disapproved of. Apparently there had been a violent row and the girl had been confined to her bedroom at the top of the house. Despite continuous running up and down to plead with her determined father she was forbidden to see her young man ever again. The parents found her dead in her room the following morning.'

∞

MR. HAITHWAITE from Ripon in North Yorkshire remembers: 'Some years ago I had caught a bus from town which stopped not far from where I live. It was about 9.30 in the evening and it was quite dark. As I walked along the road I heard a child crying over to the right.

'Thinking that the child must be in some difficulty I crossed over the road to see if I could help. I could still hear the crying, and moving along the other side of the road I saw what I thought was someone in a white coat.

'At that moment a car approached along the road so I thought that I would probably be able to see whoever it was in the car's headlights. To my surprise there was no one anywhere along the road or footpath and there was absolutely no place that anyone could have gone to. The crying had now stopped.

'I went home, mentioned what had happened to my mother and thought no more about it. A few days later a little boy who lived just down the road from our house was killed by a car on that very spot.'

∞

FROM Bradford in West Yorkshire a lady recalls when she was a young bride in 1942. 'I had only been married six months and was delighted about the fact that my new sister-in-law was very friendly towards me and used to call frequently for a chat and a cup of tea. One day she told me about a very vivid dream that she had had the night before.

'In her dream she had seen a young man, a soldier she thought, who had knocked on her door and she had invited him inside. She was surprised to see when he was next to her, that he wore a navy blue uniform with a white webbing belt and a white peaked hat. There was a red stripe running down the side of the trousers. It crossed her mind then that perhaps he wasn't a soldier but a sailor. She remembered being quite puzzled about this in the dream.

'He held out his hand, took her hand and said, "I've come to say goodbye because I must go now." He then turned away and waved goodbye to her.

'The very next day my mother and father received a telegram from the war office to say that my brother, a Royal Marine, had been killed in action by a direct hit along with six other men. They were on board Bradford's adopted cruiser, *The Aurora*.

'My brother had been on constant active service and was unable to attend my wedding and so my sister-in-law had never met him. His dress uniform was exactly as she had described in her dream.'

∞

IN 1932, Mr. Anderson of Newton Heath, Manchester, used to live in a house in Bridgewater Street, Oldham, Lancs. The house has long since been demolished and the site is now part of the local school grounds. 'It was a single house, one up, one down, no back door and the front door opened directly onto the street.

'I was about eleven years of age and one lovely warm sunny day I was playing a game of football outside in the street with a gang of my pals. The ball burst, and as I had a football upstairs in the house I told the lads that I would run up to fetch it and I'd be down in a minute.

'On entering the house, the door to the stairs was facing the main door from the street. My mother and my sister were in the downstairs room sitting on rocking chairs at each side of the fireplace and they saw me come in through the living room door which was ajar.

'I opened the door to the staircase and went up, turning round the bend of the stairwell. I stopped in my tracks when I saw a woman at the top of the stairs. She was tall and straight and she wore a long dress that covered her legs. Her hair was done up in a bun. I thought my mother had sent this woman up the stairs for some reason although I couldn't really imagine why because my mother never let anyone other than the family up the stairs as our bedroom was not a pretty sight.

'The woman seemed a bit startled, then she smiled at me and I smiled back. She came down the stairs and I had to press myself to the wall as she passed me as the stairs were very narrow. As she passed I turned to continue up the stairs but there was such a blast of coldness which seemed to smack into me that I lost my balance and fell down on my knees on the stairs. I couldn't get my breath and I'd never felt so cold in my life. I felt as if my blood was freezing up inside me. I remember thinking that I was going to die. I was fighting for breath for what seemed like a very long time but it must have been only a matter of seconds.

'Eventually I recovered and went up to the bedroom to collect the football. When I went back downstairs I was amazed to see only my mother and sister sitting in the living room. I said, "Where's that woman?" My mother asked me, "What woman?" I dashed out hoping to see her still in the street but there was no sign of her. I went all round the block followed by the lads who were only interested in getting the ball from me to continue the football match. The woman was nowhere to be seen. I even asked the gang if they'd seen a woman come out of our house as they were all waiting right outside our door. None of them had seen anyone.'

∞

MANY years ago, Doreen Bennett, a Leeds lass, was on a week's walking holiday in the Yorkshire Dales with a friend and a small brown poodle.

'We arrived very hungry at Barnard Castle. It was about 4.30 p.m. and on seeing a large notice advertising mixed grills on a cafe window, we needed no further encouragement. It was a very old building called Cromwell House Cafe.

'After a huge mixed grill with apple pie to follow, we enquired if the waitress knew of anywhere we could stay for bed and breakfast. Much to our surprise she told us that we could stay right there at Cromwell House.

'It looked such an ancient place we were not too sure but because it was getting late we thought that we'd better accept in case we couldn't find anywhere else. We were taken up the stairs to our room which had a thick heavy old- fashioned door with a large metal lock.

'During the night I awoke in horror. The hair was prickling on my head with sheer fright. The floor seemed to have opened up and there in the middle of the bedroom floor I could see about a dozen bone-thin people all stretching out stick-like arms. Their faces were so gaunt that they looked like skulls but they were alive and all the time reaching upwards as if they were trying to rise up out of the floor. I'll never forget the pleading expressions in their sunken eyes. One word came into my head – Belsen!

'I tried to sit up in the bed but I found that my body was rigid and I was unable to move. I had all my senses about me and I could see the mass of twisting limbs before me. I tried to call out to waken my friend who was fast asleep in the other bed but when I opened my mouth no sound came out. This made me go into an inner panic as I felt completely helpless.

'It was then I heard the most pathetic wailing sound. I kept looking from one tortured face to another to see who it was that was crying out. Although the sound continued I could not distinguish exactly where it was coming from. I still could not move anything except my eyes. I looked over to the far corner of the room and I saw my little dog cowering into the wall. The wailing was the sound of my poodle's terrified whimpering. I could see it virtually quivering with fright and looking at the figures.

'All I could do was just stare and stare at these tortured people for what seemed like ages but I expect that it was no more than a few seconds in reality. Very gradually the faces faded and eventually all of the bodies had disappeared and the room was back to normal. It was only then that I was able to move so I jumped up out of the bed and ran to pick up my dog which was still shaking with fright. I woke up my friend who had not heard or seen anything.

'The next morning after breakfast, the owner asked us if we would like to see the dungeons in the cellars where at one time men had been imprisoned, starved and tortured.'

∞

A LADY from Wakefield in West Yorkshire used to know a girl called Clara Gill who was a member of the same Methodist chapel and who attended Sunday school. 'She left the area and for years I never saw her. One day she came back to Wakefield to settle down. She was married and I noticed that her husband was a very smartly dressed young man although I never really got to know him very well.

'Clara died and her widower lived on his own in their little house. When I used to walk to chapel I used to pass the end of the road where he lived and on several occasions we walked part of the way together. I was always struck by how smart looking he had remained despite his lonely life.

'After a few years however he became unable to live on his own and went to stay in a local communal home. I never saw him after that.

'One day I was walking from my home into town and as I

passed a flower shop I suddenly began to wonder about this man. The only name I could think of was Mitchell but I knew perfectly well that this was not his name. I noticed, for some reason, that the time was 3.00 p.m.

'I thought no more about the matter until the next day when I again passed that same flower shop. As I passed the entrance, two of the members of our chapel came out of the shop. They were called Mr & Mrs Mitchell. We started to talk and they told me that they had just been into the flower shop to order a wreath on behalf of the chapel for Clara Gill's husband who had died the previous day at 3.00 p.m.'

∞

A LADY from Liverpool remembers when her daughter was born, 32 years ago. 'It was in the days before husbands were encouraged to stay with their wives during childbirth. The general attitude was that the men were just in the way and therefore after my husband had accompanied me safely to the hospital he was sent home with instructions to ring the ward the following morning.

'He went home and went to bed as usual but in the middle of the night he awoke with a start. There at the foot of the bed he saw his late mother who had died the previous year. She was nodding and smiling. He looked at the clock by the bedside and saw that the time was 4.45 a.m.

'At that precise moment I gave birth to our daughter. The first thing I noticed was that she had a mop of bright auburn hair exactly like my late mother-in-law.'

∞

MRS. E. Edgar, now a resident of Audenshaw, Manchester, at one time lived in Singapore. 'I had come home for a holiday just at the time of my nan's 89th birthday. My mother had arranged a party for her and of course all of her friends and relations were invited.

'On the day of the party my nan took me aside and quite calmly told me that she would not see me again. She said that she knew I would be going back to Singapore and that she was going to die very soon. I immediately got upset at her words but she told me that I was not to grieve because she was prepared to go and it would only make her unhappy if she thought that I would be miserable. She said it all in such a simple direct way that I believed her. She added that wherever she was she would be looking after me.

'I went back to Singapore and exactly three months after her party my beloved nan died. I was living in a large house with very wide stairs up from the living room. There were eight stairs up then a passage turned round and more stairs continued upwards to the next floor. One day I was just pottering about the house and I had to go up the stairs for some reason. Just above me at the top of the first eight steps I saw a flitter of light in the shape of a human figure. I watched it go up the remaining steps then turn and move along the winding passage.

'I was not sure what to make of it. I was alone in the house at the time as my husband travelled a lot and was away on business and both of my sons were out. I just got on with things and tried to put it out of my mind. A little later I had to go upstairs again but this time I was a little worried. Just as I started to walk up I saw it again – the same glimmering shape about the size of a person. It was in the exact same position and it was moving up towards the passage.

'It then hesitated, and started to glide back down the stairs coming towards me. By this time I was most alarmed. The only thing I could think of was that this light was my nan who had returned to look after me just as she had told me she would.

'I stood at the bottom of the stairs and shouted up towards the shape as loudly as I could: "Nan, I will always love you, but if it is you, you are frightening me. Please leave me alone." The light instantly disappeared and I never saw it again.

'Since that I have had only two dreams about my nan. In the first one she was crying but the second time she was laughing and looked serenely happy and contented.'

∞

GORDON, a Humberside man, remembers a story told to him by his mother: 'In January 1934, my mother was in the centre of Hull having just seen her mother onto a tramcar. She suddenly felt overwhelmed by a sense of her late father's presence. He had died four years previously. She felt that if she turned around she would most certainly see him.

'She was aware of his voice ringing in her head telling her, "Get a bus and go home." At the same time she felt as if someone was tugging at her coat to try to prevent her from going the way that she had intended to. She looked all around her but no one was touching her coat or was even near her.

'Having more errands to do before she could go home, she just pulled herself together and told herself that she was being foolish. She went on her way as per her original plan.

Within seconds, as she was crossing over the street, a mineral lorry came speeding round a corner and ran right into her knocking her unconscious. She was rushed to hospital with near fatal serious injuries and for a few days it was uncertain whether or not she would survive. She has always been convinced that her father had tried to save her from that catastrophe.'

∞

MANY people may have had an experience similar to that of Mrs Cantrill of Rotherham, South Yorkshire. 'At the time I was a young married woman with a baby and two other young children. Although my mother was dying of cancer I could only visit her rarely as my husband was at the office all day and we lived in a little village, well out of the city with hardly any bus service.

'One night I went to bed as usual and in the very early hours of the morning, for some reason, I woke up. I was very surprised to see my mother standing by the bed looking at me. Half in panic, I woke my husband who told me that I must have been dreaming and to go back to sleep. My mother had been dressed in a coat and hat which I knew well, but when I turned back round again she was gone.

'Whilst we were having breakfast the following morning, one of my sisters who lived with my mother and father opened the door and walked in. She looked at me and I said, "No need to tell me. Mummy's dead. She came to say 'goodbye' in the night." My mother's appearance in our bedroom had occurred at approximately the same time as her death.

'My older sister told me that for the last two days of my

519

mother's life, her eyes had been constantly looking round her bedroom searching for me. I couldn't get to her but she found a way to get to me.'

∞

ANOTHER short story comes from Mrs Grimmer of South Yorkshire: She reports, 'During the last war my husband was sent up to Fulford, an area of York, to a makeshift army hospital. He had tuberculosis. I had to go to Fulford with our two children and we were billeted at Park Grove.

'There was a great view of York Minster in all its glory from our room. One night we were sleeping on our bunks and I suddenly woke up. I felt completely paralysed and stone cold. I just couldn't understand what was happening to me for no matter how hard I tried to move I found it impossible. After a tremendous effort I managed to turn round on my other side. There, floating in mid air I saw the head and shoulders of an elderly lady. She had her hair piled up on top of her head and she was staring at me with her piercing blue eyes which I could see clearly. Although the room was in darkness she appeared in a luminous surrounding light and her face was brilliant as if it was somehow lit up from inside.

'My first thought was to lock the door but then I told myself that it wouldn't make any difference because being that she seemed to be just floating around without the rest of her body, she would probably be able to pass through doors. On thinking back I am amazed that I was able to think clearly about anything as I was so frightened at the time. The following day I happened to speak to a lady from downstairs. I just asked out of curiosity if she knew anything about the building. She told me that an old lady had once thrown herself off the little balcony outside my room window.'

∞

TINA of Manchester reports: 'Several years ago, when I was aged ten, my father died. A couple of months after this I used to see his face smiling in the centre of a halo of light up in the corner of my bedroom.

'At the time it frightened me even though I could hear his kindly voice saying to me, "Don't be afraid." Nevertheless I was afraid and used to run into my mother's bed.

'This carried on for about a year – not every night but about one or two times a week. By this time I had become used to seeing him and I was no longer afraid. The peculiar thing was that he no longer said anything but his face appeared smiling directly at me and very much alive.

'Ten years later, after I had married and moved away from home, my brother and his family (who had emigrated to Australia and then returned) were living at my mother's house. My niece who was aged seven at the time and had never met my father, occupied my old bedroom.

'One night she came running downstairs quite upset saying that she did not want to sleep in that room any more. When my mother asked her why, the child replied, "Daddy's daddy keeps smiling at me."

∞

PERHAPS one of the strangest stories of the north comes

521

from a lady from Kirkhamgate near Wakefield in West Yorkshire.

'We had six ponies in 1984 and since we had had a fair show season, we rented a field for a month from a farmer we were friends with in order to give the ponies some freedom. Show ponies are normally kept in the stables for most part of the time.

'One Friday evening my daughter and I went down to the field where five of them had been left to run around. They all came running towards us as usual. They were having such a great time that we decided we would leave them out overnight and check them again first thing in the morning.

'Early the following morning we were wakened up by someone thumping on the door of the house. My husband went down and was told that the ponies had got out onto the motorway and there had been a dreadful accident. Two of them had been killed outright and another two had been seriously injured and probably would have to be put down. Only one white pony, "Holly" had remained in the field and was safe. "Foxie", the sixth pony, was in the stable.

'We all got dressed quickly and went down to the scene of the accident. A huge opening had been made in the fence, possibly by vandals, but we might never know for sure. My youngest daughter's pony, "Cha-Cha" had lost one of her eyes and she had bad head wounds. The other injured animal was a pathetic sight to see. She was in foal and in a serious state of shock. She just stood still with her head dangling down towards the ground like a football. Our own vet arrived but informed us that both of the surviving ponies' injuries were so severe that they would have to be put down.

'We were all absolutely shattered and of course we

blamed ourselves for not bringing them up to the stables the previous night. After the animals had been put to sleep we went over to where they were lying on the ground to cover them with blankets until they could be taken away.

'My daughter Karen looked down at her pony "Cha-Cha". As she stood there, an icy feeling crept over her. At that very moment, my other daughter Elaine saw "Cha-Cha" rise up from the ground shrouded in swirling mist. The solid body of the animal still lay dead on the ground. She could only see the top half of "Cha-Cha" in the mist.

'On the following Tuesday afternoon my husband was driving me down to the stables to feed our two surviving ponies, "Foxie" and "Holly". Just as we were approaching the stables "Cha-Cha" ran right across the front of the car. My husband had to jam on the brakes making the car screech to a halt. The pony had just loomed out from the hedgerow and dashed right across the roadway and through the opposite hedge. We were both shaking with fright. He turned to me and said, "Cha-Cha".

'"Cha-Cha" was jet black all over except for a little white star on its forehead and it was the only black pony we had ever owned. We both got out of the car immediately and looked all over the place. There was no sign of "Cha-Cha" but up by the stables we were surprised to see "Holly" running about in a very excited state.

'We quickly got "Holly" back into the stable. We could not understand how she had got out as there were no signs of any break-in and her stable door was still shut.

'I couldn't help wondering if "Cha-Cha" had come back to collect her, or had she guided "Holly" back to the stable?'

OVERSEAS

MR. COLE, presently living in Essex, England served in France in the last war and was stationed at Eisenhower's Advance Headquarters on arrival into the outskirts of the recently liberated Paris.

'The Command Headquarters used by the German High Command had been in outbuildings of the Palace of Versailles, mainly in the old stables, and these were speedily converted to our use. Living accommodation was very scarce for a variety of reasons, therefore temporary sleeping quarters were found in the old Satory Barracks on the hill overlooking the main palace until something better could be found. It was here, during a period in late 1944, that I experienced what could appropriately be called a proper Winter's Tale, though it was absolutely true.

'Paris proper was still out of bounds to us so we set up a makeshift Warrant Officers' and Sergeants' Mess in a disused store at the far end of the main barrack room. Since electricity was rationed for the capital to a couple of hours a night, I was forced, as Mess President, to do the stocktaking by the light of a flickering candle.

'I had just finished one night and I was awaiting the arrival of the bar steward when the lights came on earlier than expected. I became aware of the grubby condition of my hands, previously unnoticed. I went to the rear washroom which consisted of a couple of cold water basins (no toilets) apparently installed by the outgoing German Army.

'Whilst I was washing in the freezing water by the light of a bare low watt bulb, I was aware that someone else was using the other basin in the far corner. He never said a word to me but I noticed that he was wearing a dark greatcoat. With the soap in my eyes I commented over to him about the bitterly cold night – in suitable army parlance.

'Not receiving any answer, I turned to get a better view of him as I dried my face. He just continued to wash his hand and did not even think it worth his while to acknowledge my friendly chit-chat. I was just about to discuss his parentage for being so surly, when he disappeared.

'At that moment, the corporal bar steward walked in from the corridor and asked who I had been talking to. I explained as best I could that a tall bloke in a heavy coat had been washing his hands in the other basin and I'd had a few words with him. I then said the man had somehow vanished. He shrugged his shoulders and muttered something under his breath about "first signs". Then, in no uncertain terms, he pointed out to me that nobody had, or could have, passed him in the corridor without him seeing them.

'I dismissed the episode until nearly eight months later when I was the British Office Commandant of Berlin and I met a Warrant Officer of the unit that took over the barracks when we moved out. He asked me if I knew that the barrack room was reputed to be haunted by the ghost of a Colonial soldier who had committed suicide rather than join Napoleon's Army at the front.'

∞

A CANADIAN, Jean Gordon, was on holiday at her

parents' home in Buckie, Banffshire, Scotland, in 1948. She had emmigrated to Canada on her own in the year 1921 when she was only 17 years of age.

'It was a long 27 years later before I was able to get home to Scotland to see my parents and family. I was overwhelmed when I reached Buckie and saw the magnificent house which my parents had bought on dad's retirement from the railroad.

'I arrived at the house about 4.00 p.m. feeling a bit tired but very excited at seeing mother and dad and some of my family again. My bedroom was on the first floor at the right hand side of the building. Around 11.00 p.m. I went to bed and soon fell asleep.

'I felt my arm being shaken so I opened my eyes and saw that daylight was just breaking. I turned round and found a wrinkled old lady, very tall, bending over me. She wore black and had leg-of-mutton sleeves and her neck-piece was made of white lace. I was rather agitated at being awakened in such a way and I looked down at her hand, which was still shaking my arm, to see that it was very bony.

'The first moment I saw her I was in such a sleepy state that I just assumed that she must be a friend of my parents, but then as it sank through to me that the mode of her dress was so antiquated I felt a tingle of fear. The feeling that all was not normal took a hold of me and as the panic spread throughout me I let out a loud scream. She let go of me and started to back away but all the time she kept staring at my face which really unnerved me. I got myself up to a sitting position in the bed and watched as she floated backwards and then just merged into the wall and the next second she was gone.

'I was so disorientated by the woman that I wanted to

find out where she could have gone. I knew that I had seen her in my room and I had felt her shaking my arm so she must have gone somewhere. I got out of bed and looked all around the room and even moved a heavy dresser to see if there were any hidden exit doors behind it but there were none. I assumed that no one could have heard my scream, so in a most perplexed state, I went back to bed, wondering about the thing I'd seen.

'Next morning when I went downstairs I asked them if they had heard my scream but no one had. My mother asked me what had happened so I related everything about the old lady. I was a bit surprised to see how lightly my mother took this. She then told me with a laugh that I must have seen the ghost. I was not prepared for this and by my expression my mother must have guessed as much.

'She went on to tell me that because all of the family had become so used to living with the ghost, she had ceased to be a threat. Seemingly the fisher folk of Buckie had always referred to my parents' property as The Haunted House because there once had been a terrible lovers' quarrel in one of the rooms and the woman involved had met her death in a most mysterious manner.

'Later that day my mother took me to the nearby cemetery to see the grave of the woman who had died as a result of the quarrel. On first sight we were both amused to see that the cemetery attendants were carrying out some work on her grave and they had dug up the sods which had been covering her coffin. These where piled high up by the side of the grave. My sense of humour soon changed to a foreboding feeling as a bizarre thought occured to me: when the workmen had unearthed her coffin could she have

527

wandered out of that grave and into my bedroom?'

∞

JANE Brewin, a lady from Cirencester in England went to Ireland to stay at a house not far from Dublin. She relates that, 'Caroline and Brigid Montgomery were cousins of my father, so they were my cousins once removed. All their lives they had lived about 12 miles outside Dublin and had made a lovely garden in what must have been an old sandpit. It was hollow-shaped, open towards the south, and looked towards the huge Sugarloaf mountain.

'The cousins died in the 1940s and the house then had a succession of owners. In the 1960s it was bought by a Mr. & Mrs. Fitzgerald. Mrs. Fitzgerald was a keen as well as learned gardener and she and her husband set about restoring the garden after its years of neglect.

'A few years ago they invited me over to see them. They wanted me to tell them about my relatives and the garden they had created. Taking tea with them on my arrival they told me about a recent visit they had made to Canada to see their married daughter. They had gone in the summer, but because there was so much unemployment in the Irish Republic they had worried about leaving the house empty. They had heard that many empty houses had been broken into so they had asked a colleague of Mr. Fitzgerald if he would stay in the house in their absence. He was delighted to do so since the house was close enough to Dublin for him to travel to work and he knew that he would enjoy being out of the city during the summer months. However, the man made one stipulation: He was no gardener and he refused to touch the garden or get involved with it in any way.

'When the Fitzgeralds returned from Canada they found

everything in order and they were pleased to find that their friend had obviously enjoyed himself. After the preliminary greetings the man asked them, "Who is the little old lady who wanders in the garden? I never managed to get near enough to speak to her."

'The Fitzgeralds could think of no old lady so they asked the old man who had lived in the next house for years and years if he had noticed any strange lady in their garden during their absence. The old man replied, "I saw her but it was only old Bridget Montgomery, fussing over her garden as usual."

∞

CHARLES from Karatina, in Kenya, Africa, tells of how his father was one of the first Indians who settled in the Nairobi area. His father had been a hard-working man and through his efforts he had built a bungalow. 'He came to like that bungalow as he liked his life. He had three sons and I was the eldest of all.

'As time went by, he became very ill and eventually died, but just before he drew his last breath he gave us all one last command; "Don't ever sell the bungalow – I built it for the family."

'Time went on and my two brothers and myself all found suitable wives and we all bought our own new modern houses and settled down to life with our own families.

'After my mother died, there was no one left living in the bungalow so my brothers and I decided that the only wise thing to do would be to sell the property and share out the money equally between the three of us.

'I started to look for a buyer and one day I met up with an

African businessman who became interested in viewing the property. I had shown him photographs of the exterior and an appointment was set up so that he could see the inside of it. The day came for me to take the businessman round the bungalow but that very same day my wife gave birth to a baby boy. The baby had not been expected for another two weeks but when it came early it upset all my plans and as you can imagine my main concern was to be with my wife and new son. With all the confusion I completely forgot about my appointment to show the man round my late parents' bungalow.

'The following day I went to see the businessman at his office hoping that he would forgive me for not turning up the previous day and that he would be understanding in view of the circumstances. We met and shook hands and I immediately started to apologise saying, "I am sorry that I could not keep the appointment yesterday because.." The man interupted me by saying, "It's okay, the man you sent showed me everything."

'I didn't know what he was talking about and asked him what he meant. I wondered for an instant if one of my brothers might have been at the bungalow without my knowledge, but then I remembered that I had the only set of keys with me all the time. In any case I knew that neither of them was in the area because they were unable to come to my home to celebrate the birth of my son. My house is quite close to the bungalow.

'I did not talk for a while as my mind was trying to work out who could have been at the bungalow to show this man around. The man, seeing how puzzled I was, tried to throw some light on the matter.

'He said that when he had approached the bungalow in

his car, he was met by an old Indian man with grey hair. The thing that he had noticed most about the old man was that there was a bit cut off his earlobe. I asked the businessman to give a full description of the Indian and he described my father down to the last detail. He then went on to give a precise description of every single room in the bungalow, all accurate in every detail, so I knew that he must have been inside the property to know these facts.

'However, although he seemed to identify my father to perfection I just could not believe that he could have seen a man who had been dead for years. I made no comment about who I thought had shown him around the house and I did not of course tell him anything about my father or the fact that he was dead.

'The businessman then said something which made my hair stand on end. He told me that although he had been treated with courtesy by the Indian who took pride in showing him all around the bungalow, the old man then told him that he was sorry but the bungalow was not for sale.

'Since my brothers and I agreed that it would be my responsibility to find a buyer for the bungalow because I was the only one living in the area, I felt that I would have to do everything I could to push the sale through. I could see that the businessman had been most impressed by what he had seen so I asked him if he would mind coming back to my own house so that we could talk over the details of the sale, and I assured him that there must have been some misunderstanding and that the bungalow was most certainly still up for sale.

'When we arrived at my house we got down to talking but the story he had told me about being shown round the bungalow was still bewildering me. I went to a drawer and took out some old family photographs and showed them to the businessman. He immediately pointed to my father saying that this was the old Indian man who had shown him round the property.

'At that stage I'm afraid my expression must have given me away because instantly the man seemed to guess that there was something strange going on. I admitted to him that this old Indian man was my father and that he had died some years previously. The moment the businessman heard this he jumped up from his chair and made to leave my house saying that he was no longer interested in buying the bungalow because he knew that it would always be haunted by my father.

'I felt very odd when I had to relate the story to my brothers about how I lost the sale on the property. We gave the matter a lot of thought and between us we came to the conclusion that if father was going to scare off all our would-be purchasers like that then perhaps we'd better change our thinking. We decided then that the best thing to do would be to forget about selling the bungalow and to rent it out instead.

'Within a matter of days we found a very worthy tenant and to this day the bungalow has been rented out and over the years it has been the source of a steady income for all of our family – not a great deal, but money that we would not otherwise be receiving on a regular basis.

'My father had always been a strong-willed man and had always been able to win his way. It seems that even death had not changed him.'

∞

A STORY comes from Co. Kildare, Ireland, from Mr.

Patrick Joe Coyle: 'The following account comes from my late father who told me that a man called Mike Deeley from a village in Co. Kildare went to a fair with two young bullocks. He was unmarried and lived with his elderly parents.

'It grew late and the young man had not returned the seven miles home and his parents started to worry. They sat up till well after midnight, then went to bed trying to convince each other by various suggestions what the explanation of their son's absence might be. They had not entirely ruled out drink, and they anticipated his return the following morning showing the after effects.

'The next day when there was still no sign of the son old Mr. Deeley became quite cynical thinking that his boy had just run off with the money from the sale of the bullocks. Both parents were upset as they had never looked on their Mike as a potential thief.

'In those days many people left Ireland for America to seek their fortune so the Deeleys assumed that this must have been what had happened but they felt badly let down by the fact that they had not been informed about Mike's plans to leave the country. At the back of Mrs Deeley's mind, however, there was still a lingering doubt as she always claimed that her son would never intentionally upset her like that. On her suggestion a thorough search was made of the area, but there was no trace of Mike.

'Days passed into weeks and the weeks into months. Then, as the years passed on, the father, and later the mother, died, still without a single word from their missing son. Twenty one years went by and the name of Mike Deeley was all but forgotten except by a few of the old timers who would mention now and then, "Whatever could

533

have happened to Mike Deeley?" As is the way in rural Ireland the people are never short of an explanation and some of the old lads would say that he must have skipped it to America and that any day he would be back to the village sporting his fortune.

'Around that time several men had returned to their original homes in that part of Ireland after having done their 21 years service in some city in the States and retired on a grand pension. Always when one such man would return the stock question would be, "Did you see any sign of Tom Deeley's son in America?" as if America was just the size of our village where everyone knew each other.

'One day a number of men were cutting peat on the outskirts of our village when they came across a body which had been buried there. It had been perfectly preserved by the turf. Word went round the village like a flash for a door to be brought to the peat field. That was the normal means in Ireland at that time whereby a corpse would be carried. The body was placed on a wooden door and was left at the side of the road surrounded by locals waiting for the police to arrive.

'The village was rife with rumour and suggestion as to the identity of the body in the bog. On the way to the scene, the two policeman had picked up a returned emigrant in their horse-drawn police cart to give him a lift to his destination as they had encountered him on the road walking with two heavy suitcases. The inspector told the stranger that they would be pleased to take him the further three miles to the cottage he was aiming for but on the way they would have to stop to attend to a bit of police business that had cropped up.

'The stranger said that he quite understood the situation

as he himself had just spent 21 years in the Boston Police Force. He thanked the policemen for their kind offer of the lift to the cottage and agreed to wait in the van until they had attended to the matter in hand.

'At that moment one of the old timers came on the scene to see what all the fuss was about. He took one look at the face of the corpse and instantly recognized the features of the long lost Mike Deeley. He made his discovery known to the policemen who then made a close examination of the body and saw that foul means had brought about the death.

'Then the strangest thing happened. Whether it was a natural or an unnatural procedure I am not sure, but a gush of water spouted from the mouth of the corpse. Things have strange ways of coming to light, especially in Ireland, and the country folk around the corpse looked upon this as an omen. It might well have been the result of an accumulation of water within the body. Nevertheless, because suspicions had been aroused, some of the people began murmuring that whoever killed Mike Deeley must have scarpered off, probably to America. These remarks made the policemen think about the passenger they had in their cart.

'When they were lifting the door upon which the corpse was laid out, up onto the cart, they noticed that the stranger had gone into a severe state of shock. The inspector wondered at this since being that the stranger had been a seasoned policeman in the Boston Force he should be well used to seeing the odd dead body. There was something fishy about the way the man was staring at the face of the corpse with a look of abject fright on his face.

'Because of the stranger's reaction he was told by the inspector that due to the circumstances surrounding the identity of the corpse all people who had resided in the area at the time of Mike Deeley's disappearance 21 years earlier would be taken in to the police station for questioning. The stranger broke down on the way to the police station and admitted that he had murdered Mike and robbed him in a desperate effort to acquire the money he needed to help towards his fare to America all those years ago. He had buried him in the field not thinking that anyone would ever find the body in a million years. He had kept in touch with his relative in the village over the years and when there was no report whatsoever about the missing Mike, he assummed that his secret was secure for ever.

'The returned emigrant was charged and found guilty of murder and was later hung. Afterwards Mike Deeley's brother was asked how he felt. "It was great," he replied, "not to hear that they have hanged a man, but to know that my brother was not a thief after all." He added, "Wasn't it the pity though that the ouldfella [meaning his father] had not survived to hear the proof."

∞

MRS. Buller had an experience which, for years and years, she was afraid to discuss with anyone: 'I was very ill with a serious chest condition. The first thing I noticed was that my bedroom furniture looked as if it was leaning to the left. The next thing I remembered was being near the ceiling looking down at myself, watching myself talking to my two sons. All I could say was, "I can't see the ceiling – I can't see the ceiling," over and over again.

'I was very aware of the fact that I was hovering in mid air and I was overwhelmed by the marvellous feeling of lightness. Everything was at ease, I felt like a feather peacefully drifting and the best bit of all was that there was no pain whatsoever – just a lovely feeling of contentment. I remember thinking that I could hardly find words to describe the exquisite state that I was in. I looked down again at the other me who was stretched out on the bed and although I knew perfectly well that it was my body I just kept saying to myself, "Look at that stupid woman down there behaving like that!" I had no compassion for her at all and I felt so detatched from that body it was as if I was watching somebody else on the bed but at the same time I knew that it was me. Because I felt so fit and well and extremely alert from my vantage point I found it hard to believe that I had once been trapped inside the body of that woman on the bed.

'I don't remember much about going back into my body but I found that my husband had taken me downstairs and he was making me comfortable in front of the television saying that there was a good film on. The next thing I knew I was back up on the ceiling again and once more I could see the other me sitting there. I then became aware of watching the television again thinking that I had no idea what the film was about. With this came the realization that I was not on the ceiling any more and for some reason I began to cry. My children had never ever seen me cry before but the tears just flowed and flowed. It came to me at that point that the reason I could not see the ceiling earlier was that I was up there.

'On the following Saturday afternoon, I was sitting in my lounge at about 2.10 p.m. I know the exact time because I had looked at the clock to check, wondering if my eldest son would be home. He was married and serving with H.M. Forces in Germany where he lived with his wife and baby son. The next instant I found myself hovering near the ceiling. There was something very strange about everything though and when I looked down I did not recognize anything but suddenly I noticed that there was a photograph on the wall. It was a picture of my little grandson like the one which had been sent to me only bigger and in a frame. I remember being given a jolt as the realization swept over me that I was in Germany in my son's flat. I had never ever been to Germany in my life and had never seen any photographs of his flat but I just knew – goodness knows how – that I was there. I could see no sign of my physical body this time nor could I see any other people.

'I floated into the hall of the flat and then noticed where the bathroom door was open and I could see another door beside it which was closed. The kitchen door was open and I felt myself drift in there where I noticed that everything was neat and tidy and I took special notice of the colour scheme and the dishes. I then looked into the open lounge but there was no one in there either. I noticed that there was a clock on the wall and saw that it read 3.10 p.m.

'I floated along the corridor until I reached a child's bedroom which I knew must be where my grandson slept. There was a playpen on the floor with a pink elephant cuddly toy in it. I remember thinking that it was an unusual colour of toy to give a little boy as I would have expected it to be blue. At that I thought, "Well there's no point in phoning him if there's nobody at home", then the very next instant I found myself back in my own lounge again.

'Four hours later my son telephoned me. I asked him some questions about his flat and he was astounded to hear me describe the entire flat including the baby's bedroom. He confirmed that the playpen was indeed in the middle of the floor and that there was a pink toy elephant in it. He explained that this was a present to the baby from their neighbours.

'I told him there was just one more thing I wanted to check with him; "Do you know that the clock on the wall of your lounge is fast by one hour?" He assured me that it was not fast so I must have been mistaken. It was after I put the receiver down that I realised that the time difference between Britain and Germany in the summer time is exactly one hour.'

∞

HELEN Swire was working in West Africa in the 1950s in a place called Warri on the Niger Delta. 'I lived in a company house, the gardens of which ran down to one of the tributaries of the Niger. It was the residents' custom to sit out in the evenings on the paved patio alongside the river, sipping cool drinks and chatting.

'Africa is never quiet. Even at night there is continuous music and laughter from the workers' quarters, the sound of bullfrogs and the thousands of insects which live in the bush, also the splashing of paddles from canoes which pass up and down the creeks.

'One evening I was having a drink with my neighbour, and just relaxing after a day's work in the intense heat. Suddenly, we both stopped talking and became aware of a deathly silence. There was no human voice, no rustle of insects, no movement on the river, not even a whisper, but the complete and utter absence of sound. Despite the heat of the tropical night, we both shivered and I could feel my skin break out in gooseflesh.

'After about five minutes, thankfully the normal sounds of the African night began to return. I heaved a deep sigh of relief. My neighbour, a Geordie, and a most practical and down-to-earth young man, admitted to me that the hair on his scalp had risen during the silence as had mine. We saw nothing but we were both overwhelmed by an indescribable atmosphere of evil which had descended on the place.

'Next morning when I mentioned the matter to my African houseboy he was very subdued and informed me that very bad ju-ju was about last night. Ju-ju is a kind of curse. Africans are very superstitious and if a person has a ju-ju put upon them they become very frightened and in extreme cases people have literally been frightened to death.

'The particular area where the incident took place is believed to be subject to hauntings by spirits which are said to be present in the river. The natives always used to sing in a loud chanting fashion as they came up the river and its tributaries in their canoes in an attempt to scare off these spirits. There was a fish festival every year when all the local tribesmen would travel up the river in their canoes, their bodies highly decorated by certain paints, colours and dyes which were meant to neutralize the power of the spirits.'

∞

HAROLD Hampson is a man who never had any time for what he calls 'spooks' and has always dismissed stories about anything unexplained as codswallop, but now he's not so sure. 'Last year my wife, daughter and myself all went to New Zealand to visit my son and his family.

'He had only recently immigrated and had purchased

eight-and-a-half acres of land in a very isolated spot. It was six miles to the nearest village, a place called Takaka, near Golden Bay on the northern tip of South Island. My son had cleared all the scrub and trees, and had cultivated the land to grow vegetables and fruit.

'My son had almost finished building a house for his family on the grounds and had completed two bedrooms by the time we arrived there. As he had a lot of work to get through on the building side, my wife, daughter and myself agreed to take the burden of the cultivation work away from him so each day we used to busy ourselves with tilling the land and planting all sorts of vegetables – sweetcorn, fruit, etc.

'We had been working on the land one particular morning and even though it was fairly early it was stifling hot. I was not quite acclimatized and felt a bit tired so I told my wife that I was just going into the house to have a lie down for a while.

'I drew the curtains to keep out the brilliant sunlight, settled down and closed my eyes to have a cat-nap. After no more than a few moments something made me open my eyes. From up in the corner of the shaded room near the ceiling a wicked looking face zoomed down to within a few feet of me. It was the most wicked looking face I had ever seen. He had dark skin like dried prunes, black rotted teeth and a fuzzy matted beard and long bushy hair. He gave me a sneering grin then shrank back into the corner of the room where he had come from. Three times this awful face zoomed down on me and then it disappeared. I went out of the house into the sunshine again but I decided not to mention my experience to anyone in case they became alarmed.

'A few days later my son told me that over 100 years ago the land he had bought had been a Mauri settlement and there was supposed to be a burial ground on the land. I could not get that face out of my mind and it struck me that it must have been a Mauri tribesman. I kept wondering why I should see such a thing and got the impression that I was being given some kind of warning.

'Within that week my wife took ill. I was very worried about her, so worried in fact that I arranged to return to England straight away. Before we had gone to New Zealand she had been perfectly fit and well. Very shortly after we got home she died.'

∞

AN ex-Singapore resident tells of the night a friend came into her house looking as white as a sheet. 'He was a big brawny R.A.F. policeman but he was reduced to a quivering jelly.

'He told us that he'd just come off duty and had got to the bottom of the hill which led to our houses when he saw a Malay girl standing at the corner. As it was a very dark night, he stopped and asked her if she wanted a lift. She said nothing, but got into his car. She was dressed in a sarang and had a flower in her hair, the perfume of which filled his car.

'When they got to the top of the hill our policeman friend turned round to ask the girl where she wanted to go to but she had vanished. He jammed on his brakes and sat there stunned. He then noticed that a frangipani flower was on the passenger seat.

'You can imagine how he felt. It took a long time for him

to get over it and he swore us to secrecy as he knew the ribbing he would receive if his mates got word of the incident. Needless to say he never gave anyone else a lift at night. He never even told his wife about the incident.

'We learnt later that just before our houses had been built, a Malay girl had been killed on the spot where he had picked up the stranger.'

∞

EILEEN, an English lady, had travelled to India one year to visit the family of her husband who had come to Britain several years earlier. Eileen was particularly looking forward to meeting her Indian mother-in-law as the woman had always begged her son, in her many letters, to bring his wife out to see her.

'We were not all that well off at the time so the only way we would ever manage the trip would be to go overland in our battered old blue van, taking ferry boats where necessary, and hopefully working our way when funds ran scarce. We set off with just the minimum of belongings and soon we were on our way.

'Everything went well considering our mode of travel, and apart from the expected inconveniences we were quite happy with our progress. After many weeks we reached the Khyber Pass with 500 miles still to travel. We were running very low on petrol so we pulled up to try to buy some. We were asked to produce a ration book. We had no idea what this meant, then the horror of horrors hit us when we were informed quite officially that because petrol was in such short supply there was no chance of us being sold any without a ration book. Even the people with ration books were being severely restricted.

'We sat in our old van quite devastated knowing that our tank was almost empty. We did not even have anything like enough to go back to the border and it looked like we would not be allowed to progress. We felt utterly helpless.

'Suddenly a strange wave of energy seemed to devour me. I ran out of the van up towards the official who was guarding the petrol. I started screaming at this man at the top of my voice telling him that he just had to give us some petrol. My husband came running up behind me wondering what the commotion was. I truly do not know what got into me that day as it was so unlike me to cause a fuss. My husband just stood and stared in disbelief at my irregular behaviour.

'The official started speaking loudly back to me but because I did not understand his language I had no idea what he was saying, having always relied on my husband to be my interpreter. I thought, by the tone of his voice, that he was arguing with me. This made me go into an absolute frenzy and I screamed and yelled blue murder into his face, bellowing at him to let me have some petrol.

'He suddenly stopped talking and stretched out his arm towards me. He then gestured for us both to follow him and he led us into a little building and told us to wait. He went into a back room and a few seconds later he came out carrying a can which he handed to us, explaining to my husband that it was enough petrol to at least get us on our way. I'm sure he only wanted to get rid of me screaming and yelling at him. We were overjoyed at receiving the petrol and thanked him and I must admit that I felt deeply ashamed of the way I had behaved.

'My husband poured the petrol into the tank and noticed that it could not have filled more than about half the tank. We had no idea how far this would take us but at least we could try to make it to the next petrol station and then see what could be done.

'It was very heavy going over that territory as the road was nothing more than a dirt track which made driving quite arduous. However, we plodded on hoping for the best. We reached the next petrol point but because the van seemed to be going fairly well we felt that maybe we should keep going while we could, and the petrol gauge reading was just under the half way mark.

'We travelled on without stopping for several hours and we both began to wonder at the petrol gauge being still just under the half-way mark. We assumed that it must be broken and we expected to run out of fuel any minute but since it was beginning to get dark we agreed that we would just keep driving until the petrol ran out then we would have a sleep in the car and wait for help. There was little else we could do as we were travelling down an endless road which was totally deserted of any towns or villages. The funny thing was that the old van showed no signs of struggling and just kept going.

'My husband drove all through the night while I slept, and in the early morning as dawn broke I woke up absolutely amazed to find that my husband was still driving and the petrol mark was still just under half full. Leaving the engine running we quickly changed seats so that he could have a sleep and I took over. Later on we changed places again just before we approached my husband's village.

'It was with great joy that he ushered me into his parents'

home but our joy quickly turned to sadness when we were informed that my Indian mother-in-law had been taken seriously ill. Within minutes of being introduced to her she died.

'A bit later that day, amidst the upheaval caused by the death in the family, with relatives and friends pouring into the house, my husband whispered to me that he would take me out to purchase a few items. In his sudden grief, I think he just needed to get away from the house for a little while.

'Without thinking, we got into our blue van but no matter how many times we tried we could not get that van to start. We just sat there in tears.'

∞

PATRICK Joy brings yet another story from Ireland and relates: 'I was born in Co. Kerry in 1934, taught at the national school in Killorglin, and that was about the sum of it till I started work. Like my brothers, I worked for my father who was the town blacksmith.

'The story begins when my brother Seamus took to the drink in an attempt to brow-beat my father who always drank too much. At least that was Seamus's excuse. A card game was played most nights at the local pub, but it was well known that these games were usually fixed by a gang of lads we called the bright boys. They used to wait until the unsuspecting players were well and truly sozzled when they would raise the stakes and of course they always came out winning.

'At that time there were two routes to our home which was only a mile away. We could take the main road which was fairly well lit until we got to the outskirts of the town

546

when we had to rely on the lights from the odd cottages scattered along the way. The other way home was along the railway track which we usually joined at the nearest point to the pub which was by the exit to the local cinema.

'Nearly every night Seamus and I walked along the railway and our conversation would inevitably revolve around the fact that each night poor Seamus always seemed to lose money at the cards. We concluded between us that the only way he could hope to beat the bright boys would be for him to cut down on the drink. We also drummed it up between us that we would try to beat them at their own game by using their kind of tactics. The idea was to rig up some of his pals to join in the game with fixed cards. We put our plan into practice the next night and of course Seamus won every game. Then he sportingly bought every one of the bright boys a drink, taking care just to have coke ourselves.

That night we decided to go home by the main road. We were both cold sober as we had purposely kept off the booze so that we could concentrate on the cards and get one over on the bright boys. As we approached Carter's Shed which had once been a stable for the horses of the gentry, a huge black dog raced out from a doorway and stood right in front of us.

'Seamus was well used to animals and had a great way with them so he attempted to persuade the dog to move so that we could get past. We walked forward but the creature reared up on its hind legs and appeared more like a horse than a dog. It was then that we got really scared and I could feel my hair stand on end. Seamus looked over at me and whispered that this thing was no ordinary dog. We edged over a bit to see if we could slip past but there was no way that the beast was going to let us pass.

'We looked at each other and then very slowly started to move backwards, too frightened to turn our backs on the thing. We walked backwards for quite a time until we could see that the thing was not going to follow us. Then we turned round and ran as fast as we could back to the town without stopping once for breath. We got to the railway and made our way home by that route.

'We told the rest of the family about the dog the minute we got home but of course they all roared and laughed at us and none of them believed us, except for my mother. She was very serious about what had happened and told us that it was a warning for us and that we should not be gallavanting around the town at that hour anyway.

'I just did not know what to think about it and tried to put it out of my head but Seamus was so affected that he took to asking the priest for advice and also one of his old teachers who he was still very friendly with. From that day on we never ever went near Carter's Shed again.

'The years went by, Seamus got married and then took his family out to America. One night I received a telephone call from him. He told me that he had just finished doing some work for nuns at the local convent and he had just got into his car to drive home when suddenly the same black dog rushed out in front of him to prevent him taking his normal route home. He was petrified as he recognized the same creature by the way it reared up on its hind legs just like a horse, and he knew that the nuns did not keep any dogs so there was no mistaking the beast. He naturally tried to drive past but the animal kept leaping up on to the bonnet of his car making it impossible for him to proceed.

'He remembered my mother's words about it being some kind of warning so he did what we had done all those years earlier – he turned the car round on the roadway and drove home by a different route.

'He had only been home about ten minutes when news came to the house that there had been a terrible crash on the road and there was a big pile up of cars. This was the road that he would surely have been on had the dog not prevented him.'

∞

MR. JOHNSON M. ARAN from Kagumo in Kenya, Africa, is a schoolteacher by profession having started teaching in 1982. He has travelled extensively in Africa and has remained great friends with one of his tutors who related to him the following experience: 'One time my tutor went from Mombasa to Pakistan for further studies where he stayed for two years. Before he left Africa he had left his car with a friend who agreed to keep it in good condition and check it for rusting, etc. His two years' course completed, on the night he was due to leave Pakistan he telephoned his friend to inform him that he would be back shortly and to make sure the car would be ready for him.

'He arrived back in Mombasa and went straight to his friend's place to collect his car. They had only a soda together as my tutor was longing to see his own family and did not want to spend too much time before going home.

'His house was on the mainland Kilifi, and therefore he had to cross the old Nyali pontoon bridge. Before he crossed over onto the bridge a girl waved him down for a lift. By this time it was quite dark and he hesitated, but feeling a bit sorry for the stranded girl he stopped and opened the door of his car for her. She got in and he drove off but just as the car was halfway over the bridge the girl opened his car door while the vehicle was still moving and jumped out. He jammed on his brakes as he was sure she must have been very badly injured, and got out of his car expecting to find her stretched out on the road.

'Instead of that he saw the girl step up onto the safety bars of the bridge. He was terrified that she was about to commit suicide so he rushed up to her calling out not to jump.

'As he reached her, she just stepped off the bridge. He looked over and saw that she was gently floating downwards towards the water. He then watched her walk across the surface of the water as if it was a solid road. He just stared and stared, hardly able to believe his eyes as the girl walked further and further down mid-stream until she disappeared into the darkness. My tutor stood on that bridge for ages in a state of shock just staring down at the water. The loud bleeping of other motorists eventually brought his attention back to the fact that his car was holding up a long line of traffic on the bridge. He got back into his car and to this day he still doesn't know how he managed to drive himself home as his hands shook so much.

'On his arrival at his house he could not say one single word to his family, who were all convinced that he had become deaf and dumb. His wife went into a state of hysterics and some of the neighbours, hearing her loud screaming, came in to see if they could help. They arranged for my tutor to be taken to hospital where he was thoroughly checked over and it was found that he was in deep shock. He was kept in hospital that night for observation and thankfully the next day he had recovered sufficiently to tell the doctors what had happened.'

∞

A FISHING lady named Lorna was once on a holiday in Norway with some friends. 'They stayed at a large house in the mountains which we used as a base for our fishing trips. The house was owned by the uncle of one of my friends who normally travelled with us on these trips but that year he had suddenly been taken ill and was unable to leave his home in London.

'One day I had been out walking on the mountains and returned to find the house empty so I sat down in the dining room to have my supper. The window looked out onto a verandah where there was an assortment of chairs where we all used to sit out in the sun. My host always used to sit in one particular rocking chair out on the porch every day when he was staying in the mountain house. While I was having my supper I saw the rocking chair begin to rock back and forwards. This went on for some time so I went outside to see if a sudden high wind could have sprung up but outside all was calm and still except for the chair which kept rocking back and forwards with no one sitting in it.

'After supper I went down to the river to find my friend who was fishing as I had not seen her since breakfast that morning. When I reached her she had just caught a fish but she seemed very depressed. I asked her what was wrong and she told me that there had been a telephone call from London earlier that day to inform her that her uncle, my host, had just died.'

PETER and his wife Doreen went to stay at a friend's house just outside Sydney in Australia. The first night they went to bed in the comfortable guest bedroom on the ground floor. 'We fell asleep but I was wakened in the middle of the night by heavy footsteps trudging up and down the staircase, the foot of which started just along the corridor outside our bedroom. The next morning I asked Doreen if she had slept well and she told me she had. I was waiting for her to tell me that she too had heard the footsteps but she never mentioned it so, not wishing to frighten her, I kept quiet about what I had heard. Being that I was a guest in the house I did not like to say anything to my host so I just kept my mouth shut about the footsteps.

'I settled down to sleep the following night trying not to think too much about the previous night's activity and after reading for a while I drifted off to sleep. A thundering thumping noise wakened me up once more. It went on and on up and down the stairs, up and down, for ages. I was nearly out of my mind with the noise but what really amazed me was the way my wife continued to sleep right through this pandemonium as if nothing was happening.

'This went on for about half an hour and it took every ounce of self-control not to roar out to anyone who might be listening to stop the din. I eventually got to sleep again and in the morning, just like the morning before, my wife made no remark to show she had heard anything unusual. Something still prevented me from reporting the tramping footsteps to my host.

'On the night before we were due to leave, I was again wakened but this time I heard not a sound but I could feel icy fingertips running up and down my back. I turned round quickly to see if my wife had touched me but she was fast asleep beside me and I could still feel the freezing cold fingers on my back. I broke out in a cold sweat and lay down on my back and pulled the bedcover right over my head to try to block out whatever was touching me.

'As soon as I did this the fingers left my back. I had just heaved an enormous sigh of relief when suddenly I felt almost winded as something thumped me on my ribs. Once more I felt a tremendous punch in the ribs but by this time I'd had enough. I just screamed out telling whatever it was to clear off and leave me alone except my actual terminology was somewhat more forceful than that.

'My wife sprang up in the bed with fright wondering who I was shouting at. I told her not to worry. From that moment I had no further trouble but I got the distinct impression that the entity had made its point by getting me to recognize its existence and would now be happy to let things be.'

Full unabridged version
Watch out!

A unique collection
of true ghost stories

by
Peter and Mary
Harrison

Published by Sinclair
1990

ISBN 1-872149-03-0

Quote this number to your favourite bookshop

THE MYSTIQUE OF LOVE

by
Peter and Mary Harrison

OUT SOON

Watch out for

II

by
Peter and Mary
Harrison

ISBN 1-872149-04-9

Quote this number to your favourite bookshop

Peter and Mary are presently researching their next book. If you have had an encounter with the unexplained, please send your true story to PETER & MARY HARRISON at their publishers in Wellingborough, the address is:

SINCLAIR PUBLISHING LTD
VICTORIA HOUSE
123 MIDLAND ROAD
WELLINGBOROUGH
NN8 1LU